UNDERSTANDING REFORM IN MYANMAR

D1357966

MARIE LALL

Understanding Reform in Myanmar

People and Society in the Wake of Military Rule

HURST & COMPANY, LONDON

First published in the United Kingdom in 2016 by
C. Hurst & Co. (Publishers) Ltd.,
41 Great Russell Street, London, WC1B 3PL
© Marie Lall, 2016
All rights reserved.
Printed in India

Distributed in the United States, Canada and Latin America by
Oxford University Press, 198 Madison Avenue, New York, NY 10016,
United States of America.

The right of Marie Lall to be identified as the author of
this publication is asserted by her in accordance with the
Copyright, Designs and Patents Act, 1988.

A Cataloguing-in-Publication data record for this book
is available from the British Library.

ISBNs: 9781849045803

This book is printed using paper from registered sustainable
and managed sources.

www.hurstpublishers.com

For my brother Nay Win Maung, without whom
none of this would have ever happened

CONTENTS

Acknowledgements   ix
Cast list   xi
Abbreviations   xvii

Introduction: Reforms, Civil Society and the Challenge of
Democratisation in the Wake of Military Rule   1

1. How Myanmar Got from 2005 to 2010—The Role of Civil Society   13
2. The Elections and the New Opposition—Validity and Public
   Disenchantment   43
3. National Reconciliation with the NLD   67
4. The Peace Process   93
5. Economic Reforms and Re-engagement with the International
   Community   133
6. The Reform of Myanmar's Education System   159
7. The Rise of Buddhist Nationalism   185

Conclusion: The Challenges of Democratisation in Light of the
                2015 Elections   209
Epilogue: The 8 November Elections   221
Annex   227

Notes   235
Bibliography by Chapter   309
Index   323

ACKNOWLEDGEMENTS

My journey to Myanmar started with my father telling me about his one and only trip to Burma as a World Health Organisation official in the summer of 1971, just weeks after I was born. His story of travelling to the ethnic hills and his description of the Shwedagon were part of my upbringing. I took my first steps in the country in 2000, travelling as a tourist from Calcutta. From then onwards I was obsessed with going back. It is therefore fitting that my first thank you goes to Razeen Sally, who one drunken evening in a London wine bar mentioned that I should meet Professor Robert Taylor, who was organising for foreign academics to teach at Myanmar universities. It is to Bob that I owe my real introduction to the country. He took me under his wing and mentored my engagement with the country. It is through Bob that I met Dr Kyaw Yin Hlaing in January 2005, who introduced me to the other boys who founded Myanmar Egress. I thank both for my introduction to Myanmar and its agents of change.

My most profound thanks go to the founders of Myanmar Egress, in particular Ko Tin Maung Thann, Ko Kyaw Ni Khin, Ko Sonny Nyunt Thein and U Hla Maung Shwe, with whom I worked for the best part of this past decade. But of all I owe most thanks to Dr Nay Win Maung, who adopted me as a sister and to whom this book is dedicated. I miss our conversations so much. Thanks also go to his mother, Mummy, who still treats me like her daughter. Without her guidance, both to her son and the military cadets, which include President Thein Sein and many of his closest ministers whom she taught at staff college, I don't believe any of what we witness today could have happened.

Myanmar Egress grew into a bigger place, and the sayas were replaced by the younger generation of leaders. I have to thank Ma Nan Theingi, Ma Khin Moe Samm, Ma Thei Su San and Ma Phyo Thandar for their friendship and support. My immense gratitude goes also to my research team: Nwe Nwe San, Thein Thein Myat, Lwin Thet Thet Khaing and Yin Nyein Aye, who for four years worked hard on the projects I led. They were often supported by Swann Lynn Htet and Yeh Tut Naing. I owe the team so much when it comes to the original data included in this book. Nwe Nwe San has been much more than just a research team leader, and she and her husband Aung Htun epitomise the change agents of this younger generation who are dedicated to the future of their country.

There are many other friends I made over the years of travelling to Myanmar. I want to thank with all my heart Ma Ja Nan Lataw, Ma Susanna Hla Hla Soe and Mi Kun Cha Non for their friendship and support in my work with ethnic groups, both armed and unarmed. Ma Thanegi, who gave me my Burmese name, remains one of my closest friends.

When I started travelling to Yangon, Sjoukje Zilstra and her son Wei Pyo gave me my first home. When they had to move out of Golden Valley due to the influx of foreigners and the rise in rents, Lyndal Barry and Myo Gyi gave me my second home in Yangon. Thank you both for having me in what I affectionately call the commune.

Once Nay Win Maung died and was no longer picking me up at the airport, my faithful taxi driver U Ba Swe has been there every time, welcoming me with a smile.

Thanks go also to Derek Tonkin, Bob Taylor, Emily Spears Mears and Romain Caillaud for commenting on various chapters of the book. Ashley South, who also read parts of this book, has shared some of the moments in this research journey and I am deeply grateful for his friendship over the past five years. It is due to this group of colleagues and friends, and Michael Dwyer and the team at Hurst, that the book finally saw the light of day. All errors, however, are mine alone.

Finally I need to thank my husband Viren Lall, who put up with my crazy travel schedule, for his unwavering love and support over our twenty years together.

CAST LIST

SLORC/SPDC

SPDC State Peace and Development Council was the official name of the Myanmar military regime that seized power in 1988 and ruled till March 2011. From 1988 to 1997 the SPDC was known as the State Law and Order Restoration Council (SLORC).

Senior General Than Shwe Chairman of the Union of the SPDC, the ruling military junta of Myanmar from 1992 to 2011. Commander in Chief of the Tatmadaw (Myanmar Armed Forces). Head of the Myanmar regime 'troika'.

Vice Senior General Maung Aye Vice chairman of the SPDC, the ruling military junta of Burma from 1993 to 2011. Maung Aye was the second highest ranking member of the SPDC. Number two of the Myanmar regime 'troika'.

General Khin Nyunt Former number three of the Myanmar regime 'troika', Chief of Intelligence and Prime Minister from 25 August 2003 to 18 October 2004. He was put under house arrest in 2004.

Thura Shwe Mann Speaker of the Myanmar Parliament since 2011. Previously he replaced General Khin Nyunt as number three of the Myanmar regime 'troika'. He also served as joint chief of staff of the Tatmadaw.

Prime Minister U Thein Sein Former military commander who was Prime Minister from 2007 to 2011. He became President of Myanmar in March 2011 after the November 2010 elections.

USDP-led government

USDP The Union Solidarity and Development Party was formed on 29 March 2010 and is the regime party. It was created out of the USDA, an organisation formed by SLORC in 1993. As of 30 April 2007, the Association had 24 million members. All assets of the USDA were transferred to the USDP, leading to the disbanding of the USDA.

President U Thein Sein Former Prime Minister, see above.

Vice President (one) Thiha Thura Tin Aung Myint Oo Previously Minister of Military affairs and generally seen as a hard-liner in the new government. He resigned the vice presidency in May 2012.

Vice President (two) Dr Sai Mauk Kham An ethnic Shan medical doctor who was chairman of the Shan Literature and Culture Association. He is widely seen as the 'ethnic politician' of the USDA.

Vice President (Admiral) Thray Sithu Nyan Tun The incumbent Vice President of Myanmar, and previously Commander in Chief of the Myanmar Navy. He was elected on 15 August 2012 to replace Tin Aung Myint Oo, who had resigned for health reasons.

Speaker of the House Thura Shwe Mann See above.

Minister U Aung Min Union Minister, Office of the President. Chairperson of the Myanmar Peace Centre, and hence responsible for the peace process. He is a former Minister for Railways of Myanmar and a retired Major General in the Tatmadaw (Myanmar Armed Forces).

Minister U Soe Thane Union Minister, Office of the President. Former Minister for Industry-2 of Myanmar, responsible for economic reforms. He previously served as the Commander in Chief of the Myanmar Navy, and Chairman of Myanmar Investment 2010–13.

General Min Aung Hlaing Current Commander in Chief of the Tatmadaw (Myanmar Armed Forces).

'Opposition' and 'opposition' parties

Daw Aung San Suu Kyi General Aung San's daughter. Needs no introduction.

NLD National League for Democracy, led by Daw Aung San Suu Kyi. Founded in September 1988 and won the 1990 elections. The party continued to operate but its members were harassed. The NLD refused to take part in the 2010 elections, but did register for the 2012 by-elections.

NDF National Democratic Force, led by U Khin Maung Swe. A political party created by former members of the NLD who chose to contest elections in 2010. The NDF's adoption of the peasant bamboo hat, which is the traditional symbol of the NLD, created some controversy. Daw Aung San Suu Kyi remains very angry with the break-away party who defied her wishes to boycott the 2010 elections.

Ethnic parties Those that won seats in the 2010 elections include the AMRDP—All Mon Region Democracy Party (Mon), the PSDP—Phalon-Sawaw Democratic party (Karen), the PNO—Pa-O National Organisation (PaO), the WNUP—Wa National Unity Party (Wa), the SNDP—Shan Nationalities Democratic Party (Shan), the CNP—Chin National Party (Chin), the RNDP—Rakhine National Party (Rakhine). Other ethnic parties contested but did not win any seats.

Civil society (selection of organisations mentioned in the book)

Myanmar Egress

Dr Nay Win Maung Medical doctor and journalist. Publisher of *Voice* and *Living Colour* magazine. Co-founder and Chairman of Myanmar Egress. Died of a heart attack on 31 December 2012.

U Tin Maung Thann Aquaculturist and consultant. Vice president of Myanmar Fisheries Federation. Co-founder and president of Myanmar Egress. Currently with the Myanmar Peace Centre.

U Hla Maung Shwe Vice president of UMFCCI and businessman. Co-founder of Myanmar Egress. Currently with the Myanmar Peace Centre.

Dr Kyaw Yin Hlaing Academic (NUS and later Hong Kong). Co-founder of Myanmar Egress. Currently with the Myanmar Peace Centre.

U Sonny Nyunt Thein Travel agent and businessman. Co-founder of Myanmar Egress.

U Kyaw Ni Khin Architect and businessman. Co-founder of Myanmar Egress.

U Ye Mya Thu Businessman based in Mandalay. Co-founder of Myanmar Egress.

Shalom Foundation (Nyein Foundation)

Ma Janan Lahtaw Daughter of Reverend Saboi Jum, who was instrumental in the 1990s ceasefires. Assistant Director of the Shalom Foundation. She coordinated peace-building work across Myanmar.

CAST LIST

Metta Development Foundation

Established in 1998 and developed projects in Kachin, Shan, Karenni, Karen and Mon States. Former Metta director was Daw Seng Raw.

Karen Women's Action Group

Ma Susanna Hla Hla Soe A women's rights activist and founder of the Karen women's action group that has been campaigning hard for the inclusion of women in the peace process.

Ethnic armed groups (selection, information taken from www.mmpeacemonitor.org)

NMSP and MNLA New Mon State Party and Mon National Liberation Army, founded in 1958; operational area: Thaton, Paung, Chaungsone, Moulmein, Hpa-an, Kawkareik, Kyeikmayaw, Mudon, Thanbyuzayap, Ye, Yayphyu, Three Pagoda Pass, Mergui-Tavoy and Kyar-Inn-Seik Gyi. Estimated strength 800+ (2,000 reserve).

KNU and KNLA Karen National Union and Karen National Liberation Army, founded in 1947; operational area: Than Taung, Taungoo, Nyaung Lay Bin, Hlaing Bwe, Hpa-an, Hpa-pun, Kawkareik, Kyar-Inn Seik Gyi, Kyeikdon, northern part of Tanintharyi region. Estimated strength 5000+. Signed NCA on the 15th October 2015.

DKBA Democratic Karen Benevolent Army, founded in 1995; operational area: PanTawMee, Myaing Gyi Ngu, Kama-moung, Hpa-pun, HLaing-bwe township. Estimated strength 4000. Signed NCA on the 15th October 2015.

DKBA 5 Democratic Karen Benevolent Army Brigade 5, founded in 2010; operational area: Three Pagodas Pass, Hlaing Bwe and Kyar-In-Seik-Gyi townships, Manerplaw (former KNU headquarters). Estimated strength 1,500+.

KNPP Karenni National Progressive Party, founded in 1957; operational area: Loikaw, Shar Daw, Ho Yar (Pharu So township), Daw Tamagyi (Dee Maw So township). Estimated strength 600+.

PNLO and PNLA PaO National Liberation Organisation and Pa-Oh National Liberation Army, founded in 2009; operational area: Hsi Hseng, Hopong, Nam San, Lan Khur and Mawk Mai in Shan State. Estimated strength 400+. Signed NCA on the 15th October 2015.

RCSS/SSA (South) Revolutionary Council of Shan State, Shan State Army South founded in 1964/1996; operational area: Mong Ton, Mong Hsat in Eastern Shan State, Mong Pan, Mong Nai, Laikha, Kunhing, Lawksawk, Maukmai, Mongkaung, Nam Sang in Southern Shan State, Kyaukme and Nam Kham in Northern Shan State. Estimated strength 6,000+. Signed NCA on the 15th October 2015.

SSPP/SSA (North) Shan State Progressive Party/Shan State Army, Shan State Army North, founded 1954/1989; operational area: Nam Kham, Langkho, Hsipaw, Kyauk Mae, Mong Hsu, Tang Yang, Mongyai, Kehsi, Lashio township. Estimated strength 4,000+.

TNLA Ta'ang National Liberation Army, founded in 1992; operational area: Naung Cho, Kyaukme, Hsipaw, Kutkai, Namtu, Mann Ton, Namhsan, Mong Mit, Mongoke in Northern Shan State. Estimated strength 1500.

USWA and UWSP United Wa State Army and United Wa State Party, founded in 1989; operational area: Pangsang, Mongmau, Pangwai, Nahphan, Mongpawt, Hopan. Estimated strength 20,000/25,000.

NDAA National Democratic Alliance Army, Eastern Shan State (Mongla group); operational area: Mongla, Shan State (Special Region # 4). Estimated strength 3,000+.

KIA and KIO Kachin Independence Army and Kachin Independence Organisation, founded in 1961; operational area: 5 brigades across Kachin State and Northern Shan State. Estimated strength 7,000 to 10,000 (excluding the KIO's MHH and MKM civilian militia forces).

CNF Chin National Front, founded in 1988; operational area: Thantlang township, Tlangpi village tract, Dawn village tract and Zang Tlang village tract. Estimated strength 200+. Signed NCA on the 15th October 2015.

ALP Arakan Liberation Party, founded in 1968; operational area: Northern Rakhine and Karen States. Estimated strength 60–100 (2,000 party members). They are a part of the Arakan National Council—ANC. Signed NCA on the 15th October 2015.

AA Arakan Army, founded in 2009; linked to Kachin conflict and largely depicted as a product of the KIA as its soldiers were trained at the KIA Academy. Claims to have 2500 troops under arms.

ABSDF All Burma Student Democratic Front, founded in 1988; operational area: KIA and KNU controlled areas. Estimated strength 600+ (about 200 in Kachin State). Signed NCA on the 15th October 2015.

Myanmar Peace Centre

Created in 2012 to support the government in the peace process. Key personnel include Dr Kyaw Yin Hlaing (see above), U Hla Maung Shwe (see above), U Tin Maung Thann (see above), U Kyaw Soe Naing (Tin Maung Thann's friend), U Aung Naing Oo (former exiled dissident and head of the Vahu Development Institute), Dr Min Zaw Oo (former dissident and academic).

Other organisations/people mentioned in the book

AUSAID Australian Agency for International Development, later renamed and integrated with the Department of Foreign Affairs and Trade (DFAT).

MPSI Myanmar Peace Support Initiative, led by Charles Petri working with Dr Ashley South and Mi Kun Cha Non (amongst others).

BC British Council.

ABBREVIATIONS

ABFSU	All Burma Federation of Students Union
ACDE	Action Committee for Democratic Education
ADB	Asian Development Bank
ASEAN	Association of South East Asian Nations
BCP	Burmese Communist Party
BGF	Border Guard Force
CBOs	Community Based Organisations
CCA	Child Centric Approach to education
CESR	Comprehensive Education Sector Review
CSOs	Civil Society Organisations
EAGs	Ethnic Armed Groups
EPIC	Education Promotion Implementation Committee
ETWG	Education Thematic Working Group
FES	Friedrich Ebert Stiftung (Foundation)
FESR	Framework for Economic and Social Reform
FNS	Friedrich Naumann Stiftung (Foundation)
FPTP	First Past The Post (electoral system)
ILO	International Labour Organisation
IMF	International Monetary Fund
KAS	Konrad Adenauer Stiftung (Foundation)
LID	Light Infantry Division
LNGO	Local Non Governmental Organisations
MDRI	Myanmar Development Resource Institute
ME	Myanmar Egress
MEC	Myanmar Economic Corporation
MEC	Myanmar Education Consortium
MEPE	Myanmar Electric Power Enterprise

ABBREVIATIONS

MFF	Myanmar Fisheries Federation
MI	Military Intelligence
MIC	Myanmar Investment Commission
MNCs	Multinational Corporations
MNEC	Mon National Education Committee
MOGE	Myanmar Oil and Gas Enterprise
MPC	Myanmar Peace Centre
MPT	Myanmar Post and Telecommunications
NAG	Nargis Action Group
NBF	Nationalities Brotherhood Foundation
NCA	Nationwide Ceasefire Accord
NCCT	National Ceasefire Coordination Team
NEMC	National Energy Management Committee
NGOs	Non Governmental Organisations
NPT	Nay Pyi Taw, capital of Myanmar
NRC	National Registration Card
PDSG	Peace Donor Support Group
PEPC	Parliamentary Education Promotion Committee
PR	Proportional Representation (electoral system)
SEEs	State-owned Economic Enterprises
SEZ	Special Economic Zone
SITAN	Situational Analysis
SLORC	State Law and Order Restoration Council
SPDC	State Peace and Development Council
TCA	Teacher Centric Approach to education
TRC	Temporary Registration Cards
UEC	Union Election Commission
UMEHL	Union of Myanmar Economic Holdings Ltd
UMFCCI	Union of Myanmar Federation of Chambers of Commerce and Industry
UN	United Nations
UNESCO	United Nations Educational Scientific and Cultural Orgaisation
UNICEF	United Nations Children's Fund
UNFC	United Nationalities Federal Council
UPWC	Union Peace-making Work Committee
WB	World Bank
WGEC	Working Group for Ethnic Coordination

INTRODUCTION

REFORMS, CIVIL SOCIETY AND THE CHALLENGE OF DEMOCRATISATION IN THE WAKE OF MILITARY RULE

Myanmar is reforming. In the country where for decades life seemed to have come to a standstill, everything is changing at breakneck speed. Positions and policies are fluid and nothing can be taken for granted any more. The military might not have returned to the barracks, but at least it is no longer a troika of military generals calling the shots. What we are looking at is a changed country.

Myanmar today seems to be planets away from the Myanmar of ten years ago—the time at which this book starts. There are many very visible changes in Yangon, and increasingly around the rest of the country: from new infrastructure, the increased pace of life, the growing middle classes, to the changed atmosphere with regard to political and social engagement. Today traffic jams fill the streets with new, imported cars, and Yangon resembles a giant building site. Everyone is rushing around with mobile phones. The 'international community' is present both in the aid and the investment sectors. The World Bank has opened its offices, and Western and Asian development partners make regular trips to Nay Pyi Taw to help with capacity-building at an official level. This includes the police being taught how to be polite and how to live up to its motto, 'May I help you?'[1] Daily (uncensored)[2] newspapers criticise the government, MPs in parliament debate new laws, holding the executive to account. Sometimes this even results in rows between the powerful speaker of the house[3] and the president.

All this is the result of positive reforms, but there is also another side to the story that is unfolding. There is a widening gap between rural and urban Myanmar, at social, economic and political levels. Inflation has made the income divide between the urban middle classes and rural poor much starker. Land is now at a premium, so peasants are losing their livelihoods to development schemes, not least due to the establishment of special economic zones (SEZs) that are being created to bring more foreign investment to Myanmar. Social justice has not been sufficiently part of the reform agenda, despite it being promised as a pillar by President Thein Sein in his inaugural speech, and reiterated in his 2015 New Year message. The only difference from 'before' is that now those who have been wronged can protest. So there are loud and visible protests about land ownership all around the country. There are also protests about many other things as well, for example the new education law that is decried by the NLD. The fact that protests are not beaten down by security forces is new too, and in some cases the government has even started to listen.[4]

Are the reforms real?

In the course of 2015, and in light of the elections in November, there has been a big debate about the reforms engendered by President Thein Sein's government since 2011. Both inside and outside the country questions arise as to how far these reforms are real, far-reaching, long-lasting, irreversible etc. The international and domestic press abounds with articles speculating and debating each and every move the government makes, and every word Daw Aung San Suu Kyi utters about what the government did or did not do. On the face of it, as described above, Myanmar has changed remarkably. Just four years ago, in January 2011 before the handover of power to the new government, there was little aid and foreign investment, hardly any development, and widespread ethnic conflict in the border areas. Civil society had to operate with a low profile and stay clear of politics. Anyone advocating or working for change was taking significant risks. Newspapers were heavily censored and private papers only appeared once a week. Owning a mobile phone was considered something of a luxury, as the distribution of SIM cards was tightly controlled. One did not discuss politics or critique the government in public, as it was too dangerous. After all, there were scores of political prisoners languishing in jail on decade-long sentences. Fast forward to today. Who ten years ago would have thought that U Shwe Mann would team up with Daw Aung San Suu Kyi in parliament against the President's Office? Who would have imagined that all ethnic armed group leaders would meet together with the government in Yangon to negotiate a nationwide ceasefire? Anyone suggesting this would have been labelled insane.

It is clear that overall the reforms have had a profound effect. But critics say that the reforms have stalled and that much less change can be seen since 2013. Clearly the Myanmar government chose to tackle the 'low-hanging fruit' first, focusing on visible changes and 'quick wins'. The reforms that have followed, such as structural economic reforms and changes in the education system, do not have immediate visible results; and it will take a few years, if not longer, to show any effect. The newly formed 'democratic' bureaucracy that needs to be learned and mastered has also hampered the speed of the reforms. Now laws and by-laws are extensively debated in the parliaments, then sent to the president who sends them back asking for amendments, resulting in a slow game of ping-pong that can really frustrate those who simply want to get on with the process of change.[5]

More serious is the charge that the reforms are not real. Many, including Daw Aung San Suu Kyi, say openly that deep-seated transformation would require a change in the constitution, that Daw Aung San Suu Kyi should be allowed to stand for president and that the army should relinquish its 25 per cent representation in the legislative assemblies. Those voices also say that unless this happens before the elections in 2015, then the reforms would have been only cosmetic.

But this would be a misunderstanding of the intentions of the current government and the aims of the reforms. The reforms were never meant to create a Western-style democracy, but rather to develop a 'discipline-flourishing democracy'. The government and the army remain in control as they expected to. The constitution was written so as to secure the role of the military, and safeguard those who had changed from uniforms into civilian clothes. Anyone who followed the 2003 'roadmap to democracy' and read the 2008 constitution would have understood this.[6] It was therefore a surprise in the course of 2011 to see that the new civilianised leadership did not want to maintain the status quo, and that within government the 'reformers' led by President Thein Sein saw the need to change the circumstances in which the country was mired.[7] It was this desire—to 'unstick' Myanmar—that engendered a reform process that has allowed for more inclusive decision-making, for a peace process and for economic changes that will eventually benefit the majority of Myanmar's population. However, a Western-style democratisation process was never planned.

This does not mean that what has been achieved should be deemed a failure. Clearly it is not. Quite obviously the country has changed dramatically. If criticising the reforms, it might help to remember what Myanmar was like ten years ago. At that time Morten Pedersen summarised the challenges facing the junta-led regime as: national reconciliation and dealing with differences of opinion by peaceful means, state building, civil service reform, overcoming budget constraints, and the empowerment of ordinary people.[8] These challenges remained constant until 2010. After decades of stasis the Thein Sein government finally started work on all the issues listed above, with some surprisingly successful results.

And whilst it is easy from a Western perspective to decry the reforms as a failure that has not delivered democracy on a platter, this is a misinterpretation of the mindset of the leadership whose aims differ from the aspirations of the NLD[9] and the West. It is on the basis of this understanding that this book seeks to uncover and explain the origins and reasons for the reforms as they were planned (as opposed to how they are wished for by others). The book focuses on key turning points between 2005 and 2010 that led to the current transformation programme, a period that has been under-researched. Subsequently the book maps the main reform priorities of the new government, explaining how they are linked to each other and what has been achieved as a result of the efforts of this government, amounting to a first small step in the direction of 'democratisation'.

The challenge of 'democratisation' in the wake of military rule

As mentioned above, a Western-style democratisation process was not planned, whereas an Asian-style controlled and more inclusive participatory 'democratisation process' has been what President Thein Sein has delivered over the last four years. It is this version of 'democratisation' that the book aims to describe and discuss, and it has to be clear from the outset that what is happening in Myanmar cannot be measured by Western standards, but rather judged by local and Southeast Asian views. As a process, 'democratisation' is highly complex and involves shifts in many different spheres of governance and social relations. There are multifaceted priorities that include ending armed conflict, introducing economic reforms and some form of participatory politics, as well as allowing ordinary citizens freedom of speech and association. As Morten Pedersen said in 2005: 'It is the totality of these processes that matters, both for the sustainability of democracy as a system of government and for progress in human security and welfare.'[10] Looking back at the time before 2011 from the 2015 vantage point, a picture emerges that has the trappings of such a democratisation process. However, its path has not been without obstacles. This book aims to describe these obstacles, how they were dealt with and what challenges remain in the process of embedding the new system.

INTRODUCTION

At this point it is useful to have a brief look at the actors who engendered the reforms. Mary Callahan describes how President Thein Sein, Lower House Speaker U Shwe Mann and General Min Aung Hlaing emerged as key personalities in the new leadership. She notes that they are still all male, ethnic Burman, retired or active-duty military officers. They had been hand-picked by the retiring Senior General Than Shwe, who did not seem to realise the reformist tendencies amongst some of those whom he placed at the helm of a new system. How the reformists managed to prevail over the more conservative elements is described in Chapter 3, but it is pertinent to mention here that part of President Thein Sein's success was based on a significant step of separating the non-military government functions from the military high command that remained under the leadership of General Min Aung Hlaing.[11] This move, as described by Mary Callahan, created a new political space that became jointly owned by the new civilianised government as well as new political actors, such as the NLD, the Ethnic Armed Groups and civil society. It also allowed the new political actors to strengthen the newly formed institutions. This move was only possible because of General Than Shwe's retirement, which in turn allowed the new president to establish and act upon his reform priorities. First in line was the national reconciliation with Daw Aung San Suu Kyi and the NLD, and their reintegration into the political spectrum. Second came the peace process with the armed groups. President Thein Sein used the fluidity of the new political space and the retreat of the senior generals to appropriate policy-making prerogatives that had previously rested with the military high command.[12] He took a considerable personal risk in doing so, but could base the changes on an already developed civil society and private sector businesses that had been pushing for change for almost a decade. In offering political and economic change, the new president was in tune with the emerging urban middle classes, who had worked hard to push the boundaries as far as possible under the previous regime. It is to his credit that President Thein Sein was able to tune into the calls for non-revolutionary change and push through a programme that has today brought about the greatest transformation of Myanmar since 1962.

Why this book?

This book makes three contributions. First of all it aims to fill a gap in the literature about the origins and start of the Myanmar reform process. Few researchers travelled to Myanmar in the decade preceding the 2010 elections and therefore there is a distorted picture that was created by aid agencies sitting in Thailand on the border as well as by activists and the press. Whilst much of the awful situation they reported on the border was true, it did not give a full picture of what was happening inside the country, far away from the combat troops fighting ethnic armed groups and persecuting ethnic minorities. A lot was happening in Yangon as of early 2005 that would shape the reforms post 2010. This book aims to describe a large part of that picture. In doing so it locates itself at the heart of a few civil society organisations that emerged in the mid 2000s and were able to shape events. This viewpoint is unique as well as contested. Clearly, the same events could be (and are)[13] interpreted very differently by those who were members of the NLD, heavily persecuted at the time. However the story of Myanmar Egress and other ethnic civil society organisations is real and needs to be told. The views expressed in this book are clearly written from a perspective of the organisations that struggled to make change happen, choosing not to take the path of confrontation, protest and revolution, but rather trying to push the internal boundaries as far as possible, often at great personal risk to the leaders of these organisations. In choosing this path, they were not hampered in the same way as the NLD (or any other political party for that matter), simply because they managed to stay mostly clear of politics in public, but also because they were able to create new alliances with those who would eventually come to power post 2010 and who shared their views on gradual non-revolutionary transformation.

Civil society—key driver for change

This book's second contribution is the mapping of the role of civil society in Myanmar. It argues that civil society was and is key to the transformation and reform process since the start. It also puts the voices of ordinary Myanmar individuals who shaped the changes at the heart of the narrative. The changes started internally, bottom-up. Eventually these organisations and their leaders did receive some very limited international financial support, but mostly under the radar. Whilst today the changes look top-down and elite-driven, one should not forget where they originated nor underestimate the ties that have been created between the government elite and those civil society organisations that are at the origins of the reforms. In sum, it was the space created inadvertently by the military junta that first allowed civil society to occupy and define that space. As time progressed and new alliances were formed, some key civil society organisations were able to shape events by exercising important influence. As the new executive has evolved, certain individuals and groups, who emerged out of the Myanmar CSO landscape, were able actively to drive and define change. This does not mean that the military has in any way retreated as a key stakeholder in the process.

More is said about civil society in Chapter 1, but given that civil society is the main protagonist of this book and has been key in engendering and maintaining Myanmar's reform process, it is worth describing what is meant by this term in the Myanmar context. It is important to remember that civil society in Myanmar is far from homogeneous. Most civil society leaders will disagree quite vehemently about pretty much everything. However, in the decade preceding the 2010 elections, many were able to form alliances with each other, and their common aim for a changed, better Myanmar made many of the disagreements fade.

Civil society is often defined as the space between the state and family, which is autonomous and separated from the state.[14] Steinberg says that in the case of Myanmar, civil society 'is best more narrowly defined' to include 'non-ephemeral organisations of individuals banded together to pursue a common purpose or purposes through group activities and by peaceful means'.[15] This definition therefore excludes political parties, armed groups and the business sector. The term does not exist in Burmese and is usually left in English.[16] When SLORC/SPDC came to power, they severely restricted the space for civil society to develop, starting with the decree that assemblies of more than six people were illegal. Those who wanted to form non-political social welfare organisations were required to register their organisations with the Ministry of Home Affairs.[17] However, space did eventually open up. The development of 'modern'[18] civil society in Myanmar happened first in the ethnic regions due to the 1990s ceasefires that are described in more detail in Chapter 1. Many were based on actions taken by faith groups involved in the ceasefire dialogue process.[19] By the early 2000s a large number of local initiatives were active across the country, focusing on welfare and religious activities[20] but also on education and the environment. These were mainly self-help groups that assisted the poorest of the poor, who had no other recourse, as the state was not providing many of the most basic social services.[21] These types of organisations were mostly referred to as Community Based Organisations or CBOs. A 2003 survey cited by Kramer estimates the number of local CBOs/NGOs at the time at 270.[22] Later changes in the military intelligence structures and Cyclone Nargis helped more organisations develop. Since there were so many new organisations, many of which needed financial help from embassies or

INGOs, Paung Ku was established in 2007 by a consortium of international and local agencies in Myanmar as one of the main organisations helping to bridge the gap and allow small local NGOs to access international funding.[23] Paung Ku was not only able to help smaller local NGOs with finance, but also INGOs and donors to start accessing the wide network of CBOs beyond that tiny fraction of elite-driven urban civil society initiatives. Such funding streams allowed for civil society literally to 'bloom' in the pre-election period.

In 2010 Mary Callahan wrote about the thousands of local NGOs that were not linked to the NLD and that were changing the social landscape of Myanmar. Part of the change were the links that the leaders of such organisations had created with regime officials in order to be able to function. At the same time such links served to educate the officials on global and humanitarian issues. This process managed to 'push back the boundaries or arbitrary power and uncontrolled force'[24] that had dominated the way Myanmar functioned until then. Callahan remembers how her fieldwork uncovered the way in which these disconnected organisations wanted to promote empowerment, advocacy and democracy, without linking themselves to the NLD.[25] This was the start of what was later dubbed 'the third force', heavily denounced by exile activists, campaign groups and the media.[26]

Civil society in Myanmar is multifaceted. When discussing civil society in Myanmar it is important to remember how the different organisations emerged and that there are different 'types' of organisations, some of which emerged out of the reform process and others which preceded the reforms and were instrumental in initiating the reforms. Today some of the more established and well networked CBOs and CSOs use formal and informal channels to influence policy-making around many of today's most contested issues including land reform, environmental protection and private investments.[27] Some CSOs and CBOs have been created by 'alumni' of the original organisations, such as Myanmar Egress.[28] In other cases coalitions of interest formed themselves spontaneously in opposition to issues such as the Myitsone dam or the two land bills[29] that are seen as favouring large corporations over the small farmers who have tilled the land for generations. These coalitions do not necessarily become formalised organisations, but according to Mark SiuSue one public campaign through which farmers were able to voice their concerns about the new proposed legislation was considered so effective that other groups replicated the campaign around the country and created a sort of 'secretariat' to coordinate the campaign.[30]

What is interesting to note is how the relationship between CSOs and the government developed over the years. Whilst the NLD as a political party was persecuted for decades, the emerging local NGOs, CBOs and CSOs needed to form local alliances and personal relationships with officials within the regime in order to function. How this was pioneered in 2005/6 is described in Chapter 1. Today most civil society leaders are only able to have the social and political impact they seek because of the networks and social relationships they have created over the years. These networks have also helped convert officials into allies and champions of the cause. Myanmar's structures always operated on networks—originally socialist party and military networks. What is interesting is how civil society leaders appropriated this model, creating new networks which now dominate policy-making. In doing so these organisations are now able to complement the role of the government, bridge the gaps between citizens and the state and become the channels of communication between society and the government.

Rewriting history

This book has a third and final aim. Often when events inside a country remain unrecorded by Western observers, history tends to be rewritten, with very little understanding of the local circumstances. There is already a policy discourse on the extraordinary success of the Western sanctions policy, allegedly forcing Myanmar to open up. Nothing could be further from the truth. Sanctions if anything made the initial change process much harder. Enough has been written on the ineffectiveness of sanctions and how the leadership remained unaffected—it does not need to be rehashed here.[31] President Thein Sein's government certainly wanted sanctions lifted, but this is not *why* the reforms started or *how* they started. The book recounts and reviews the true motivations behind the reforms, challenging the dominant narrative that only ever saw a part of the full picture.

Looking into the future

2015 is a key year in Myanmar history: the country is due to go to the polls in what will possibly be the first free and fair parliamentary elections[32] since independence with all stakeholders participating. The officials and policymakers in Nay Pyi Taw are clear that the reform process will be totally discredited if these elections are rigged in any way. They are also aware that this means they could lose power. Those interviewed for this book expressed that their only aim between 2011 and 2015 was to use the time to cement a new

Myanmar where peace and prosperity would be able to take root and grow with subsequent governments. As such, the peace process and economic reforms have been key to the change process.

This book draws on a decade of intense work and engagement within Myanmar at the heart of the key civil society organisations that were the origins of the reform process. The original data used emanate from fieldwork between 2005 and 2015. The views and voices of key civil society leaders, including a number of ethnic civil society organisations, allow for a 'worm's-eye' view of the change process. I have been travelling to Myanmar several times a year since 2005, working with various local NGOs, training key civil society leaders, and I have been with Myanmar Egress since it was founded in 2006. As a result I was fortunate first to see the change process from its early days, and later to have unprecedented access to the key CSO and political figures involved in the reforms through the local networks that were created prior to 2011. I have also worked with ethnic civil society organisations since 2005 and therefore had access to the key leaders of the EAGs as well. This has allowed me to hear both sides of the argument, especially with regard to the ongoing and rather fraught peace process.

Since 2011 I have led large-scale funded research projects on education, decentralisation, citizenship, ethnic political parties and the peace process.[33] Aside from the literature cited, all chapters draw on original fieldwork data, some of it collected across the country with the help of a Myanmar research team.[34]

Structure of the book

This book charts Myanmar's reform process, starting in 2005 after the purge of General Khin Nyunt in 2004. His arrest allowed a handful of new, education-oriented civil society organisations to develop and lead an unprecedented reform process from within. Chapters 1 and 2 cover how Myanmar got from 2005 to 2011, specifically looking at the role of civil society. Chapter 1 focuses on the political importance of the early ceasefires agreed between the main EAGs and General Khin Nyunt which allowed civil society in ethnic regions to develop. It covers the seven-step roadmap, the changes within Military Intelligence after 2005, the creation of Myanmar Egress (ME) and how ME used new policy networks to challenge the military network that was in power. This chapter also looks at the civil unrest ('saffron revolution') of 2007, Cyclone Nargis and the resumption of international aid, and how this new

INTRODUCTION

engagement with the West empowered civil society organisations. The chapter ends with the referendum on the constitution.

Chapter 2 focuses on the pre- and post-election periods and how young people and civil society organisations felt about political participation. In providing a reinterpretation of this period that has really only sketchily been described before, the book aims to show through the drama and crises of these five years how new actors emerged to lead civil society organisations and push for non-revolutionary change.

After these two background chapters, the book follows the reforms thematically in the order of priority given by President Thein Sein at the start of his new government in 2011: national reconciliation with the NLD, peace with the ethnic armed groups, economic and education reforms.

Chapter 3 focuses on the start of the political reform by analysing General Than Shwe's legacy and the division of power at the centre of the new government which resulted in a 'battle' between reformers and hardliners in Nay Pyi Taw during summer 2011. The chapter reviews the national reconciliation process and how the NLD was reintegrated into the political fold through discussions with Daw Aung San Suu Kyi, and what led up to the president meeting Daw Aung San Suu Kyi and posing for the press under General Aung San's photo.

Chapter 4 focuses on the second presidential priority of peace with the EAGs. It reviews the early negotiations with the different groups and the issue that led to conflict in Kachin State in the summer of 2011. It also explains how ethnic demands differ between groups. A key aspect of the peace process is the struggle between the presidency, parliament and the army, as well as the differences between the UNFC and the Working Group for Peace. The role of the Myanmar Peace Centre, U Aung Min, U Soe Thein and the role of Norway's MPSI are discussed in light of the lead-up to the first EAG meeting in Laiza and the first joint negotiations with the government in Myitkyina in 2013. The chapter ends with discussion on the state of the negotiations of the Nationwide Ceasefire agreement before the November 2015 elections. The chapter also gives detailed views on the process from all stakeholders, including the government, the EAG leaders, civil society leaders and ordinary people who took part in a survey.

Chapter 5 reviews the economic reforms and re-engagement with the international community. It discusses the currency reform, the return of the IMF and the World Bank, as well as the role of the international community, especially Japan, but also new relations with the US and the EU.

Chapter 6 discusses the situation of state education today, explaining how Myanmar's diverse education system (state, monastic, private and ethnic) has developed over the last decade. Drawing on a survey of over 200 teachers, the chapter explains the current issues and the aspirations of those who work in the sector. The chapter then goes on to discuss the competing reform processes between the CESR (Ministry of Education), EPIC (the Presidency), NNER (NLD) and the Parliamentary Committee led by Daw Aung San Suu Kyi and U Shwe Mann. The role of the development partners (UNICEF, AUSAID, DFID and EU) and their relations with the different education stakeholders (and how they try to influence the new education system) is also discussed. The issue of ethnic education systems and mother-tongue education is explained with examples drawn from Mon, Karen and Kachin States.

Chapter 7 looks at political and nationalism issues that have emerged during the reform process and have marred the early successes. This includes the debate around who is a Myanmar national, who has the right to live in Myanmar, the issue of the Rohingya, the role of religion in defining national identity, the census and the views of ordinary citizens, as well as the radicalisation of the Sangha (monastic community of Buddhist monks and nuns).

The Conclusion looks at the changing politics and role of political parties in light of the upcoming 2015 elections. It reviews the debates around constitutional change and the power struggles between the presidency, the parliament, Daw Aung San Suu Kyi and the chief of staff.

1

HOW MYANMAR GOT FROM 2005 TO 2010

THE ROLE OF CIVIL SOCIETY

Winds of change

It is always difficult to pinpoint the exact origin of change. Many different elements feed into change, and in Myanmar the complex interplay of different political actors in the 1990s makes this even more challenging. However, one event and one year stand out, without which none of what followed could have happened. In the autumn of 2004 General Khin Nyunt, then Prime Minister and Director of Defence Services Intelligence or Military Intelligence (MI) and former third in command of the junta's troika,[1] was arrested on charges of corruption.[2] The entire intelligence corps was discharged with him.[3] Not much information is available on the motives and circumstances of these arrests, but Khin Nyunt had already fallen from grace earlier, as he was demoted from number three to the much less powerful position of Prime Minister in August 2003. He was seen as having become too powerful and too popular. According to Kyaw Yin Hlaing there was a long-standing struggle between the army and the intelligence corps. A clash occurred between intelligence and army units in Muse (on the China border, north-east of Myanmar) in September 2004 and senior army officials came to the conclusion that the intelligence corps was becoming too powerful.[4]

Khin Nyunt had built up a parallel power structure that was widely perceived as a threat to other junta leaders. His difficult relationship between 1997 and 2004 with the junta's number two, General Maung Aye, also contributed to his arrest.[5] Khin Nyunt was politically important, as he was the instigator of the seven-step 'roadmap'[6] that would eventually lead to the 2010 elections, the architect of the ceasefires signed with many ethnic armed groups in the early 1990s, and he was the darling of the few Western agencies that operated inside the country in the 1990s and early 2000s. His personal agreement with the ICRC's regional director David Delapraz (based in Delhi at the time) opened up all of Myanmar's jails to ICRC inspections.[7] With regard to the wider population, he was known to tour the country and address complaints and issues personally. Consequently many, both Burmese and foreigners, saw him as a 'liberal' or a potential 'reformer'. However, despite this overall reformist impression, he was also the merciless head of military intelligence, responsible for the political prisoners numbering over 2,000 who languished in Myanmar's jails. During his rule anyone in the Bamar heartland who dared speak against the regime was followed by his agents and at risk of arrest.

At the time of Khin Nyunt's arrest, there was a fear that the National Convention which had operated on and off for a few years to write the basic principles for a new constitution would not be reconvened and the ceasefires would collapse, bringing new turmoil to Myanmar. This especially worried the few Western agencies that had projects or offices in Myanmar at the time. That same year, Robert Taylor[8] described the country as stuck in 'political stalemate and societal stasis'.[9] Taylor said that:

> ... among the societies of Southeast Asia, it [Myanmar] is the only major country which appears nearly six decades after independence not to have yet resolved the consequences of its past in order to build a more prosperous and open society for its people. The legacy of civil war, separatism, ideological conflicts, socialism, under-investment, inadequate infrastructure, and other consequences of an overemphasis on security have created a poverty stricken society in crisis in terms of health and educational provision.[10]

Looking back ten years later, it is clear that it was impossible to imagine the changes and the transformation that were about to occur.

Myanmar's reform process took off with Khin Nyunt's arrest,[11] but in order to understand how things evolved after the winter of 2004, one has to take a look at two of Khin Nyunt's legacies that were to shape the subsequent process: the ethnic ceasefires of the 1990s and the emergence of the seven-step roadmap.

The 1990s ethnic ceasefires—the first step

Myanmar had suffered from an ongoing civil war since its independence in 1948. As of 1979, funding from China dried up for the ethnic rebel movements that had originally been led by the Burmese Communist Party. By the late 1980s some of the ethnic armed groups (EAGs) became open to negotiating with the regime. Prior to this, the military junta's objective had been to defeat all opposition through the military,[12] but the military leadership changed tack. In the 1990s, General Khin Nyunt devised and led a ceasefire process that resulted in eighteen armed ceasefires between the army and different EAGs of the following ethnicities: Kachin, Kayah (Karenni), Shan, Rakhine, Mon, Wa, PaO and Palaung.[13] By 2006, twenty-five groups had agreed ceasefires with the SPDC.[14] The basic agreement between the regime and the armed groups was that the ceasefire groups would be allowed to keep their arms and control their territories until a new constitution was put together. Khin Nyunt believed that the system he was proposing would allow ceasefire leaders to re-enter politics as heads of political parties.

With each agreed deal, more troops were freed up to fight in the areas where no agreement had been reached. Beyond the opportunity offered on the political spectrum, the economic angle was also important as ethnic armed groups were now able to exploit the natural resources in their areas not only to finance conflict, but also to develop their areas. The hope was that once the rebels stopped fighting the army, the people in the region could pursue their traditional agriculture and live normal lives without regularly having to flee the violence. In turn the army promised to support improved health and education services as well as infrastructure.

> While the precise details of the ceasefire agreements the regime separately negotiated with different armed groups have never been public, a growing body of data suggests that the number of joint ventures extracting gems, precious metals, minerals, tropical hardwoods and other valuable resources dramatically increased in each of the former conflict zones immediately after a ceasefire was declared. Significantly, most of these joint ventures were not formally registered companies; rather, they were ad hoc entities that opportunistically linked military and commercial interests together in a particular place, though rarely on equal terms. Typically these entities partnered members of different Tatmadaw field battalions, different ceasefire groups, state owned enterprises, and local entrepreneurs, especially those with access to foreign capital via transnational personal networks.[15]

Given that all the field battalions are expected to be economically self-sufficient, joint ventures certainly helped as they allowed the battalions to collect rent or protection fees and a percentage of the commodities extracted.[16] Smith has described in detail the 'new economic complexes' that included government departments, ceasefire organisations, as well as non-ceasefire groups that became involved in logging and gem mining, changing the economies of many of the ethnic states.[17] The rebel forces were allowed to become a kind of local militia, retaining arms[18] and governing their territories.

As a part of the ceasefire movement, a Border Area Development Programme was initiated in 1989. In 1992 this became the Ministry for the Progress of Border Areas and National Races. The Ministry built hospitals, health centres, bridges, dams and more than 430 schools as well as thousands of miles of roads in the border townships, including ceasefire areas.[19] The ceasefires were presented as part of the policy of 'national reconsolidation' and, according to Senior General Than Shwe, were 'the most defining characteristic of his government's rule'.[20]

After decades of conflict, the ceasefires improved physical security for the inhabitants of the border regions and allowed basic economic development to take place in areas that less than a decade previously were war zones. As a result there was also a re-emergence of civil society networks and indigenous language schools. Civil society organisations and NGOs developed, but they were limited to development, educational and health issues and had to stay well clear of politics. Some of these organisations had emerged directly out of the ceasefires, for example Shalom was set up by Reverend Saboi Jum, and his daughter Ja Nan later extended the work beyond Kachin State to other ethnic states. Ashley South explains with hindsight that 'the previously missing or dormant civil society has, over the past decade, come back to life especially in areas where ceasefires between armed ethnic groups and the military are in place'.[21] Already in 2001 Seng Raw, the founder of Metta, expressed her frustration that Western governments did not recognise the political significance of the ceasefires and what they had achieved. She said:

> It is important to stress that, in principle, as one of the key elements in the peace process, the former SLORC government—now the SPDC—and the ceasefire groups have agreed upon the institution of development projects as one of the most vital ways to stabilize the peace and foster reconciliation. From the perspective of ethnic minority groups, this is another important proof of political recognition—and it is through such agreements between previously opposing parties that it is trusted that peace and reconciliation can eventually be brought to the entire country.[22]

Aside from giving space to civil society to develop, another successful measure in certain ceasefire areas was opium eradication. Due to Chinese and UN pressure, the ex-CPB National Democratic Alliance Army (MNDAA) announced a ban on growing and processing opium in 1997 (although the ban was not effective until 2002), and drug-trafficking on the Shan–China border therefore greatly reduced.[23] Conversely, the ban led to increased internal displacement in the Wa and Kokang areas as livelihoods were forced to change. At the same time the ceasefires allowed the military to militarise areas previously affected by conflict. There continued to be instances of forced labour in areas close to ceasefire zones, and welfare services remained painfully under-resourced. Extraction of natural resources (mainly timber, but also gold and jade) increased, and mining was poorly regulated, damaging the environment. Most importantly the ceasefires did not lead to a more sustained dialogue or political peace process[24] and fighting continued in some areas, most notably Karen State where no ceasefire agreement had been reached between the regime and the KNU.

All ceasefire groups were part of the National Convention, which reopened on 14 May 2004. The government hand-picked most of the 1,000 plus delegates. Over one hundred delegates represented the twenty-eight ceasefire groups.

> As noted, the ceasefire groups were a mixed bunch, enjoying varying degrees of legitimacy. Nevertheless, they did share a number of common concerns, and in their deliberations at the National Convention were able to develop coherent positions on several key issues. If nothing else, the ceasefire groups' participation in the convention created opportunities to focus on the centrality of the 'ethnic question' in Burmese politics. Whether or not their demands were accepted, in expressing their concerns, the ceasefire groups laid important groundwork for the future.[25]

Their main demands included increased legislative and administrative power for local governments, the formation of local ethnic security forces and a federal union of Burma. In the end these proposals would not be included in the draft constitution, which led to further problems and threats by certain groups to take up arms again.

The emergence of a 'roadmap to democracy'

As mentioned above, Khin Nyunt was also the architect of the seven-step roadmap.[26] The roadmap was announced in August 2003 and the SPDC staunchly refused to provide a timetable for the next stages. The first step was a reconvening of the National Convention that had been suspended in 1996.[27] Daw Aung San Suu Kyi would not accept the conditions on the NLD's participation in the National Convention spelled out by the SPDC, so she was not allowed to attend and the NLD boycotted the process.[28] The speed at which this roadmap was progressing was labelled 'glacial'[29] as the National Convention and its drawing up of a new draft constitution took fourteen years. In January 2006, the National Convention Convening Commission Chairman, Lieutenant General Thein Sein,[30] noted that fifteen chapters of the draft constitution had been completed, comprising around 75 per cent of the work.[31] The National Convention finally drew to a close in 2007.

At the same time that the roadmap was slowly moving forward, the SPDC also started to organise itself administratively by developing the USDA (Union Solidarity and Development Association, founded in 1993),[32] which was being groomed to become a political actor for the planned elections. All civil servants were expected to become members of the USDA, and the organisation focused mainly on public campaigns supportive of the regime.

In November 2005 the SPDC announced to everyone's surprise that the government would be shifting the capital to Nay Pyi Taw, near Pyinmana at the centre of the country. There was much speculation about why this move was taking place. As Pedersen reminds his readers, 'In traditional Southeast Asia the establishment of a new capital often marked the founding of a new dynasty. [...] Than Shwe, it appears, is walking in the footsteps of the kings of the past.'[33] Aside from building a brand new capital with all the trappings, including wide avenues, gardens at the centre of every roundabout, ministries and a very large presidential palace, all supplied by limited amounts of electricity (Yangon regularly suffered severe power cuts), Than Shwe also removed the government officials from Yangon, and hence from all the action that was starting to brew underground. This was fortuitous as with the removal of the officials, any overseeing by intelligence and police services became more sporadic and less intense. All in all this also contributed to the consolidation of a reform movement amongst civil society groups.

The Western diplomats in Yangon[34] at first speculated that the military was worried about a potential US military strike, but actually what was probably more accurate was the suspicion that Than Shwe saw himself as the last king in Myanmar and wanted to secure his legacy and his family's future. By mid February all ministries had moved. There was great reluctance and some resistance to this move, as the families of the officials had their children in schools and their spouses at work in Yangon. The train journey departure times to and from Nay Pyi Taw were made particularly awkward (often in the middle of the night for a twelve-hour journey), so that no one could simply jump on a train after meetings and go home.[35] The capital was barely finished at the time of the great move, with most core buildings still being built well into 2008/9.[36]

The rise of a 'new' civil society and a business-minded middle class

Khin Nyunt's arrest led to the second phenomenon: the rise of a 'new' civil society in Yangon. Civil society has always excited in Myanmar. Kyaw Yin Haing depicts how the Sangha[37] was the backbone of Myanmar's civil society across centuries. Focusing primarily on education and people's spiritual development, it was the parallel societal structure, not only during Myanmar's military dictatorships, but already well before this under British colonial rule and prior to that under Myanmar's monarchy. However, the Sangha is expected to be apolitical. Monks and nuns are not allowed to vote, let alone become actively involved in politics. It is this separation between the religious and the secular world which allowed monasteries to continue to function during the junta era. The 'new' civil society that emerged in 2005, however, was not linked to religious institutions, was secular and quickly turned political, albeit not overtly so. The 'space' for this was created by the fact that the risk of arrest clearly diminished drastically after Khin Nyunt and his chief MI agents were removed. It took the government several months before they were able to set up a new intelligence service that was seen as loyal to the junta and not loyal to Khin Nyunt. In January 2005 Myanmar was essentially operating without an intelligence system, and people felt more confident talking to each other about possible change and ways forward as their country was increasingly being left behind in a fast-advancing ASEAN. An embryonic middle class, using education and business networks as vehicles for change, underpinned the emergence of these groups.

Since the early 2000s some private supplementary schools[38] had started to operate in Yangon. Attending government school was compulsory, so the private schools operated in the afternoons, evenings and at weekends outside the official school timings. These schools suffered a number of severe setbacks through government crackdowns.[39] At one point around 2004/5 they were told that they were only allowed to teach English and IT, as all other subjects were sufficiently covered by the government system. According to the Myanmar government website at the time:

> [...] though the private sector has not yet formally been granted a status of setting up Universities with privileges to confer degrees, it has increasingly played an important role in the education market in consonance with the adoption of market mechanisms in the country's economy. The Private Tuition Law of 1964 permits setting up of private schools to teach single subjects per se. Permission is not granted to set up private schools to teach the full curriculum.[40]

The schools that had been set up decided to teach science and maths as part of IT and all other arts and social science subjects under the rubrics of English. The policy as to what could or could not be taught in private schools evolved over the years as their numbers increased. In fact such policies seemed at first to change quite arbitrarily and without much warning.[41] The larger schools operated as registered businesses and were less affected than the smaller community-based outfits, which did not have the same kind of recognised status.

With Khin Nyunt gone, these schools suddenly felt the freedom to teach more of what they wanted: some schools catering for the early years even set out to offer a full curriculum during the day, offering an alternative to government schools; some even started to employ foreigners. This was quite a revolutionary idea, as all Myanmar children at the time were required to attend government schools and foreigners were not really allowed to teach.[42] However, the 'market' for private education and supplementary schools grew quickly from early 2005 onwards. Private schools sprang up at pre-elementary, elementary, secondary and higher education level to cater to the popular demands of the market for English language, computing, accounting and business-related training. Some of them offered a wider curriculum, some focused on just a few subjects. These private organisations, sometimes calling themselves schools and sometimes education centres, were also engaged in preparing students for examinations held by overseas universities and professional institutes. They became the hallmark of the transformation across Myanmar's burgeoning middle classes who wanted change. One of the first people to open a private school in Myanmar was Ko Tar, who credits education and the desire to improve education as the instigator of subsequent changes. He maintains that the changes in the ethnic areas after the ceasefires showed people in Yangon what was possible. Education went hand in hand with grassroots leadership training, and in the Bamar heartland monastic schools were the next torchbearers of the movement. He remembers how in that period monks were sent to attend seminars on 'consumer protection' and 'consumer rights' in Penang, Malaysia. 'But actually it was all about human rights.'[43] In the end a new education movement sprang up across monastic schools linked to Paung Da Oo monastery in Mandalay. The abbot U Nayaka had been close to Khin Nyunt and therefore was in some sense protected. After Khin Nyunt's arrest, all had to tread more carefully, but as long as education was not perceived as political they were able to continue.

Education was also the catalyst for the movement of new civil society organisations which emerged in the wake of Khin Nyunt's arrest. Many realised that whilst children would now be able to get more than just government education, young adults would be left behind. After the 1988 and 1990 student protests the universities had largely been closed. Undergraduate provision had been moved outside the cities into remote areas, and distance university education was encouraged: officially to enable the poorer students to study at home, but mostly to avoid students from getting together and becoming politically active. A whole generation was unable to access education beyond the metric examination, and the quality of government education, especially tertiary education, had fallen dramatically over the decades of isolation, due to under-investment and lack of contact with the outside world. The generation that was the last to complete their university education before 1988 realised that they had been the lucky ones, and that those who came after them would never have access to any form of higher education. Now in their forties or older, some started to think about how the country could and would be able to change, but how a growing number of uneducated young adults would make change ever more difficult.

At this point it is important to discuss the role played by the main German foundations active in Myanmar at that time. Whilst all Western aid and economic relations had been suspended in light of the junta's crackdown in 1988 and the subsequent issues regarding the non-acceptance of the election results of 1990,[44] the two larger German political foundations—the Konrad Adenauer Stiftung (KAS, linked to the CDU) and the Friedrich Ebert Stiftung (FES, linked to the SPD)—still had funding streams for Myanmar. One of the main links was established between Dr Kyaw Yin Hlaing (who was based at NUS in Singapore at the time) and KAS (regional HQs in Kuala Lumpur, Malaysia) to enable foreign academics to come and teach intensive courses to Myanmar junior academics at Yangon University. This programme ran for the first time in the summer of 2004 with academics mainly based at the National University in Singapore. In the summer of 2005 the programme ran again, this time including an academic from the University of London and one from the Hiroshima Peace Institute in Japan, and the team was able to teach not only in Yangon but at Mandalay University as well. The academics between them offered updates in anthropology, international relations, political economy, history and research methods, and despite being recorded, they could say anything and teach what they wanted. KAS money was used to purchase suitcases full of books to bring into the country, and these were then left for the university libraries. Most of these books would have been photocopied and passed on amongst academics, as it was impossible at that time to purchase books from the outside. The programme ran again in 2006, only in Yangon and only for Yangon University academics, with an even wider variety of international staff and a larger offering of subjects. In the summer of 2007 the teaching programme ran into some trouble as the permission to teach at the university was withdrawn.[45] However, teaching did eventually continue, this time at Myanmar Egress, Myanmar's first adult training and research institute.

The creation of Myanmar Egress (ME)

Myanmar Egress has been pivotal in the country's reform process. In the course of 2005 six friends got together and decided that if change was going to come to Myanmar it was only going to happen by expanding the space from within, and not through either a revolution (as had been attempted in 1988) or through pressure from the outside (as the sanctions had been attempting since the 1990s). The idea of an institution that would serve as a training institute, a think tank, a liaison office for reform-minded military government officials and as a catalyst for change can be credited to Dr Nay Win Maung a medical doctor who had left medicine first for business and then left business for journalism.

The main aim of Myanmar Egress was first and foremost the training and education of young adults—the generation that had not had the chance to go to university, and those who could be catalysts for change. All knew that change was on the cards. The roadmap clearly showed that within a few years there would be a new constitution and elections—and although tightly controlled by the state, this also meant the retirement of the two most senior junta leaders, Than Shwe and Maung Aye. It was in light of this that ME wanted to see how far the internal boundaries could be pushed and to prepare the younger generation to make the most of what change might be on offer.

Although Dr Nay Win Maung had studied medicine,[46] he was unhappy practising and therefore decided to work in business. At first he was part of a group that sold timber to China until a policy change banned the export of Myanmar teak, and he is said to have lost close to $150,000. He then started a new business in journalism. He first launched the magazine *Living Colour*, and being friends with Khin Nyunt's younger son Dr Ye Naing Win, he was able to secure a publishing licence. As Myanmar went through economic reforms, he also created a weekly newspaper, *Voice*.

Nay Win Maung and Tin Maung Thann met shortly after Nay Win Maung finished his metric exams. Once Tin Maung Thann came back from having completed his masters in Aquaculture at AIT (Asian Institute of Technology) in Thailand in 1996, he and Nay Win Maung started to meet frequently, often driving around in a car discussing politics. At the time it was not safe to discuss how the country could change in public places, whereas in a car they could not be overheard. Both were convinced that something had to be done to break the political impasse. These discussions went on till 2003, by which time they had started to devise a strategy and were thinking of recruiting others. U Hla Maung Shwe was the first to be brought on board. He was a friend of Nay Win Maung's and had direct links to General Shwe Mann through his business in the Irrawaddy delta and his family connections (his brother had studied at staff college with Shwe Mann).

In 1998 the government decided that professional federations were needed, and the Myanmar Fisheries Federation (MFF) (originally the Fisheries and Aquatic Technicians Association) became the first political platform for ideas to be aired and exchanged. Tin Maung Thann was on the executive board and by 2005 was able to organise public lectures for an audience much wider than the MFF members. At the time Tin Maung Thann's main aim was to establish a successful tilapia business, which he saw as a way of feeding more protein to Myanmar citizens. His involvement with the MFF was therefore in the first instance professional, but he also realised what a powerful platform such an association could become. UMFCCI and other associations also started to send their members, and the various associations were able to network with each other. This was a highly risky proposition at the time. Dr Nu Nu Yin, a professor in business administration and Nay Win Maung's friend, started to give public lectures every other week at MFF. Established organisations and businesses known to the organisers were used to recruit the audience. The public lectures were first on business-related topics so as to escape the intelligence services radar. Gradually the lectures took on a different tone, discussing issues related to state and nation building, but still very much under the cover of business topics and titles.

In parallel, the core network that was to start Myanmar Egress kept growing. Nay Win Maung met Kyaw Yin Hlaing in Brussels in 2005 and brought him on board. Nay Win Maung's childhood friend Kyaw Ni Khin, a successful architect who was involved in hotel training, joined as well. Later Nay Win Maung also brought Sonny Nyunt Thein to the group, a neighbour and travel agent who had had trading activities with Germany and whose third wife was German. Kyaw Yin Hlaing brought his childhood friend Ye Mya Thu from Mandalay to the group, but U Hla Maung Shwe and Kyaw Ni Khin already knew him through business connections. Between 2005 and 2006 the group started to discuss creating an organisation, and the name 'Egress' was chosen as 'the way out'.

In the summer of 2006 the Burma Studies conference was held in Singapore. The conference venue was so close to Yangon that it was relatively easy for Myanmar nationals to attend, and Kyaw Yin Hlaing organised the attendance of local civil society representatives. A meeting was held over dinner at the Royal Thazin Restaurant, where Nay Win Maung, Kyaw Ni Khin, Tin Maung Thann and many others were present. The idea was that this conference would for the first time have a substantive voice from inside Myanmar rather than being dominated by foreign researchers or those based on the border. Most of those who went to Singapore were not academics. Yet they all presented papers on issues regarding the situation of Myanmar's civil society, education and other issues in which they had been involved. Ma Ja Nan Lahtaw[47] from Shalom was there as one of the representatives of ethnic civil society. Others included Dr Khin Zaw Win, a dentist and former political prisoner, who after his twelve years in jail (and upon his release after Khin Nyunt's arrest) decided to get involved in education; and Kyaw Thu, who had worked with the free funeral service, amongst others. Members of the MFF were also well represented. The conference was an occasion at which local Myanmar civil society actors were able to showcase what work they were doing, bringing them closer to the German foundations[48] that were ready and willing to fund programmes to support change, and creating a better network with each other.

The conference was also the first time ever that activists and exiles based out in Thailand were able to meet with a large group of civil society actors from inside the country. Despite the conference-based socialising, this did not result in a meeting of minds. It quickly became apparent that the biggest fault-line was between those who were working for change from inside the country and those who were working on the border, with the latter group castigating many from inside Myanmar as junta collaborators. There was however a break-through at some point, as the conference is tipped today as the starting point of the 'Bangkok process':[49] this was Nay Win Maung's brainchild for a system by which change agents inside would start to engage with activists in exile.

Later in 2006 the ME founders held their first meeting, with Aye Mya Hlaing taking notes. They decided to rent the back offices of the Thamada Hotel. ME was registered as a business, which because of Kyaw Ni Khin's position in hotel training could have a hotel school status for a while, so that teaching and training were not heavily scrutinised. (When the offices were renovated, some teaching kitchens were built—but never used.) One evening in June 2007, at an auspicious time,[50] the board of Myanmar Egress was put up on the wall of the offices, while still being painted in green and blue by workers. The renovation works were still going on and the paint was barely dry on the walls when Nay Win Maung moved the offices of *Voice* and *Living Colour* into the premises, and Tin Maung Thann and Sonny Nyunt Thein also moved their offices into the building.

Now that ME had an office, the group decided to offer a number of social science courses. There were disagreements at first as to what kind of teaching and training this should be. Kyaw Yin Hlaing's aim was to train people with academic potential. He also maintained that the other ME founders did not have an academic background and therefore might not be able to teach at higher education level. The other founders, in particular Nay Win Maung and Tin Maung Thann, wanted to use ME to create political space and develop a political and social identity amongst the young middle-class Myanmar citizens who had missed out on 'proper' education. The idea was to recruit those who were enthusiastic, even if they had limited skills and few qualifications, and develop them into change agents. Nay Win Maung and Kyaw Yin Hlaing fought, but the final agreement reached at the Fuji Coffee House was that ME would accommodate Kyaw Yin Hlaing's summer school as E001, and a new course would be designed for those with no foreign language skills called E002. Tin Maung Thann had been a training expert so set to work with Nay Win Maung to design a course that would include political and social sciences, focusing on what could not be accessed at the time, and offering an exposure to political economy, development and leadership skills. ME's aim was also to train for social and political mobilisation, which resulted in a second disagreement between Kyaw Yin Hlaing and Nay Win Maung.[51]

E002 became ME's flagship course, run three times a year with three months' duration. Nay Win Maung taught well over 100 hours and Tin Maung Thann taught 68 hours during each session. Through their networks, ME recruited others to teach as well; Tin Maung Thann categorised them as 'the best brains in the country'. Funds were a challenge, and at first ME ran business workshops to get seed money to pay the teachers.[52] After three successful courses had run, the German foundation FES offered 50 per cent funding. The rest was paid by those candidates who could afford it, costing on average $100 per person per course. Many were on scholarships as they had no means to pay the fees, so the FES money and the collected fees had to cover all the candidates. There were mostly three types of students: those who wanted to continue with their studies, those who wanted a career change, and those who were already working as NGO workers or activists. Recruitment happened through the networks of students who had completed the course, snowballing the number of applications. From the second cohort onwards, the newspaper *Voice* also carried an advertisement for the course. In the end the number of students wanting to enrol far exceeded the number of places and all candidates had to be interviewed for the final selection. Some of the graduates of early courses then joined ME as staff for research and training.

Funding for ME remained a challenge. The other German foundation, KAS, continued to fund the summer school (E001) that had emerged out of the academic training offered at Yangon Universities, but that was for training in English mostly by foreign academics who flew in for a couple of weeks every summer. In order to expand and have an effect, ME needed more than pocket money. The directors—Nay Win Maung, Tin Maung Thann and Sonny Nyunt Thein—met with a friend[53] in Bangkok to write the first ever funding proposal for an EU funding stream that would allow ME to teach hundreds of students. Tin Maung Thann famously said, 'I want one million dollars from this', and he was confident that he would get it. The application did indeed get funded, and ME was able to set up its first suite of courses and employ some core staff, mainly graduates of the first E002 batches. The back of the Thamada Hotel started to look like a small private university with students coming in and out at all times of day. With the help of more funding from FES, a special residential course was set up for young people from the ethnic states who also slept on the premises.

Within a year of its foundation, ME had funding from multiple European sources and the directors were well connected across the diplomatic circles in Yangon. All Western agencies hoping to support change wanted to be on good terms with ME. Many foreign diplomats could not believe their eyes and ears that an independent institution was teaching—often with foreigners at the helm—without any impediments from the government. Though not widely advertised, ME was starting to develop policy documents which they hoped would influence the changes that were expected to happen through the roadmap. All of this of course also brought criticism, as some (including many of those in exile) propagated the rumour that ME was supported and sponsored by the government and was peddling the regime's ideas. However, the truth was more complex than that.

As important as their own networks, created over many years and with the help of meetings at MFF, were the connections the founders had been able to establish with the regime. The Minister of Agriculture Htay Oo (Shwe Mann's successor in the Irrawaddy delta, south-west command) was their main connection within the system, and ME communicated directly with him. Nay Win Maung had been arrested once for a few weeks in 2002, after writing a paper, but managed to create a connection with the Intelligence Officer who interrogated him. This connection with Special Branch was later used again to keep ME's activities safe.

According to Tin Maung Thann,[54] Nay Win Maung, U Hla Maung Shwe and himself understood the mindset of the military and therefore did not cross any 'red lines'. Their behaviour was based on well-calibrated moves to test the boundaries, but not to end up in jail. When the regime found that the group was going too far, they were harassed. At one point all three had to complete interrogation forms, and although they were not arrested, they thought they would be. Later they heard that the Special Branch chief had instructed the lieutenant colonel responsible at the time to treat them with respect.

Two other military connections helped ME through the early years. Nay Win Maung's father had been a military officer and a trainer at the Tatmadaw's staff college in Pyin Oo Lwin (Maymyo). His mother had also taught there; many of the most senior generals of the regime in those years had had her as an instructor, and their respect for their teacher in some way protected Nay Win Maung.[55] U Hla Maung Shwe also had military connections. His brother had been a classmate of the junta's third in command, General Shwe Mann. Shwe Mann had replaced Khin Nyunt and was younger than the two older senior generals; it was said that he was more open to new ideas, but he was not an overt reformer. Information could thus be passed through U Hla Maung Shwe's brother to the top of the pyramid. Even so, there were many times when local administration and military intelligence took issue with the ME directors. Nay Win Maung was interrogated a number of times; and Sonny Nyunt Thein's wife remembers two officers arriving at her home one evening who, after being asked to have dinner, with many apologies removed Sonny's passport. Aye Mya Hlaing, a close friend of Nay Win Maung who later joined the ME teaching staff, also had connections to MI and made sure that the communication channels between MI and ME remained open. However, sometimes ME did land itself in hot water; this was more often than not the case when Kyaw Yin Hlaing engaged with research or projects that raised questions with local officials. In the summer of 2007, for example, some ME students were on a research project conducted by Kyaw Yin Hlaing collecting (what was probably seen as sensitive) data in Lashio. The police in Yangon raised the issue with Nay Win Maung and Tin Maung Thann, who had to call in a number of contacts and favours to avoid any of the students being arrested. However, ME was mostly able to teach and train without impediment.

Aside from training and teaching, ME's activity in writing policy papers became of increasing importance. Over the first years at Egress, Nay Win Maung wrote between 600 and 700 strategy papers addressing political and economic issues that were sent to Shwe Mann. Only one of these managed to get to Than Shwe, as it was on the US policy towards Myanmar at the time when Than Shwe was trying to avoid meeting the UN special rapporteur Gambari. Two papers, one on military intelligence and one on the role of the special branch, were forwarded to Maung Aye.

In parallel to ME growing in Yangon, the ME directors started to engage with the outside world. What was termed the 'Bangkok process' started during 2007, after the first meeting of Myanmar and exiled activists at the Singapore conference of 2006. Military Intelligence had been severely weakened through the arrest of Khin Nyunt, and Nay Win Maung believed after the Singapore conference that it was safe enough to start travelling and developing networks with exiles and others abroad. An invitation to Wilton Park was one of the first international engagements, and others followed. Tin Maung Thann was offered a short Chevening fellowship through the British Embassy, and also joined Nay Win Maung at the Wilton Park conference. Through more international travel the ME founders, but especially Nay Win Maung and Tin Maung Thann, were able to establish personal relationships with prominent exiles such as Aung Naing Oo,[56] Zaw Oo and others. They managed to organise regular meetings with exiles and international donors in Bangkok. Nay Win Maung convinced people to come, even if at the start many had negative views of ME. His view was, 'If we can engage with educated exiles, this will be useful for the change process.'

In parallel to the Bangkok process, there was a 'Bangkok dialogue': one meeting a year between 2007 and 2010 with Tin Maung Thann, Debby Aung Din Taylor, Thant Myint Oo, the World Bank, IMF, ADB and UN representative Dr Noeleen Hayzer, who worked for UNESCAP. These meetings were about bringing macroeconomic change to Myanmar. The culmination of these meetings was an invitation to Professor Joseph Stiglitz to come and give a very high-profile lecture in Nay Pyi Taw in 2009. The generals present listened to Stiglitz's ideas about economic change, and it is understood that this had a significant policy effect when the new government took over after the elections.

2007: the 'saffron revolution'

The world did not take much notice of the changes in Myanmar between 2005 and 2007, but in September 2007 the news from Myanmar exploded onto TV screens as hundreds of monks started protesting in Yangon. The West coined this the 'saffron revolution'.[57]

At first the protests were a response to the fuel price increases of August 2007, resulting in people being unable to pay the bus fare to get to work.[58] The fuel price increases also affected the price of food. This in turn led to the beginning of expressions of dissent and protests, mainly in Yangon, surprising both the international community and the regime. The focus was on economic hardship, not on issues pertaining to democracy. Back in October 2005 the regime had increased the price of both petrol and diesel by more than 900 per cent[59] and basic commodities had gone up by 10–20% within a week; but there had been no reaction. The 2006 price hike meant that diesel went up from 1500 to 3000 kyat per imperial gallon and petrol from 1500 to 2500 kyat per gallon, while compressed natural gas (increasingly used by taxis, buses and for cooking) went up by 500 per cent; this time there were small protest marches, including a few leaders of the '88 Generation student group.[60]

The different reaction of the public was attributed by Horsey first to the increase in poverty and second to a changing political landscape, with increased social activists and the released 1988 student leaders having established the '88 Generation student group. It was also probably due to the fact that since Khin Nyunt's arrest in 2004 there had been fewer politically motivated arrests and people were feeling more 'secure' and possibly even willing to 'test' the regime. However, these protest marches were relatively small and quite sporadic. Bystanders seemed sympathetic but did not join in, and the protesters were unable to galvanise the wider population. The regime did not send in the army or riot police, but used Swan Arr Shin, a civilian militia[61] organised by the USDA, to break up the gatherings. The international media soon started to report on the events that were unfolding. It is unclear at which point these demonstrations that had started as economic discontent movements were first reported as being political protests,[62] but within a few days more and more demonstrations erupted and the issues shifted from economic hardship to political issues, including the freeing of Daw Aung San Suu Kyi from house arrest.

On 5 September 2007, a street demonstration took place in Pakokku, in which several hundred monks from a local monastery took part. Swan Arr Shin was deployed again, but this time a few live rounds were fired over the heads of the monks and some of them were severely beaten. The next day officials went to apologise, but also to ask the monks not to take part in any further demonstrations. The officials were taken hostage and their vehicles were set on fire. After the officials were released, the situation escalated significantly. On 9 September, a newly established group called the All Burma Monks' Alliance presented demands to the authorities: 'that they apologise for the Pakokku incident; reduce commodity and fuel prices; release all political prisoners including Daw Aung San Suu Kyi and those detained for the recent protests; and enter into a dialogue with democratic groups with a view to achieving national reconciliation and resolving the suffering of the people'.[63] If the authorities did not comply, the monks would issue a religious boycott. As the deadline passed, monks began taking to the streets with the leading monk holding his begging bowl turned upside down, signifying the religious boycott. On 18 September, 300 monks gathered at the Shwedagong pagoda in Yangon. The authorities tried to block the marches but were unsuccessful. On 22 September, a group of monks stopped in front of Daw Aung San Suu Kyi's house, where she seems to have been allowed to appear at her gate to greet them.

By 24 September the demonstrations in Yangon had swelled to 100,000 people, led by tens of thousands of monks. The authorities were getting increasingly uncomfortable and announced that the demonstrations had to stop or else steps would be taken 'according to the law'.[64] Violence was first used on 26 September, with smoke grenades, baton charges, rubber bullets and live rounds. There were arrests and that night troops stormed a number of monasteries. Demonstrations continued in Yangon and were met with continued violence. Many were insulted and an unknown number were killed, although it is believed that the casualties were not as high as in 1988. By 1 October, the demonstrations had been brought under control. The authorities now focused on night raids and arrested thousands of those who had taken part, many of whom had been filmed in action. The detainees were held in makeshift detention centres around Yangon, interrogated and classified into different categories according to which they were either released or imprisoned.

The main difference between these demonstrations and the protests in 1988/90 was the use of electronic media. In the late 1980s all camera footage taken by tourists was confiscated at the airport and not many images remain. This time, despite the fact that there were few tourists in Yangon at the time, many locals had cameras in their homes and were able to email the footage to friends and family abroad. Much footage was filmed from the JICA offices in

Sakura Tower and the UN offices in the Traders Hotel.[65] Journalists, many under cover, also entered the country. The world was able to watch what was happening on Yangon's streets live on TV. The regime also used electronic media to its advantage, filming and identifying the protesters and their leaders. There was no bloodbath,[66] but those involved were subsequently arrested during night raids. Monasteries were also raided at night and young monks who had taken part were arrested and de-robed, despite public revulsion. Much of the brutality took place behind closed doors. No one really knows how many were arrested or beaten, and how many lives were really lost.

It is interesting to note that during the protests it was General Shwe Mann, the junta's number three, who chaired most of the National Security Council meetings and that neither Than Shwe not Maung Aye attended many of them. There are rumours that Maung Aye was against a too heavy-handed response towards the demonstrating civilians and monks. According to Win Min[67] the army's standing orders were to use firepower as little as possible, quite in contrast to 1988. However, Win Min's sources also say that on 25 September Than Shwe asked regional commanders to use violence 'decisively'. Different levels of violence were used in different parts of the country, and the fact that the Bureau of Special Operations chief for Yangon, Lieutenant General Myint Swe, is a nephew of Than Shwe's wife will have put him under pressure to use violence. The commander of Light Infantry Division (LID) 77, Brigadier General Win Myint, based in Bago but assigned to Yangon during the crackdown, appeared more lenient. As a result LID 66 based in Pyay was called to Yangon, and the pre-dawn raids of the monasteries and the serious shooting occurred after they arrived on 27 September. There was far less violence in Mandalay. However in Kachin State, where there were very few protests, the reaction of the northern commander Major General Ohn Myint was very harsh. Troops raided the monasteries in Myitkyina and Bamo on 25 September and more than 200 monks were detained.

Myanmar Egress did not close during the protests. On the day when one of the largest demonstrations by monks took place, the students wanted to go out and be part of the movement. Nay Win Maung, Kyaw Yin Hlaing and Tin Maung Thann convinced them not to join the rally, saying that nothing would change through street politics. Tin Maung Thann recalls that he explained: 'We know our system and the level of tolerance of military and we can see how this will end and don't want you to be victims.' All the students accepted and none went out. However, they were encouraged to take pictures and post blogs to transmit breaking news.[68] ME even provided a few digital cameras.

It was the first big test for ME, but also one that showed the directors the power of citizens' reporting, planting the seed for the mass communication course that would subsequently be developed and offered by ME.

In response to the demonstrations, obligatory mass rallies were organised around the country by the USDA. The regime did not respond to the economic issues that had originally triggered the demonstrations. It is also rumoured that the Military Intelligence had earlier submitted a report highlighting the economic plight of the people, suggesting that the problem of the gap between expenditure and income needed to be addressed immediately. However, it is also said that Than Shwe did not take this problem seriously.[69]

At the time many inside and outside the country believed that the violence signified that the country had taken an irreversible step backwards and that civil society would not be able to continue its work. Many civil society organisations kept their heads down. The feelings on the street after the 2007 protest were of increased caution. After two and a half years of some feeling of increased 'social space', people were afraid again. The sentences received by those involved in the protests were beyond all proportion, many exceeding twenty-five years in jail.

Despite this, the regime that same year appointed a new minister, Minister Aung Kyi,[70] to restart a dialogue with Daw Aung San Suu Kyi:

> ... the government announced that Senior General Than Shwe would meet Aung San Suu Kyi directly if the latter stopped confronting the government and stopped calling the international Community to impose economic sanctions. The junta even appointed a cabinet minister to liaise with Daw Daw Aung San Suu Kyi and representatives of the junta have taken place, and she is being allowed to meet with certain party members.[71]

In fact only a few weeks after the demonstrations life was very much back to the way it had been before the protests, and while those arrested certainly faced the wrath of the authorities, the expected tightening around civil society activity failed to materialise.

2008: Cyclone Nargis

During the night of 2 May 2008, tropical Cyclone Nargis reached the Ayeyarwady delta with winds of 200 km per hour and waves 3.6 m high that swept away everything in their path across hundreds of kilometres. The winds caused major destruction in Yangon. The population most affected were the fishers and farmers of the delta whose livelihoods were swept away overnight.

Given that 22 per cent of rice was being produced in the delta, this would have a significant effect on both the Myanmar economy and local livelihoods. There had been warnings on national TV and over the radio, but no evacuation was undertaken and most people were taken by utter surprise, as such a storm had not hit Myanmar in living memory.[72] The storm caused unbelievable havoc:[73]

- 2.4 million people affected with 800,000 internally displaced
- 84,537 dead, 53,836 missing (presumed dead) and 19,359 injured
- 450,000 housing units totally destroyed, 350,000 damaged
- 50–60 per cent of public schools damaged or destroyed
- 75 per cent of health facilities damaged
- damage amounting to around US$ 1.75 billion and losses (reduction in economic activity) estimated at US$ 2.26 to US$ 2.38 billion (taken together the total came to about 21 per cent of Myanmar's GDP for the previous fiscal year)
- over 1.3 million acres of farmland flooded with saltwater

To the outside world the Myanmar government seemed in the first instance paralysed and then slow to respond. The actual government response was never reported in the Western press and ignored in the reports that came later.[74]

On the day Nargis struck, a state of emergency was declared in five states and divisions before a full assessment of the damage could be made. Prime Minister General Thein Sein convened a meeting of the National Disaster Preparedness Central Committee (NDPCC).[75] The government then dispatched the 77th and 11th LIDs to Yangon division while the 66th LID, stationed at Pathein, was assigned to help in the delta. According to Taylor, 40,000 troops were said to have been mobilised for relief and rehabilitation activities.[76] The USDA, the War Veterans Organisation and the Myanmar Women's Affairs Federation were mobilised, in addition to the police, fire brigade and the Red Cross. According to Tin Maung Maung Than, the government made 50 billion kyat available and tasked different ministers, military commanders, the USDA and cronies to provide relief and start the reconstruction efforts. The reconstruction materials were to be provided at an especially low price. Private companies were allowed to import construction materials without paying tariffs, and also allowed to import diesel (it had been a government monopoly).[77] Cronies were allocated different areas across the delta and ordered to reconstruct. By 16 May, more than 5,600 tons of relief supplies had been distributed via army trucks, ships, helicopters and planes, as well as by 500 private contractors' vehicles and ships of the Inland Water Transport Board.[78] By this time, many private individuals as well as monks and indigenous NGOs and self-help groups had either preceded or reinforced the work of the government in distributing aid.[79]

Western governments, however, immediately condemned the Myanmar government for not reacting fast enough and for not allowing international relief efforts to enter the country. The US and France both had naval vessels in the vicinity and insisted that they should be allow to dock to administer help to the victims directly. Being denied access, the French foreign minister invoked 'responsibility to protect' (RTP) to justify a humanitarian intervention, but this did not receive sufficient support from the international community, including at the UN. In contrast to the Western reaction that started a confrontation with the Myanmar government, the neighbouring Asian countries sent rescue teams as well as material assistance and were allowed access without much fuss. Since they did not criticise the government and stuck to ASEAN's non-interference principle, the government did not feel threatened by them. According to Taylor, the government reported that it had received and despatched 183 persons from India, China, Thailand, Lao and Bangladesh to provide medical relief.[80] Singapore, under ASEAN Chairman George Yeo took a lead in the Nargis efforts.[81] A Tripartite Core Group (TCG) was created, chaired by Myanmar, bringing together the UN, the ASEAN secretariat and the Myanmar government.

International NGOs such as UNICEF, WHO and Save the Children with offices in Yangon responded quickly as well and cooperated with their Myanmar counterparts. Those organisations that were not granted permission to access the delta linked up with citizens' initiatives and local NGOs who were able to travel to the restricted areas.[82] The restrictions imposed on INGOs and Western agencies threw up a lot of incomprehension. However, the logic at the time seemed that the SPDC not only wanted to avoid any Western interference in their internal affairs, but also wanted to avoid the inflationary gap that emerges when a disaster area becomes the base for INGOs who are able to pay much higher rents and price out LNGOs and local inhabitants.[83] Despite the difficulties between the Western governments and the Myanmar authorities, airlifts of supplies to Yangon airport were allowed. International aid flights commenced, arriving at Yangon's Mingaladon airport on 7 May, the first from Thailand. The first relief supplies from the United States arrived by US Air Force aeroplane on 12 May. The US military flew 185 airlift sorties with military aircraft between 12 May and 22 June.[84]

There was also an outpouring of public support, with many citizens setting up organisations to travel to the delta with relief goods. LNGOs such as Metta Development Foundation responded quickly, building on their already existing programme in the delta.[85] Metta is reported to have reached over 249,500 people across 380 villages in the first three months.[86] Myanmar Egress became involved in the relief operations on the first day. Tin Maung Thann remembers arriving at the office, where there was no electricity and no water, but around 200 alumni had converged as they wanted to do something. The official government policy was that individuals could not simply go to the delta freely; no relief could go to the delta without permission.

Than Shwe had assigned cronies to help deliver aid and then rebuild. Pyabon became Htay Myint's responsibility. U Hla Maung Shwe's company was assigned to the same area, and this became ME's point of entry. Htay Myint provided fifty truckloads of goods and U Hla Maung Shwe provided ten; with the help of the alumni they reached fifty villages in five days distributing the material on the way. No one had any relief experience. ME opened a field office and dumped everything in Pyabon, sending three volunteers to each village to ask them to set up village relief committees, each with five village elders who could make an inventory of what was needed and sign up the families that required help. They then endeavoured to provide what the village committees asked for by issuing slips, after which village representatives came to Pyabon to pick up the goods. This system turned out to be quicker than what the international relief agencies were doing. A few days later Myanmar Egress set up the Nargis Action Group (NAG)[87] and coordinated aid distribution in several districts. They recruited Bobby, an AIT graduate who was working in the Wa region with ECODEV. He and Zaw Zaw Han, who had also worked with ECODEV, were assigned to develop NAG and run crash courses in fieldwork. MFF also became involved and decided to organise a damage assessment exercise in which 120 alumni became involved. ECODEV got the logistical service contract from UNOPS to provide logistical support for damage assessment. They created the first grid to locate and access each and every village. ME's foreign links were also used as Sonny Nyunt Thein's wife Kerstin started fund-raising to buy boats, livestock and construction materials for a number of affected villages. This was only one example of many such similar actions in which Myanmar expatriates mobilised funds and people to help.

ME also became involved at policy level, convincing Shwe Mann to issue the first three visas for international assistance. An unofficial office was set up inside the British ambassador's residence, within walking distance from the ME office, to coordinate between the Western relief efforts and the government,[88] working particularly closely with the British first secretary and DFID. Tin Maung Thann, Nay Win Maung, the US embassy 2nd secretary and other US officials negotiated with the government to allow the relief flights to come to Yangon. Once this was agreed, U Soe Thein and U Myint Swe were at the airport to meet the 7th Fleet commander who was on the first plane.

Western governments had warned there would be a second wave of deaths through disease if they were not granted access, but this never occurred. A few weeks later the electricity pylons had been re-erected by the army, and aid organisations from Thailand, Bangladesh, India, Japan and other Asian countries were busy making inventories of what different villages had received and still needed. The networking through handheld computers between these different organisations and often also with LNGOs was unprecedented.[89] The Myanmar Information Management Unit (MIMU) was set up to support coordination in the delta as of May 2008.

> Initially working closely with OCHA, the MIMU trained information associates in all five hub offices on the standards, practices, and procedures of information gathering, and promoted the dissemination of information products to humanitarian partners in the Delta through the hub offices. The resulting products, updated regularly, became crucial to enabling coordination, and understanding the scope of the damage, as well as where relief efforts were being provided.[90]

This resulted not only in trained personnel but also in data and information being available for the first time in such detail to local and international NGOs.

In the end the horror of Cyclone Nargis allowed for a myriad of LNGOs to be born, to develop and to be networked with each other.

> New local organisations that were created included Link Emergency Aid & Development (LEAD), which had started as a volunteer organisation distributing emergency aid to the Delta. Later on the organisation started to implement livelihood projects with support from international donors. Ar Yone Oo ('Morning Dawn') was also set up in the immediate aftermath of Cyclone Nargis. Using church connections, this local organisation provided emergency aid in Yangon and the Delta. Like LEAD, the organisation has expanded since, and plans to implement projects in other parts of the country as well.[91]

Civil society that had previously lived in the shadows was suddenly out in the open, linking in with INGOs, getting funds and more often than not engaging with government agencies as well. The learning curve for many was steep but unprecedented, and was to leave a legacy in terms of an interconnected civil society network that was ready to harness the process of change in a way the government would never be able to imagine.

2008: the constitution and rigged referendum

Cyclone Nargis was particularly badly timed as the government had planned for the new constitution to be put to a national referendum on 10 May. The announcement had been made 91 days earlier through SPDC Announcements 1/2008 and 2/2008. These proclaimed that a national referendum to ratify a new constitution would take place on an unspecified date in the coming month of May and that elections to implement that constitution would be held on an unspecified date in 2010.[92] The draft constitution went on sale on 9 April. Both domestically and internationally there was an expectation that the referendum would be postponed because of the cyclone. However, this did not happen and the regime pressed ahead with the referendum, only postponing it by a few days (to 24 May) in Yangon and the areas affected by Nargis.

The NLD campaigned very hard for a rejection of the constitution because of the contentious provisions: that 25 per cent of the seats in parliament would be reserved for the military; the military would remain completely autonomous and manage its own affairs; an immunity clause protecting the junta and any other government personnel from being persecuted for any act 'carried out in the execution of their respective duties'; the requirement for the president to be 'well acquainted with the affairs of the Union, such as political, administrative, economic and military'; the candidate not to be allowed to have a foreign spouse or children; and lastly any amendment of the constitution requiring more than 75 per cent of the vote in parliament, making any change without military approval impossible. The campaign for a 'no vote' was widespread across the opposition groups and made an appearance through posters and graffiti, playing 'hide and seek with the authorities'.[93] The government countered this with arrests, and involved the USDA and the Swan Arr Shin in leading a 'yes' vote campaign.

Many of those who were part of the 'third force' were divided. On the one hand the constitution on offer was not what they wanted, but many also realised that this was 'the only game in town' and that this was an unprecedented offer for some form of change.[94] The alternative on offer was not a better constitution, but a continuation of the political and societal stalemate described by Taylor in 2004. A 'yes' majority was ultimately recorded by the government, and the subsequent anger expressed by these groups was because this had been achieved through fraud. Most townships went to the polls on 10 May: officially there was a 99.06 per cent turnout with 92.4 per cent support for the new constitution. Then 47 townships in Yangon and the delta voted on 24 May: officially there was a 93 per cent turnout with a 92.9 per cent supportive vote and only 6 per cent negative votes. Advance votes cast by officials constituted 4.6 million votes, or 17.3 per cent. The numbers simply did not reflect the reality on the ground.

The NLD lost its 'no' campaign but decided to reject the constitution nevertheless. They released a statement on 22 September rejecting the referendum result and calling for parliament to be convened with the representatives elected in 1990.

Whilst there were many domestic and international complaints about Myanmar's government in 2008–9, there were some positive results as well. The year 2008 was when the ILO, led by Steve Marshall, was able to negotiate an agreement with the Ministry of Labour to put in place a mechanism by which victims of forced labour would be able to challenge their situation and find redress.[95] The framework of assistance delineated in the Post Nargis Recovery and Preparedness Plan (PONREPP) handed over the responsibility to the Ministry of Social Welfare, Relief and Resettlement, with other line ministries, such as the Ministry of Health, the Ministry of Education, the Ministry of Agriculture and Irrigation, the Ministry of Progress of Border Areas and National Races Development Affairs involved as well (Tripartite group, Monthly Recovery Update, May 2010). Suddenly INGOs and LNGOs had to cooperate with the government agencies, and the government agencies were willing to work with them. Nargis became the catalyst for LNGOs and CSOs to develop and start work on many different issues. A local Myanmar observer at the time estimates that by 2009 more than 200 LNGOs and hundreds of CSOs were involved in humanitarian aid, poverty reduction, rebuilding livelihoods, sustainable development, the environment, gender rights, HIV-Aids and education.[96] He also estimated that the founders and staff of these organisations spanned the whole spectrum of Myanmar society and included activists with a record of political dissent, former political prisoners as well as the loosely grouped third force, business people and former civil servants still close to the government. None of these organisations could work without some form of link to the government. He explained:

> When a LNGO decides to try and work in an area, it needs to identify local government representatives, USDA leaders, traditional leaders, potential allies (doc-

tors, lawyers, engineers, teachers, civil servants, etc.), and to collaborate with local CBOs (and help create them where they don't exist). In many cases, the networks built by civil society organizations are stronger and more efficient than government networks. Often, government representatives end up serving as members of civil society networks, which, civil society members say, gives them a better image of themselves, since they feel they are useful to the community and feel, one more paradox, empowered.

Nargis can therefore be credited with changing the dynamics between CSOs and the 'official sphere'. Whilst for many the government remained either the enemy or an impediment (impossibly lengthy registration processes, for example), the local government contacts that the CSOs and LNGOs had to start working with had become necessary partners in the endeavour to develop the work of the organisation. However, even if LNGOs had worked out operating mechanisms either to cooperate with or to bypass the government, they often suffered from lack of funding. According to the Tripartite group, Monthly Recovery Update:

> ... many respondents from LNGOs said international groups competing for the same money who don't always understand the local situation were the biggest obstacles. One respondent said, 'when denied funding, we were told it was because we'd never had a grant that big before. How can you have money if nobody will give it to you?' while another said, 'INGOs should shift their attitudes toward smart support of local groups.' [...] In terms of funding, both INGOs and LNGOs agreed that more funding specifically ear-marked for local groups is needed.

ME was one of the few organisations that seemed to receive continuous international funding, having established a track record through its training programmes and its help in the relief efforts during Nargis. Although there were now many new NGOs on the ground, the international community often did not know who to fund and seemed to prefer to stick with the three or four organisations it had worked with previously.[97]

After Nargis, a new course on Project Cycle Management was established at ME, born out of the needs that had been established by the crisis. A 'mini E002' was also developed for under-qualified community leaders from areas outside Yangon, bringing ever more students to the Thamada Hotel.

One year to go

In 2009–10, the last year before the elections, politics in Myanmar seemed to speed up and to become increasingly complicated and colourful. Daw Aung San Suu Kyi's house arrest was due to come to an end, but on 4 May 2009 an

American citizen, John Yettaw, swam across the lake to her house.[98] She was arrested on 13 May, charged with breaching the conditions of her house arrest; he was charged with illegally entering a restricted zone, breaking immigration laws. Yettaw was sentenced to seven years, including four of hard labour.[99] Daw Aung San Suu Kyi received a three-year jail sentence that was immediately commuted by Than Shwe to eighteen months of house arrest. The supporters of Daw Aung San Suu Kyi maintained that this incident had been staged by the regime to keep her under house arrest until after the 2010 elections, but it is likely that this was just the action of a very disturbed individual. Relations between Daw Aung San Suu Kyi and the regime did eventually improve during the course of that year, and meetings with Minister Aung Kyi continued.

> In late September 2009, in a letter sent to Than Shwe, Daw Aung San Suu Kyi offered to work for the lifting of sanctions. She also asked for permission to meet with European and US envoys to understand the nature of sanctions. Soon after the letter was sent to NPT, Minister Aung Kyi met with Daw Aung San Suu Kyi. Although the issues discussed in the meeting were not made public, that Daw Aung San Suu Kyi was allowed to meet with European Union and US envoys indicated that there might be a thaw in relations between the government and "the lady" ...[100]

On the ME side of things, Nay Win Maung had increased his contacts with Western embassies, especially the US, in which he provided briefings on possible post-election scenarios and who in the Myanmar regime would potentially support reforms. Informing foreign governments was not without risks and became really dangerous with the increased prominence of Wikileaks, especially the large amount of US classified materials dumped on the web in 2009. At this point Nay Win Maung realised that his previous briefings with his US contacts might be discovered by the regime. For the next few months he kept two bags packed by his door: one in case of being notified that he had to leave the country at short notice, and the other ready for arrest and a long stint in jail.[101]

The regime was facing its own challenges. Now that the elections were around the corner, the ceasefires that had been agreed by Khin Nyunt had to be revisited and the government hoped that the EAGs would either give up their weapons or transform into border guard forces under Myanmar army command. A few small groups, with few men under arms, complied, but the larger armed groups resisted. There had been no political dialogue since the ceasefires had been agreed and they had no intention of giving up their arms until their political demands were met. This proved to be an unplanned headache for the government, leading to renewed fighting in some areas, notably against the Kokang in 2009 on the China border, sending 30,000 refugees into China. Whilst the army won that fight, China was not pleased and all ceasefires were now at risk.[102]

Another element of 2009–10 was the extreme drive towards privatisation that gripped the government. The regime oversaw the sell-off of around 300 state-owned assets and enterprises to private owners, including mines, factories, agricultural processing plants, ports and airlines and government real estate. The reasons were not impending economic reforms, but they made sure that the retiring military elite would be able to secure enough money before leaving power.[103] At the same time the civilian economic elite of cronies close to the military rulers was being cemented. According to Sean Turnell:

> The two military conglomerates, the Union of Myanmar Economic Holding Limited and Myanmar Economic Corporation, dominate the economy and reportedly secured the largest share of privatised assets. Other buyers of these assets are either regime connected individuals or friends with close ties such as Tay Za's Htoo Group, the Max Group of companies headed by Zaw Zaw, and Steven Law's Asia World company. Chinese, Indian and Thai firms have also been present, as well as a broader ASEAN influence, with Singapore, Malaysia and Indonesia involved.

The last year before the elections was a particular busy one for LNGOs and CSOs as they became involved in the election process. No one was quite sure how much would actually change after 2010, but those on the ground wanted to give their best efforts to supporting change. The next chapter will focus on the work done by LNGOs in training up Yangon's middle classes in preparation for the vote, as well as the elections and how the government changed after November 2010.

2

THE ELECTIONS AND THE NEW OPPOSITION

VALIDITY AND PUBLIC DISENCHANTMENT

Preparing for elections under military rule

Prior to 2010, politics and political participation had remained firmly out of bounds with the threat of heavy jail sentences for anyone challenging the system or becoming involved in party politics. Surveys by Kyaw Yin Hlaing of business people and students found little enthusiasm for political participation, given the risks to themselves and their families.[1] There had been so much active avoidance of politics that political literacy was very low—even in urban centres and amongst the middle classes. People were very aware of politics but saw it as dangerous.[2] The crushing of the 1988 uprising had created a state of fear, which meant that ordinary citizens preferred to avoid political processes. The crackdown in 2007 was still very much on everyone's mind. Two popular political mindsets could generally be encountered on Myanmar's streets. One was, 'Sit on the side, say negative things but don't get involved' (*Bay Htine, Bu Pyaw, Bar Hma Ma Lote*). This phrase reflects 'passive politicians' who focused on the negative and looked for whom to blame, but did not search for any possible solutions to the problems they talked about. The other common view was, 'Don't get involved and entangled with politics so that you won't get fired' (*Ma Hlote, Ma Shote, Ma Pyote*).[3]

Given the history of military rule, there was little experience of harnessing a multi-party political system or in fact any understanding of citizenship in terms of rights, responsibilities and political participation. Parts of Myanmar society—such as the Sangha and other religious leaders—have been constitutionally excluded from political participation, as they are not allowed to vote or stand for elections.[4] Given that most of the non-state education, focused especially on the poor, is provided in monastic schools and that religious leaders of all faiths are seen as pillars of society, this helped to distance society further from political processes. State education has not imparted much with regard to the elements of citizenship either, focusing on duties and nationalism.[5] The history and events of the 1980s, including their state and civilian violence, are not debated or discussed, leaving the younger generation largely ignorant of the last time when large parts of urban Myanmar became politically active. Yet despite a lack of education and preparation, the population was propelled into a political process, starting with the referendum of the highly controversial 2008 constitution and the subsequent 2010 elections. The lack of experience and political literacy seems to have been seen by the regime as an advantage, as it allowed them to keep the playing field uneven and control the process.[6] However, coming closer to the elections, the official tone started to change. Throughout 2010, most of the public debate about the elections was between publications that advocated participation and those that questioned their legitimacy and were behind the 'no' campaign. Newspapers were allowed to be surprisingly free and open with their comments, even if they did not support the elections. According to U Pe Myint,[7] certain newspapers such as *Voice*[8] advocated participation, whilst others, including his own, questioned the process of change. This was an incredible improvement on the past. Previously all references to politics were oblique and the avoidance of politics was essential for a journalist's survival. However, with the advent of the elections came a change in discourse in the state-sponsored press, from fear to responsibility. Politics was not only legal again; the state media depicted the elections and citizen involvement as a national duty:[9] 'The success of elections is concerned with the image of the State as well as every citizen. So, the State, the people and the armed forces are to prevent those attempting to disrupt the elections.'[10]

This 180-degree turn reflected Myanmar's understanding of politics and leadership, which does not accept dissent. After decades of actively avoiding politics, citizens were urged, even commanded to support and protect the political process and to engage with the state. These elections were in effect not 'optional', and a boycott (as advocated by the NLD) would be seen as an affront to the same powers that had previously suppressed any form of political participation. It was in light of this that a number of informal small pre-election surveys were quietly conducted to establish what people thought of the state, the process it was proposing and how ready they felt to go to the polls.

Pre-election political awareness—the difference between urban and rural areas

As mentioned above, prior to elections people avoided politics. Although the 2010 elections were controversial and perceived as a sham, the attitude with regard to politics in urban Myanmar changed quite dramatically during the course of 2010. Talking about politics was no longer taboo, and it was even cool and popular to be knowledgeable about political parties and their campaign. According to a pre-election survey conducted by Myanmar Egress and published with the help of the Friedrich Naumann Stiftung (FNS) in Bangkok (2011), 87.4 per cent of those surveyed stated they would vote and only 10.9 per cent that they would not vote.[11] A CPCS survey concluded that there were six main perspectives on the streets, ranging from not believing that the elections would be fair, and that the regime was engineering the elections only to maintain power, to views that the elections would somehow bring some form of change. These views also included many from ethnic groups such as the Rakhine, Mon and Shan groups who at first had said that they would not participate, but then changed their minds after attending pre-election training or visits to Cambodia organised by civil society organisations. Those who did engage with the pre-election training started to believe that a boycott would actually mean a missed opportunity. The most optimistic view included those who believed that this could become a means to advance ethnic agendas, create and expand organisations and networks and even engage positively with the government. However, according to CPCS, negative views seemed to dominate, with some even saying that the elections would not take place at all and others that civil society and opposition parties had no time to prepare, rendering the exercise meaningless.[12]

Another small survey[13] conducted in 2010[14] (six months preceding the elections) concluded that political awareness was much higher amongst the urban educated middle-class youth compared to the rural population (in this case a sample from the delta) and that this would impact on how people would vote.[15] Figure 1 is taken from that piece of research.

The difference between the urban areas and the delta was startling, as only 20 per cent of the rural sample expressed high or very high levels of political awareness—this despite the fact that at the time of the survey the elections were only six months away. The picture painted by this research clearly

Figure 1: How Politically Aware Are You? Yangon/Delta

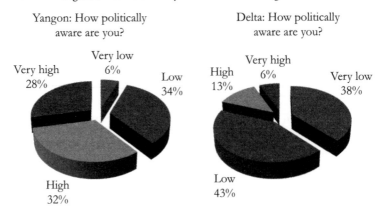

reflected the legacy of authoritarian rule during the last decades. It also pointed to another problem: how people who had for decades been denied any form of political literacy, living far from the urban centres where change was taking place, would almost overnight have to become active voters and in some cases active political representatives ready to stand for election.

But whilst the urban population and especially the urban young were engaging in the process and debate around the elections, there was a widespread lack of knowledge when it came to the real parameters of citizenship, especially with regard to 'rights' and what to expect from the government after the elections. Given this lack of political literacy, a small number of CSOs, some of which focus on ethnic issues, started to become actively involved in advocacy and political awareness building, as well as basic citizen education. These CSOs based in the urban centres started to offer courses in voter education, on the content of the constitution and other electoral and politically related fields, with the aim of preparing the wider population for some form of participation.[16] These were the first steps towards making parts of the population more conscious of political processes. Individuals were to be empowered to use the limited system that they were being offered. ME became particularly involved in the pre-election training, offering a 'quick fix' package over three weekends (six days in total) to provide civic education and engagement—basically a short version of their E002 course. The EU and FNF funded this, and in the two years preceding the elections ME managed to train 40,000 people across the country. There was also another education package on offer at that time, called ODPD (Organisational Development and Process Development), offered separately from the general voters' education and introducing a political strategy manual. This was for a more limited number of people. Whilst ME focused on voter education across the country, other CSOs[17] mainly offered courses in Yangon. What was interesting is that there was no government interference in the process, and although the CSOs involved had to be careful and risks were certainly taken, the process was basically not interfered with by the authorities.

The emergence of new political parties

Training the urban population was not sufficient to get a political process going. In order to make the most of the elections, new political parties were needed. At the time of party registration for the 2010 elections, ten parties were officially registered and had to decide whether to remain in the political realm. However these ten did not represent the wide ethnic range of people, and neither were they equipped to engage in politics at the ethnic state level. The government released the legislation that would govern the election on 8 March 2010. The five laws included the functioning of the Election Commission (EC), the party registration and how the representatives to the National Legislature would be elected. The commission was appointed three days later and then issued a series of by-laws related to the electoral procedures.[18]

As of 2007 the ME leadership had been convinced the elections were going to happen within a few years and that political parties would emerge. These, however, were likely to be created and supported by the regime. A series of strategy sessions were organised by ME involving many other civil society organisations. The result was an internal policy called the 'Shwepyitaw document', intended to build the big picture of the process and try to create political parties that would not be products of the regime. ME started a pilot getting civil society organisations together to sound them out about political participation, but did not explain to the ME staff helping these gatherings what the ultimate objective was, for fear of arrest and harassment. The initial money for these meetings was provided by U Hla Maung Shwe and FNF and other small grants. As a next step ME invited the potential groups, starting with the Rakhine literature and culture associations. This involved six separate groups that were put in one room; after a six-hour meeting the RNDP (Rakhine Nationalities Development Party) was born. Strategy meetings were held in Cambodia with leaders of ethnic civil society groups, in order to discuss matters that would have been too sensitive in Yangon.[19] Ultimately nine parties, mainly ethnic parties (Rakhine, Karen, Shan and Chin) emerged from this process.[20] ME further helped the new-born party fill out the necessary forms. However, the new parties needed money; so fifteen cronies were approached and convinced to support some of the new parties by providing the necessary funding. But private money was also raised, and U Hla Maung Shwe, Nay Win Maung and Tin Maung Thann even borrowed money to make sure the new parties could register and pay the fees for the candidates they were going to field in the elections. ME then started on the campaign training. In order not to fall foul of the regime, USDP party members were trained alongside the other political parties.

The regime was also getting ready for elections. Under the party registration law, neither civil servants nor members of the military are allowed to be members of a political party. Therefore in late April 2010 Prime Minister Thein Sein and more than twenty ministers and deputy ministers resigned from the armed forces and applied to the election commission to register the USDP as a political party. According to ICG they however remained ministers, and the election commission controversially decreed that ministers were not civil servants.[21]

In order to register as a political party,[22] lists identifying all party members had to be submitted to the authorities; and no party was allowed to function without a minimum membership number of 1,000 for national parties and 500 for regional parties. This resulted in rather unorthodox practices in some areas, notably the Chinese border, where allegedly Chinese residents were being offered ID cards to be able to register as political party members and then vote.[23] Parties were also required to contest a minimum of three constituencies in any legislature, and needed advance permission from the election commission to make any changes, such as amending their manifesto/policies, their constitution or their structure.[24] Beyond this there were steep costs to register the candidates—$500 per head meant that many parties were in the end not able to register as many candidates as they had originally planned. In some cases parties had to select wealthy candidates who were able to cover their own registration fees.[25] By June 2010 42 parties had registered:[26] five were parties that had contested in 1990;[27] 60 per cent of the parties (25/42) aimed to represent a single ethnic minority group, or a geographic area dominated by a single group.

When it came to fielding candidates, the National Democratic Force (NDF) prepared to put up 161 candidates across three parliaments. The Union Democratic Party (UDP), another opposition party, was fielding only three, mostly because of the fee each candidate had to pay. According to *The Irrawaddy*, the UDP announced that its leader, Phyo Min Thein, had quit his post in protest at the lack of election law reform.[28] The ethnic party that submitted most candidates was the Shan Nationalities Democratic Party (SNDP) which submitted 157 candidates to the Election Commission. At this point in the process, however, it was unclear how many candidates of the opposition parties the Election Commission would approve through the stringent vetting process.

The other interesting phenomenon in the election process was that a number of ethnic parties were able to field four sets of candidates, despite there just being three parliaments. The ethnic minorities living outside their birthplace were able to vote for a candidate in the place where they lived as well as in their home ethnic state, depending on the percentage of the ethnic population in the city of residence.[29]

At the time, Ashley South commented:

For many parties—particularly those representing smaller ethnic communities—the election is an opportunity to demonstrate their political significance, serving to reinforce ethnic identities. For some parties associated with communities that have long-standing histories of insurgency, such as the Karen, the formation of non-armed political groups represents something of a 'declaration of independence' from the politics of border-based insurgency. [...] Elsewhere (among the Karen community, for instance), more than one party has emerged. It will be interesting to observe whether inexperienced political leaders—who do not always enjoy smooth relationships—will be able to agree among themselves how best to cooperate. Depending on demographics and local conditions, some areas will lend themselves to tactical coalitions—with parties agreeing to endorse each other's candidates in order not to split the ethnic vote.[30]

The NLD boycott and the creation of the NDF

Daw Aung San Suu Kyi was still under house arrest as the elections were being prepared. However, as of early 2010 there were meetings between her and the government liaison officer U Aung Kyi.[31] Details of these discussions are not known, but they did restart a dialogue, and observers in the country and outside wondered if the NLD would stand in the elections.[32] At that time the NLD also announced that it would expand its Central Executive Committee from 11 to 20 members. According to Mizzima this was to allow younger members into the party's policy-making body.[33] There were again speculations that this move was related to preparing for the elections.

However, on 6 April 2010 the NLD announced that they would boycott[34] the elections. The following 'Six Points' by Suu Kyi were reportedly conveyed through her lawyer U Nyan Win to senior NLD party members prior to their decision on 29 March 2010 not to seek a continuance of NLD party registration: 1. She does not accept the 2008 Constitution and upholds the 'Shwegondaing Declaration'. 2. She does not accept the junta's unjust and one-sided Political Party Registration Law, which is undemocratic. 3. She said that the NLD is neither her property nor anyone else's. 4. She does not favour or accept any attempt to create factions within the party. 5. She would like to say to the people that she is committed to democracy and will continue her struggle. 6. She will not recognise that the NLD is abolished, even if it is dissolved by the military regime.[35]

The Shwegondaing declaration that had been passed in April 2009 rejected the 2008 constitution:

> A State Constitution based on the democratic principles is required to establish a democratic state. The not yet in force Constitution (2008) of the State Peace and Development Council contains provisions that are not in accord with democratic principles. Therefore the emergence of the Constitution which is acceptable to all the people including the ethnic nationalities is urgently required.

The declaration also demanded the recognition of the 1990 elections:

> At the present, recognition in some way of the People's Parliament, which is the outcome of the 1990 election, is urgently needed in accordance with the Section 3 of the People's Parliament Election law. Only then the democratic traditions can be maintained. Otherwise the State Peace and Development would seem to be breaching their own laws and regulations enacted by themselves.[36]

The decision not to take part in the elections led to a split in the party as U Khin Maung Swe led the faction that did want to contest and that became the NDF. Whilst arguably the splitting and weakening of the NLD had been part of Than Shwe's plan, this move not only divided the party, but also divided society.

Hans-Bernd Zöllner's work depicts how the NLD, Myanmar's traditional opposition, perceives politics. He argues that debate and discussion do not necessarily form a part of the political spectrum, not even within a democratic party. Traditionally the Burmese will expect complete adherence to party leadership and principles—whether they are in power or in the opposition.[37] Internal debate, especially across hierarchies, is not tolerated. Suu Kyi's 'personal' views were treated as a virtual instruction to the NLD and therefore the voting was unanimous. Those who were opposed to the boycott did not dare vote against Suu Kyi' wishes.[38] Nonetheless, the NDF was formed almost immediately, and Suu Kyi was furious. Zöllner locates the issue of local notions of respect and political acquiescence in Myanmar's political history as starting with Aung San and anti-colonial political movements. In essence he argues that when the Burmese speak about 'democratic politics' they mean something quite different from the Western concept.[39] The rejection of the election laws followed a similar non-democratic pattern. Daw Aung San Suu Kyi publicly expressed her dismay at the laws that did not allow prisoners to stand, vote or be members of a political party, and as a result the NLD unanimously rejected taking part in the elections, without any room for dissent within their ranks.

The reverberations of this decision across Yangon society were stark. Daw Aung San Suu Kyi called the election laws unjust[40] and the NLD portrayed those who were willing to take part in the elections as traitors. This resulted in a lot of name-calling between the more radical NLD followers who claimed to take the moral high ground and the 'moderates' who wanted to participate in order to change the system. At the time, a Myanmar watcher living in Yangon wrote:

> Make no mistake: the moderates won't change their opinions, and they will indeed participate. Not for any lack of respect for Aung San Suu Kyi, the NLD, political prisoners or democratic values. But because just as deep inside as they love democracy, they believe there is no credible alternative to participating to the slow, painful and frustrating process that is underway. They do respect radicals, and they feel for their suffering. They see their different approaches as being complementary. But calling them names is not going to help.[41]

Even the ICG called Daw Aung San Suu Kyi's reaction to the elections laws a missed opportunity. Continuing to operate as a party would not have required any expulsion of imprisoned members, including Daw Aung San Suu Kyi.[42] The Election Commission could have clarified whether Daw Aung San Suu Kyi's status of house arrest qualified as a prison term or not—the one possible restriction on her standing as a candidate, and issues relating to other political prisoners could have been worked on. But the NLD seemed more concerned with the moral high ground, rather than practicalities or what might be good for the country as a whole. Once de-registered, the NLD then suggested that it would transform itself into a social organisation, 'working on social welfare programs for the people as well as programs to provide aid and protect people from suffering ... our party won't just sit and watch'.[43] This created consternation across other civil society organisations, who had until then operated rather freely, and who were worried that if the NLD joined their ranks, all CSOs would in the future be monitored for political activity.

Looking at the elections before November 2010—to vote or not to vote?

In an unpublished paper,[44] Mael Raynauld describes the situation on the ground in Yangon in the summer of 2010 as difficult:

> The pro-democracy forces are split on the topic of the elections, and the strategy to follow. Several parties, under the leadership of the NLD as a whole and Aung San Suu Kyi in particular, have preferred to lose the legal status they enjoyed (and that in no way protected them from repression) rather than participating to a process they see as a sham. These parties represented the 'historical' opposition, in the sense that they commanded legitimacy gained during and after the 1990 elections. Other parties have appeared, many of which share common individual members with the now (legally) defunct 'historical' opposition. These parties would agree on most of the analysis that led their colleagues to boycott the elections, but their conclusion is drastically different. They feel there is no alternative to accepting the process as it is, for the military does enjoy complete control over it, and as no such opportunity has been available in over two decades.

This reflects Dr Nay Win Maung's analysis, which described the political and electoral spectrum as split into three camps. At one end of the continuum he located the pro-regime USDP:

> ... that supports the status quo, engages in rent seeking behaviour, refuses to acknowledge Myanmar's economic problems and does not recognise the need for the government to be legitimate or accountable in the liberal democratic tradition. At the other far end of the spectrum are the conventional democratic opposition forces. These are 'zero sum' players who refuse to contest the elections. In the middle sit the so-called 'third force' groups, who are largely moderate and pro-election. These opposition parties are made up of civil society actors and ethnic groups.[45]

Whilst in Myanmar civil society actors grappled with the rapidly changing reality, the elections were decried in the West, even before they had taken place. There were a number of wrong assumptions made by many about the Myanmar election laws that reinforced the rejection of the Myanmar change process in the West. According to Derek Tonkin, these included that: (a) Suu Kyi is debarred from standing for election because of her former marriage to an Englishman, Michael Aris; (b) hundreds of thousands of monks have been deprived of the vote for political reasons; (c) the 1990 elections were to a governing parliament. The Burmese Perspectives goes on to explain in detail that Daw Aung San Suu Kyi is actually ineligible as a presidential candidate due to the nationality of her sons, that (as explained above) the Sangha never had the vote, and that the 1990 elections were to a body that was to write a new constitution that would have to be approved before any transfer of power could take place.[46]

Unknown to most at the time, ME had set up an unofficial and underground election monitoring system that was funded by the EU. There were three stages to the process: pre-campaigning, campaigning and the election day. Monitoring involved the establishment of a database on a website,[47] media monitoring with an election bulletin and report cards. Report cards involved so-called 'citizen reporting', where individuals/citizen groups/civil society networks and Egress alumni were asked to report back to a focal observer. Egress expected that there would be five citizen reporters to each focal observer, with a total sample size of 1,000 (which included citizen reporters and focal observers) in Yangon. Citizen reporting took place in 27 of the 35 constituencies in Yangon, around 30 constituencies in Mandalay and also some constituencies in Magwe Region, Shan State, Kachin State and Rakhine State. Members of the business community and candidates (both elected and defeated candidates) were also asked to contribute to the monitoring process. It was hoped that this process would allow ME to determine how free and fair the elections were in the places that they were able to monitor. Clearly this activity was not discussed until well after the elections were over. The report that emerged from the election monitoring campaign was never made public, but offered a good insight into the infringements that had taken place during the campaign, and on the day, but also confirmed that there was also a reasonable amount of good practice across the country.[48]

The elections

On 7 November 2010, Myanmar went to the polls for the first time in twenty years to choose from a total of 37 political parties standing for more than 1,100 seats across two houses of parliament and 14 local legislative assemblies for the seven states and seven regions.[49] The parties included the pro-regime USDP, the NUP representing the regime that had ruled the country between 1962 and 1988, and a plethora of other, smaller parties, including the NDF—the splinter party from the pro-democracy NLD. They also included a large number of ethnic minority parties that were focused in particular on the representation of their ethnic group and were standing not across the whole country, but primarily in states where they had potential constituents. A small number of ethnic political parties had not been allowed to register, the most prominent example being the three Kachin parties, which left the Kachin people with no one to vote for.[50] The elections were not held in a few townships, either because of armed conflict (some areas in Karen and Shan States) or because the ceasefire groups did not allow the voting to take place in the territory they controlled (as in the Wa-controlled districts).

The playing field was seriously tilted in favour of the USDP, which was able to field candidates in almost all constituencies, whilst the pro-democracy parties were limited to far fewer candidates, largely because they had so little time to raise funding for registration fees and election expenses and to set up and organise their parties and secure membership. The elections also had the controversial feature of advance voting, whereby many officials and members of the armed forces were instructed to vote before 7 November. The elections were therefore not expected to be in any sense fair.

On the day, reports from across the country show that on balance the behaviour at most of the polling booths allowed for a free choice. There were also reports of isolated infringements, and the USDP is heard to have offered new clothes, coffee and snacks as incentives.[51] Mostly, however, especially in the urban areas, people were able to vote as they pleased. The counting in each polling station was in many but not all cases held in front of party representatives and members of the public and registered wins for opposition and ethnic minority candidates alongside those of pro-regime candidates. On the night of 7 November there was cautious optimism.[52] The following morning, however, a number of constituencies reported that the counting of the advance votes showed they were largely cast for the USDP, quite possibly under pressure, and had nullified a number of wins. When the regime announced winning around 80 per cent of the seats, a number of those who believed they had been elected the night before found that they had lost to the advance ballots.

The Union Solidarity and Development Party (USDP), the main pro-regime party, 'won' over 75 per cent of the seats across all assemblies. The National Democratic Force (NDF), the NLD break-away faction, did quite badly. However, the ethnic minority parties, especially in Shan, Chin and Rakhine States, did comparatively well nationally and were well represented in their own regional assemblies. Since none of the pro-democracy parties adequately contested the regional assemblies, pro-democracy ethnic political parties took a large number of these seats in the ethnic states. 'In Chin State, the USDP won 29 per cent of seats while the Chin Progressive Party and the Chin National Party each won 21 per cent. In Rakhine State, the USDP won 30 per cent of seats while the Rakhine Nationalities Development Party won 38 per cent.'[53] It is also worth adding that although the turnout at the elections was an average 77 per cent for the two national and one regional assemblies, this did reflect an almost 20 per cent boycott by voters who would have been willing to select a 'democratic' party if the NLD had agreed that they could do so, but felt that they had to boycott because that was Suu Kyi's wish.[54]

The USDP won 884 of the 1,156 seats open to the electorate. In the Nationalities Assembly (the upper house), the party took 77 per cent (129) of the elected seats, and in the People's Assembly (the lower house), it won 79 per cent (259) of the elected seats.[55] See annex for full results.

The *New Light of Myanmar's* 24-page supplement published on 17 November reported the ballot count for each parliamentary seat. According to Special Rapporteur Quintana's report, the Election Commission had reported voter turnout exceeding 100 per cent in some constituencies and declared two pro-government candidates winners in constituencies in Kachin State where elections had been cancelled.[56]

The results certainly surprised those who had observed the voting and counting on the ground. Those who had supported the elections were stunned, depressed and felt that all their hard work had been for nothing. Campaign groups from the 'no' vote, the NLD and other anti-election forces said that this was no surprise. Yet despite this let-down, the elections still mattered. People in Yangon reported being upset—but they also said that the teashops were buzzing with political talk.[57] The biggest win was that politics was legal once again, and many were openly supportive of legally accepted opposition parties. Some parties, including the NUP and the RNDP, were even considering taking the matter of overturned wins through advance votes to court.[58] Whilst there was talk of a potential boycott by those unhappy with the rigging, Myanmar's two largest ethnic parties said that they would claim their seats in parliament despite their unhappiness with the process. The Shan Nationalities Democratic Party (SNDP)[59] and the Rakhine Nationalities Development Party (RNDP)[60] said, 'We will take our seats in Parliament even if other parties boycott it [...] We want to use our position inside Parliament to improve the living standards of our Shan people.'[61] In the end all those elected took their seats, and after years of waiting the new political process began. Not long after the elections, Thant Myint U said, '[this is a] clear watershed, there is no turning back, and what happens over the coming months may be critical in determining the nature of Burmese politics and society for many years to come.'[62]

The new system

With hindsight one can see what a catalyst for change these elections were, despite being neither free nor fair on the day. They heralded the inauguration of a new and complex political structure with three national assemblies. The National Parliament is bicameral: the lower house (Pyithu Hluttaw) has 440 members, of whom 330 are elected by voters according to their township, and 110 appointed by the military; the upper house (Amyotha Hluttaw) has 224 members, consisting of 12 elected representatives from each of the seven states and seven regions (168 members) plus 56 military appointees. Representation at township level is in the lower house and state/region representation in the upper house. Whilst 25 per cent of the seats across the houses are reserved for the military, the hierarchical military status quo of the three supreme generals that ruled the country was replaced by a presidential system. Given that the military has been a stakeholder in Myanmar politics since independence, a total break with the armed forces was never part of the plan.[63] The problem of military seats was compounded by the fact that a number of military have shed their uniforms in order to stand, meaning that military representation is in reality much larger than the allocated quota.[64]

Members of both houses sit for a five-year term. The constitution also provides for the two houses to combine and sit as the Union Assembly, and it is this combined body that elects the president. On the same day voters also elect regional assemblies in each of the seven states and seven regions. One of the most important changes was the establishment of the fourteen regional legislatures, as a first step to limited decentralisation and devolution. The new regional assembles were particularly significant because they represented a potential new power base, with new members of parliament and a new civil service infrastructure to support the new institutions—in essence a new and legal political space where there was none before and a new ethnic dimension of politics. It raised the possibility of ethnic communities and ethnic parties having a greater say over their affairs, as well as a new political space that had not existed before.

> While this may not make local governance less authoritarian, it is likely to make it somewhat more responsive to local needs. Ethnic communities are likely to have enhanced opportunities to promote their cultures and languages, using, for example, local media and the education system. And it is difficult to imagine foolish decrees from central government—such as uniform quotas for bio-diesel production or enforced tea-growing at the expense of more suitable and profitable crops—being implemented unquestioningly.[65]

Basically this was going to be a more fractured system of power, with checks and balances, making the whole process of decision-making less hierarchical and more complex.[66] Despite the fact that the pro-regime USDP kept overall control and would be supported by the military members, the new parliamentary system represented a structural change, from a military junta to a presidential system that had new institutions and would require changes in governance. The biggest issue actually lay in the inexperience of the MPs and their parties in local governance and the real possibility of personal disagreements that could scuttle the effects of these changes. Richard Horsey listed the main changes in the system,[67] including Than Shwe having retired from day-to-day political affairs, the elected parliaments allowing for legal opposition parties, some level of decentralisation through the regional legislatures, and a new constitution that provided a basic legal framework.

Parliaments were convened on 31 January 2011.[68] The first session of the two houses of parliament was very short, lasting only fourteen days, and on many days the sittings were so short they were labelled the '15 minute parliament'.[69] In part this was because the business of the parliament was to elect speakers, the president and to administer oaths to office. Since there were no objections, there were no discussions; and things happened quickly and almost by decree. The Union Parliament composed of members of both houses elected the president and the two vice presidents after both houses and the military had proposed two candidates each for the three posts on 4 February. U Thein Sein, the former prime minister, was elected president. Sai Mauk Kham,[70] a Shan doctor proposed by the Amyotha Hluttaw (Upper House), and Tin Aung Myint Oo, the former Secretary 1 of the SPDC since 2007 who had been proposed by the military,[71] were elected vice presidents.[72]

Later the parliament developed much longer sessions that dealt with questions and proposals, and though the procedure to submit questions was complicated, interesting issues were raised, including sensitive topics such as land tenure, the registration of CSOs, the censorship board, discrimination against ethnic minorities in civil service recruitment, illegal gambling, the citizenship cards of Muslim residents in northern Rakhine State and the lack of labour unions.[73] These were issues that could never have been raised before. Some issues even resulted in immediate action, as 25 CSOs had their registration approved rather quickly after the issue had been raised.[74] According to Horsey, the opposition MPs raised most of the questions in the first fifty days of government, but since the agreement of a majority of MPs is needed for the issue to make it to the floor, this showed that USDP and even military appointees were agreeing to debate what were seen as rather sensitive issues.

There was another new phenomenon in Myanmar politics. The president started to give speeches. In his first three addresses the president made the agenda for his five-year term public. The inaugural speech to the Union Assembly was given on 30 March, the speech to the new government the next day and the speech to the Central Committee for Progress of Border areas and National Races on 23 April 2011.[75] The presidential priorities included:

- National unity and end to conflict
- National reconciliation with the NLD
- Economic reforms
- Closer cooperation with NGOs, INGOs and the UN
- Tackling corruption

He also announced on 31 March that the government leaders would not take their allotted salary increase for the moment, in recognition of the fact that many were still battling poverty in the country.[76] In the event President Thein Sein started with economic measures, including a reduction in export tariff, an increase in pension rates, reining in public spending, streamlining government services.[77] His next steps were the recognition of poverty, lifting restrictions on microfinance and unifying the various exchange rates. More on this in the economic reforms chapter.

President Thein Sein's ambitious agenda was quite in contrast to the outgoing Senior General Than Shwe's last words, who clearly saw this transfer of power as a continuation of the old system:

> The democracy system introduced to the Union of Myanmar is still in its infancy. Therefore, it is required of the entire national people to safeguard and build together the newly-introduced democracy system, which has been adopted with the combined efforts of the government, the people and the Tatmadaw. In the process, it is mandatory for all national brethren to tackle any forms of disruptions to the new system.[78]

It was noteworthy that President Thein Sein also spoke about the difficulties of uniting all the citizens, including those who did not support the SPCD's transition: 'there are so many individuals and unlawful organizations inside and outside the nation that do not accept the State's Seven Step Road Map and the Constitution. [...] They are all citizens of our country. Therefore, they have to accept our government as their government constituted with national races of their own.'[79] He also asked people with 'different ideas and concepts, to work closely in matters of (the) same views in the national interests', reminding everyone that the 2008 Constitution would not be eternal: 'According to Chapter (XII), the people have been vested the rights to amend the constitution in line with procedures.' It is significant to note that he promised:

to show our genuine goodwill towards those who have not accepted the constitution because of being sceptical about the seven-step Road Map in order that they can discard their suspicions and play a part in the nation-building tasks. Likewise, we need to convince some nations with negative attitude towards our democratization process that Myanmar has been committed to see the interests of the nation and the people to serve those interests only in the constitutional framework and not to try to disrupt the democratization process outside the constitutional framework and harm peace, stability and the rule of law. The Union Government will welcome all actions done within the constitutional framework but prevent and take necessary action against all actions done outside the constitutional framework. Democracy will promote only hand in hand with good governance. This is why our government responsible for Myanmar's democracy transition will try hard to shape good administrative machinery.[80]

The scene seemed set for radical changes.

Unfortunately, after the rigged elections, the West did not believe any real change was on its way and Myanmar remained under sanctions. Most Western governments still believed that Than Shwe was pulling the strings behind the curtain, and the short parliamentary sessions, the lack of immediate change and the rejection of the new system by the NLD underscored this position. In light of the unchanging Western position, Myanmar's 'new' legitimate and democratic opposition—the eleven small and ethnic parties[81]—decided to take an anti-sanctions stand and put out an official statement on 11 March 2011:

> ... One may be impatient of the speed of the transition undergoing in this country. But, it needs to recognise (sic) that a space for political process has formed, that a new generation of leaders is about to take over, and that the political parties like us have been elected into the parliaments. It is important that the international community, and notably the EU, realises that there is an evolution unfolding in this country. Therefore, the EU should rethink its current approach of isolating Myanmar. [...] we ask the EU and its member states to refrain from 'recommendations' advising against tourism, against trade and against investment ...

However, despite the fact that standing for elections had taken so much effort and courage, these elected representatives and their parties soon found that their voice was being ignored by the international community. Their statement in opposition to the NLD's policy was not taken into account by any Western government, whose policies preferred to reflect the NLD's position. In effect these new opposition leaders were being given less status than the NLD, despite the fact that the NLD at that time was no longer even a legitimate political party and could only play the part of an extra parliamentary opposition.

Sanctions remained in place. The West's policy remained unchanged, greatly disappointing the parties who had signed the declaration. One Myanmar writer at the time cited three reasons why Western policy was not changing:

> One, westerners who have a very shallow understanding of the political and economic situations of Myanmar, but in their conceit think they know everything about it, many without having set foot in the country. [...] Two, the Myanmar exiled activists who are like beggars: the political deadlock and problems in Myanmar are their begging bowls. In order to continue enjoying the millions of funds they get for making noises, they need the problems in Myanmar to continue to exist. [...] Since 1988, there has not been a single act done by the exiled activists which had benefited the people of Myanmar, setting aside for the moment that many of their acts actually harms us. Three, western politicians and media people who realize the world-wide popularity of Daw Aung San Suu Kyi. They prefer her to remain a victim because this way the former can continue to use her image as a free, efficient and easy PR tool. [...] The last two groups know the reality of Myanmar's political situation but they are benefiting too much from our problem to have any desire to see it dissolved or even to ease up. Their intentions are self-serving and deliberate.[82]

But it was not only the political parties who were disappointed and cynical. Now that the excitement and activity around the elections had subsided, many young people across Myanmar's urban populations were disillusioned with the results and unsure about what the future would bring. However, many believed that things had changed.

Post-election views: reflecting back, and looking into the future[83]

In order to get a clearer idea as to how the elections and the immediate post-election transition had been perceived, the research that had been conducted before the elections in the spring and summer of 2010 resumed in early 2011 with three focus groups[84] of mainly young people in Yangon. The results showed a very different attitude from the one that had reigned in Myanmar prior to 2010. There was a clear interest in getting more involved in politics— even if many of the respondents said they needed to remain cautious. But the traditional reluctance to take part in politics was not there amongst those interviewed. It was as if the election campaign had ignited their imagination.[85] Out of the 11 respondents of one group, 8 had campaigned in some form: either for the 'I vote' campaign, the 'no vote' campaign, and/or for a political party. In another group 6 out of 10 had campaigned. The participants of the Karen focus group had not campaigned at all. But all members of the groups spoke about the importance of the political processes the election had engendered and their political interest. One participant mentioned: 'I am more politically aware now that I am 22 years old. I have never voted before. I came to know how and why to vote. Political awareness is a process.' Another added: 'Before 2008 I was not interested in politics. I had no political awareness. The constitution started my awareness and my education. Then came voters' education and other civic education. More awareness is very good for me.'

Many across the three groups said that both awareness and participation were more prevalent amongst the youth and those living in urban areas and that people, especially young people, were less afraid. They confirmed that what was happening in Yangon was not a countrywide phenomenon: 'Political awareness depends on location. In Yangon people have awareness, but in the provinces everything is different.' If political participation is to become once again part of daily life, the problems of the poorer and rural parts of the population who are not educated and struggle for their daily livelihoods have to be taken into account. One participant mentioned: '70 per cent of the people are not educated. What about them? How do they understand citizenship?' Another said: '[...] People have to struggle for basic needs. When people are starving, then they are not interested in rights and duties; and political participation is far, far away.'

The rest of the discussion was about the future and whether the legalisation of parties would encourage greater political participation. The young people across the groups were quite divided on this. Some organisations still did not want to engage with people who were members of political parties, and whilst this might have been a hangover from pre-election policies, it still affected the way politics was viewed: 'Taking part in politics is still not "safe" or accepted. There was a singing contest[86] and you could not take part if you were a member of a political party. The Alliance Française asks you to tick a box if you are a member of a political party.' This type of reporting obviously shows that even foreign organisations based in Yangon had not yet moved to a post-election mindset.

Some respondents were positively inclined when speaking about the future. Those who spoke positively pointed to the fact that civil society had had more space recently and they felt that this was the first step in policy changing. Others spoke more about the role of knowledge—or the lack of it. Education and the development of civil society were both seen as the key, which would help move things forward. And time for everything was essential: 'I believe political participation will go up. Slowly.'

Not all were positive, however: there were sceptical and negative voices across all groups, including both Bamar and ethnic minority participants. They spoke about the role of the army, and the possibility of having to do military service, something that scared all of them, especially the girls. They also discussed the division between the opposition who had been pro-elections and those who had been anti-elections, and that young people were not allowed the necessary space to be active participants in the process. The fact that the last point was mentioned a number of times reflects Myanmar's age-old hierarchical system which threatens to be a cultural obstacle to change: 'For citizenship to change, political parties need to give space to young people.' Leadership was also seen as crucial in determining the future path; one participant put it succinctly: 'The three pillars [rights, duties, political participation] are accepted, but more important is for them to be accepted by the leaders. We need leaders, we need a campaign, demonstrations and the right to raise our opinion as they get more awareness on these issues.'

Whilst the young people had mixed views both on the elections and what the future would bring, civil society leaders on the whole were satisfied with the changes that had happened and expected to push on for further transformation. Despite being disappointed with the way that the elections had been held, and the unfairness of the rigging, CSO leaders pointed out that one of the main outcomes of the elections was that the new opposition parties had decided to try to bring change within the structures allowed by the regime and gained popular support. Civil society organisations, loosely known as the third force, were central to the creation of these parties, as well as the civic education Myanmar citizens received, and they had also dramatically increased in importance. They cautioned that people needed to press on and reminded those who had been disappointed by the elections that no one had ever thought the process of change would be easy.

As part of the evaluation of post-election views, three leaders who had been involved in voter and political party training were interviewed. One of them was Dr Nay Win Maung; the other two were leaders of ethnic CSOs. When asked about how the elections had affected them personally and how they perceived the possibility of political participations, all three had similar views that the political process is one that needs to be learned by all. Even if the process is an imperfect one, it still needs to be engaged with. In one case the interviewee spoke about how the process increased agency, as the acquired education was then passed on to other groups in a kind of snowball training method. Another spoke about the new and increased political space that had made some form of campaigning possible. Nay Win Maung explained how, despite their imperfections, the elections were important: 'The elections have changed the view of politics in the country. And they have changed my own awareness. I have witnessed the increased space, especially in urban centres like Yangon and Mandalay. I have witnessed the political space and the political campaigning. This was formerly not possible.' One of the ethnic leaders concurred, explaining how it had changed her and her community: 'The elections have changed me very much. Because of the elections we had to learn the law. We attended the [name removed] foundation voters training. We became trainers. We trained people from Yangon and Karen State and staff went to the delta. We put in much effort because of this awareness. To that end we also need education.'

All three had interesting things to say about political awareness, the understanding of political participation across the country and how the wider population had been affected. One in particular pointed to the role young people needed to play as the new system developed. Both education and patience were needed to see some of the changes through, but in the end young people would understand that there were options in this new system with political parties, options that had not existed in twenty years. Even the NLD's 'no vote' campaign was not seen as having been negative, as it had engaged the youth in what was in effect a political process. Despite being sceptical of the constitution, one of the ethnic leaders acknowledged: 'Citizens have a role to play. In two ways: some citizens can take part as politicians and some can take part as participants—voters. This was new. This was brand new for me. I have never voted before.' As long as the opposition parties continued to raise motions on behalf of their constituents and were perceived as active, then parties would be perceived as a vehicle.

In fact the role of political parties would be critical in maintaining political momentum, but here also lay the problem, in that most of those elected had never been exposed to politics before and did not necessarily have the capacity to take on their new responsibilities. ME was able to develop a short programme entitled 'Public policy training for ethnic change agents' that ran from 6 January to 6 April 2011, trying to plug some of the gaps.[87]

When speaking about the future, the positive seemed to outweigh the negative. Political literacy was seen as the key for subsequent development. What had been done in the pre-elections training was necessary but not enough. As in the youth focus groups, the needs of the largely uneducated rural population were seen as a key impediment to an inclusive development of citizenship, and all three emphasised that unless education and capacity building were expanded around the country, there would not be much hope for a democratic Myanmar in the future. 'We need to facilitate the awareness of being a citizen of the country. Capacity building for this is essential. Education is needed.'

In their own words, the three civil society leaders put the election process in perspective—as a necessary step for the system as a whole to change. None of them advocated radical change or revolution, and all emphasised the time it would take for the wider population to be able to take part in the process and become politically literate. What was seen as essential, however, was their role and the role of their various organisations in the process of change and development. These civil society organisations (and there are many across the country, of various sizes) are key to providing the necessary education. The next step in their view was for them and those they educate to engage with the political parties and the new system as it was being set up, and try to influence it as much as possible.

Nay Win Maung stressed again the need for patience. Given time, policy gaps allowing for more agency would be found and things could change: 'This is a transition. The leaders will need to learn how to function. Politicians, political parties all need training. From an ethnic perspective we need to think where we can find space for ethnic grievances. Once people learn, they can find gaps. There is need for further education.'

All three were hopeful that the new government would mean some form of change, and all three were curious to see what form it would take. They did not have to wait long. After the elections two momentous events took place: one very much in the public eye, the other well away from the press and the outside world. The first event was the release of Daw Aung San Suu Kyi in Yangon, the second was the fight between reformers and hardliners within the government in Nay Pyi Taw.

The release of Daw Aung San Suu Kyi

Six days after the elections, on 13 November, Daw Aung San Suu Kyi was released at the end of her sentence of house arrest that had begun in May 2003.[88] She was welcomed by crowds and became active immediately. According to the report filed by Special Rapporteur Quintana, Daw Aung San Suu Kyi started to meet with and speak to a wide range of interested parties immediately. The Special Rapporteur spoke with Daw Aung San Suu Kyi by phone on 11 January 2011, when she is supposed to have assured him that she would work towards national reconciliation and dialogue with the government.[89] Quintana in the same report lamented that despite the release of Daw Aung San Suu Kyi, another 2,189 political prisoners remained in jail and that some ceasefire groups were in the process of re-arming, expecting armed conflict to resume.[90] More on Daw Aung San Suu Kyi's release and her new engagement with the government will be discussed in Chapter 3, which covers the national reconciliation process. The issues related to the re-arming of the EAGs and the resumption of conflict will be covered in Chapter 4, looking at the peace process.

The new government embattled

The structure of the new government did not come about by chance. Than Shwe pitched potential reformers against hardliners as a careful design for balance of power, so that not too much change could take place too quickly. As the ICG put it: 'In order to avoid disruption, a careful "diffusion of power" has been organised by installing four power centres all related to the military: the presidency, the military, the parliaments and the leading party.'[91] However, the new president had promised change. The parliament closed for the Thingyian (Burmese Buddhist new year in April) and during the summer not much seemed to be happening in Nay Pyi Taw. Many both inside and outside the country believed that with an immobile parliament and no word from the capital, it could all have been a farce. What few knew was that an epic battle of wills was taking place in Nay Pyi Taw between the reformers and the hardliners. President Thein Sein emerged more or less victorious from the battle: in his speech to the nation in August 2011 he appeared with Daw Aung San Suu Kyi under the portrait of General Aung San to lay out and start the change process he had promised early on that year when he was made president. The nation awoke that morning to a picture in the press that no one could have dreamt of before. It was the start of the promised national reconciliation process.

The next chapter looks at the first presidential priority, national reconciliation between the regime and Daw Aung San Suu Kyi and the NLD, including the run-up to the 2012 by-elections and Obama's visit to Myanmar.

3

NATIONAL RECONCILIATION WITH THE NLD

The release of Daw Aung San Suu Kyi and her return to politics
(Nov 2010–Jan 2012)

Six days after the elections, on 13 November, Daw Aung San Suu Kyi was released from her house arrest that had begun in May 2003 after the Depayin massacre.[1] Whilst she had had some increased engagement with the regime after 2007, her house arrest had been extended by eighteen months after the Yettaw incident in 2009. Despite international pressure and her limited negotiations with the government on the reductions of sanctions, she was not released even a day early. At the time many suspected that having her under house arrest during the elections had been a regime priority, and that the election dates had been timed especially to precede her release. Now that the elections were over, it was safe for her to be free again. Crowds of her supporters were at the gates to welcome her. On 14 November an even larger crowd, of around 10,000 people, gathered in front of the NLD headquarters shouting 'long live Suu Kyi' and listened to her saying:[2]

> It's not enough to think only of oneself or one's own family. I want to reiterate this. Please don't have the attitude that politics do not concern you. My father has said that before, that you may not be concerned with politics but politics will be concerned with you, you can't avoid this [applause]. Everything is politics. Politics is not just coming here and supporting us. The housewife, who is cooking at home, also has something to do because she is struggling to feed her family with the money she has [cheers]. Struggling to send children to school is politics. Everything is politics. No one is free of politics. So saying that politics does not concern you

67

and that you do not wish to be involved in politics is a lack of awareness of politics. So I ask the people to try and understand politics and to teach us. We must teach one another.[3]

Daw Aung San Suu Kyi became socially and politically active immediately, starting by meeting with a few ethnic leaders on 16 November when she suggested the idea of organising a second Panglong[4] meeting so as to bring peace to the country and foster unity amongst different ethnic groups. This suggestion was not well received at government level, and even some ethnic party representatives voiced reservations.[5] After all, her stand after the 1990 elections had been that the recognition of these polls was of a higher priority than the ethnic grievances; she is alleged to have said at the time: 'democracy first—ethnic issues can be sorted out after'.[6] In addition, she had been under house arrest for so long that many rightly believed that she did not have a clear idea of the development which the country had achieved during that time.

One of the first things she did was to file a petition with the high court to have the NLD reinstated as a political party. But this was denied at the end of January 2011 as the NLD had not registered for the 2010 elections, and therefore remained an 'unlawful association'.[7] Fighting to reinstate the NLD as a political party also brought up questions of internal reorganisation, as the NLD's senior leadership is made up largely of men in their 80s and 90s and no one had dared make any changes whilst she was under house arrest.[8] Daw Aung San Suu Kyi made it very clear that she respected the sacrifices her elderly party team had made and that the top ranks of the Central Executive Committee would not be replaced or even re-energised with some younger members. The NLD remains strictly hierarchical; even her leadership and her decisions will remain unchallenged, and using democratic means to take decisions within the NLD would be out of the question. As Hans-Bernd Zöllner explains in his work on the NLD, the tendency of unanimous elections (and subsequent unquestioning following) of a political leader is rooted in Burmese tradition.[9] In his article he cites Daw Aung San Suu Kyi herself referring to a Buddhist text to defend this tradition, which had been used to legitimise the rule of the Burmese kings: '[t]he agreement by which [the] first monarch undertakes to rule righteously in return for a portion of rice crop represents the Buddhist version by social contract'.[10] Dissent and disagreement, as seen already when the NDF split off, is therefore unacceptable, even though the NLD claims to be democratic. It was going to be no different after her release.

Daw Aung San Suu Kyi's early activities included a visit to a home for HIV patients run by an NLD activist,[11] as well as giving press interviews and meeting foreign diplomats. Most of her activities at the time drew much domestic and international attention, especially through the media. It was almost as if she was trying to see what she could do and what the old regime—about to hand over power in March 2011 to the new government—would allow her to do.

Internationally people were clamouring for her voice, wanting to hear what she had to say after having been shut away for so long. On 28 January, just two and a half months after her release, Daw Aung San Suu Kyi gave a speech at the World Economic Forum in Davos via a video link:

> Over the past few years, despite my isolation from much of the world, I have been able to follow closely the global response to the economic downturn through listening assiduously to radio broadcasts. [...] I would like to speak on behalf of the 55 million people of Burma who have for the most part been left behind. We yearn to be a part of the global community [...] I would like to request those who have invested or who are thinking of investing in Burma to put a premium on respect for the law, on environmental and social factors, on the rights of workers, on job creation and on the promotion of technological skills. [...] I would like to appeal to all those present at this gathering to use their particular opportunities and skills as far as possible to promote national reconciliation, genuine democratization, human development and economic growth in Burma that our people may in turn be able make their own contribution towards a safer happier world.

This attitude of still not openly encouraging Western economic engagement with the country was also reflected in the NLD papers on the Myanmar economy, which maintained that the sanctions had not affected the Myanmar economy[12] and therefore should only be lifted if the 'violations of human rights and lack of democratic practices' come to an end.[13] Her comment that sanctions 'had not affected the Myanmar economy' was bolstered by the argument that they had impacted on the generals who were pressing for their removal. There was no official reaction from the government, but it is understood that they were not pleased with Daw Aung San Suu Kyi's attitude on sanctions. After all, some of the negotiations she had had with the regime touched on this and earlier, during her time under house arrest, she had promised to cooperate with the government to end sanctions, at the time even asking General Than Shwe for more data and information. In sum, the deep divisions between the NLD and the government remained stark, and at the time it was unclear how they could be bridged.

Whilst Daw Aung San Suu Kyi was keen to re-enter the political process immediately, many things had changed on the ground since she had been put under house arrest. At that time the NLD was regarded both domestically and internationally as the only opposing force to the regime. By 2010 the political landscape had been transformed completely, especially with regard to a more plural opposition which now also included legally elected ethnic parties. In 2010, when she stepped out from her house arrest, she was no longer the only option for those who wanted change. It is unclear how far Daw Aung San Suu Kyi recognised this at the time. In her meetings with various CSOs she emphasised the role the NLD would play in Myanmar's future, and certainly did not credit anyone with the work that had brought about the changes during her 'absence'; so relations between her and other civil society organisations started on a rather tense footing.[14]

However, it seems that she did recognise that the army was a relevant stakeholder in the new system. She said to the Western press: 'We have not ruled out cooperation with the military. But we have to talk about it, how do we effect a smooth transition and in how many stages. [...] We're not saying no more military on the scene any more.'[15] In fact in a Radio Free Asia interview she was cautious about how the military might be treated in the future: 'It is important to consider carefully whether one would send the military government before the ICC (International Criminal Court) as a means of applying pressure on them, or because one holds a grudge against them. It would not be good for the country if such an action were taken because of a grudge. I only want to create a situation in which there would be no reason for sending anyone from our country before the ICC.'[16] In the same interview she also expressed the hope that the armed forces would participate in the second Panglong conference she was advocating.

However, in a number of interviews she remained adamant that the results of the 1990 elections needed to be recognised, despite the fact that the 2010 elections has rendered these results void:[17]

> If I may express my opinion with regard to the 2010 and 1990 elections, we cannot discard the results of the 1990 elections. The reason is not because the NLD won the elections or because the NLD wanted to hold on to its victory. It is to respect the will of the people. It is also because we agree to the principle of democracy, which is having a high regard for the wishes of the people.[18]

Besides the recognition of the 1990s election results, the status and position of the NLD continued to be a headache. Just before her planned tour of the country at the end of June 2011, the Myanmar government sent a stern letter to her, reminding her of the illegal status of her party.[19] The authorities wanted Daw Aung San Suu Kyi to take a stand on whether she wanted the NLD to return to the legal political fold or decide if the NLD was to morph into a social welfare organisation, which still required registration.[20]

Despite these differences, the government continued its engagement with her, even facilitating her attendance and that of around 3,000 NLD members at the Martyrs Day commemoration on 19 July.[21] On 25 July, Daw Aung San Suu Kyi met with Minister Aung Kyi for a private discussion.[22] Not much was revealed about their deliberations, but a joint statement was released stating rather blandly that 'the two sides are optimistic about and satisfied with the dialogue'.[23] It was hoped at the time that this new series of talks might be different from the ones that had been held after 2007. What was different was the fact that there was a statement to the press about it. A few days later on 28 July, after conflict re-erupted between the KIA and the Myanmar army, Daw Aung San Suu Kyi wrote an open letter (see Annex) to the president and four armed groups calling for an immediate ceasefire and stating that she did not believe that the force could resolve the ethnic conflict and that this would be 'harmful' to all concerned parties.[24] Interestingly the government did not condemn Daw Aung San Suu Kyi's initiative as interference, and Minister Aung Kyi confirmed that the ethnic conflict issue was one that was under discussion between them. Aung Kyi and Daw Aung San Suu Kyi met again on 12 of August. Their joint press statement said that 'the two sides will cooperate in pursuing stability of the state and national development' and that 'the two sides will avoid conflicting views and will cooperate on reciprocal basis'.[25] This seemed to point to an improvement in the relations between her and the government. So much so that on her first political excursion outside Yangon to Bago the next day, Daw Aung San Suu Kyi accepted government security and avoided confrontational language in her speech.[26]

The turning point: Daw Aung San Suu Kyi meets the president

Relations were soon to improve even more. On 20 August people across Myanmar awoke to a now famous photo of the president standing together with Daw Aung San Suu Kyi under the portrait of her father, General Aung San, symbolising national reconciliation. Until that day photos of Aung San were not seen in the press.[27] His memory had been expunged from the public domain, largely to avoid legitimising his daughter. This first meeting between the president and Daw Aung San Suu Kyi had been arranged as part of the second National Workshop on Reforms for Economic Development, convened by the president's chief economic adviser U Myint in Nay Pyi Taw. This was the second in the series of its kind. U Myint's paper focused on corruption, a topic that had been taboo previously.[28] Daw Aung San Suu Kyi was seated at a VIP table and both ministers and prominent businessmen came to chat with her during a break.[29] In the evening, she was invited to dine with the president and his wife.[30] The meeting had not been announced, creating maximum surprise the next morning across the country. In part this was possibly the case because it had been so difficult to get Daw Aung San Suu Kyi to agree to come. According to the go-between, senior members of the NLD did not want Daw Aung San Suu Kyi to go to Nay Pyi Taw, especially alone. It was only at very short notice, just before she was picked up early that morning to fly to the capital, that all was put in place.[31]

After her meeting with the president, Daw Aung San Suu Kyi made her most positive statement about the new government thus far, saying that she believed he wanted real change.[32] It became clear that the ice was thawing on both sides and a new future was being contemplated when the Speaker of the Pyiduangsu Hluttaw (Union Parliament), U Khin Aung Myint, told Radio Free Asia in September that Suu Kyi 'is the daughter of General Aung San whom we all love. She is welcome if she joins the Parliament.'[33]

That same month Daw Aung San Suu Kyi undertook her second trip outside Yangon to Bagan. This was a private trip and upon return she published her reflections in the weekly paper *Pyithu Khit*. The same newspaper carried an article about her father, General Aung San, written by the NLD leader Win Tin.[34] The ban on news articles about her or her father had stopped, showing the first signs of a thawing of media censorship.

The meetings with U Aung Kyi continued. In October a joint communiqué was released stating that: 'They discussed steps being taken by the President to grant amnesty, means and ways on bilateral cooperation in conservation of the Ayeyarwady river, endeavours of the government to build eternal peace with armed groups within the framework of law and cooperation in ensuring community peace and prevalence of law and order.'[35] This was more than had been revealed previously. Clearly Daw Aung San Suu Kyi was being asked about her opinions on the new policies, and she seemed keen to cooperate. Shortly after that last meeting, at the end of October 2011, the NLD announced to everyone's surprise that it would probably re-register as a political party and contest the 2012 by-elections.[36] NLD spokesman Nyan Win said the re-registration would happen under an amended party law that dropped certain clauses to which the party had objected.[37] By 1 December, Daw Aung San Suu Kyi made the news public herself, stating that she hoped to run for parliament, provided the re-registration of the NLD was accepted.[38] On 18 January Aljazeera reported that she had registered to run for a seat in parliament in Kawhmu, a rural constituency in the delta south-west of Yangon.[39] Shortly after, at the end of the month, she again addressed the World Economic Forum in Davos via video link, where Industry Minister U Soe Thane was present. Daw Aung San Suu Kyi said she was not able to attend as she was busy preparing for the by-elections on 1 April. Her message was positive and optimistic: 'A year on I can say we have taken steps toward meeting those challenges.' She said that 'an important step that will take us nearer to a truly revolutionary breakthrough will be the inclusion of all relevant political forces in the electoral and legislative processes of our country'.[40] Her message and attitude showed how far things had moved on in the year after her house arrest had ended.

The new government: President Thein Sein's other reformist moves (Jan 2011–March 2012)

Whilst national reconciliation was the new government's first priority, the reform agenda that President Thein Sein had outlined included many other issues. Improving the international perception of Myanmar was high on the list as well. Over the early months of 2011 there had been increased collaboration with different UN agencies. This followed improved collaboration between the government and UN agencies after Cyclone Giri had struck the Rakhine coast in October 2010. Even in the aftermath of the elections and the transfer of power, the UN emergency services were able to report that it had been much simpler to deal with the government than when Cyclone Nargis had struck two and a half years earlier. The post-cyclone relief efforts continued into spring 2011, becoming the responsibility of the new government after the transfer of power.

At an update meeting on the UN Strategic Planning Process,[41] Bishow Parajuli, UN Resident/Humanitarian Coordinator in Myanmar, informed the donor and aid community about the regular series of consultations that had been held with the government beyond the relief efforts of the cyclone, and specifically informed them that at a meeting in late February an agreement had been reached that the UN engagement in Myanmar would be around four strategic priorities: 1. Encourage inclusive growth (both rural and urban), including agricultural development and enhancement of employment opportunities. 2. Increase equitable access to quality social services. 3. Reduce vulnerability to natural disasters and climate change. 4. Promote good governance and strengthen democratic institutions and human rights. It was the first indication that the UN would work more closely with the UN than it had ever done before, facilitating UN work rather than obstructing it.

The parliament (and the country) closed down for the Thingyan holiday in April 2011. Before reopening at the end of August, a lot of behind the scenes engagement ensued between different UN agencies, including the ILO helping the Labour Ministry to write international standard labour legislation that would be submitted to the parliament in the new term. Some local CSOs were also involved, but not much detail about these early meetings between government and the CSO sector is publicly known. However, those sitting on the outside had no idea that so much activity was going on in Nay Pyi Taw. Many believed that the parliament, once reconvened, would not be very active and would simply play the role of a rubber-stamping authority. However, once the parliament was reconvened on 22 August 2011, countering general expectations, debates quickly became very lively and the topics covered included issues that had till then been seen as sensitive and would not normally have been discussed, let alone debated. The topics included conflict in ethnic areas, amnesty for political prisoners, reinstating licenses for activist lawyers and ending *in camera* trials at Insein prison. For the first time in history, government ministers had to explain government behaviour and MPs had to deal with constitutional matters of local importance.[42] Bills on local democracy, labour unions, micro-finance, environmental conservation and the registration of private schools were submitted. Complaints about the registration process of CSOs were aired.[43] Gwen Robinson wrote many articles on the new government and the reforms, describing the parliament as an 'engine for the sweeping reforms of President Thein Sein [...] Relatively junior MPs have grilled cabinet ministers in marathon sessions, while nearly 20 multi-party parliamentary committees have flexed political muscle over the shape of legislation.'[44] For the first time, journalists from non-state media outlets were allowed to observe the debates from the galleries and report on them, giving the country and the world a unique insight into the democratisation process.[45]

A number of other things changed as well: on 16 August 2011 daily propaganda slogans disappeared from the state newspapers,[46] and the next day President Thein Sein gave a speech to government, business and non-government organisations, urging exiled Burmese to return home.[47] The president explained that those who were not under criminal investigation would be welcomed and that those who had committed crimes would be treated with leniency. It became clear that the president wanted members of domestic civil society as well as those who had worked on the border to join hands to build something new. It was not the first time that the president had called upon local CSO leaders to support change, but what was unprecedented was his call for those in exile to come home and be part of the change process. This was followed by President Thein Sein's most spectacular 'reform': the suspension of the Myitsone dam project in early October 2011.[48] The move surprised the domestic population and international observers, as well as the Chinese government whose joint venture it was.[49] The dam in Kachin State was the largest out of a series of seven dams to be built by the Chinese, at a cost of $3.6 billion. The 6,000 MW of power was also earmarked for China. The dam had become an issue rallying Myanmar nationals from all walks of life who were worried about the environmental effects. The dam would flood an area the size of Singapore, displacing 10,000 locals. The president made a stand against the Chinese, and this was seen as a show of strength, with policy departing from the previous pro-Chinese regime. This move was politically astute as it allowed ordinary people to believe that the president was able to stand up for them, for the country, even to the powerful Chinese government. An alliance of different CSOs had been protesting about the construction of the dam. Instead of being herded off the streets, the CSOs felt that their protests had been heard. This was a first step of change in the relationship between government and LNGOs. Many young people at the time expressed wonder as to how the system was transforming, and many started to admire the president for his courage.[50]

Another gesture of reconciliation and progress was the various prisoner amnesties and releases, including increasing numbers of political prisoners. On 16 May 2011, 58 political prisoners were released. The amnesty also included a reduction of all prison sentences by one year. On 11 October this was followed by the release of another 240 political prisoners (as part of a larger amnesty of criminal convicts), including the comedian Zaganar who had been arrested in 2008 for criticising the government's response to Cyclone Nargis. He had organised collections of charitable donations himself and was later accused of 'illegally giving information to the press and causing public alarm'. Upon his release he said: '... if I do something wrong they will send me back. I'm not happy today because there are so many of my friends still in prison.'[51]

Later, early in January, another 36 and 302 political prisoners were released. They included former general Khin Nyunt released on 13 January 2012[52] and well-known dissidents U Khun Htun Oo (chair of Shan National League of Democracy), Min Ko Naing ('88 Generation student group), Htay Kywe and the monk U Gambira (leaders of the 'saffron revolution' in 2007).[53] This fourth amnesty brought the total number of political releases to 477. In January 2012 all death sentences were commuted to life imprisonment.[54]

Western governmental reactions to the budding reforms were generally positive. In August 2011 Derek Mitchell appointed a special representative and policy coordinator on a dual track of engagement and sanctions policy, changing decades of US policy towards Myanmar. In September the IMF sent a delegation to help with the exchange rate reforms.[55] This was followed by Hillary Clinton's visit in November 2011. Finally in November 2011, at a summit in Bali, ASEAN announced that Myanmar would take up the ASEAN chair in 2013.[56] This announcement underlined the international recognition the reforms were being given in the region and resulted in a surge of domestic pride. From an international perspective this move was also seen as potentially risky, as the reforms had just started and were not yet embedded or in fact seen as irreversible.[57]

Despite the positive reactions to the reform process across many governments, there emerged a serious movement asking for a UN Commission of Inquiry to be set in place to look at the human rights abuses and alleged war crimes that had been committed by the Myanmar government.[58] The movement was led by a lobby of exile groups and human rights organisations that had written to President Obama in July 2011. This was followed by a report by Human Rights Watch documenting summary executions, torture, the use of convicts as army porters and as human shields. The debate continued throughout the rest of 2011 and early 2012, even Daw Aung San Suu Kyi giving her support to the movement.[59] Although there was considerable pressure for a UN Commission of Inquiry on human rights abuses, Western governments gave only limited support, knowing full well that China and Russia would oppose any such inquiry and that it would be counterproductive at a time of incipient political reform to seek fresh confrontation. As a result, the campaign slowly petered out.

Just short of a year after taking office, the president addressed the Union Assembly to outline the achievements and future plans of the government in its first year. The speech was transmitted live on national television. He was candid, recognising that much was still to be done to achieve the aims he had outlined eleven months previously. He shared the credit of the changes with '... all the stakeholders, including political parties, civil society, members of the Hluttaws [legislatures], the judicial pillar, the fourth estate media, national race leaders, and the Tatmadaw [armed forces]'. Noting that action counted more than words, he said: 'our people have suffered under various governments and different systems, and the people will judge our government based on its actual achievements'.[60] The speech was given a month early, most probably due to the campaign and preparations for the 1 April by-elections.

NLD campaign and Daw Aung San Suu Kyi visits across the country (March 2012–April 2012)

In March 2012 the election campaign for the by-elections started in earnest. The NLD was contesting all the available seats and Daw Aung San Suu Kyi was campaigning vigorously around the country. Thousands came to hear her message and see her, often standing for long hours in paddy fields under the sun, waiting for her to arrive. The seat she was contesting had been vacated by Soe Tint, who was appointed Deputy Minister of Construction in the new government.[61] Her rural constituency of Kawhmu was also being contested by the local doctor who represented the USDP and who had promised to focus on local issues, trying to capture the votes of those who questioned whether, given her national and international status, Daw Aung San Suu Kyi would be able to engage with the needs of the constituency.[62] According to an interview conducted by *The Independent*, U Aye, a member of the NLD since 1989, responded to this by saying that Daw Aung San Suu Kyi '... will focus on policies and the system. Other leaders can change things here... This will not be her main job.' However, she clearly needed a constituency in which to stand. Since Daw Aung San Suu Kyi was not a local resident of Kawhmu, the party chose to register her at the home of Kyaw Swar Min in Wah Thin Kha, whose community was mostly made up of Karen farmers.[63] This might have been a bit unusual, but the local community was very proud to host her.

The NLD also had to select another 43 candidates for the remaining constituencies.[64] This resulted in some local controversies as many of those selected personally by Daw Aung San Suu Kyi seemed to be chosen on the basis of how much time they had spent in jail, and were not based on other, possibly more important competencies. In Mandalay the candidate chosen was not the one who held local support, resulting in local activist incomprehension and disappointment. The person who had wanted to run for the seat had collected local signatures to support his case, but was told that Daw Aung San Suu Kyi had chosen someone else and that he was just required to help in the campaign.[65] Another criticism resulted when the NLD refused to cooperate with other smaller parties, especially in ethnic areas, where fielding NLD candidates was going to split the vote and weaken the ethnic parties. Again, this did not go down well with local ethnic leaders who had hoped that the NLD would show solidarity with other opposition parties.

During the campaign Daw Aung San Suu Kyi went on a whirlwind tour, trying to visit as many constituencies that were going to vote as possible. Her rallies drew large crowds of supporters wherever she went.[66] The constant campaigning however took their toll, and a few weeks later Daw Aung San Suu Kyi cancelled her trips outside Yangon due to increasing ill health. After being stuck in a boat on a sandbank whilst travelling to Myeik in the south, she ended up having to be put on a drip. Kyi Toe, deputy officer of the NLD, announced: 'According to the advice of her family doctor Tin Myo Win, she will take a rest at home. She should not travel far for trips any more.'[67] Not long after, Daw Aung San Suu Kyi delivered the NLD campaign speech on TV, which was part of the government provision that allowed contesting parties to address the nation for fifteen minutes on TV and radio. She called for constitutional reform, the 'democratic rights of the people' to be better protected, a freer media and a stronger judiciary, free from political interference. Reflecting her party's rule of law stand she said: 'All repressive laws must be revoked.'[68]

Given the rigging of the 2010 polls, the 2012 by-elections were being carefully watched by the international community. In March, President Thein Sein invited representatives from the European Union, United States and ASEAN to send observers to monitor them, announcing: 'This coming by-election is a first-ever election which will be held by the new government and the world will be watching us. [...] I would like to urge our people to help us have a free, fair and clean election. [...] All political parties must accept the people's decision, whether win or lose.'[69] This was an unprecedented step in a country that had been ruled by the military for so long and whose ruling elites had never allowed any international organisation or other country so much as a comment on its internal processes. Despite this the US state department stated that they did not think the process would meet international standards for complete transparency.[70] It was for the government to prove itself—and so the scene was set for an unprecedented poll that included for the first time Myanmar's most famous former political prisoner as a candidate.

The by-elections and NLD win, 1 April 2012

The NLD won the 1 April by-elections unequivocally, taking 43 of the 44 seats they had contested.[71] What was remarkable was that the NLD also won the four seats in Nay Pyi Taw that were seen as a military stronghold.[72] Two of these had belonged to President Thein Sein and first Vice President Tin Aung Myint Oo.[73] Daw Aung San Suu Kyi won the Kawhmu township seat with over 85 per cent of the votes.[74] The USDP and the Shan Nationalities Democratic Party (also known as the White Tiger party) won a seat each. These polls made the NLD the largest party after the USDP. In terms of overall votes the NLD garnered a 66 per cent share, while the USDP managed only 27 per cent.[75]

The results surprised those who had expected some level of rigging. However, this vindicated the government's promise of free and fair elections, leaving a profoundly shocked USDP,[76] and the ethnic parties and smaller democratic parties licking their wounds. USDP leader Htay Oo attributed the NLD victory to Daw Aung San Suu Kyi's popularity as the daughter of Burma's independence hero, trying to downplay the NLD success. Nevertheless it was clear to all at home and abroad that the USDP would now face a tough challenge in 2015.[77] The NLD victory speech set out its main aims as the rule of law, internal peace and constitutional amendments.[78]

Possibly as a result of the polls, the government changed the military's representations in parliament.[79] On 22 April, the Election Commission announced the replacement of 59 military-appointed MPs (39 in the People's Assembly and 20 in the National Assembly) with higher-ranking officers.[80] Majors were replaced by 8 brigadiers, 14 colonels, and 37 lieutenant colonels.[81] The press immediately speculated that this was to counter the new NLD MPs, but allegedly the Commander in Chief Min Aung Hlaing decided that he needed more independent thinking personnel in the legislative assemblies.[82]

However, despite the successful elections, things did not start smoothly for the NLD MPs elect. As parliament resumed on 23 April 2012, the NLD MPs refused to attend the first session, protesting that they could not take the necessary oath that required them to 'safeguard' the 2008 constitution.[83] They would be prepared to 'respect' the constitution, but not 'defend' it.[84] Despite the fact that Daw Aung San Suu Kyi insisted that this was just a technical problem, there was now a new political deadlock.[85] No one knew how this would be resolved, and there was some level of public disquiet, with voices starting to say that the NLD was being unreasonable. The problem threatened to escalate as the MPs were coming close to the maximum period in which they would be able to take the oath, risking otherwise to be disqualified.[86] In the end the NLD had to back down and their MPs attended parliament on 2 May and were sworn in, ending the impasse 'as a gesture of respect to the desires of the people'.[87]

The government continues reforms[88] (April 2012–Oct 2012)

After the 2012 by-elections, further government-led reforms followed. Two were of particular importance: the abolition of press censorship and the commitment to rid Myanmar of all child labour and child soldiers by 2015. Both issues had led to heavy criticism in the international press and across foreign governments. The president knew that these issues needed to be rectified.

In one of the president's speeches, he had referred to the media as the 'fourth estate' and said he recognised the importance of the media's role and respected it.[89] At first a certain number of topics such as sports and culture no longer needed scrutinising, but the president decided to go the whole way and on 20 August 2012 the censorship board, officially known as the Press Scrutiny and Registration Department, was abolished. Tint Swe, head of the PSRD, said that 'Censorship began on 6 August 1964 and ended 48 years and two weeks later. [...] From now on, our department will just carry out registering publications for keeping them at the national archives and issuing a license to printers and publishers.'[90] Internet rules were also relaxed, with many previously unavailable websites freely available. The abolition of official censorship opened the door for exile publications such as *Mizzima* and *The Irrawaddy* to come and set up shop in Myanmar in the course of 2012 and 2013. However, the removal of censorship also resulted in an outpouring of hatred, especially on blogs and social media, towards the 'Rohingya' or Bengali Muslims. This had been a long-standing problem that had been suppressed, but started to re-emerge in light of the newly won public speech and press freedom, leading to fears of anti-Muslim riots across the country.[91]

The second momentous improvement was the culmination of several years of work by the head of the ILO, Steve Marshall, in getting Myanmar to commit to a schedule that was to abolish child labour. The ILO had previously managed to put in place an agreement with the government through which families could complain directly to the ILO if children had been enlisted as soldiers, or if they were suffering from other forms of forced labour. This complaints mechanism for forced labour abuses had been in place since 2007, and the mechanism allowed the ILO to act as a go-between for the family and government once the case had been verified.[92] Outcomes varied from the discharge of under-aged soldiers (and their release from prison if they had tried to desert) to cases where compensation was paid for injuries and loss of life. The project was so successful that, starting with just a handful of cases brought by very brave families, the ILO has now registered more than 2,000 complaints, including issues of under-age recruitment into the army to traditional forced labour, bonded labour, human trafficking, land issues that lead to forced labour, forced cropping, portering in conflict zones, forced recruitment into the military and into infrastructure projects.[93] The ILO had also helped the government rewrite its labour laws to international standards over the summer of 2011, bringing them to parliament that autumn. The relationship between the ILO and the government had strengthened through the complaints mechanism described above, leading to senior army officers having direct and personal contact with Steve Marshall in Yangon. This had led to mutual confidence, allowing the ILO to achieve more than any other UN agency in the country before the 2010 elections. According to the ILO report,[94] an MOU was signed in March 2012 providing a framework for ILO support for the objectives of abolishing forced labour and freedom of association and social dialogue. The five other areas that the ILO would be working on included: employment opportunities and vocational skills, especially for youth; labour legislation and labour market governance; enterprise development; labour migration; and addressing employment and labour issues in specific sectors. Myanmar's new Labour Organisation Law came into force in March 2012, and by October 2012 they had registered 264 workers' organisations and 13 employers' organisations.

One result of the reforms the government was undertaking was the strengthening of the lower house of parliament, whereby the legislative branch of government started to understand how it could 'check and balance' the executive branch. Parliamentary Speaker U Shwe Mann became increasingly aware that his parliament could counter the president, and he started to use this as a political tool when his previously close relationship with the president started to degrade. In one instance the president's suggestion that village heads should be elected by a show of hands was rejected by the legislature, who decreed it had to be a secret vote. In another conflict, far more complex, the issue arose over a ruling by the nine judges of the Constitutional Court when they ruled that the committees of the legislature were not 'Union level' (meaning state) bodies. The lower house disagreed, as this would limit the powers of such committees; more than two-thirds signed a petition to impeach the judges, despite the fact that the president suggested instead amending the constitution for increased clarity. Before the impeachment could occur, the nine judges resigned.[95] The ruling had come in response to a request from President Thein Sein to clarify the powers of parliament's committees. The threat of impeachment showed the lack of political maturity of Myanmar's body politic and the lack of understanding that the Constitutional Court was a 'watchdog' over the political establishment. The threat to impeach was also related to charges of inefficiency—for example the delayed foreign investment law had undergone more than 90 amendments.[96] Speaker

U Shwe Mann believed that the decision of the judges affected what work MPs were able to do, and therefore supported the impeachment move.[97]

In July 2012 the first Vice President U Tin Aung Myint Oo, regarded as a 'hard-liner', resigned on health grounds. The suggested replacement, General Myint Swe, previously Chief Minister of Yangon Region, turned out to have an Australian daughter-in-law which therefore disqualified him.[98] Finally Navy Admiral U Nyan Tun was confirmed and sworn in. This change was followed by a cabinet reshuffle in which the president moved his closest ministers to the presidential office, giving U Aung Min, who had been Minister for Railways, responsibility for the peace process; and U Soe Thane, Chairman of the Investment Commission, responsibility for economic developments and industrialisation.

Joining the government, becoming a politician (June 2012–Nov 2012)

President Thein Sein's government took very seriously the NLD joining parliament. In August 2012, Daw Aung San Suu Kyi was appointed chairperson of the newly formed Committee for Rule of Law and Peace and Stability, underlining a new era of cooperation with the NLD. It immediately received petitions and requests from citizens regarding land records and land disputes, an issue that had not yet been addressed by the reform process.

Whilst the West tried to define the NLD's role in parliament as that of an 'opposition', this is not the way the government perceived it. In Myanmar, joining the parliament meant becoming part of the system, and the NLD was expected to support the reform process, not sit on the sidelines and criticise it. From the government's perspective, this has not been entirely successful. As Robert Taylor put it, looking at the post-2012 election scenario:

> Aung San Suu Kyi is also a new actor in her own right and brings the NLD with her. She seems increasingly to be in thrall to the existing order. She is doing nothing to threaten stability. She is actually doing very little indeed. Her party seems largely moribund despite its presence throughout the country. It has announced no policies but mainly goes along with things proposed by others in the legislature. [...] There is no evidence yet of policy thinking by her or her party, hence my belief that she will be led by the bureaucracy if she ever comes to power.[99]

Despite being elected and joining parliament, Daw Aung San Suu Kyi still cautioned against foreign investment. In June 2012, at a meeting in Bangkok organised by the World Economic Forum, she said: 'Would-be investors in Burma, please be warned [...] Even the best investment laws would be of no use whatsoever if there are no courts that are clean enough and independent enough to be able to administer those laws justly. This is our problem: so far we have not been aware of any reforms on the judicial front.'[100] U Than Htay, Myanmar's Minister of Energy, also attended and was actively encouraging foreign investment at that same meeting, especially in the special economic zones that Myanmar was preparing to develop, showing a rift between the two sides. President Thein Sein had been expected to attend that meeting but is said to have cancelled after Daw Aung San Suu Kyi was given a prominent slot to speak. Cracks between the president and Daw Aung San Suu Kyi were slowly starting to show.

Daw Aung San Suu Kyi's travels continued throughout the summer, on a seventeen-day tour of Europe where she was feted and received like a head of state. But given the strain, she was then unable to attend the opening of parliament in July, reconvening after a two-month break. The NLD spokesperson said she was 'too tired' but that her health was satisfactory.[101] Not much was reported about this high-profile absence, but it must have irritated the government who had tried to accommodate her special needs since the elections. The irritation did not end with this incident. Calling Myanmar 'Burma' had raised some government eyebrows, and she was asked to use the country's official name of Myanmar. At a press conference on 3 July she remained defiant: 'I call my country "Burma" as we did a long time ago. I'm not insulting other people. Because I believe in democracy, I'm sure that I can call it as I like.'[102] As Derek Tonkin noted at the time: 'Suu Kyi may well be right in terms of Burmese law, but probably not with respect to diplomatic practice and international law. She is however serving notice that she does not wish to represent her State officially in any context at the present time, which many might regret.'[103] However, despite Daw Aung San Suu Kyi's uncompromising attitude towards certain issues, she also started to make positive statements about the army, something which came as a surprise to many of her followers. Her position at the time of her release had been that she held no grudges, but when she started to speak about how much she loved the armed forces, many wondered if this attitude was for political purposes, preparing her future to share power with one of Myanmar's most important stakeholders. In an interview on *Desert Island Discs* on Radio 4, she said: 'The truth is that I am very fond of the army because I always thought of it as my father's army. [... I thought my father] was the father of the army and that all soldiers were his sons and that therefore they were part of my family.'[104]

The domestic and international admiration of Daw Aung San Suu Kyi continued unabated for most of 2012. However, as Daw Aung San Suu Kyi was making the transition from pro-democracy 'icon' to practical politician, some of the choices she made came in for severe criticism. This started with her positive comments about the army who had imprisoned and maltreated hundreds if not thousands of NLD supporters and party members. Four other issues followed. The first was a revelation that the NLD had accepted money (a total of 200 million kyat/US$ 235,000) from pro-regime cronies Sky Net, Air Bagan and AGD Bank. Whilst she is said to have explained that she did not want to hold personal grudges, she thought that crony support for the NLD and other charitable organisations was useful and contributed to the democratic reform process. It seemed that she did not see this as an issue that could tarnish her reputation.[105]

Much worse was to come. Over the autumn of 2012 activists had been complaining about a copper mine, the $997m joint venture between the Chinese Wan Bao Mining Company and a Myanmar military company, asking for it to be shut down as it caused environmental damage and health problems. The protesters also signalled that the project, signed before the elections, had not undergone parliamentary scrutiny. It is possible that due to the suspension of the Myitsone dam, protesters hoped the president would hear them. They held a demonstration against the Chinese joint venture of the Letpadaung mine on 29 November, and the police used force to break it up, including white phosphorus, leaving many with severe burns. President Thein Sein appointed a commission to inquire into the incident, to be chaired by Daw Aung San Suu Kyi. The commission's report was released in March 2013, acknowledging that the smoke bombs the police had used contained phosphorus but suggesting that the project should continue so as not to create tensions with China and discourage foreign direct investment. This was despite the fact that the report acknowledged that the project was not creating any local jobs and did not have adequate environmental safeguards in place. No punishment was demanded for the violent police force.[106] When Daw Aung San Suu Kyi visited the area, hundreds of angry farmers heckled and walked out on her as they saw her as representing the establishment and no longer protecting their rights.[107]

The third issue that created criticism of Daw Aung San Suu Kyi was her stand on the resurgence of conflict in Kachin State. It seemed that despite being critical of the government on certain issues, such as economic reforms, she was reluctant to condemn the actions of the army in Kachin and Northern Shan States, which at the time had displaced some 75,000 people. In London, when asked by a student why she showed such reluctance, Daw Aung San Suu

Kyi remained neutral: 'We want to know what's happening more clearly before we condemn one party or the other'; this greatly angered the Kachin community both in Myanmar and abroad,[108] and was not to be the only time she tried to avoid taking a stand on human rights.

The fourth issue that brought in a lot of criticism was her lack of views on the status of the Rohingya and the Buddhist violence against the Muslim community, which started to make headlines in the course of 2013.[109] Part of the issue has been Daw Aung San Suu Kyi's neutrality, her efforts seemingly to please certain members of the former regime and her refusal to upset the Buddhist Bamar majority,[110] as well as her obsession with changing the constitution, so that she can develop her political future. In addition, the lack of clear policies and manifestos from the NLD has not been helpful. As Vikram Nehru, senior associate at the Carnegie Endowment for Peace, explains: the NLD 'needs to flesh out and test its stance on human rights, tensions in ethnic minority areas, relations with the military and the appropriate role of the private sector, foreign investors and the government in the development process'.[111]

Obama's visit to Myanmar, 19 November 2012

The year ended on a high when President Obama came on his first visit to Myanmar. This move endorsed the reform process: he spoke at Yangon University to say he was optimistic about the future and promised that the US would support Myanmar in its remarkable reform journey. On this trip he also met President Thein Sein and visited Daw Aung San Suu Kyi. Just a year seemed to have made a lot of difference. As Robert Taylor put it:

> After years of being held up as one of the outposts of tyranny and the only pariah government in Southeast Asia, by the end of 2012 Myanmar was being toasted as a newly reformed champion of political opening and democratic transition, a model for persisting 'tyrannies' to emulate. What a difference a year makes. The 2008 Constitution of the country is now seen as a worthy document, but in need of amending, and the government of President Thein Sein, formed after the 2010 general elections, which were roundly condemned as a fraud and sham by Western nations, is now heralded as the friend of everyone and the enemy of none. Western political leaders, from British Secretary of State for Foreign Affairs, William Hague, at the start of the year, to U.S. President Barack Obama near the end, queued to have their pictures taken with President Thein Sein, with a side trip for another photo opportunity with Nobel Prize winner, Daw Aung San Suu Kyi, the leader of the National League for Democracy (NLD).[112]

The constitutional issue: the Lady wants to be President

The first NLD party congress was held on 8 March 2013. Whilst Daw Aung San Suu Kyi commands immense popularity across the country, she had been criticised, as discussed above, for her silence on the ethnic violence in Rakhine, for supporting the continuation of the Chinese-owned copper mine and for accepting donations from business tycoons who were seen as cronies of the former regime. With regard to NLD party politics, criticisms started to abound as well. At the end of 2012, 500 NLD members in Pathein in the delta left the party in protest, because they felt the leadership was authoritarian. This was not the first time that such concerns had been voiced. There was talk of conflict and disunity within the NLD, though not much reported on, as many of the Myanmar press felt they could not criticise Daw Aung San Suu Kyi, who remains a national and international icon. But despite an unspoken ban on public criticism, complaining voices were getting louder. The party congress hoped to show a positive, democratic and unified image, in order to silence some of the critics. However, it failed to do so. Daw Aung San Suu Kyi was re-elected as chairperson, with no one else contesting the position.[113] The 'elections' of the Central Executive Committee (expanded from 7 to 15) and the voting of the 120-strong Central Committee were not seen as democratic. Given the issues raised by members and the youth, there had been an expectation that some 'younger blood' would be included in the NLD leadership. These hopes were dashed as Daw Aung San Suu Kyi stated that it was 'impossible to leave the old, experienced members behind', that new members had been chosen because of their previous relationship with the party, for their capacity, and that some of the new members chosen would have to come from ethnic minorities. As such she retained a direct hand in the selection of the executive committee, a less than democratic practice. Some who support the party and would like to see the NLD win in 2015 said in private conversations that Daw Aung San Suu Kyi 'does not listen to anyone'. Yet the domestic and international focus remained on Daw Aung San Suu Kyi's personality and her decisions, rather than the NLD's policies on the economy, health and education. Despite the congress, party policies were only outlined in the broadest of terms. However, one policy priority that has dominated the NLD remained and became clearer and more pronounced—changing the constitution.

Changing the constitution has been one of the most important debates that emerged after the 2010 elections and was brought to the fore when Daw Aung San Suu Kyi started to say that it was unfair that the constitution contained an article that barred her personally from the presidency. Article 59f forbids any of the president's family from being foreigners, and therefore bars Daw Aung San Suu Kyi from the presidency due to her two sons by her late English husband.[114] The NLD also opposes Article 109, which guarantees that 25 per cent of the seats in parliament are reserved for the army. This is especially important, because according to Article 436 any constitutional amendment requires 75 per cent support in parliament, and therefore in practice the support of the military MPs. Daw Aung San Suu Kyi started touring the country, speaking at rallies that supported her wishes for constitutional amendment and garnering support from the wider public. At that time she reportedly threatened to boycott the next elections unless her demands are heard.

Leaders of the ruling party in government had different views on changing the constitution. It seemed that after a series of breakfast meetings[115] Daw Aung San Suu Kyi had brought Myanmar parliament speaker U Shwe Mann to her side, as he declared his support for changing Article 59f, saying 'I would personally be glad if Ama Gyi [i.e. Daw Aung San Suu Kyi] becomes president.' But later Shwe Mann explained that changing Article 59f is not the first priority. At the time it looked as if he would be the biggest beneficiary if Suu Kyi were not allowed to stand for president, as he has expressed interest in the post himself. However, the point he made is important: there are more urgent revisions needed in light of the peace process. Much more important are suggested amendments regarding power-sharing between the states and the centre, as already brought forward by the parliamentary committee. This is indeed essential in light of the government negotiating a national ceasefire agreement with the EAGs (discussed in Chapter 5). One of the main demands of the ethnic armies has been a greater level of federalism, especially regarding power over natural resources located in the ethnic states and issues pertaining to the use of mother-tongue languages.

The government set up a committee of MPs to review the constitution, made up of representatives from the military, as well as MPs from the USDP, NLD, the Chin Progressive Party, the All Mon Region Democracy Party, the Shan Nationalities Democratic Party, the Rakhine Nationalities Development Party, the Phalon-Sawaw Democratic Party, the Pa-O National League, the National Democratic Force and National Unity Party. In August 2014 the committee confirmed that they had reviewed all the suggestions proposing amendments for more than 450 of the 457 articles, including Article 436. The committee had received 28,000 suggestions for amendments, but also claimed to have received a petition signed by over 100,000 people who did not want to see the constitution changed. It certainly seemed as if the committee did not want to change either article, resulting in a stalemate between what the NLD wants and what the committee suggested. A smaller committee of 31 mainly USDP MPs was formed to make the official recommendations to parliament based on the committee's report. They came back negatively as well, voting against changing Article 59f.

In the meantime Daw Aung San Suu Kyi decided to rally the crowds across the country in a systematic way to challenge the government, hoping to be still in time for the 2015 elections. On 27 May 2014, in front of around 3,000 supporters in Nay Pyi Taw at the start of the movement, she urged supporters to 'test' the country's parliament, starting a two-month petition campaign to change the constitution. This was despite receiving a warning letter that she was in breach of the oath she had taken as an MP. The campaign was jointly organised with the '88 Generation student activist group to form a joint committee comprised of Win Htain, Nyan Win, Ohn Kyaing, Win Myint, Han Thar Myint, Tun Tun Hein and five members of the '88 Generation group: Min Ko Naing, Ko Ko Gyi, Mya Aye, Jimmy and Pyone Cho. The petition campaign was organised from the NLD's offices across the country.[116] At the start of the campaign she said: 'I'm asking you to join us because we want to introduce a peaceful tradition that can bring change. [...] Let's test whether parliament reflects the opinions and attitudes of the people.'[117] The campaign ended on 19 July 2014, Martyrs' Day, after rallies in Yangon, Mandalay and many other demonstrations around the country. The campaign's main focus was on changing Article 436 (rather than 59f), which requires more than three-quarters of the parliament votes to approve any amendments, and gives the military MPs a de facto veto on any constitutional change. It is clear that despite the focus on Article 436, this is still about Daw Aung San Suu Kyi wanting to become president. Her position is that if the constitution can be changed, then Article 59f can be changed later as well. The government was well aware of this. The rallies also led to a change in Daw Aung San Suu Kyi's tone vis-à-vis the military. In one of the Mandalay rallies she accused the armed forces of incompetence: 'The government has always said the Burmese (Myanmar) still don't deserve democracy. They (the military) have ruled the country for nearly 50 years, and if they have failed to educate people the norms of democracy during that period, they'd better not keep governing the country now.'[118] This is quite different from the conciliatory notes that she had struck in the first year after her house arrest when she referred to the army as her family.

The campaign collected over 5 million signatures. Daw Aung San Suu Kyi also sought support internationally. However, this resulted in a backlash.

Presidential spokesman Ye Htut lashed out at the US government for support-ing constitutional change: 'It is not the concern of the United States. It is inappropriate for us to tell how the US should amend their constitution and likewise the US should not dictate how it should be amended.'[119]

Her repeated calls for tripartite talks between the president, Commander in Chief Min Aung Hlaing and herself were finally partially met when on 31 October 2014 the president called a four-way meeting between himself, the military, the parties and the parliament. The invited representatives included the two vice presidents of the Union (U Nyan Tun and Dr Sai Mauk Kham), the Speakers of the Pyithu Hluttaw (Thura Shwe Mann) and Amyotha Hluttaw (U Khin Aung Myint), the Commander-in-Chief of the Tatmadaw (Senior General Min Aung Hlaing) and his Deputy (General Soe Win), the Vice Chairman of the Union Solidarity and Development Party (U Htay Oo), the Chairwoman of the National League for Democracy (Daw Aung San Suu Kyi), the Chairman of the Shan National League for Demo-cracy, also representing the United Nationalities Alliance (Khun Htun Oo), the Chairman of the Shan State Nationalities Democratic Party, also repre-senting the Nationalities Brotherhood Federation (Sai Aik Pao), the Chairman of the National Democratic Force, also representing the Federal Democracy Alliance (U Khin Maung Swe), a member of the central executive committee of the National Unity Party (U Thein Tun) and the Chairman of the Union Elections Commission (U Tin Aye). This new dialogue potentially aimed to find a solution to the deadlock around constitutional change and the 2015 elections. The president also wanted to talk about the successes of the reform process and the many challenges that remained ahead. In his speech he said, 'I would like to suggest that all political forces work in concert to ensure that the political transition will be smooth, that the 2015 elections will be free and fair, and that there will be a peaceful transfer of power.' Despite being a positive first step, the meeting was sharply criticised by Daw Aung San Suu Kyi and the NLD, as they felt that with so many stakeholders present no real dialogue could be had. They felt that the meeting should have been a four-way meeting that only included the president, the Speaker of the House U Shwe Mann, Chief of Staff General Min Aung Hlaing and Daw Aung San Suu Kyi herself. The president however maintained that any dialogue about the future had to include the political parties as well.

The NLD campaign to change the constitution might have collected large numbers of signatures, but it proved unable to change hearts and minds within the government. On 25 June 2015 Myanmar's bicameral parliament, the Pyidaungsu Hluttaw, held a crucial vote on whether to change articles 436, 59f, 59d, 60c and 416a of the 2008 constitution. The vote came on the back of three days of parliamentary debate, with 75 MPs registering to take part in what was seen as crucial discussions. So many in fact wanted to speak that all parties, including the NLD, had to reduce the numbers of those allowed to discuss the bills.

The Amytha Hluttaw (224-seat Upper House) and the Pyithu Hluttaw (440-seat Lower House) together hold 664 seats, of which 31 are currently not filled. For the proposed constitutional changes to be accepted, at least 475 votes in favour were needed. In the end only article 59d gained enough votes, changing the terminology from the president needing to have 'knowledge of the military' to 'knowledge of defence'. Votes to amend Articles 436 and 59f fell short, only gaining 61 per cent (388 votes) and 58 per cent (371 votes) in favour respectively.

The amendment process had originally been proposed by the USDP in March 2013 and moved very slowly, mostly behind closed doors. As the elections approached and the six-party talks failed to bring about any agreement on constitutional change, it was interesting to see that USDP leader and Speaker of the House U Shwe Mann wanted to be seen as a reformer. The speaker made it clear that any change would only come into effect after the next elections; however, he seemed to use this process to improve his own reputation in light of the elections and to show that the USDP can work in coalition with other parties. This move seems to have cost him the future support of the military.

Daw Aung San Suu Kyi did not use the failure of the vote to reiterate the threat that the NLD might not take part in the elections later in 2015. In April 2015 she declared that the NLD might boycott the elections if the constitution was not amended. Such behaviour, as she well knows, would result in the NLD being deregistered and barred from any political activities. In a press conference held immediately after the results of the ballot, the NLD pointed out how the military had used its seats to block the reforms and stressed again how the military did not want the country to change. Daw Aung San Suu Kyi also criticised the USDP for not presenting wide-ranging reforms, stating that she had given up hope that the six-party talks with the president and others would yield any tangible results before the elections.

It was always a long shot to expect that the military MPs would agree to changing the constitution. Chief of Army Staff Min Aung Hlaing has reiterated that he feels the country is not ready for such monumental shift and that the military MPs still have an important role to play. Altering Article 436 would have removed the military's veto power, something the army is not yet willing to accept. However, looking at the numbers, it is clear that the USDP and the military MPs no longer necessarily hold the same position. Given that the NLD and other parties hold few seats, it appears that a majority of the USDP MPs voted for change, showing that politics in Myanmar has changed quite dramatically over the past five years, even creating what seemed to be a new political rift between the regime party and the military.

Not long after the vote on constitutional change, the new political rift became much clearer. The rift was less between the USDP and the military and more one between USDP members supporting U Shwe Mann versus those who supported the president and the military. Between 12 and 13 August 2015 an internal party coup removed U Shwe Mann as chairman of the USDP. The dramatic incident involved a night raid by the police on party headquarters. The next day the Central Executive committee was reshuffled, allowing for pro-president MPs to gain the upper hand.[120] Much of the speculation has focused on Shwe Mann's close relationship with Daw Aung San Suu Kyi as a part of the reason for the purge; but a more important reason for his falling out with the president will have been his refusal to let both presidential ministers U Aung Min and U Soe Thane stand as USDP candidates in Kayah State.[121] Shwe Mann had rejected the candidatures of other retired senior officers that the military had proposed as well, upsetting both the president and the chief of staff. Daw Aung San Suu Kyi publically supported Shwe Mann, calling him an 'ally' and promising to work with him.[122]

The intra-party coup was followed by more parliamentary drama: their wrangling over the 'right to recall the local MP' bill that was being debated at the same time. The Union Election Commission had asked parliament to pass the bill the same day that U Shwe Mann was removed as head of the USDP. Some observers wondered if the party was going to remove him as an MP as well. Eventually the MPs who supported U Shwe Mann, including the ethnic MPs, the NLD and his allies within the USDP, voted to suspend the bill rather than debate it and Shwe Mann stayed in post both as an MP and as Speaker of the House.[123] On 28 August 2015 parliament held its last session and then suspended further meetings until the elections to be held on 8 November.

Coming to the end of President Thein Sein's term in office, Daw Aung San Suu Kyi is firmly part of Myanmar's political spectrum. In that sense 'national reconciliation' has indeed been achieved. However, she is still as far from the presidency as she was when she stepped out of house arrest in November 2010. The elections in November 2015 will be a test of how President Thein Sein's government can handle the power the NLD is likely to gain at the polls. It will also be a test for the NLD to see how far they can manage their side of the 'national reconciliation' deal.

4

THE PEACE PROCESS

Background

Myanmar is home to more than 100 ethno-linguistic groups, with an estimated population in 2012 of 58 million people—although exact numbers are hard to come by. Non-Burman communities make up at least 30 per cent of the population.[1] Under the 2008 constitution, the country is divided into seven predominantly ethnic nationality-populated states, and seven Burman majority regions (previously called divisions). The basis of Myanmar's contemporary ethnic conflicts lie in the colonial system of government, which led many tribal groups in hill regions to believe that they were not part of Burma.[2] The British helped define Burma's ethnic diversity by mapping the various ethnic groups. In 1992 the military government catalogued 135 'national races' (*lu myo* in Burmese).[3] This classification derives from the colonial era when the British took advantage of ethnic power struggles to establish their authority, and consolidated their grasp on the country by allying with local elites. During the last Anglo-Burmese war, the British destroyed Burma's monarchy along with the administrative structure of pre-colonial Burma.[4] The favouring of ethnic minorities and the advent of American Baptist missionaries, who worked first with the Karen and later with the Kachin and Chin tribes, led to a 'divide and rule' system which underlay British power.[5] Taylor also argues that the British were responsible for the politicisation of ethnicity in Burma.[6] The British developed a separate administration for the Kachin and the Chin through the Kachin Hill Tribes Regulation and the Chin Hills regulation 1894 and 1896 respectively.[7]

The colonial state's reification of ethnicity had significant political implications, as ethnic groups wanted to maintain control over their populations and territories. At independence the different groups needed a common ideology that would support the state. This was particularly difficult as the various ethnic groups felt they had had a special status under British rule, which they were unable to maintain after independence, when the Bamar majority ended up controlling the political process. Ultimately a unified, inclusive movement supporting the new state was never developed. General Aung San succeeded in bringing some of the minorities together at the Panglong conference in 1947 to form a union, but without the support of the Karen who only attended as observers. The constitution that emerged was 'tenuous' as 'the Shan and the Kayah States were theoretically able to secede from the union after a ten year trial period and referendum'.[8]

1948–89 ethnic conflicts and the Burmese Communist Party

Taylor and others have argued that it was the post-colonial rulers' championing of Buddhism as a state religion, particularly under U Nu (1960–62), that was interpreted as an attack on minority identity,[9] especially affecting predominantly Christian groups such as the Kachin.[10] Alan Saw U and others have argued that in addition to this, the central government discriminated against all non-Bamar groups politically, economically and through specific suppression of their culture, language and religion.[11] The conflicts started almost immediately after independence, with Karen armed rebels fighting just outside Rangoon.[12] Western concern at the time was largely directed towards the ethnic groups with sizable Christian populations. In the course of the conflict, they gained foreign support because of their status as the Christian 'underdog'.[13] Taylor adds to this the concern that had grown out of alliances that many Karen, Chin and Kachin had developed with the British forces fighting the Japanese.[14] Some ethnic groups, including the Kayah, the Kachin and the Chin, supported the Union government in 1949 and wanted rebellions suppressed.[15] This later changed. The late 1950s and 60s saw a new wave of ethnic nationalist movements emerge, in response to the government's perceived 'Burmanisation' policy,[16] increased militarisation and human rights abuses in ethnic areas that led to political grievances that have been held to this day.[17] In addition, the Tatmadaw saw itself increasingly as nation-builders rather than soldiers[18] and the second military coup in 1962 brought Ne Win to power. His 'Burmese Way to Socialism' brought economic isolation and no solution to ethnic issues, with more rebellions flaring up across the country. As of the 1960s, the government waged what it saw as counter-insurgency campaigns, also targeting the civilian populations in ethnic areas to break the EAGs. The brutality and systematic nature of the human rights abuses that continued into the 1990s in certain areas has been documented by a number of INGO and human rights agency reports over the years. The civil war led to large numbers of displaced people across the entire Myanmar border area, both inside and outside Myanmar. At the heart of the government policy was the 'four cuts' strategy designed to undermine the capacity of the ethnic armed groups by cutting their supplies (food, funds, intelligence and recruits etc.) and their supply routes. This was supported by the Tatmadaw having to be more or less self-sufficient when in the field[19] and therefore living off the villages they travelled through, often forcing villagers to give up whatever meagre supplies they had and also using locals for porter duties. Villagers were often caught in the middle, as the EAGs used similar and often equally brutal tactics to try to control their areas.[20]

As of the 1970s, armed ethnic groups started to lose control of their once extensive 'liberated zones', increasing the humanitarian crises in the borderlands with Thailand and China.[21] The cold war also encouraged separatism, insurgency and smuggling. China in particular was deeply involved in funding groups who supported the Burmese Communist Party (BCP) and consequently was instrumental in prolonging the war, which lasted until the late 1980s. 'Until 1989, the Myanmar Army had been fighting two inter-connected civil wars—one against the ethnic nationalist insurgents and another against the Communist party of Burma.'[22] According to Martin Smith, the BCP collapsed due to ethnic mutinies but also due to the funding from China reducing significantly in the late 70s and grinding to a halt at the end of the Cold War.[23]

The 1990s ceasefires and the development of civil society

In 1988 a democratisation movement took hold around Myanmar, and the socialist regime led by General Ne Win was brought down, leading to a breakdown of the bureaucracy and widespread instability across the country. As of 1989, the military government made efforts with ethnic armed groups to secure ceasefires. As mentioned in the first chapter, General Khin Nyunt led the process and he proceeded to negotiate with each armed group separately. The government negotiation team ultimately achieved ceasefires with around twenty armed groups without signing written agreements, except with the KIO, who were the only group who insisted on a written document.[24] The military government of the time did not initiate a political dialogue, allegedly because they were not an elected government, promising this would take place in the future.[25] Later, when the EAGs were indeed invited to take part in the National Convention, they found that their views would scarcely be taken into account.

During ceasefire periods in the 1990s and early 2000s, ethnic armed groups received special economic opportunities and some rights for resource extraction in their respective areas to ease the lack of development in their areas.[26] However, according to South many local communities lost large amounts of land (and associated livelihoods), confiscated by the army, either due to its self-support policy, or due to local authorities and business groups establishing 'development projects' or unsustainable natural resource extraction.[27] Neither side made any efforts to achieve DDR (disarmament, demobilization and reintegration), SSR (security sector reform) or dialogue activities that would transform the ceasefires into a peace process. No code of conduct was established and both parties extended their troops to secure the territories they controlled at the time. General Khin Nyunt, commander of Military Intelligence, developed a substantial relationship with most ethnic armed groups through limited trust-building activities, becoming the major liaison link between the government and the EAGs. Despite occasional clashes the ceasefire was broadly maintained. As discussed in Chapter 1, in 2004 the government deposed General Khin Nyunt from his position, deeply impacting the ceasefire agreements and leading to renewed clashes in certain areas.[28]

Overall the agreed ceasefires did hold[29] and resulted in the development of civil society networks that were instrumental in bringing increased services to the local communities—most of these were actually organised and run by the EAGs themselves, replacing in large part the absent state services. Since the beginning of the 1990s, religious organisations and a few NGOs started community development programmes for the people at the grassroots level in some ethnic states.[30] Shalom, the NGO based on the concept of a 'just peace' headed by Reverend Saboi Jum and his daughter Ja Nan Lahtaw, was not the only non-governmental organisation that has helped first the Kachin people, and later other ethnic groups.[31] The Metta development foundation was established in 1998 and developed projects in Kachin, Shan, Karenni, Karen and Mon states. Metta director Daw Seng Raw stated that, 'Many ethnic groups feel extremely disappointed that in general foreign governments are not responding to the process of these ceasefires or indeed even understand their significance.'[32] Lahtaw argued at the time that it was essential that border areas were developed equitably, that people needed access to education and increased infrastructure that was not only used for either the army or the Chinese to encroach on more land and natural resources.[33] Given these developments, and unlikelihood at the time of elite level political change, Ashley South argued that civil society could become an engine for democratisation.[34]

In 2007 Smith said that 'by any international standards, the achievement of ceasefires with so many insurgent groups, in one of the most conflict torn countries in Asia, has to date been unexpectedly smooth and stable'.[35] He also argued that due to the simplicity of the agreements and the economic development, there was general popular support. Aside from increased services and limited economic prosperity for ordinary people, some EAG leaders also enriched themselves cultivating 'commercial relationships well beyond their immediate mountain strongholds,'[36] creating an economic interest in the established order that would later impact on the peace process. In any case despite the numerous ceasefires, conflict continued in certain areas of Myanmar—not least in the south-east where no ceasefire had been reached with the KNU, but also with the Karenni National Progressive Party (KNPP) and the Shan State Army (SSA-South).[37] These conflicts continued, fuelled by genuine political grievances as well as 'greed agendas' of the Tatmadaw and the EAGs who were becoming rich through the illegal cross-border trade.[38] The continuing conflicts also resulted in large refugee flows, primarily to Thailand but also to India, Bangladesh, Malaysia and China.[39] The worst situation was on the border with Thailand. By the mid 1990s, as a result of decades of armed conflict in the south-east of the country, tens of thousands of mostly ethnic Karen refugees were living in several small camps spread out along the Thailand–Burma border. In addition, an unknown but significantly larger number of Karen and other civilians were internally displaced in Burma, and about 2 million Burmese migrant workers (many of them Karen) were living a precarious existence in Thailand with a very uncertain legal status.[40]

The big change regarding the dynamics between the EAGs and the regime came as the 2008 constitution was promulgated after the highly controversial referendum. Since there would be only one army after the handover of power to the civilianised government, the regime suggested in April 2009 that the EAG transform into border guard forces (BGF) that would be under the direct control of Tatmadaw commanders. For the 326 soldiers in a BGF battalion, 30 would be from the Myanmar army including the deputy commander and the quartermaster.[41] This had been part of the broad plans to make the roadmap work. This move resulted in an argument between the regime and some EAG leaders exposing fundamental differences between the EAGs and the government regarding the nature of autonomy in ceasefire areas, and questioned the perceived legitimacy of the state and its armed forces. To many the expectation of laying down their arms and submitting to Tatmadaw command was tantamount to a surrender, therefore unacceptable, and trust between the EAGs and the government was further eroded.

Among the 25 EAGs,[42] the less powerful ones had little choice: five groups transformed into border guard forces and 15 groups transformed into militias. However, five larger EAGs resisted transformation into border guard force or militia, including the Kachin Independence Organization (KIO), the New Mon State Party (NMSP), a breakaway DKBA faction, the United Wa State Army (UWSA) and the Kokang (MNDAA).[43] The Kokang were quickly punished with a military campaign that sent thousands of local residents running across the border into China in 2009, forcing the Kokang to back down. However, at the time the Tatmadaw did not take similar action against the other groups as they were militarily stronger. In February 2015 of course the Kokang conflict erupted again as the ousted leader Pheung Kya-shin attempted a comeback in February 2015, leading to a new outbreak of fighting that directly impacted the discussions on the Nationwide Ceasefire Agreement, discussed later in this chapter.

The issue with the KIO/KIA

After a ceasefire agreement with the government in 1993, the KIO followed the government political roadmap and participated in the National Convention. Although the representatives from ethnic minorities had little influence, the KIO continued to participate and cooperate with the government. In 2007, KIO submitted a 19-point proposal to the National Convention for consideration in the new constitution, but the government did not take any notice of the demands. As a result the referendum on the constitution faced stiff resistance in Kachin State. However, in 2008 the KIO backed the constitutional referendum, on the understanding that they would be allowed to participate in the 2010 elections—but as will be seen below, this deal was not fulfilled, with no credible Kachin party participating in 2010.[44] In 2008–9 the KIO also faced the demand to transform their troops into a border guard force, but rejected the scheme. They retained their weapons and kept their troops under their command chain, starting a re-armament and recruitment process.[45]

Despite the increasing rift between the Kachin and the regime, there were different ideological positions within the group regarding the political process on offer. This became obvious when the government promulgated the political parties registration law. KIO leader Dr Tu Ja, who was vice chairman of KIO, resigned from the KIO and organised the Kachin State Progressive Party. However, given the resistance of the KIA to the border guard idea and other difficulties between the Kachin and the government, the party was denied registration both in Kachin State as well as in the areas of Northern Shan State where there is a substantial Kachin community. To the consternation of the local Kachin community, Dr Tu Ja, being a pragmatist, then decided to apply to run as a USDP candidate. He was rejected due to his recent ties with an armed group. Not allowing the Kachin their own political representation gravely impacted the relationship between the government and the KIO (ICG, 2011, p. 6). By late 2010, the tension between the KIO and the government became serious. The government used the term 'insurgent group', resulting in an escalation of tension between the parties. In February 2011 a Myanmar army officer was shot by the KIA, raising the tension between the parties to an even more serious level.[46] In May 2011 the Tatmadaw Light Infantry Battalion fired mortar rounds close to the KIA Battalion 25 HQ, KIA brigade 5. Tatmadaw troops were deployed further, close to KIA troops. On 8 June the KIA captured a Tatmadaw police officer, and later a captain and a lieutenant. On 9 June the Tatmadaw arrested a KIA liaison officer, Lance Corporal Chyang Ying. Chyang Ying died due to injuries that the Tatmadaw said had occurred on the battlefield, but the KIA maintained had been sustained under torture.[47] The repeated clashes between the KIA and the Tatmadaw near the Myitsone hydropower project led to the collapse of the seventeen-year ceasefire. On 12 June the last KIO liaison office closed in Myitkyina. The government announced an ultimatum for the KIA to withdraw their troops from the project region; this was not heeded and clashes between the two sides gradually increased, culminating with the hydropower dam being blown up.[48] This was followed by the destruction of roads and bridges across the state. Over the summer there were three rounds of peace talks between the KIO and a team from the Kachin State government, on 30 June, 1 and 2 August 2011. The KIO indicated that they were not ready to sign a new ceasefire without neutral witnesses and without a public commitment from the government to starting a political dialogue with all groups, in effect turning the clashes into a sustained war that was to continue for many months.[49]

South confirms that the reasons behind the resumption of armed conflict in Kachin areas are complex and contested. They include opaque political–economic and geo-strategic factors,[50] such as the economic interests of the Northern Command of the Tatmadaw, the geo-political and economic interests of the KIA/KIO and the influence of the Chinese, who do not want to see Western competition for the exploration of Kachin State's natural resources. In addition, the newly created middle class that emerged after the 1990s ceasefires allowed Kachin State to develop economic and political networks nationally and internationally, creating a Kachin diaspora that also plays a crucial role in Kachin nationalism, and therefore in the continuation of the conflict.[51]

The resumption of armed conflict between the two parties and other armed groups in northern Myanmar in mid-2011 caused the displacement of over 100,000 civilians, forced to flee the Tatmadaw offensive operations.[52] Most fled to the China border, and many stayed in camps outside the KIA stronghold of Laiza. The speech of the president on 17 August took a hard line towards the KIA. The president blamed the KIA for the destruction of the infrastructure in Kachin State and accused the KIA of not allowing the residents to grow rice on time as they had to flee. He said that Christian associations, cultural and literary associations in Kachin State had written to him to bring the armed conflict to an end and restore peace as soon as possible, and he defended the right of the Tatmadaw to launch defensive attacks.[53] The conflict continued and the army shelled the KIA strongholds, coming close to Laiza, where the KIA leadership was based. The flow of refugees continued unabated. It was a horrible winter, with many internally displaced suffering cold and hunger. However, the local Kachin population is said to have supported the continuation of the conflict—as did the Kachin diaspora abroad.

In early March 2012 the tone of the president markedly changed.[54] In his state of the union address to parliament on 1 March he said that the desire of government was to share rights among the national races and enjoy equality; he pointed out that trust was a vitally important factor in the national reconsolidation process. He spoke about a three-step process to realise peace—starting with dialogue at state level, then dialogue at union level, expanding this dialogue to include cooperation development activity, opening liaison offices and engaging in a political process. The third step was an agreement that would be signed in parliament with all political players represented.[55] It is this change of tone that eventually led to the peace process.

The start of the peace process—the second presidential priority

The second presidential priority, mentioned in President Thein Sein's speech at the start of his new government, was peace with the EAGs. In late 2011 and through 2012, the new government agreed, or renegotiated preliminary cease-fires with ten of the eleven most significant EAGs, representing the Wa, Mongla, Chin, Shan, PaO, Karen, Karenni, Arakan/Rakhine and Mon.[56] Early negotiations went well, but it became clear very soon that the original three-step blueprint was not going to work. The government would have to be flexible and work towards the inclusion of all groups, including the KNU who had never signed a ceasefire before, as well as the KIO/KIA with whom conflict had resumed.

The most important move towards the initial peace process was the government dropping the demand that all EAGs had to become border guard forces. One of the first groups to sign with the government were the Wa. There was a four-point 'initial peace agreement' between the USWA and the Shan State government, listing the conditions: 1) preserve a ceasefire between the two sides; 2) establish liaison offices to maintain communications; 3) commit to obtaining advance agreement from the other side before carrying arms outside respective areas; and 4) agree to further talks on peace and development issues to be held with the national-level peace-making group at a mutually convenient time. Later it was also agreed that the USWA would maintain its close relationship with China, on whom they rely for currency, communication, schools, even using the local Chinese time-zone.[57] The USWA talks were followed by talks between the Shan State government peace-making group and the National Democratic Alliance Army (Mongla), resulting in a similar four-point agreement. This was followed by talks with the 5th Brigade of the DKBA and the Karen State government peace-making group. There was one additional point stipulating where the group could establish its base. Then contacts were made with the KIO, SSA-S, SSA-N, KNU, NMSP, KNPP and Chin National Front (CNF), offering the same four-point agreement. However, these armed groups were not prepared to return to the *status quo ante* of 2009, as they wanted political talks and not a ceasefire that would not lead to a political solution.[58] An additional problem was that the negotiators with the EAGs in the northern part of the country, U Aung Thaung and U Thein Zaw,[59] did not have the trust of the EAG leadership. Both were seen as hard-liners, and not close to the president. The EAGs worried that the negotiation process would not be reported in full to the president. By contrast, in the south the president had sent U Aung Min, the railways minister with whom he had a very close relationship, and so the process was much smoother.

The special role of the KNU ceasefire

Out of all the early ceasefire agreements and re-affirmations in 2011–12, the most difficult at the time, and the one perceived to be least likely to succeed, was an agreement with the KNU. The KNU rebellion was the longest insurgency in the world, lasting 63 years, starting just months after independence at the end of January 1949.[60] Over the years there had been a number of talks between them and the government, but the Karen demand of a free Karen state of 'Kawthoolei'[61] was not acceptable to the regime. There were talks also with General Khin Nyunt around 2004, when the Karen delegation was led by head of foreign affairs P'doh David Taw,[62] but in the end they did not lead to any tangible results,[63] and the Tatmadaw waged an unrelenting and brutal campaign in Karen State, sending thousands of refugees across the Thai border.

The new government insisted that it was open to negotiate with all EAGs. The KNU had its first meeting with a government peace representative in Mai Sai, Thailand in November 2011. This led to a consultative meeting in Hpa Ahn with the Karen Peace Committee and the Karen Baptist Convention, and further meetings over the next two months. Overall, the Karen in Myanmar as well as the diaspora abroad voiced scepticism and lack of trust in the process. According to Nant Bwa Bwa Phan, the KNU European representative (and also of the Burma Campaign UK and the European Karen Network), there was little trust:

> After more than 60 years of conflict, you would expect the hundreds of thousands of Karen people worldwide who were forced to flee their homeland to be very hopeful and excited about the talks, and perhaps even discussing returning. But that isn't the impression I get from the Karen people around the world I have spoken to. Instead, many people are very sceptical. There are many reasons for this. First, we know from experience in the past 60 years that governments often talk peace while waging war. There have been five previous occasions when official ceasefire talks took place, and every time the government effectively just demanded surrender.[64]

However, despite this, a formal ceasefire was indeed signed on 4 January 2012, and on 11 April 2012 the KNU opened a liaison office in Kyaukkyi (Bago Region, KNLA 3 Brigade) as part of its peace-making agreement with the government. This was unprecedented. U Aung Min (still railways minister at the time), Bago Region Security and Border Affairs Minister Colonel Thet

Tun and KNU General Secretary Naw Zipporah Sein opened the office together.[65] Not all factions within the KNU and across the Karen community supported the peace talks, and internal divisions over the process remained. However, the KNU was now part of a large number of EAGs that had started to engage in the new peace process with the government.

Supporting the process: the creation of the Myanmar Peace Centre (MPC)

The Myanmar Peace Centre was a Myanmar Egress brainchild. Already at the end of 2010/early 2011 Tin Maung Thann had started to draw a prototype peace process on the whiteboard in his office. In order to support the government in its endeavour for peace, a centre would be needed to do research, as well as offer the necessary space for armed groups to meet with government officials.[66] Funding was going to come from international donations. At first there was no money, and ME supported U Aung Min in his preliminary negotiations with the EAGs as well as they could.[67] Once the idea took form and meetings between the government and the EAGs started, the EU and the Japanese government became the largest donors to MPC. The Japanese focused primarily on infrastructure, renovating and building new offices to host the 120+ staff, whilst the EU funded the necessary programme and salaries of those who would work there. The Myanmar Peace Centre (MPC) was opened on 3 November 2012 and is headed by U Aung Min (President's Office Minister) and run by U Soe Thein (President's Office Minister) and U Khin Ye (Home Affairs Minister). Key senior staff include the chief executive U Kyaw Soe Hlaing (Tin Maung Thann's friend from AIT), Dr Kyaw Yin Hlaing (Myanmar Egress), U Hla Maung Shwe (Myanmar Egress), U Aung Naing Oo (Vahu Development Institute, returned from exile, and previously with the ABSDF) and Dr Min Zaw Oo (another ex-ABSDF member). MPC's main role has been to institutionalise the government's role in the peace process, and with donor support to undertake a wide range of activities related to the negotiation of ceasefires, political dialogue, coordination of humanitarian and development assistance in conflict-affected areas, and public outreach as well as research, policy advice and capacity-building in order to resolve the long-standing conflicts between the government and the EAGs. Over time it developed into a secretariat for the presidentially-mandated Union Peace-making Work Committee (UPWC) which supports the work of Minister U Aung Min. The centre also serves as a focal point for international partners and CBOs, facilitating dialogue between the government and non-state actors. There are a large number of international donors and partners.[68] The MPC did not win much trust among ethnic nationality communities, who tended to regard this as a Burman and male-dominated, pro-government institution. However, it became a useful centre for meetings, with some EAGs even being able to stay there during their trips to Yangon. More recently MPC started to bring together CSOs and representatives of various political parties in order to brief them on the peace process, sometimes with U Aung Min himself conducting the briefings. This was done in order to facilitate dialogue between different groups about the political dialogue that would follow the signing of a Nationwide Ceasefire Accord, as well as the implications the peace process has on the elections. U Hla Maung Shwe explained the regular meetings in terms of the 'Bangkok process' (discussed in Chapter 1), started by Nay Win Maung so many years earlier, which brought all the different stakeholders to one table for open discussions about the way forward.[69]

The views of the government on peace

'There can neither be peace without democracy nor democracy without peace.' President Thein Sein[70]

When President Thein Sein embarked on the peace process, he decided to surround himself with a group of ministerial advisers who had previously served as military commanders in ethnic states, who knew the difficulties in each state and who were positively inclined towards making peace, some even with reasonable relations with the leaders of some ethnic armed groups. The ministers of electrics, forestry, immigration, and livestock, fisheries and rural development became formally engaged in the process by joining the Union Peacemaking Working Committee, which also includes U Aung Min (Minister of the President's Office and chief peace envoy of the president, previously railways minister), U Soe Thane (Minister of the President's Office and responsible for economic reforms), the Deputy Attorney General, a USDP representative and the first vice president.[71] As such these leaders are the architects of the government's peace process, drawing on first-hand experience of the armed conflict in the ethnic states.[72] In order to give an inside view of how the government viewed the peace process, long conversations were held in Nay Pyi Taw and Yangon to discuss peace and the legitimacy of the process as well as the actors. Overall the views they expressed in the conversations held in Nay Pyi Taw and Yangon between December 2013 and August 2014 were aligned, and apart from the representative of the USDP there seemed to be a desire towards genuine and lasting peace.[73] One of the ministers[74] explained that, 'Each and every citizen wants peace and this is the inclusive process,[75] so if we have a successful peace process it will be invaluable process for the whole country.' It emerged through the conversations that there was only a limited recognition amongst the ministers that some EAGs still challenge the legitimacy of the government, but this was offset by a recognition that the government had to create its own legitimacy through the peace and reform process:

> There is partial legitimacy, but with the national reconciliation process, if there is progress they will have much more space to engage with the community and they can build up through peace dividends. They will have a chance to take part in the political process, build political legitimacy. Because of the peace building process, many ethnic groups have been more recognised more in terms of culture and traditions, there will be many dividends, own rights will be much more recognise, create moral legitimacy.[76]

Reflecting back on the causes of the conflict,[77] the ministers explained that the EAGs took up arms because of inequality, and because they could not have their political demands fulfilled by the previous government due to a lack of political will. However, they felt that both the government and the armed groups have changed:

> Many believed armed conflict was the only way to get their way, but now new blood have international exposure. They have a vision for the future, and they intend there will be no place for armed conflict in the future. They will be able to convince the old guard. Armed struggle is not the answer for political demand.[78]

But meeting the ethnic aspirations would be hard, and as one minister confirmed, the peace negotiations were not yet addressing the underlying issues of the conflict. Confidence-building and political dialogue would be needed to address grievances, as well as reforms. U Aung Min was very clear: 'Ceasefire is not peace. We need to come with political settlement for grievances, through a political dialogue.'

A few ministers presented the wider reform process as a major vehicle to address the issues related to peace and conflict. In many ways this showed that there was still an important gap between the grievances of the armed groups, which relate more to national identity and decentralisation/federalism, and the government, which hopes that economic and political reforms and the economic dividends these bring will go a long way in cementing peace. But the gap seems to be reducing, as there was a general recognition that the political process has to be inclusive and that democratic practices mean that ethnic demands will be heard and protected. 'Peace building process is integral part of democratisation process, which is reform. [They] Cannot be separated. We need social sector reform and education in remote areas. [This is an] Integrated process. [They are] head and tail of same process.'[79] The ministers spoke of freedom of speech and an all-inclusive political process, as if it was nothing new and the most obvious development in the world. However, when it came to issues related to decentralisation, there was a sense that the ministers were still uncomfortable with this concept and they wanted to emphasise that decentralisation had to be controlled. The Deputy Attorney General mentioned that any discussion on secession could not be on the table. One of the ministers said that whilst the principle of decentralisation was permissible in principle, the state governments do not yet have the capacity to deliver services, and that even the central government does not yet have the necessary capacity. Therefore decentralisation needed to be balanced and he believed that the Myanmar diaspora, as well as the ethnic diaspora, should come back and help build the country anew. U Aung Min was able to explain the government's vision with regard to peace and the reforms most succinctly:

> As you know, peace is important. Without peace no democracy, no development. Peace is the underlying thing we need to solve. The president realises it. When we embarked on this he had categorised into the sectors. Political reforms are very important. Creating of space for civil society, platforms for political parties and peace process is included in the political reforms, but more important political parties and space for political life. When I started with peace process I thought peace would be it. In working with the problems associated with it, peace building is related to state and nation building. You cannot take out education or health care reforms. State and nation building and the type of society we are trying to create.

And of course there are major challenges. Like U Aung Min above, many involved in the peace process realised that simple development would not be enough; they realised that the aspirations and demands of the diverse groups were different; they realised that trust was difficult to build.[80] 'It is hard for the one armed group to build trust when they have been shooting at each other until recently. Both sides need exposure to international norms of peace building process.'[81] Trust is also hard to build on the army's side, where they were taught for sixty years that the EAGs were the enemy, and how many people they had killed and how many weapons captured. The army, U Aung Min says, was not part of the process at the start because they did not believe it would succeed. Their involvement increased as they saw the 'fruits of the process'.

Part of the challenge is the issue surrounding the legitimacy of the EAGs. Whilst no armed group can represent the entirety of their ethnic group, the ministers agreed that the grievances, aspirations and demands at the table are those of a majority of ethnic people, even if there are frictions within. The Tatmadaw of course is struggling with the UNFC demand for a 'federal' army,[82] which the deputy attorney general says is impossible. But this does beg the question of what will happen to the armed groups after the political dialogue and whether they will be able to enter political life.

When asked if they believe the peace process would be successful, the ministers agreed that it would take time. 'No government has achieved peace overnight.'[83] The government could not force anyone to sign what they did not wish to sign, and whilst a nationwide ceasefire agreement was desirable and a government aim, it might also be possible to start the political dialogue process with those who were ready to sign, if others were not. However, they believed that the nationwide ceasefire would be reached in the current government as trust and confidence had built up between the teams. There was a worry amongst some that post-2015 there might be a new government and the same team might not be in place.[84] Personality politics in Myanmar means that much of the trust has been built between the EAGs and U Aung Min, whom they believe to be sincere. He himself has committed his political life to achieving peace and making sure the process is sustainable. 'I want to try and do as much as I can, mainly because the people who comes after us will have to implement the peace process and so that they cannot turn back so that the process continues into the future.'

Regardless of the outcomes, the relevant ministries saw their work in ethnic areas as underpinning the new Myanmar that is being created. For example, the portfolio of the Ministry of Electrics is to give access to electricity across the country, and the intention is to have a 50 per cent electrification rate across the country before 2015, including in the remote areas in Kachin, Chin and Shan States. Where necessary, work would be coordinated with the EAGs. The Immigration Ministry's work is also directly related to the peace process, as they have to register all IDPs and refugees and deal with Myanmar citizenship for those exiles who return and want to regain their citizenship status. The Immigration Ministry was directly responsible for the announced invitation for returnees. The minister explained that out of the 125 cases, 10 per cent had already been granted and another 35 cases would be granted the next day. The minister has also had consultative meeting with various groups (including the ABSDF) about returning and creating one-stop shops in Karen, Mon, Kayah and Shan States to facilitate getting NRC cards.[85]

International involvement

MPSI

After over sixty years of conflict and no political dialogue following the 1990s ceasefires, the ethnic stakeholders did not believe that the new government would have the political will to deliver peace. The biggest issue has been that of trust. For communities and ethnic armed groups to start believing that President Thein Sein was serious in delivering peace, tangible proof needed to be provided at community level on the ground. The government of Myanmar was aware that they did not have the financial capacity, nor the logistical ability, nor indeed the legitimate authority with the conflict-affected communities to deliver such tangible results. As a consequence the Myanmar Peace Support Initiative (MPSI) was initiated in March 2012. The government of Myanmar requested the help of the Norwegian Minister of Foreign Affairs to mobilise international support for the peace process. According to the MPSI's independent review, the Norwegian government 'took a considerable political risk that no other international actor was able or willing to take at this time'.[86] In response to the request, the Norwegian government launched a 'light and flexible initiative that would test the sincerity of all parties to the agreements being made'.[87] Charles Petrie, the former UN Humanitarian Coordinator and Resident Representative in Myanmar from 2003 until December 2007, was asked to lead the initiative. Asking Petrie back to Myanmar after he had been declared *persona non grata* by the Myanmar government in 2007 was an important signal that the government of Myanmar was serious about both peace and change.[88] The idea of MPSI was to work with key stakeholders (particularly conflict-affected communities, CBOs and EAGs) to identify projects that would be locally delivered, building trust and confidence in the peace process. The idea was also to test the peace process, how much space was available for the types of activities that could address stakeholders' concerns and hopes for the future, and communicate this learning to the international community and where possible the government (through the MPC).

The 'peace architecture' that emerged in the course of 2012 included the Peace Donor Support Group (PDSG), chaired by Norway, an International Peace Support Group (a forum for international and national NGOs active on peace issues), and the Myanmar Peace Centre. Donors to MPSI projects are mostly members of the PDSG, and apart from Norway include Finland, the Netherlands, Denmark, the United Kingdom, Switzerland, the European Union and Australia.[89] MPSI was not meant to be a mediation agency nor a funding agency for projects. Rather it was an organisation that was meant to link the elite-driven peace process between the government and the armed groups, as well as international aid agencies, with the affected communities on the ground.[90] According to its own self-evaluative document entitled, 'Lessons learnt from MPSI's work in supporting the peace process in Myanmar, March 2012–March 2014', the initiative 'facilitated projects that build trust and confidence in and test the ceasefires, disseminated lessons learned from these experiences, and sought to strengthen local and international coordination of assistance to the peace process'.[91] MPSI pilot projects delivered assistance to conflict-affected people living in very isolated areas, including food, medicines, tools and school supplies. This was also recognised as an important way to test the ceasefires. In addition more than 100,000 people received national identity cards, which allow citizens to invoke basic rights such as access to education, voting etc., and enable freedom of movement without fear to access their land, go to markets and meet with family in government-controlled areas.[92]

MPSI's main aim was to ensure local participation and to respond to the requests and needs of the conflict-affected communities. As such, local NGOs and civil society actors were involved at all stages of all projects, and projects had to be requested by local actors to ensure community buy-in.[93] MPSI projects and pilot projects were undertaken across five ethnic states (Chin, Shan, Mon, Karen and Kayah) and two regions (Bago and Tanintharyi) and delivered in partnership with seven Ethnic Armed Groups (KNU, NMSP, ALP, CNF, KNPP, SSA-S/RCSS and DKBA), thirteen local partners (four of which are consortia), and nine international partners.

At the start of the peace process the international community had limited knowledge and little information about the situation in the conflict-affected areas and did not necessarily understand the local dynamics on the ground. MPSI's staff, all with expertise of the various Myanmar conflicts, were tasked with helping the international donors understand how best to respond and also helping the armed groups and affiliated organisations engage with international aid agencies.[94] This resulted in a number of challenges, as most ethnic armed groups had never submitted proposals for international support before and there were unrealistic expectations about the level of support and how quickly funding could be accessed. 'There was limited understanding of how the international aid infrastructure works, how to explain their needs in terms that donors could respond to, and how to adhere to accountability requirements.'[95] Even local CBOs, often the key implementing partners, had limited project development and management skills.[96] This challenge was more often than not poorly handled by the international development partners, many of whom had arrived well after the start of the reforms and peace process (and therefore with no knowledge of how things had been before 2011).

The Myanmar government also had unrealistic expectations as to how quickly large-scale interventions in ceasefire areas could be implemented. Driven by a desire to show quick 'peace dividends' (often referred to as 'quick wins') and to demonstrate that the peace process was credible to affected communities, MPSI was under pressure to facilitate such government-led initiatives in conflict-affected communities.[97]

What emerged out of MPSI's work was a better understanding of how all stakeholders in the peace process needed both support and capacity-building and that this would become more important once the political dialogue started.[98] Other things that were learned through MPSI's work, in what is really a locally-driven peace process, were that there are vast differences on the ground between conflict-affected communities across Myanmar and that solutions that work in one area are not always appropriate elsewhere. Even though this is a locally-driven process, outsiders, even Myanmar officials or other ethnic representatives, did not necessarily understand the challenges faced by individual communities. Local context seemed to matter more than many aspects in this process. However, across conflict-affected communities issues relating to land tenure security[99] and business interests[100] still worry all those who return or aspire to return to their original land.

Nevertheless, the review and evaluation of MPSI's work also showed that beyond the concerns expressed, the ceasefires had a positive effect on communities. MPSI was able to facilitate a listening project that considered the experiences of Karen, Mon and Karenni (Kayah) communities before and after the ceasefires, and the results showed that there was less fear and that lives in the previously conflict-affected areas had notably improved.[101]

The Nippon foundation

MPSI has not been the only conduit for foreign involvement in the peace process. As mentioned above, the EU has funded a large part of the programmes run at MPC, and other individual donors have also been involved. Nevertheless, in terms of direct involvement in the peace process, especially with regard to EAGs and ethnic communities, the second most important player has been the Nippon Foundation. Their main focus has been the improvement of the livelihoods of remote communities. In June 2012

Sasakawa Yohei, chairman of the Nippon Foundation (and also of the Tokyo Foundation and the Sasakawa Peace Foundation), was appointed 'ambassador for the welfare of ethnic minorities' and asked to coordinate the assistance programme. The foundation claims to be working closely with the UNFC, and $3 million has been donated in emergency aid to support education and health care in EAG-controlled areas.[102] The projects supported by the Nippon Foundation are often opaque, and not much information is available in the public domain.[103] There have been instances where ethnic communities have allegedly complained about Japanese projects (possibly Nippon Foundation projects) as being too allied with the state and not necessarily meeting their needs, but it has been difficult to verify these claims as there is so little information in the public domain.[104]

Until Cyclone Nargis, the government of Myanmar had been very reluctant to let international agencies become involved in Myanmar internal affairs. In the aftermath of the cyclone that devastated the delta and damaged much of Yangon, the regime had resisted what it saw as too much Western interference in particular. ASEAN and other Asian support were deemed acceptable, but it took much negotiation for the international community at large to be allowed to help. With this in mind, it is interesting to note that although the reform and peace processes are essentially domestically driven, the acceptance that a useful role can sometimes be played by international development actors has been accepted across the board. As U Aung Min put it:

> The support of the international community is very important because I believe the internationals want peace also. In the past they worked with ethnic armed groups. Despite right intentions there were negative consequences also. Now what I try to do is to build trust with the international organisations through my work. And this trust, like all trust building is an on-going process. But at this time if I have to look at international community process, we have not got the whole support yet.

Others agree with him, saying that the role of the international community in de-mining, building shelters, supporting the IDPs and other humanitarian assistance is essential for the peace process to be successful. However, not all promised assistance has as yet been received, and the government remains resistant to any international involvement with regard to mediation.

Negotiations between the EAGs and the government

Two main groups have dominated the ethnic side of the peace process. The more hard-line United Nationalities Federal Council (UNFC), based in

Chang Mai, rejects the 2008 constitution and brings little trust in the peace process to the table. The other is the more pragmatic Working Group for Ethnic Coordination (WGEC). The UNFC's alliance does not include all the main EAGs, whilst the WGEC is more broad-based and gets support from Harn Yawnghwe's[105] Euro-Burma office. There have been increasing tensions between the groups as the UNFC has tried to position itself as the main negotiator with the government, despite the opposition of some EAGs.

Both alliances have emerged out of previous ethnic alliances and collaborations. In August 2001 the Ethnic National Council (ENC) had been established (as the Ethnic Nationalities Solidarity and Cooperation Committee) to improve cooperation between all ethnic nationalities and EAGs. As the 2010 elections were to change the political status quo, the ENC organised a conference at which the CEFU (Committee for the Emergence of Federal Union) was created. It was made up of three ceasefire groups, the KIO, the New Mon State Party (NMSP) and the SSPP/SSA, and three non-ceasefire groups, the Karen National Union (KNU), the Karenni National Progressive Party (KNPP) and the Chin National Front (CNF) and later went on to represent 11 EAGs.[106] In February 2011 the CEFU was renamed the United Nationalities Federal Council (UNFC);[107] it wants to establish a Federal Union of Myanmar, and has clear political aims and claims to represent all EAGs, small and large.[108]

In August 2011 the president offered peace talks. In September that year an ethnic conference was held, and the UNFC and the ENC came together to discuss how to respond to the president's offer. There were different opinions: the ENC thought that the president's offer was pragmatic and that as a first step the EAGs should talk to their own respective state governments, as not all situations in the conflict zones were the same. The UNFC disagreed and said that even at a preliminary level the EAGs should go collectively. This was the beginning of very different understandings of how to move the process forward. Finally there was a sort of agreement that the individual armed groups could speak to the state and union government unilaterally to start the process, but that for a political dialogue they should go collectively. In February 2012, after a number of EAGs had signed or renewed individual ceasefires with the government, the EAGs held another conference. They formed a committee and each state sent their representatives, seven per state plus another seven, called the 'intellectual group'.[109] The groups prepared an ethnic peace plan that was submitted to the ethnic nationalities conference in September 2012. The next step was the formation of the Working Group for

Ethnic Coordination (WGEC) which prepared the framework for political dialogue, including the agenda, the composition, the mandate, the structure, any transitional arrangements, and also its core principles as well as the comprehensive ceasefire proposal. The paper was finished in March 2013 but in April 2013 a meeting resulted in another disagreement. At that time some who were part of the working group proposed to form a negotiation team for dialogue. The UNFC maintained that they already had a negotiation team. However, not all EAGs are part of the UNFC, and the negotiation team proposed by the WGEC would have been all-inclusive. The KNU was split, as those who did not wish to sign an agreement with the government sided with the UNFC. In June 2013, the UNFC withdrew from the WGEC and declared it no longer relevant as its work had been done. The UNFC insisted that it would be the only negotiator with the government, as the WGEC was more of a network than a formal alliance. The KNU and the RCSS did not want the UNFC to control the negotiations with the government, as this could impact on the gains they had already achieved and force the EAGs to have to accept policies that were not in their interest.[110] In the end the RCSS and the KNU teams came to meet the government at MPC on 23 August 2013, assisted by the Euro-Burma Office, and agreed in principle to negotiate a 14-point National Ceasefire Accord.[111] The UNFC was angry that ethnic unity was falling apart. Given the intra-ethnic group issues, the KIO organised the first ethnic conference at its headquarters on the Chinese border in Laiza at the end of October 2013. It was hoped that this would bring all groups onto the same page again. The government allowed all EAGs to travel there and attend. This was a very significant step, as earlier the government had refused to accept multilateral negotiations on the ethnic side. EAGs, as illegal organisations, were not allowed to meet to discuss a common position and certainly not allowed to cross government-controlled territory to do so. This time they had the government's 'blessing'.

The UNFC did not come to Laiza,[112] and proceeded with its own agenda, but individual member EAGs came. There the National Ceasefire Coordination Team (NCCT) was created (now representing 16 armed groups) and an 11-point strategy to guide EAG negotiations was created.[113] What was unprecedented was the fact that the EAGs were able to meet with the consent of the government.[114]

It is important to note that the UNFC position and the ceasefire became the latest in a series of issues around which factions in the KNU coalesced, resulting in deep divisions and public debates. Since the fall of its former headquarters at Mannerplaw in 1995, the KNU has been fragmented along ideological, personality, ethno-linguistic, clan-based, religious, economic, neo-patrimonial and geographic lines. A more 'flexible' approach by the KNU was only made possible because the 13th Congress in late 2012 elected a new 'pragmatic' leadership. This group has sought to be forward-leaning in the peace process, seeing the ceasefire as an opportunity for the KNU to reinvent itself, with the alternatives being continued stagnation in the borderland jungles and refugee camps.[115]

Subsequently the EAGs met with U Aung Min, MPC representatives and Myanmar army officials in Kachin State's capital of Myitkyina to present their 11-point agenda. This meeting was again unprecedented as it was the first time that the government had met with an alliance of EAGs rather than on an individual basis; it was also the first time that the Myanmar army had become involved. However, the inclusion of the army also resulted in a more hard-line approach from the government side, eroding some of the trust that had been built up between the groups and U Aung Min over the previous two years. The army brought along its own proposal and a clear gap emerged between the government's position and what the EAGs wanted; at the time it was unclear how this would be bridged.[116] The nationwide ceasefire that was scheduled to be signed in November was therefore postponed until after a further meeting, which would be held in Hpa-An, Karen State, in December 2013.[117] The Hpa-An meeting did not actually take pace and was replaced by a gathering similar to the one in Laiza between 20 and 25 January 2014, but this time held in the KNU stronghold of Law Khee Lah.[118] Further meetings between the EAGs and the government followed in April and May 2014. In April it was agreed that the various drafts of the National Ceasefire accord would be merged and then work would start on a joint document. The problems that would emerge from this exercise were differences on policies as well as definitions and wording. The work continued at a meeting in May with a Joint Nationwide Ceasefire Drafting Work Group that was made up of nine NCCT leaders and nine from the government side.[119] It is said that in May the government offered a lot of compromise and that a deal was not far off. However, the EAGs were not able to accept what was on the table at the time and needed to return to Laiza to meet with all the ethnic leaders.

In Laiza in July 2014 there were more disagreements. The NCCT wanted to form a steering committee for the whole process, so that this body could solve policy problems. The UNFC insisted that they should be that steering committee, but the KNU objected. The steering committee was not formed, whereas the NCCT organised the top ethnic leaders as if they were a steering committee. The EAGs tried to 'unblock' the remaining problems in Laiza by looking at different alternatives, so that the NCCT would be able to apply these when meeting the government. An informal closed-door meeting in Myitkyina with U Aung Min and some MPC representatives followed the Laiza meeting, where the remaining problems were discussed. A breakthrough seemed elusive. Whilst the aims and objectives of the NCCT and the UNFC were the same, their working methods were different. An ethnic representative of the NCCT said after the August 2014 meetings: 'We are more difficult than the government as we come from 16 organisations and we have our own concerns. Government answer within hours and we cannot.'[120]

During the summer of 2014 the nationwide ceasefire agreement draft that was being worked on was not available to the public. It was described by Aung Naing Oo[121] in a Myanmar Times article as having seven chapters, over 120 pages, and that it had taken over nine months for the negotiation parties to come up with that version, which was quickly superseded.[122] As Aung Naing Oo explains, this was not a simple ceasefire deal; it was a first political document setting out with a pledge to achieve durable peace based on equality and dignity.[123] Since 75 per cent of the document had been agreed, it was hoped that the next few rounds of negotiations would focus on resolving the missing definitions of disputed terminology (such as federalism, federal army, revolution, union, existing laws) as well as completing and agreeing the rest of the document. However, three main issues delayed a final agreement: first, the disputes between the various EAGs; second, the army introducing new demands—its six points[124] that included adherence to the 2008 constitution and submitting to national sovereignty; and third, the increasing disagreements on the structure and form of the political dialogue that was to follow the signing of the nationwide ceasefire agreement.[125] Both sides claimed that the goalposts had been moved. The army felt that the demand with regard to a 'federal army' changed the playing field;[126] the EAGs felt that the army was going back on previously agreed ground.

The disagreements between the various EAGs continued. At a Chiang Mai meeting of the UNFC in September 2014, the KNU decided to walk out and suspend its membership. The KNU claimed that the UNFC decision-making procedure was top-down and that they wanted to be able to take the decisions that were important for the Karen people on their own, without being subject to the politicking of other EAGs.[127] The KNU itself was split over this, as several of its senior members were also senior executives of the UNFC. The

Karen Women's Organisation came up in support of the KNU faction that sided with the UNFC in support of ethnic unity. However, those of the KNU who staked their political credibility on an agreement with the government and a peace process that would lead to political dialogue did not want to be held hostage by what they perceived as the hard-line position of the UNFC, which they felt was holding back the process. This clearly highlighted that the UNFC cannot and does not represent all EAGs.[128] This disunity remained problematic for the peace process, as negotiations stalled. Things were not helped by an aggressive incident in Kachin state when on 20 November 2014 the Tatmadaw shelled a cadet college in Liza, capital of the KIA-controlled area, killing 23 cadets[129] and injuring 13. Apparently the incident was never properly explained by the Tatmadaw command.

By early 2015, eight points out of 106 still needed to be agreed, despite the president having expressed his hope of signing the National Ceasefire Agreement on Myanmar's Union Day, 12 February 2015.[130] As it became obvious that the NCA would not be signed then, a meeting was arranged that would put in place a formal Deed of Commitment with the government promising to build a democratic and federal Union. So instead of signing the NCA on the 68th Anniversary of the Panglong agreement, the president promised to work towards a federal system—a momentous move, given that the term 'federalism' had until then been deemed unacceptable by the government. The surprise of the day was that the president actually signed the Deed, although originally this had not been planned. Vijay Nambiar, Special Adviser to the UN Secretary General for Myanmar, who was in attendance, stated:

> This is an historic moment as it is the first time that a President of Myanmar has formally signed a commitment to build a democratic and federal union. We are convinced that President U Then Sein's declared commitment will further strengthen the reform process in Myanmar and create a conducive environment for the continuing efforts to reach a Nationwide Ceasefire Agreement.[131]

The two vice presidents, the two speakers of parliament, 16 union ministers, 55 political party leaders, 29 ethnic affairs ministers, and three lieutenant generals also signed. Chairman Saw Mutu Sae Poe signed on behalf of the KNU, General Yin Nu signed on behalf of the KPC (a breakaway group from the KNU), General Moshe signed on behalf of the DKBA and Chairman Sao Yawd Serk signed on behalf of the RCSS/SSA-S. Other armed groups present to celebrate Union Day declined to sign, many saying that the deed needed to be discussed first.[132] Commander in Chief Min Aung Hlaing was not present having just returned from Malaysia.[133] This of course only served to underline what was seen as divisions between the executive and the army, and the fact that General Min Aung Hlaing was not present and did not sign eclipsed the fact that he had asked others to do so on his behalf.

On the very same Union Day, possibly timed so as to coincide with this meeting, conflict erupted in Shan State on the China border as the Kokang armed group, the Myanmar National Democratic Alliance Army (MNDAA), tried to seize Laukkai, the main town in the Kokang Self-Administered Zone. Two non-Kokang armed groups, the TNLA and the Arakan Army (AA) supported the MNDAA. This was to complicate the peace process further. However it also had a second effect—galvanising Bamar public opinion behind the Tatmadaw who were under attack. In the spring of 2015, ordinary Yangon residents started to criticise the EAGs more, siding with the Tatmadaw.[134]

Despite the new fighting in Shan State, the Deed of Commitment did breathe some new life into the NCA discussions, and just a month and a half later on 30 March, the final draft NCA text was agreed between the governments and the 16 EAGs involved in the talks.[135] The atmosphere at MPC was positive and the president (who had earlier helped unblock the last textual disagreement) flew to Yangon to sign the draft agreement. From the government's side everything was agreed. Now all that was left to do was for the ethnic representatives to take the text back to their leaders and get their agreement for the NCA to be signed by all. Unfortunately things were not to evolve that simply. It took a long time to arrange that meeting and in the meantime new clashes and problems emerged.

On 29 March 2015 fighting erupted between the Arakan Army (AA) and the Tatmadaw. The AA was generally seen as an offshoot of the KIA.[136] Now the Tatmadaw was in conflict with the AA in two areas (on the Chinese border and in Rakhine state) and the AA was not even a 'recognised' EAG.

All EAGs were due to meet to discuss the agreed NCA draft. In May the UWSP, which had not even taken part in the peace process and was not part of the NCCT, invited some of the armed groups to Pangsang. However, given that not all groups were present, the agreement on the NCA had to wait for another few weeks.

The EAG top leaders finally met at the KNU Headquarters in Law Khee Lar from 2 to 9 June 2015.[137] There were 108 representatives and observers from 17 Ethnic Armed Organizations, 11 members of the Nationwide Ceasefire Coordination Team (NCCT), 5 members of the NCCT technical assistance team, and others such as the Special Adviser on Myanmar to the UN Secretary General, Mr Vijay Nambiar, the Special Envoy on Asian Affairs of the People's Republic of China, Mr Sun Guoxiang and Mr Yuji Mori of the Nippon Foundation of Japan. The top leaders did not agree the approved draft of the NCA that had been signed between the UPWC and the NCCT. Instead they decided to create a 'Nationwide Ceasefire High-Level Delegation' with fifteen leaders of the Ethnic Armed Organizations that would meet with the government to renegotiate twelve amendments of the NCA. The new group would include hard-liners who were unhappy with some of the concessions that had been made on their behalf. The summit also agreed that none of the sixteen NCCT members would sign unless all were permitted to sign, and that non-NCCT armed groups should also be allowed to sign.[138]

The EAGs were aware that these conditions would make the NCA difficult to achieve. One of the biggest sticking points was the conflict in Kokang, as the government did not want to include the three armed groups (AA, MNDAA and TNLA) fighting there until they had signed bilateral ceasefires.[139] Another issue included the number and nationalities of the international observers who would be invited to the signing of the NCA.

The new 'senior delegation' met with the government in Chiang Mai on 3 July 2015. This was followed by two rounds of discussion from the end of July to early August in Yangon, where agreement on most of the 12 points was reached and the text finalised. The only real remaining issue was that of the signatories and the EAGs' insistence that all groups be invited to sign.[140] The government remained opposed to the inclusion of the three EAGs that were fighting in Kokang—the MNDAA, TNLA and the Arakan Army (AA).[141] The president agreed to meet senior delegates of the EAGs on 9 September, trying to break the deadlock. He said 'that he was in direct contact with the MNDAA leader, was open to a bilateral ceasefire with the TNLA after which it could sign the NCA, and that the AA had the option of being included in the NCA under the auspices of another Rakhine armed group, or the KIO in whose territory it operates'.[142] This was however rejected by the EAGs in question. At that same meeting the president said: 'I'd like to stress the importance of peace in the transition to democracy. [...] Without peace, it is not possible. I hope today's summit will pave the way to signing the nationwide ceasefire agreement by the end of September.'[143] He proposed an end of September signing, but the EAGs said they would need until mid October to discuss the details. The commander in chief was not present as he was on an official trip to Israel. This again did not help matters as the EAGs interpreted his absence as a negative signal.

It is becoming clear that whilst the government has been trying very hard to reach an acceptable deal and nationwide ceasefire accord, there are still too many detractors both within the EAGs and the Tatmadaw. The Tatmadaw seems to have lost interest after the EAGs asked to renegotiate the NCA draft that was agreed in March 2015. The chief of staff has at best been 'lukewarm', but still seemed on board till March 2015. The EAG leaders seem to be divided over whether to hand the 'political victory' of a peace agreement to President Thein Sein so close to the elections. Some EAG leaders understand that they are unlikely to get a better deal with the next government, whilst others prefer to wait and see who will be in power from 2016 and are willing to take the risk that much of what has been agreed will be lost. There is of course also the fear amongst many EAGs that once they sign, they will lose economic power and political influence. This is particularly the case in light of the fact that the main stakeholders in the political dialogue that would follow the NCA would be the political parties and the CSOs.

In the end the NCA was indeed signed by eight of the fifteen recognised armed groups on the 15 October 2015 in Nay Pyi Taw.[144] Despite the fact that the other EAG refused to sign, this was still a momentous occasion, especially as the President and the Chief of Staff both signed in front of over 1000 guests and international witnesses.

EAGs' views on the peace process

Views on the peace process vary dramatically between different ethnic armed groups. There are some who are more hard-line and others who are more open to the negotiations. There are those who see this peace process as a unique opportunity and hope that the government is sincere, and others who are ready to remain in a conflict-laden environment. 'Hard-line' and 'soft-line' positions have changed over the years according to context and circumstances, but often the more hard-line groups are supported by hard-line diasporas who do not directly suffer the consequences of the conflict. This is particularly the case with the KIO/KIA, where both the local Kachin population as well as those abroad do not want to see their ethnic leaders compromise.[145] There are differences within groups as well, generally on tribal, linguistic and religious lines; none are homogeneous. In part these differences of opinion between and within groups have been the main challenge over decades, as ethnic armed groups had never before come together as a united front to negotiate with the government.[146] The differences are of course based on the individual histories and experiences of the conflict. What is interesting is that the KNU, the armed group that fought continuously and for the longest time, seems to have a more open view towards the peace process than some of the armed groups that never went back into active conflict after the 1990s ceasefire agreements. However, many of the Karen civil society organisations have been uncomfortable with the KNU's negotiating position and this has created new splits and disagreements within the Karen community. In order to tease out the different positions and issues, interviews were held with senior members of various armed groups.[147]

Mostly the groups interviewed agree on the causes of the conflict as being lack of equality, self-determination, freedom and democracy over decades: 'Inequality, lack of self-determination, Bamar imperialism, culture and literature not recognised by Bamar, even though we fought for independent in 1948 with them.' (DKBA)

This of course was compounded by lies and what has been seen as a breaking of the Panglong agreement that guaranteed ethnic self-determination at independence. Today the groups are looking beyond the grievances and all are taking part in the government peace process, even if, as with the KIA, the war is still actually going on.

One of the biggest issues in the current peace negotiations is the legitimacy of the actors and stakeholders. The armed groups are not recognised as legal entities by the government, because of the illegal association law (and not being 'registered') as well as many having their HQs in neighbouring Thailand or China. However, the EAGs derive their legitimacy from their own ethnic people whom they claim to represent. Again, this is contested as some groups hold elections of a sort (e.g. the KNU and KNPP) and others do not (e.g. the KIA): 'When you talk about the armed groups, there will be differences between us. Like KNNP, we are elected. Not selected. Some don't have an election process. But for us we have armed wing and political body and every 4 years we have party congress and we elect our leaders at the party congress. [...] we have moral and legal legitimacy...' (KNPP)

Others operate in multi-ethnic environments, yet only represent one ethnicity, meaning that not all ethnic groups in one state are represented by the same armed group. Despite this, most groups interviewed spoke about their de facto legitimacy, that their people supported them and some of the historical antecedents and colonial recognition that came before the existence of the modern Myanmar state: 'Ethnic armed groups claim our legitimacy from historical existence pre Panglong and legally not only the law from the postcolonial period, also from the colonial period. This gives us a strong mandate like the Chin Hill Regulation of 1896 or the Kachin Hill Tribe Regulation of

1894 and the Federated State Act of 1921. This is the legal legitimacy that we brought to Panglong.' (CNF)

The legitimacy issue is reversed when it comes to the government. The EAG do not recognise the government they are negotiating with because of the 2008 constitution and the way the 2010 elections were held. 'We did not accept the 2008 constitution but they approved through referendum and they formed the government. We cannot accept this government and constitution but we have to make a deal with them although we do not accept the government legitimacy. [...] If we cannot change [the constitution] then we cannot get peace and civil war can start again and this will block the country's development'. (NMSP)

Although all agree that the constitution needs to be revised and that the government's legitimacy can be questioned, some groups are less hard on the government than others, saying for example that the reform process helps legitimise the current administration or that unless a deal is struck with those who are in power today, peace will not be forthcoming. 'In our country this government is not legitimate. But according to this attitude no one is legitimate. Armed groups are not registered. [...] If we compare with the past we did not have a constitution. Though the referendum may be right or wrong, this constitution is legitimate in this country, de facto legitimate. When we look back, we lived without a constitution. It is not perfect but it is better than before. The constitution is active and we have to do according to the constitution, but of course we want to amend and change it.' (KNU)

The 2008 constitution remains the sticking point, as it was drawn up without the actual participation and input of the ethnic representatives. One group in particular emphasised that a new social contract was needed. 'A Constitution is a social contract, so we need an all-inclusive process to produce the constitution. After that we can have unity and a society that will be legitimate. After that we can define more precisely who has moral or legal legitimacy.' (ANC)

Others again do not want to talk about the constitution right now and focus on how the peace process can be moved forward: 'This is a de facto government. Whether we like it or not. [...] If they regard themselves as the legitimate government and they are talking to us, whether they like it or not they recognise us as legitimate [as well]. Aung San was given legitimacy in 1946. There were so many leaders, and he was just 32 and even younger when he started. First Gen. Slim, chose him to talk as the other side, then Mountbatten. Legitimacy comes through talking, even through our enemies.' (CNF)

Opinions were equally divided as to whether the peace process was linked to the reform process. Some groups insisted that the government was making peace to be able to develop the country, and to gain international legitimacy or aid. The lack of real decentralisation as a part of the reforms that would allow for the individual ethnic identities to be preserved was seen as a major issue, many saying that the government was hiding behind infrastructure development. '[...] Culture and language are more important than the decentralisation. The current government is supporting area for infrastructure. This is not sufficient, we need the right to construct our ethnic identity.' (PNLO)

More hard-line groups see the two processes as totally separate: '... the current reforms are window dressing. Only exterior levels, no interior layers. These reform processes are difficult to link with peace process. If the process is genuinely reforming it must link into every sector. [...] Peace process is also linked to constitutional reform. There are no constitutional reforms till now. Everything comes back to 2008.' (ANC)

The fact that the government had not at the point of writing set aside any budget for the peace process and that laws regarding education were being passed before the political dialogue had started were also seen as proof that the peace and reform processes are de-linked. However, despite all the misgivings, there is a motivation amongst most to take part, many agreeing that the time has come to stop fighting and to try and resolve issues around the negotiation table. 'We have been fighting for over sixty years; it is enough, more than enough'. (ANC)

The views of their people were also a motivating factor: 'We don't want to live in the jungle and people want the NMSP to participate in this peace process. We hold regular public consultation meetings. We have public consultation meetings every year and public opinion polls and the public don't want to make simple agreement with the government because they don't believe the simple agreement, they want the right agreement. This is the motivation. NMSP budget comes from these people. We are accountable to them.' (NMSP)

There is an understanding that to continue fighting will result in a 'lose–lose' situation. 'If we do not take part, if we do not grab this opportunity, our people will suffer again.' (DKBA)

The basic ethnic demand reiterated by all groups remains democracy, equality and self-determination, and if those are not met, then fighting might indeed resume: 'Government wants ceasefire agreement. But they want just signed. Ethnic side, they want agreement and political dialogue with time frame. Previously we think that we can get before 2015 but thinking changed a little. [...] After 2015, new government and military. We can fight again or we can continue political negotiations.' (NMSP)

Opinions on the success of the peace process were divided, clearly separating hard-liners from others. Some see the government as more progressive and open than before, an improvement on the 1990s process. '[there is] No other way. No other choice. They [the government] have strong willingness for national reconciliation. The important thing is to construct trust through the process. We have to do together, to work with sincerity. Government needs to be sincere, we also need to be sincere. They need to put suspicion aside and builds trust'. (PNLO)

Others feel quite radically that the government would be able to resolve the ethnic problem themselves, simply by instituting a loose federal union, and that EAGs should not even have to ask for this as it is self-evident: 'They [armed groups] have been waiting for political dialogue but government is still avoiding political solutions. They [the government] can solve this by themselves, construct a federal state. We don't need to take part in this process. [...] Peace depends on the government.' (ANC)

All know it will take time, but a few worry that things might be different in 2015, as the political structures then cannot be foreseen. 'We hope we can reach before the end of the year. We worry a bit about this, who will be the next president. Maybe they will have other people'. (KNU)

Time and timing remain the most important issue at the moment. As the government is desperate to sign a nationwide deal and deliver on the president's second priority, the armed groups are divided on how quickly the deal can be done. Some say that it will take time because it takes time to change attitudes (citing the recent change of heart amongst the representatives of the Tatmadaw); some want more time so that the agreement is seen as waterproof and accepted by their constituents; again others are using time as a political tool to put the government under pressure. It is clear that not all realise that the peace process currently on the table might not look the same after 2015. 'Armed struggle is not the solution for Burma. This is a political problem, this should be stopped through political dialogue—it is the only way out. I deeply believe this. The government side also understands that dealing with the conflict with the army is not the right answer. Sixty years and they [the problems] did not disappear. This is the only solution. [...] The issue is time.' (CNF)

Who should be at the table? Another problem in the peace process

It would have been complex enough for the president's envoy U Aung Min to have to manage the army as well as the expectations of the various armed groups, and changing alliances between the EAGs. The sections above have shown how complex the process has been. By mid 2013, however, parliament decided to get involved. The speaker of the house and Daw Aung San Suu Kyi together decided to challenge the legitimacy of the peace process.[148] This emerged out of the many breakfast meetings that Daw Aung San Suu Kyi was having with U Shwe Mann, where they presumably were trying to forge a way forward in light of the 2015 elections and the power struggle between the executive and the legislatures.[149] As mentioned in the previous chapter, U Shwe Mann had already used parliament to challenge the positions and views of the president, something quite new in Myanmar. Daw Aung San Suu Kyi was looking for a strong ally to have the constitution amended to be able to become president. The two found common cause in the peace process, where they criticised the president for the fact that the executive led it, whereas they both felt that the parliament should have a role if the process was going to be legitimate. The attack greatly weakened U Aung Min's position vis-à-vis the EAGs, and for a while it looked as if the peace process was seriously damaged. In the end the inclusion of some parliamentarians in the process solved the crisis. However, it pointed out a major issue, which was how other stakeholders would or should be involved in what was Myanmar's most important political development. Many others had complained that ethnic CSOs, women's groups, ethnic political parties and other groups should have a say at the table. The NCCT and the UPWC however maintained that until the ceasefire had been signed, the negotiation teams had to be limited to those who were bearing arms, not wider civil and political society. They promised that others would be able to become involved when the political dialogue started. Given that the document being produced is a political document, however, and that it now looks unlikely that any political dialogue can start before the 2015 elections, many CSOs and political representatives have expressed concerns and dissatisfaction with the peace process.[150] The issue was essentially about 'deepening' the process through the inclusion of civil society and affected communities, a challenge described by Charles Petrie and Ashley South in their report on peace-building and civil society in Myanmar. The participation of civil society would be essential for a long-lasting, bottom-up and locally-owned transition in Myanmar.[151] But things are not that simple, as Bamar civil society and ethnic civil society are different, and often separate.[152]

Mainstream or Bamar civil society tend to focus on what Petrie and South call a 'cosmopolitan, democratic–progressive agenda', which they believe is too narrowly framed to include the issues pertaining to ethnic grievances and wider issues related to contested identities. They also point to the tensions between border-based and in-country-based ethnic civil society with regard to the peace process.[153] This results in a cacophony of opinions and voices, some of which are replicated below.

The views of CSOs, political parties and others

Whilst a lot of the news on Myanmar tends to oversimplify Myanmar society, dividing it into the classic black and white—military/government vs. civilians/civil society—the reality on the ground is much more complex, and constantly shifting. As with all other matters, views on the peace process differ amongst the broad category of civil society leaders, political parties and other 'thought leaders' or public intellectuals. With the exception of the NUP representatives and two 'thought leaders' whose thoughts are reflected below, those who were interviewed were either representatives of ethnic CSOs or ethnic political parties; however, their views, like those of the ethnic armed groups, varied markedly. As one Yangon-based public intellectual put it: 'Most armed groups in Myanmar hold weapons due to their different perspectives. Some oppose the government due to military coup. Some oppose government for getting federalism.' This means that the government actually has to deal with many different actors, different views and different problems.

> [the] government has to solve all kinds of problem. So the current government is looking for the way to solve these problems and the way using for peace process of this government is different from former one. [...] We recognize that this government tried for the peace with new policy, even though the fights still were happened. Having the chance of negotiation is good sign. (U Thu Wei)

Another writer (Ko Tar) also expressed a positive view about the efforts being made by the government with regard to peace, yet agreed that satisfying all differing views, issues and grievances across society was a huge challenge which the government was unlikely to be able to meet.

Whilst cautious optimism about the peace process dominated the tone at the time, there were many issues, starting with who is represented at the peace table. The parliamentarians[154] for instance all seemed rather unhappy that they had been invited to the negotiation table rather late in the day, and as one of them put it: 'only for show'. Another explained that it was actually the government that wanted to keep parliament away from the process. 'The main cause is that Members of Parliament were prohibited to be involved in it because government itself does not want to.'[155]

The same MP also mentioned that civil society leaders and religious leaders were missing, and another said that all peace talk was solely between the MPC and the armed groups and that this was not right. The late invitation for the parliament to take part can be explained either by the government trying to keep it simple at the initial stages of the ceasefire negotiations, involving only U Aung Min and the MPC, and a bit later the Tatmadaw, not wanting the process to be derailed by too many disparate voices;[156] alternatively it can of course be explained by the government wanting to stay in control of the negotiations, not wanting the only democratically elected representatives involved.

The grievance of not being invited to take part runs deep, especially with ethnic civil society organisations that were able to emerge and grow during the last ceasefire period of the 1990s. In many ways they were architects of the uncomfortable and unstable truth, and feel that they know what needs to be done to have lasting peace. The Karen Women's Empowerment Group explained:

> CSOs, women and youth groups are missing [in the peace process]. Because CSOs represent the communities, they know the communities, share information. Women groups [are missing]; during the conflict the women suffered a lot, they need to raise their voice on peace table for sustainable peace. In the KNU case, as we are civil society, we can put some things into the state level agreement such as not entering villages, women protection issues, no sexual violence, no child soldier recruitment, security for villagers. [...] Youth groups should also participate as they are our future they should shape their future by themselves by participating on process. This is part of nation building. Is like building a house. All family members should agree on this how we should shape our house. This [the current ceasefire negotiations] is the foundation of negotiation. If the foundation of the building is not good it won't be sustainable. People need to be part of from the start. Especially women. They suffered a lot. They need to be part if this will be sustainable.

The issue of women not participating is a particularly sore point. Given that the armed groups have all male representation, the ethnic women feel left out. As the Mon Women's Organisation put it: 'Women are missing. But some armed group leaders are blocking to include women. I have wanted to speak to the NMSP rep. Many have less experience than [Mi Sardar].'

When representatives of civil society organisations are asked about their role, they often refer to the president's speech—especially the one where he recognises the role of CSOs and where the skills and knowledge of CSOs are acknowledged. They wonder how they can be recognised and yet not invited to take part. Some feel that CSOs are expected to be supportive of the government policies if they are to play a role—and that the government is not yet ready for critical CSOs.

The lack of transparency and what is happening at the negotiation table is another issue. CSOs feel that both government and armed groups have their own agendas, and that only with their direct participation would the real interests of the people be represented. CSOs see their role as underpinning the peace through the building of legitimacy: 'We can have awareness raising in the community for democratic principles; how to elect leaders and government [...] Elected body can be controlled by the people. Watch groups have a role to play. [...] The peace process should be inclusive and community awareness and participation and it should be with a timeline, transparency. Actually it is none of these things.'

Political parties also think that the peace process should be more inclusive, but some agree with the government and the armed groups that the first stage—the nationwide ceasefire agreement—should be conducted between the fighting parties. Some see a role for political parties as representatives of the people at this stage, others do not, but mostly they believe that CSOs should wait to be involved in the political dialogue. 'In early stage, all people do not need to involve and this is to get ceasefire. When we get ceasefire [...] We must discuss political dialogue. Only if we get solutions from political dialogue, we get sustainable peace. So, this is very long process.' (KPP)

There is also a new rivalry for support and legitimacy between ethnic political parties and EAGs, despite their shared aims and agendas. More deliberation on this will be given in the Conclusion to this book.

Whilst the wrangling of who should take part at what point of the process results in a cacophony of voices in Myanmar's newly created political space, reflecting the country's great diversity, it is positive to see that political parties see themselves as important stakeholders in Myanmar's political future: 'We play a key role because the nature of political party is the bridge between government and public. We have constitution and the sovereignty come from public. It is theory and democracy culture. To save public from arm conflict, political parties are essential for them [which is why we should be involved now]. (NUP)

On the other side of the argument, the armed groups and the government representatives in the ceasefire negotiations seem to agree that the real role CSOs can play will come later, within the political dialogue framework. As one ethnic leader explained: 'The issue is that they have to be part of political dialogue, but the first we have to stop fighting. That is why the ones who are fighting have to reach agreement [and] then we have to design the political dialogue, [...] then the others have to be included...' (KNU)

Another armed group spoke of the 'misunderstanding' that was being compounded by the media. They felt that it was important to secure security and federal union issues first, and then once the political dialogue had started the subject experts could come in. (KNPP)

The government representatives went even further than the armed groups in stressing the important role that NGOs and CSOs would play once the ceasefire had been agreed, reflecting the president's speech. One minister said: '[The] role of CSOs in peace process is a must because the government will not be able to fulfil all requirements. The local parties, community leaders need to take part. CSOs have capacity that the government lacks, international exposure, objective analysis, can look into the future and plan. [this] will drive political dialogue to lasting peace.'

Another minister reminds us that the previous government did not care about civil society organisations, and did not understand the role that could be played by them. He sees the role of CSOs in social mobilisation and feels that ministries have to start working with CSOs to be more effective.

The president's chief peace envoy's words show how far the government has changed its attitude: 'Power used to come from the top, now it comes from the people. CSOs represent the people. Today you cannot do it without the people and involvement of the CSOs as representatives of the people'. (U Aung Min)

These changes are positive, and overall there is muted optimism about the outcomes of the peace process. One political party, however, points out that the actual causes of the conflict cannot be easily addressed as there are different perceptions on state and nation-building between the negotiating partners and this will take time to be resolved. (KPP)

Other political parties believe that many issues will be solved through economic development. Others again go back to the 2008 constitution, saying it needs to be changed for the peace process to be a success: 'They [ethnic groups] don't have rights, they don't have freedom. They want these back. They want to build a development for living standard. That's why they become armed groups. [...] But the disturbance is the 2008 constitution. The new government leads the peace process. They are making the political reforms. Peace process and constitution amendment is directly related. Only constitution amendment can guarantee the rights of ethnics. If so, there will be peace. That cannot happen within one or two years. The rights of ethnics, ethnic movement and movement of constitution amendment are totally related with peaceful development of country.' (Rakhine Party)

The parliamentarians of the Lower House agree that there needs to be self-determination, autonomy as well as power and resource-sharing across all seven states and seven regions. 'If the government implements the above effective reforms, peace will surely happen...'[157]

This is echoed by the MPs from the Upper House, who say: 'If both sides don't focus on their own goods rather than on country's goodness, this peace process will be successful.'[158]

Overall, political parties across the political spectrum say that the key to success is political will on both sides, and for that, mindsets have to be changed. CSOs are more cautious, saying that trust remains the main issue, and that they feel they cannot trust the government. One respondent even said that she felt the government was 'playing'.

The lack of understanding of the legitimacy of the ethnic grievance is reflected by the attitudes of the main Bamar parties, who take things rather more lightly than their ethnic counterparts: 'the government and armed groups quarrel related with the meaning of words, for instance federalism and revolution, leading to disagreement. This situation is similar with former times that they argued whether they should use 'Socialist Democracy' or 'Democratic Socialism'. If they really would like to help people who were affected by long-term civil war, they should not argue more about words. [...] If they argue only about legitimacy and the word 'revolution', they are doing this for their own sake not for the country.' (NUP)

Non-ethnic MPs also have less than positive views of the armed groups: '... some people think that these groups serve to get freedom for their states. Some people think that armed groups are nuisance.' And another says, 'The armed groups don't represent the local people, and they are making the peace process based on their party policies'. (MPs parliament FGD)

The issues remain trust, time and mindset, and whilst the peace process is recognised as unprecedented and positive, peace in Myanmar is not seen as a foregone conclusion amongst those who are not yet active at the negotiation table.

What people think about the peace process—some results from a small nationwide poll

An informal poll was conducted across Myanmar between the autumn of 2013 and the summer of 2014 to get an idea of what people knew about the peace process and how they felt about it. All seven ethnic states were visited, as well as Yangon and Mandalay. The total number of participants was 1,329.[159] The participants were largely a young, middle- and upper-middle-class sample, who were likely to read the newspapers and be interested in public affairs; but all classes and age groups were represented, and the survey was careful to keep a balance between urban and rural respondents.

The results point to cautious optimism, with 69% expressing satisfaction with the peace process (15% being fully satisfied and 16% not satisfied at all). A majority of 70% also supported the peace process, whilst only 30% did not.[160] The poll uncovered some critical voices as well, as 33% thought that the people of Myanmar should be involved (but only 19% thought the parliaments should be involved). Only 17% thought the international community had a role to play, whilst 54% thought the military needed to be at the negotiation table, and 60% thought the participation of CSOs was important.[161] Whilst there seemed to be a general knowledge on the overall process, when asked if they knew how many groups had signed individual ceasefires with the government, 71% did not know. Most importantly, despite an overall satisfaction with the peace and the reform process, 59% did not believe that the nationwide ceasefire agreement could be achieved before the elections in 2015.

There were some interesting variations of opinion between different groups, most notably between ethnic groups, but also notable variations depending on the level of education of the respondents. For example, 75% of most respondent categories were satisfied with the current government's reform

Figure 2

Research Areas

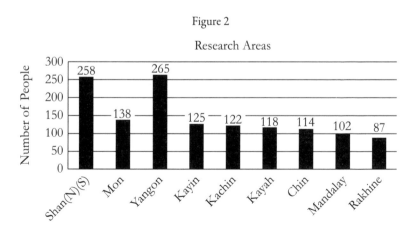

process; but only 8% of students and 4% of NGO staff were fully satisfied with it. These more educated students and NGO staff might be major supporters of the process, but they were less happy with the way it is being conducted, as shown by the fact that 40% of those with no education were fully satisfied, whilst only 4% of postgraduates were fully satisfied with the process; so there were clear class distinctions in how the peace and reform processes are viewed. The satisfaction levels also varied widely between ethnic groups, with only 2% of Kachin and 3% of Shan being fully satisfied (24% and 37% respectively being unsatisfied), whilst 25% of the Kayah and 21% of the Karen respondents reported full satisfaction, higher even than the 17% of the Bamar group. Less than 18% of all the ethnic groups (varying between 8% of the Kachin and 18% of the Mon) feel that the peace process is fully satisfying their demands.

With regard to the outcomes, more than 50% of respondents believed the participants could have a successful peace process. However, Kachin, Shan and Rakhine had less confidence, with 15%, 19% and 19% respectively feeling that the peace process would fail. Mon, Karen and Kayah had a greater belief that the nationwide ceasefire will be signed before 2015. But most of the Shan did not believe it. People from Yangon Region, Mandalay Region, Karen State, Mon State and Kayah State had higher expectations of the negotiations than those in other ethnic areas.

The bottom line

> If one were to say before the peace process was initiated three years ago that ceasefires would soon change the lives of civilians in conflict areas, few people would likely have believed it. But the truth is that the ceasefires in Myanmar have brought incredible peace dividends. They have transformed the lives of many people.[162]

Aung Naing Oo is right to say this, and is echoed by the MPSI listening project. Beyond the fourteen individual ceasefires that have been signed or reconfirmed, the process has brought together the EAGs, the government and the Tatmadaw to discuss issues face to face and collaborate and cooperate for the future of the country. This has led not only to fewer clashes and displaced people,[163] but also to some level of collaboration between the EAGs and the government in the field. The results include 800,000 ID cards being distributed in remote areas in Kachin, Karen, Mon Shan and Kayah states, new bridges and roads being built,[164] residents travelling freely, NGOs having access to areas previously off limits and villages able to cultivate their land without fear. The behaviour of the government and the EAGs is also changing. According to South, as a result of the government tolerating greater interaction between EAGs, ethnic political parties and CSOs, the EAGs are being drawn into new collaborations and are 'learning to be less hegemonic'.[165] The government is also learning to listen more to the variety of stakeholders across the country. In many ways the legitimacy-constructing project that is the peace process has changed the government's understanding of the country and they are learning how to live with different points of views.

However the peace process as it had been planned by the government took longer than anticipated, meaning that the political dialogue will now only start once the new government of 2016 has taken its seats. This could lead to a major strategy change as well as to a change of actors around the table. As of late 2014 when the negotiations with the EAGs was stuck, the government started to have more meaningful discussions with parliamentarians about the framework of political dialogue that was to follow the elusive nationwide ceasefire agreement. The fourteen stakeholders at the table of the high-level political talks at the end of October 2014 included President Thein Sein, the top two Myanmar army leaders, Union Parliament Speaker U Shwe Mann, and political party leaders including Daw Aung San Suu Kyi. However, the representatives of the armed groups were not invited. They were not invited to the six party talks a few weeks later either. In parallel the Nationalities Brotherhood Federation (NBF) met with all ethnic parties and combined four exiting proposals for the political dialogue into one single framework.[166] On 4 November 2014 an alliance of 56 political parties, formed under the Peace and Politics Implementation Committee (PPIC), agreed on twenty points they wish to be discussed as part of the political dialogue following the signing of a nationwide ceasefire agreement.[167] On 25 November the 56 political parties approved a framework for post-ceasefire political dialogue.[168] In none of the cases were the EAGs part of the discussions. Clearly—the eight groups that have signed the NCA will be part of the forthcoming process, provided the new government continues on the same trajectory. However the EAGs that have declined to sign could be marginalised and no longer seen as the main interlocutors or the main representatives of their ethnic people.[169] This could in effect significantly change the balance of power at any negotiation table after the 2015 elections.

ECONOMIC REFORMS AND RE-ENGAGEMENT
WITH THE INTERNATIONAL COMMUNITY

...We have to ensure [a] proper market economy designed to reduce the economic gap between the rich and the poor and [the] development gap between urban and rural areas.

President Thein Sein, Inaugural Address, 30 March 2011[1]

Background

The economy has been Myanmar's largest challenge[2] for the Thein Sein government. Years of isolation and under-investment coupled with a rent-seeking leadership that was not concerned with the welfare of the wider population have led to Myanmar becoming a Least Developed Country (LDC).[3] In light of the 2015 ASEAN free trade area, many of the past legacies needed to be reversed. As discussed in Chapter 3, the administration sees the political transition very much in light of economic reconstruction, so as to catch up with the ASEAN neighbours and reconnect with the world at large. Both economic and political reforms, especially the peace process, go hand in hand. However, the challenges are steep.

The country's GDP is estimated at around US$ 50 billion, and according to the latest census the population head count is just over 51 million, making the per capita income just under US $1,000.[4] Yangon is by far the largest city, with 4.6 million inhabitants. The population is mainly rural, estimated at around 70%. According to the World Bank, rural poverty was estimated at

29% compared to 15% in urban areas and 26% overall.[5] In 2012/13 agriculture accounted for 43% of GDP;[6] Myanmar is a net food exporter, mainly of rice and pulses. The sector is highly labour-intensive (it generates about 54% of employment and provides livelihoods to more than 70% of the population), with none of the capital structure and infrastructure of the neighbouring countries.[7] The manufacturing and services sectors are underdeveloped. According to the IMF, Myanmar's gas exports accounted for 21% of GDP in 2013/14, whilst other exported goods accounted for only 15% of GDP.[8] Otherwise exports include jade, wood and wood products, as well as fish, showing that Myanmar has been living off its natural resources rather than developing a sustainable economy. These figures could however be distorted. A recent report shows that unofficial and hence unrecorded sales of jade to China could have been as high as US$ 3.4 billion in 2011 (and rising), or even greater than sales of natural gas to Thailand (and now China).[9] Most of these exports are bound for China, Thailand and India. Its imports also accounted for about 16% of GDP and include petroleum products, and iron and steel coming from China, Singapore and Thailand.[10]

Myanmar had started some limited economic reforms after 1988, when it moved away from Nay Win's Burmese way to socialism, and adopted a market-based approach. Some foreign direct investment was allowed under the first FDI law (promulgated in November 1988). However, Western sanctions did not help, and for a long time there was little international capital and little economic growth.[11] Most of Myanmar's exports remained focused on agricultural produce and natural resources. In the 1990s Myanmar tried to develop a garment sector, but Western sanctions killed this off. Whilst sanctions did not affect the ruling junta, which was able to live off the exports of natural resources, sanctions did hamper the development of a manufacturing sector that would have created jobs.[12] In effect, sanctions impoverished the ordinary people, not the military leadership.[13] In addition, given the Western sanctions, Myanmar had no other option but to develop its economy eastwards. As of the 1990s, Myanmar was not cut off from the rest of the world as it had been under Ne Win's reclusive leadership, but all its relations, trade and other, were predominantly with Asian countries. Myanmar became a member of ASEAN in 1997. In 2012/13 trade with ASEAN countries accounted for around 40% of imports and 50% of exports. Myanmar also became a member of BIMSTEC[14] and the Greater Mekong Sub-region (GMS).[15] Whilst BIMSTEC is hardly functional and has not done much for Myanmar's economy, GMS has helped with some local integration across the region, including closer ties with Cambodia, Laos, Thailand, Vietnam and Yunnan province in China.[16]

Under SLORC, the regime announced impressive growth figures, especially over the last decade; however, Turnell believes the double-digit GDP growth figures reported by the government had no basis in reality.[17] Myanmar was growing, albeit slowly, unevenly and haltingly. According to the World Bank, the economy in 2012 has accelerated after a few years of moderate growth. On average, the Myanmar economy grew at 5.1% between 2005/6 and 2009/10, due to slow improvements in the manufacturing and services sector; and then at an average of 6.5 per cent since the transition. Still, this is nowhere near Myanmar's full potential.[18]

At the time of the 2010 elections the main challenges included some steep barriers to industrialisation: amongst others, the low rate of electrification around the country (only around 26% of the population had access to electricity in 2011),[19] the low levels of infrastructure including roads, but also telecommunications and IT. The road network covers 130,000 km, and is the primary mode of transport. But there are only 18 vehicles per 1,000 people in Myanmar (although this is rapidly changing). The railway network has suffered from historical under-investment.[20]

The very weak banking system was hit hard by a banking crisis in 2003, and has only just started a slow recovery process.[21] Getting credit in Myanmar has been virtually impossible, and all levels of society have had to rely on semiformal or informal money-lending systems that charge high interest rates and are largely unregulated. High levels of underemployment and unemployment of people with few skills have added to the depressing scenario. The government has been unable to raise revenue domestically.[22] According to the ADB, Myanmar has one of the lowest ratios of government revenues and tax collection to GDP. Weak institutions and important tax concessions for companies are part of the issue. Poverty explains why personal income tax levels remain so low.[23]

In addition, the decades of military rule and the lack of transparency for any transaction have made officials highly corrupt, and have increased transaction costs for any entrepreneur. The regime helped create a crony business class, entrepreneurs who secured the best deals through their connections with the military. The twelve to fifteen favoured individuals included Steven Law, Tay Za, Zaw Zaw, Kyaw Win, Thein Tun, Eike Htun, Htay Myint and Aung Ko Win, and they became the country's most powerful businessmen, owning the biggest conglomerates across all sectors, including banking, infrastructure, transport, tourism and real estate.[24] The 'Biz 15'[25] as they were known had first access to all business licenses. The crony dominance was further entrenched with the privatisation wave between 2009 and 2010, when the junta was selling off state assets before the 2011 handover of power. The transactions were neither transparent nor competitive and included a number of the Biz 15 crony companies such as Tay Za's Htoo Co., Tun Myint Naing's Asia World Co., Zaw Zaw's Max Myanmar Co., Chit Khine's Eden Group, etc., as well as two military conglomerates, UMEHL and MEC.[26] Jones (2013), who has done some work on Myanmar's cronies, estimates that they control a majority of the country's assets despite comprising just 5% of businesses in absolute terms. The rest of the business class remains predominantly small-scale.[27] The state's rent-seeking behaviour, in addition to the poor infrastructure, lack of electricity and uncertain regulatory environment, made it difficult for smaller businesses to set up or be successful.[28] In 2011 all this had to change. And rather quickly too, given the start of the ASEAN free trade area in 2015.

Starting economic reforms

President Thein Sein identified his key economic priorities as rural development and equitable growth. These priorities have required a fundamental rethinking of basic economic approaches. However, at the time of the handover, the new government policies did not seem to have a clear vision and some decisions seemed to be ad hoc, possibly because there was so much to do. The government began the dismantling of monopolies, the promotion of foreign investment, development of human resources (also asking for the return of the skilled from the diaspora), boosting electricity generation, improving export-oriented industries, transport infrastructure, tax mobilisation—all at the same time, seemingly without much of a plan.

In April 2011 the president appointed three committees to give him policy advice in economic, political and legal affairs. The Political Advisory Board is led by Ko Ko Hlaing, a retired military officer who used to work in the Research Department at the War Office of the Ministry of Defense. Police Colonel Sit Aye, former director of the Home Ministry's International Relations Department, heads the legal advisory board.[29] The Economic Advisory Board is headed by Dr Myint, a nationally respected economist who has a mandate to look at policies for poverty alleviation.[30] Then the Myanmar Development Resource Institute (MDRI) was created in March 2012. It has three separate centres: the Centre for Economic and Social

Development, the Centre for Strategic and International Studies and the Centre for Legal Affairs.[31]

In May 2011, the first of a number of economic workshops was held in Nay Pyi Taw to discuss rural development and poverty alleviation.[32] The next workshop in June, held jointly with the UN, focused on the rice economy. This was followed by the National Workshop on Reforms for Economic Development of Myanmar in August, to which Daw Aung San Suu Kyi was invited.[33] The workshop also included academics who had in the past been critical of the government. The series of workshops and meetings in Nay Pyi Taw have continued, for the first time bringing international organisations and foreign governments into the mix of Myanmar policy debate.

In the meantime the government announced pension increases, alleviating the poverty of some 840,000 pensioners and their families. The value of their entitlements had sharply fallen over the past years.[34] External oversight and scrutiny over budgets and planning have been established through two legislative committees that oversee the governments public finances: the Public Accounts Committee (PAC) vets the budget bill and the audit report, and the Planning and the Finance Committee (PFC) reviews the national development plan and legislative matters relating to the financial sector.[35] The committees have also become responsible for reviewing the executive's budget.[36] State and regional budgets have been separated from the Union fund accounts, resulting in a 'deconcentration' of budgeting and planning functions between the centre and the states/regions. There is also an Office of the Auditor General (OAG) that has purview over all the public sector, except for the Ministry of Defence. According to the World Bank, the OAG is also the entity responsible for setting accounting and auditing policy for the public sector, and has adopted INTOSAI audit standards.[37]

Exchange rates, currency and trade issues

During the course of 2011, the already overvalued kyat continued to strengthen, making life for exporters, including those in the agricultural sector, very difficult. The privatisation drive of state assets in 2009–10 had resulted in a strong demand for the kyat (as these assets had to be paid for in kyats and not dollars). According to the economist U Myint, speculative inflows of capital followed.[38] This put increasing pressure on the government and prompted it to look at the issue created by Myanmar's multiple exchange rates. The unification of these various exchange rates became one of the first priorities. Since 1977, the kyat had been pegged to the SDR at 8.50 kyats per SDR (5.35/6 kyats per US dollar),[39] resulting in a highly overvalued currency. Foreign currency earned from exports was allocated at this artificial rate to fund public import payments. Myanmar's 'export first policy' and other exchange restrictions resulted in parallel markets with various exchange rates. It has also been alleged that the artificially low rate allowed Myanmar to hide much of its export earnings, but this also eroded external competitiveness.[40] The IMF was approached for help to deal with the problem. At the time, given that the Western sanctions were still in place, both the IMF and the WB had limited mandates in Myanmar.[41] Nevertheless, a kind of plan was put in place and the government started by establishing a formal currency retail market by licensing seventeen private banks in October 2011 to operate money-changing counters at the Thein Phyu (TP) centre. In November, eleven banks were authorised to trade foreign currency with each other and domestic customers.[42] In April 2012, a managed float[43] finally replaced the peg. 'Currently the reference exchange rate is determined by a daily auction mechanism and the determined rate is allowed to fluctuate within a daily band of 0.8%.'[44] Since the managed exchange rate float has been put in place, the nominal exchange rate has depreciated slightly.[45]

A new central bank law has embedded autonomy for the central bank. Most of the private banks are trying to modernise their services as quickly as possible, by installing ATMs. Foreigners are now allowed to open bank accounts in selected bank branches. Till mid 2014 no foreign banks were operating, but a number of Asian banks had opened offices in Myanmar and were ready and waiting to open for business as soon as the banking legislation is sorted out.[46] At the time of writing nine foreign banks licences have been granted.[47] The main objective of the new monetary policy in Myanmar has been price stability.

The 2012/13 budget was the very first budget debated in and approved by parliament. It was subsequently published in the national press. This unprecedented move increased visibility and transparency, showing people what the government planned to spend its money on and what problems the government was engaging in. The budget addressed a number of important issues, including fiscal issues such as the self-financing of state-owned enterprises and changes in the tax system on imports, agricultural products, public sector employees now having to pay income tax and income tax progressively increasing.[48] The budget also provided for increasing resources to education and health and policies to try to decrease public debts.

The government also worked on formulating a National Comprehensive Development Plan (NCDP) for 2011/12–2030/31, to set out the reform and policy priorities for twenty years. The Framework for Economic and Social Reforms (FESR), a reform strategy drafted at the Centre for Economic and Social Development to support the president's policy approach to people-centred development, was adopted in late 2012, and set out ten priority reform areas for the interim period of 2012–15 that include finance and taxation, monetary policy, regulations on trade and investment, private-sector development, health and education, agriculture and food sufficiency, the governing system and transparency, mobile communication services and internet systems, infrastructure development and governance reform.[49]

Public consultations were held in Yangon with civil society organisations, political parties and the private sector in December 2012 to incorporate their views on the FESR. The president introduced the FESR at the third planning committee meeting on 28 December 2012. Specifically, the framework emphasises development of the laws and regulations surrounding decentralisation, and suggests the possibility of adding more areas to the initial list of decentralised responsibilities, possibly including health and education. FESR also stresses the need for a more 'comprehensive' policy on decentralisation.[50]

Given that much of the legislation was very old, trade in investment laws has been revised or replaced. There is a new Export and Import Law, of 7 September 2012, replacing the Control of Import/Export Temporary Law (1947). The new Foreign Investment Law, and Foreign Exchange and Management Law were also promulgated in November 2012.[51] Given the importance of FDI in Myanmar's economic development, the government has been trying to make Myanmar's investment climate more hospitable.[52] However, there are still reforms needed with regard to the State-owned Economic Enterprises (SEEs). According to the State-owned Economic Enterprise Law no. 9/89, certain sectors remain reserved for the state.[53]

Overall the reforms that were most visible and felt by the wider population included the liberalisation of imports such as cars (Yangon now boasts real traffic jams) and the slashing of red tape, making construction in particular more attractive (Yangon now resembles a large building site). According to an interview with the World Bank in August 2014, the reforms as well as the new transparency have had a real impact on Myanmar as they change how things are done. Aside from the economic impact, there is an intrinsic value to the economic reforms. However, it remains to be seen how far these reforms are truly pro poor and whether they will eventually include everybody. At the time of writing the reforms have mainly impacted on the urban middle classes.[54]

Other key sectors that have been targeted by the reform process include telecoms and the energy sector. Mobile communications in Myanmar have been particularly underdeveloped: current penetration is estimated at less than 4%, 96% lower than the average penetration of countries in Southeast Asia.[55] To develop the sector, Myanmar's Post and Telecommunications Department announced a new telecommunications law, which created four new telecommunications licenses in Myanmar:[56] 90 companies expressed initial interest and 11 were finally shortlisted. Two large telecommunications contracts were finally awarded to Telenor (Norway) and Ooredoo (Qatar) in June 2013.[57] Ooredoo was received with mixed feelings by the wider population. At the time the SIM cards were being made available (July/August 2014), there was a campaign by 969 activists[58] asking people not to buy SIM cards from a Muslim country. But there was also great excitement as the new SIM cards were much cheaper than the MPT ones, and promised easier internet access, something many urban young people needed quite desperately as the downloading time for emails and internet sites slows to a standstill at peak times during the day. Once bought, a number of people were disappointed as they found that coverage was patchy, and if they left Yangon they had to resort to MPT SIM cards again.[59] The problems did not last: at the time of writing the mobile scene is changing fast and improving considerably.

As mentioned earlier, only 26% of the population have access to electricity, and 70% of the population live in rural areas. Myanmar relies heavily on traditional biomass for its energy needs, getting approximately 75% of its total primary energy supply from that source: mainly wood from natural forests, which is environmentally unsustainable.[60] Supply of electricity in both urban and rural areas is irregular, with regular black-outs, especially in the summer when the hydropower production drops sharply. Despite having proven natural gas reserves of 7.8 TCF, the Myanmar population still suffers from an important shortfall. This is due mainly to the government using the gas for export, especially to Thailand and China, a particularly important way of raising revenues and foreign exchange during the sanctions era.[61] In early 2013, the government formed the National Energy Management Committee (NEMC) to oversee the sector. The NEMC is a minister-level committee and formulates energy policy and plans in coordination with other key energy-related ministries.[62] Industrial demand for energy is low at present, but this is set to change as Myanmar develops its manufacturing base. The main issue therefore facing the government is how to increase its energy production for the domestic market and at the same time gradually remove energy subsidies that not only constitute unaffordable government expenditure, but also distort the energy market and do not incentivise the creation of a larger and more efficient energy sector.

Special Economic Zones (SEZs)

The development of SEZs is part of accelerating foreign direct investment in Myanmar. SEZs are attractive because the costs are known and land leases are not a problem for the investor. The government enacted the Special Economic Zone (SEZ) Law on 27 January 2012. The incentives for foreign investors include up to 75 years' land use rights for large-scale industry, low income tax rates, exemption of import duties for raw materials, machineries and equipment, no restriction on foreign shareholding, relaxed foreign exchange control, and government security support.[63] Two SEZs have already been established in ethnic regions causing massive land-grabbing: the Dawei SEZ in Tanintharyi Region and the Kyaukpyu SEZ in Rakhine State. Five other SEZs are planned in ethnic regions. The third SEZ is Thilawa, near Yangon. Issues of environmental degradation, pollution and the lack of benefits to the local community have been highlighted in parliament, but the government sees SEZs as a cornerstone of the country's economic development and a way to attract FDI.

Dawei Special Economic Zone was the first one planned and started in 2008. It made headlines abroad due to the extensive land-grabbing that affected the local population, without bringing them any tangible benefits. In addition it was understood that the Thai industries with most interest in the development of this zone, so close to their own border, were primarily planning to export the industries that were too dirty and polluting for their own country. The public outcry, infrastructural problems and lack of financial backing finally resulted in the withdrawal of the Italian Thai Development Company in 2012. Given the remoteness of the region, the lack of connectivity and no proximity to trade routes, not enough international investors could be found to back the project.[64] Everything, including the transport infrastructure, would have had to be built from scratch, with much of the machinery having to be transported on mud roads, resulting in high construction costs. The other issue was lack of local labour, as so many local people have migrated to Thailand where they are paid higher wages. In order to attract local labour, wages would have to be competitive with what is paid across the border. At the time of writing it is unclear what will happen to Dawei, and it is possible that it will be scaled down.[65]

The second SEZ, Kyaukpyu SEZ, is located on an island in Rakhine State, where a deep-sea port, a power plant and petrochemical factories are planned. This SEZ is directly linked to China's Shwe gas pipeline, as the port will serve to transfer oil to China's 741 km-long oil pipeline. Both the oil and gas pipelines will pump gas and oil to Kunming in Yunnan Province. A railway linking Kunming to Kyaukpyu was also planned. China's influence in Nay Pyi Taw has meant that the SEZ has had a lot of government support, but the more recent religious violence between Buddhist and Muslim communities has hampered the project's development. At the time of writing some of the development has stalled, and the railway seems to have been suspended. However, given the Shwe gas reserves, the pipelines are being finalised although the promoter of the SEZ has yet to be announced.[66]

Thilawa SEZ, the third in the series, is by far the most promising. Located only 20 km from Yangon, the zone is well placed to take advantage of the increasing labour migration to the commercial capital, the surrounding infrastructure such as roads and electricity connections, telecom and access to electricity—all vital parts in the establishment of a successful SEZ. Thilawa is also not too far from the international airport, allowing for multinationals involved in its development to travel there with ease. The Japanese government is particularly committed to the project, and the Japanese companies will be crucial in its success.

Decentralisation

As with all great economic reform stories across Asia, decentralisation is central to its success. Until the elections, both decentralisation and federalism were dirty words as they implied reduced power at the centre and potentially independent action by individual states (and regions, formerly divisions) that could lead to the 'disintegration of the union'. However, the new government has realised that micro-management at a central level will not work if the economy is to be developed. The 2008 constitution allowed for state and region legislative assemblies that have opened up a new political, administrative and fiscal space. Since 2011 there has been greater transparency in states and regions, and the regional assemblies feel that they have some more power.[67] As mentioned above, the government established a

Financial Commission and undertook a significant deconcentration of budgeting and planning functions.[68] All finance ministers of states and regions were able to speak their minds to the union minster in a World Bank-organised workshop. According to an interview with WB staff, this occasion allowed the state and region finance ministers to be very open about the difficulties they had and what still needed to be changed, especially with regard to taxes and revenues. Clearly fiscal decentralisation still has a long way to go, but regions and states do have powers they never had before. However, the government still seeks to maintain Nay Pyi Taw's top-down leadership, and states and regions have to tread very carefully.

In addition, the new administrative relationships and the division of responsibilities as defined in Schedule 2 of the constitution are unclear. 'The formally decentralized state and region departments have an ambiguous (and changing) relationship with both their "parent" union ministries, and the new state/region government. They do not form standalone administrative units, and they do not correspond neatly with the state/region ministerial portfolios.'[69] In August 2013, the president announced five significant public administration reform initiatives to bring more order to the confused accountabilities among state and region departments, ministers and parliaments. These included increasing state/region influence over human resources and further deconcentrating major union ministries.[70]

The importance of the economic reform process is Myanmar's overall reforms

The economic reforms are very much a pivot in the overall reform process. They play two roles, signalling first to the outside world that Myanmar is changing. Myanmar's accelerated development depends on how the foreign investors are able to come in and how the government learns to partner with the West. Second, the reforms have an intrinsic role in themselves—the objective being to develop the country to its full potential. The two are interrelated, as the more the country reforms, the louder the signal to the outside world. Clearly the signal has worked as the World Bank, amongst others, believes that this is a serious endeavour and so has started to engage with the government. The pace of reforms underlies the serious intent. It is in fact the term 'serious' which keeps cropping up in various interviews. When the WB started to re-engage with the Myanmar government at the end of 2011, it planned to post its staff in Thailand. Six months later, in 2012, the staff had to be relocated to Yangon and the first ever WB office opened in August 2012. One of the first issues the Bank had to deal with was the clearance of arrears. The WB arranged for a short-term loan for Myanmar to clear its arrears of 420 million dollars to the WB and 520 million dollars to ADB. Then a long-term loan was arranged to pay off the short-term loan and start with new loans for further development. The WB staff interviewed believe that their presence lends credibility to the reform process and that this attracts more people and businesses, creating a virtuous circle. According to the interviews, many agree that U Soe Thane, Minister of the President's Office, was driving the reform process, but for the WB the Ministry of Finance remains the main interlocutor. The president guides but in the end it is the technocrats who negotiate the details and undertake the reforms they deem necessary. This is already a change in the way things used to operate, allowing for specialist input in the change process.

Bottom line is that the economic outlook is more positive than it has ever been: according to the IMF, real GDP growth is expected to hit 8% in 2015, driven by commodity exports and higher investment. As Derek Tonkin, advisor to Bagan Capital, put it:

> In fact, economic progress in Myanmar, though slow, is steady. Foreign investment is being made and the environment is no better, no worse than elsewhere. Though the political process may be going through a 'bumpy patch', overall progress is more than balanced by economic development, supported by the international financial institutions.

The issue of sanctions

In April 2012 the EU suspended all its sanctions, announcing a new chapter in its relations with Myanmar. Norway, Canada and Australia followed suit. Only their arms embargoes remained in place. The US announced that it would ease only some of its financial sanctions. The ban on the import of all Myanmar products was retained.[71] President Thein Sein's government did not understand why after the 2012 by-elections and Daw Aung San Suu Kyi joining parliament, as well as the release of political prisoners, the US would maintain sanctions at all. However, the activists in the West, some of the ethnic armed groups (including the KNU) and some former political parties, such as the leaders of the Shan Nationalities League of Democracy (SNLD), the Arakan League for Democracy (ALD) and the Rakhine Nationals Progressive Party (RNPP), campaigned against the lifting of sanctions, saying that it was too early and that the government first needed to prove itself. Some believed that a nationwide ceasefire would be an appropriate measure of the government's goodwill; others wanted the sanctions to remain in place until at least 2015, the date of the next elections.[72] In London the Foreign and Commonwealth Office announced the lifting of sanctions at a special Burma stakeholders' meeting. The Burma Campaign UK and other activists who were present were quite incensed, many arguing that the government was making the wrong decision. The FCO team seemed to hide behind the fact that this was an EU-wide decision that Britain could not stop and the sanctions were just suspended and not lifted. The announcement and subsequent discussion sounded like an apology to the activists, showing how Britain was still very much divided over the issue.[73] Debate about sanctions seems to have continued unabated.[74] Some US sanctions in fact remain. In May 2015 Congress voted to keep certain sanctions in place despite the reforms.[75]

Part of the problem with the debate on sanctions is that activists have refused to acknowledge that sanctions actually never stopped the military leadership from ruling and only harmed the general population. More recently discussions have emerged that sanctions in fact were successful, since they apparently 'forced' the new government to reform. As the first chapters of this book have shown, this is blatantly incorrect and the reforms were started for quite different reasons. Despite this, and despite evident progress, some activist organisations continue to call for sanctions. In April 2012 the Conflict Risk Network published an elaborate report decrying the economic reforms of the new government and insisting that the reforms were not benefitting ordinary people. It stated:

> Resource extraction projects have provided extensive opportunities for corruption. Less than 1% of gas revenues generally have entered the government budget. Until recently, the exchange rate was fixed around six Burmese kyat to the U.S. dollar compared to the illegal market rate of 800 per U.S. dollar. By officially recording public revenues at the lower official exchange rate—not the actual market value—military elites in control of the government have been able to siphon off profits to their personal coffers and private offshore accounts.[76]

The report[77] did agree that once the exchange rate had been unified, this practice would possibly be curtailed. It also pointed out the important nexus between the natural resources and conflict. However, rather than focusing on how both the army and the ethnic armed groups benefited from the control of natural resource extraction in their respective areas, the report preferred to accuse foreign investment companies of supporting corrupt practices:

> Projects in the energy, hydropower and mining and gems industries have the strongest links to conflict-affected areas and serve as drivers of conflict. Foreign

companies operating in these industries are generally required to operate in partnership with a state-owned Burmese firm. This requirement enables the concealment of revenues and impedes transparent disclosures of royalties, profit-sharing, signing bonuses, profits, fees and taxes, creating a deeply corrupt environment among government and corporate actors. There is a high likelihood that revenues from the oil and gas sector—including from the construction of exploration and production equipment and transit pipelines, fund the military-backed regime.[78]

President Thein Sein is deeply aware of the corrupt practices of the previous regime and has on many occasions called for clean, responsible government. In September 2013 a new anti-corruption law came into effect, replacing the former suppression of corruption law (1948). The new law resulted in the establishment of an Anti-Corruption Commission, and also requires all government officials to declare their assets.[79] Clean governance is much easier to achieve with the help of multinational investments, however, and the introduction of good practice in all industries. Myanmar joining EITI is a case in point. In its Framework for Economic and Social Reforms, corruption is mentioned several times; and joining the EITI is showcased as a way of managing its natural resources responsibly and getting rid of corruption:

> Myanmar has huge natural resources but international experience clearly shows that such resources can as often be a curse as a blessing. In order to ensure that the extraction of natural resources produces real benefits for people, GOM is presently reviewing the potential value of the Extractive Industries Transparency Initiative (EITI), a global standard for the promotion of revenue transparency. This standard requires that companies publish what they pay and governments publish what they receive. GOM is committed to early adoption of the standard, starting with an appointment of a senior government official in leading the efforts, followed by the formation of multi-stakeholder group and a secretariat to prepare the application and reporting procedures in the next two years.[80]

Many issues remain

Whilst the president and his closest team of advisers are committed to the reforms, in particular the economic reforms, there is resistance from many officials at all levels. Sometimes this is due to bureaucratic inertia; sometimes particular individuals benefit from the status quo; at other times there are rivalries within and between ministries. The president recognised this as an early impediment and mentioned it in one of his speeches: 'in this transitional period, we are working hard for transition to a new system. So, we will take punitive action against those sticking to (the) red tape system, and those without a sense of democratic spirit'.[81] There is also the issue of limited capacity: when lower levels of the administration have never had to take decisions and responsibility before, they wait for top-down instructions, lest they are held responsible for mistakes made.

Decentralisation

Whilst the Union government has been providing resources to states and regions and has encouraged an independent approach to budgeting, the constitution still does not give enough scope for real progress on the decentralisation agenda. Education and health are still controlled centrally, although some embryonic changes there are being made too.[82] The constitution is unlikely to be changed in the near future, so effective decentralisation will need a creative approach from the centre and increased capacity at region and state level, so as to maximise what is indeed possible already.

Land

One of the main issues that remain to be addressed properly by the new government is the issue of land ownership and land rights. According to BCN, land confiscation has been on the rise since the late 2000s, largely because of the development of agri-businesses, which have seen nearly 2 million acres allocated to the private sector during the SLORC years. The concerns have continued under President Thein Sein's government, as economic development and foreign direct investment require land to be made available to multinational firms.[83] Land rights protests have been prominently displayed across the local media, some activists and protesters demanding return of land that was taken in the SLORC years, others protesting more recent land-grabs. According to the law, all land in Myanmar belongs to the state, and individuals only have lease rights. The new land law of 2012 seems to have encouraged expropriation from those who have lived and worked on it in order to facilitate economic development. 'The Farmland Law stipulates that land can be legally bought, sold and transferred on a land market with land use certificates (LUCs).' There are no safeguards for those who might not have official titles, but who still have been on the land for generations. The Vacant, Fallow, and Virgin Land Law (VFV Law) legally allows the government to reallocate villagers' farm and forestlands to domestic and foreign investors. This has also resulted in monopolistic power over the allocation of farmland being given to the Farmland Administration Body (FAB), chaired by the minister from the Ministry of Agriculture and Irrigation (MOAI). According to BCN, FAB is beyond the judiciary branch, meaning that aggrieved farmers are deprived of any legal recourse.[84] This does create dangers, especially in ethnic states, where recent conflict means that villagers fled their land but could now come back and find it taken over or 'transferred' for large-scale investment. The Union government does not need state government approval for large-scale investment in the state or region, and the Myanmar Investment Commission (MIC) has considerable power over the approval and direction of foreign investment in the country, without providing recourse via formal or legal channels for those who may disagree.[85] None of this is good news for the small farmers, either in ethnic states or elsewhere, and whilst a new land policy is under preparation, the government will have a hard time balancing industrial and foreign investment priorities with the interests of farmers.[86]

Education, skills and capacity gaps

Myanmar also suffers from large skills and education gaps that will slow future growth unless tackled quickly. According to research done by McKinsey in 2010, only 5% of the country's workers had tertiary and higher education credentials, and only 15% had finished secondary education.[87] An informal survey by Myanmar Egress in 2009/10 found that even in urban Yangon, those with university degrees could not secure a commensurate job unless they had taken some NGO or private-sector training. This clearly shows that there was and still is no confidence in the government higher education system. Whilst the government has embarked on an education reform process, it will take the best part of a generation to see the effects of this.[88] And even if a lot is planned in the education sector, the government also has to work to eliminate barriers to job creation, and offer training to adults who have not been trained and cannot return to school.

Industry, infrastructure and the rest

On the industrial side, manufacturing needs a helping hand. Most of Myanmar's manufacturers are small, with ten or fewer employees. They have to import most of the machinery from somewhere in Asia. Given the lack of access to capital, much of this machinery is twenty years old or more, and the companies are unable to modernise. Economies of scale are impossible to achieve under these circumstances.[89] Given the isolation of the country for many decades, management practice has not been able to incorporate international best practice, and there is little knowledge about product development or modern engineering. This is compounded by the intermittent power supply, which also makes asset utilisation low, resulting in low productivity (single shifts, with the average daily labour hours in Myanmar manufacturing firms being only around 40% of the levels in other Asian economies).[90]

Another question that has yet to be addressed is the fate of the State-owned Enterprises (SEEs) and whether they will eventually be privatised. It is unclear how the three SEEs—Myanmar Oil and Gas Enterprise (MOGE), Myanmar Post and Telecommunications (MPT), and Myanmar Electric Power Enterprise (MEPE)—will be able to continue to operate in a modernised and reformed economy. However, the Framework for Economic and Social Reforms does state that: 'While all SEEs are now subject to operating on a commercial basis and using the market-determined exchange rate, further reforms on equalisation, commercialization and possible privatization will be undertaken in the future.'[91] The same question needs to be posed when looking at the two military controlled conglomerates: the Union of Myanmar Economic Holdings (UMEH) and the Myanmar Economic Corporation (MEC).[92]

Foreign investment was held back initially because the new foreign investment law was delayed. The law that had been drafted by the Ministry of Finance and Revenue at the end of 2011 was submitted to parliament, where the lower house asked for some amendments. The law was then stuck in the upper house of parliament, unable to finish their work on the bill before the end of the parliamentary session in May 2012. The bill was shrouded in secrecy, as the initial draft law was not made public. Foreign investors have been having difficulties with inconsistent interpretation of laws that are sometimes at odds with other laws. The WB staff interviewed believe that the domestic and foreign investment laws need to be amalgamated and that inconsistencies and clarity issues need to be sorted.

Not only in the industrial sector are there problems that need to be resolved: also in agriculture. According to Rieffel, boosting agriculture productivity to ASEAN-average levels will require improvements in almost every area: land ownership, crop credit, floor prices, extension services, research, infrastructure, etc.[93] In order to provide enough energy for development, the government might even have to renegotiate some of the gas contracts it has with China and Thailand, a difficult prospect at best. In the meantime, the government is raising revenue with three 'gem auctions' a year (jadeite, rubies and pearls), much more frequently than under SLORC. Each auction has yielded gross sales in the order of $1 billion, and some more than $2 billion.[94] The government will have to rethink its extractive industries of coal, copper, gold, iron, lead, limestone and zinc so as to make them more sustainable. Timber has already been extracted for over twenty years at unsustainable levels, and all that is smuggled (as in fact a lot of jadeite is as well, especially to China) deprives the country of well-needed revenues.

Infrastructure also needs more attention. To date Myanmar is unconnected by rail or road to any of its neighbours. The border infrastructure on the Chinese border is best, largely because it has been developed by China. The Indian and Thai borders are woefully underdeveloped. Whilst new mobile phone companies have started to improve the telecommunications sector, the telephone and internet penetration are amongst the lowest in the world. According to Rieffel, when the new government came to power, Myanmar's internet access was limited to 'a single gateway to the global fibre optic network and 1GB per second of bandwidth'. Most websites are now unblocked but there are no extra gateways, making the internet connections very slow.[95]

Myanmar has yet to realise and utilise its geographical advantage to the full. The Western press might dub it the 'last frontier' where millions can be made by those willing to take risks, but in order to become competitive with the Asian markets, the problems listed above need to be addressed quickly. The decades of under-investment need to be reversed, and the private sector alone will not be able to do it. The government has realised that it has a role to play in facilitating changes, but its role is wider in that it has to strengthen the institutions that will make the necessary international investment in Myanmar stick and be successful. It also needs to reduce the urban–rural service provision and infrastructure gap, and remove bureaucratic hurdles that keep the costs for FDI high.

Despite all these issues, Myanmar's economic landscape changed dramatically between 2011 and 2014. With Western sanctions suspended, a large number of international and multinational companies have started to come to Myanmar. The press has dubbed Myanmar 'the last frontier' where big money can be made. Myanmar's natural resources and growing middle classes are a big attraction. Given that there are social and economic needs at all levels, there is definitely a big market place for any company that wants to sell or produce goods. However, Western companies not only have to contend with the issues described above, but with small mundane issues such as the lack of hotel rooms and office space and the lack of internationally-educated and English-speaking local employees, driving salaries up for those who do have relevant skills and qualifications, and leading Myanmar companies to suffer as the best staff leave for better opportunities, and better working conditions opened up by MNCs.

The winners and losers

The many changes will not only have winners, but also losers. Till now crony businessmen dominated the Myanmar economy. They will continue to dominate for a while, as they were strengthened just before the handover of power in 2011; but their role will diminish over time and their political power will wane as the political reforms succeed. Cronies, however, do not seem to fight the new system. Rather they seem to have rebranded or repositioned themselves, some speaking to the media and others reaching out to Daw Aung San Suu Kyi, offering funds. As Myanmar's economic model changes, and personal connections that are still important today decrease in value, their position will have to adapt and change as well.

The military owns vast holding companies—UMEHL and MEC that were mentioned above. These companies monopolise many markets, and some foreign investment had to be through joint ventures with them. However, in the long run it is unclear how both conglomerates will continue to operate, and how far the joint ventures will change their business practices. The presence of Vice President-1 Tin Aung Myint Oo, a hard-liner personally selected by the former dictator Than Shwe, who had very close links to the old business elite, was an obstacle to the reform process. However, he resigned due to health reasons and departed in July 2012. In the same way, the old guard of the military holding companies will eventually retire and the younger generation will have to choose whether to go with the reform process or to resist it.

Role of the international agencies/development partners in the reform process

As of 2012 the international community, especially the Western countries and Japan, became fully engaged in Myanmar's reform process. After the 2012 by-elections, the government was seen as serious, and even before sanctions were dropped, Western powers and Japan started to normalise their diplomatic relations. The Nay Pyi Taw Accord for Effective Development Cooperation signed in January 2013 allowed for donors to coordinate and collaborate in supporting the reform process.[96] As mentioned above, the World Bank and the Asian Development Bank sorted out Myanmar's debt arrears problems, and this in turn brought additional aid and relief from the Paris Club, Japan and Norway, resulting in a total of $6 billion of debt relief given to Myanmar by January 2013. ACLEDA Bank plc set up a new microfinance institution in March 2013 with the aim of providing loans to more than 200,000 people by 2020. At the end of 2013 Myanmar became a member of the Multilateral Investment Guarantee Agency, which provides risk guarantees to investors.

The role of the development partners has become important in two ways: first it provided validation for President Thein Sein's vision and what the government was doing. Internationally there was still scepticism as to whether real change was happening. The support of the INGOs and the development partners underscored the progress. Second their involvement was crucial in providing the technical assistance that Myanmar needed. As Myanmar approached its second wave of reforms, the government had to identify what specific help it needed and which development partners were there to provide advice on how the funds should be spent by bringing international best practice to the table, creating a partnership with common goals. In addition, the reform process needed the financial support that can only be provided by the international community. The international community in turn knows that the further the government reforms go, the harder it will be to roll them back. The reforms in some way have developed a life of their own.

Discussions in Yangon showed that the development partners have been surprised at how far they have been able to go despite the fact that the military is still a dominant player. Their main aim is to make sure that Myanmar does not become aid-dependent. The approach has to be one of sustainable development, which helps the private sector develop and allows people to take opportunities forward. Many of the development partners see their role as helping the Myanmar government with private-sector development, and the discussions with Nay Pyi Taw focus on policies, policy advice and technical assistance, but not on more aid. The government has the same attitude and the foreign economic relations department is weary of more debt, so whilst grants are welcomed, loans are not seen as the best way forward.[97]

One of the main development partners is the EU, and as a part of EU support the company IMG was tasked to support the economic reforms with two projects. The first IMG-led project was conceived in a time of sanctions shortly after the elections, in early 2011, but was broadly focused on Myanmar reforms, as the new government was coming in. Although the international community did not perceive the leadership as fully legitimate, there was a feeling that change was happening and things were moving forward. In 2012 the reform process had started, but there was no hard evidence yet that it would stay the course. At the time the World Bank and ADB were discussing the clearance of arrears and Japan was re-engaging, but the UN was still working under a restricted mandate. The EU started looking at 'soft' entry points to support the economic reform process. A second IMG project was planned to help Myanmar with meeting its Millennium Development Goals (MDGs), and to do that government capacity had to be improved. Much support had already gone into CSOs, because working with the government had been impossible. Now with the new government in place there was a window of opportunity to cooperate. The second programme started in January 2013, complementary to the previous project, after the release of the political prisoners, the suspension of the Myitsone dam and the reduction of censorship had taken place. During the first six months specialists came to assess the situation and to discuss needs with eleven ministries, including amongst others the Ministries of Commerce, Finance, Science and Technology, Health and Forestry. With the Ministry of Forestry a project relating to forestry and environmental conservation was conceived. A second area of development was found in helping improve trade. The project was to help change the enabling environment for general systems preferences (GSP), the removal of tariffs. Even though Myanmar was classified as an LDC country, it had not been able to access any privileges, including the standard 0% EU tariff, due to the Western sanctions regime. However, in order to trade with the EU, food safety standards, timber legislations, weights and measures needed to be sorted out. The project was to give technical advice on this. The emerging advisory institution MDRI, specifically the Centre for Economic and Social Development (CESD) that was advising the president on economic affairs, was also supported under that same grant. IMG worked with economic advisers and helped set up an advisory institution that could provide advice on call. Some economists, especially the civilians, were quite surprised when they were asked to help. After the creation in November 2012 of the Myanmar Peace Centre (MPC), it too was supported. The EU was trying to support institutions that could further policy reform and improvement, as well as offer the Myanmar government help to get in line with international and regional regulations, treaties and norms.

The experience of the IMG-led projects is an example of how the partnerships between aid agencies and the Myanmar government had to be developed slowly. At the start some ministries were reluctant to admit to a reform process. Some were not sure how far it would go and if it would stick. Many had memories that after 1988 an economic reform process had been initiated, but had never been fully implemented. Meetings were held mainly in Nay Pyi Taw (the EU did not have an office in Myanmar at that time). Approaching the ministries offering help and trying to assess needs solicited two types of responses—either a keen interest in collaboration, or a total rejection of help. Those who were positively inclined knew exactly what they needed and wanted. Ministries would talk about needs of the country first, then ASEAN and then international norms.

> It was interesting how excited some were to engage. They had lists of issues where they needed technical assistance. At first I thought they would not be interested in international treaties and agreements. They were very interested on getting everything sorted with the ASEAN economic community that starts 2015 and they were very aware of the ASEAN chairmanship and wanting to be working to be able to host it with a sense of pride and some experience and knowledge.[98]

But the reforms were only really accepted after the first presidential reshuffle, which gave more powers to the reformists and side-lined the hard-liners in the government. This created a critical mass of officials in Nay Pyi Taw, and the fear of sitting 'on the wrong side of the fence' was largely removed. Some ministers started to show a real sense of pride in being able to catch up, and it even created a new sense of urgency to get things done before 2015. Myanmar government staff who had been cut off from access to knowledge and information and restricted in what they could change and improve were suddenly able to access knowledge and international good practice, resulting in great enthusiasm at a personal level and great momentum at an institutional level to enact policy change.

The EU has had to balance international advice carefully with knowledge on the ground. The IMG projects tried to pair international consultants and Myanmar specialists, so as to get maximum buy-in by stakeholders. Some ministries remained more difficult to collaborate with than others, mostly because of individuals and their views rather than the ministries themselves.[99] Sometimes ministries felt that they had a particular technical weakness that they did not want to have exposed, or worried that they would be looked down upon, and some were afraid of change. Another difficulty was the constant commute to Nay Pyi Taw at a time when there were restrictions on foreigners living in Nay Pyi Taw. The EU also had to learn how to deal with the formality of planning that has been institutionalised in Nay Pyi Taw. Planning had to be done at a high level to get meetings organised, sometimes taking weeks if a minister had to be involved. However, once the project was agreed, things could go quickly.

Overall the EU projects have had a broad reach. They have helped improve public financial management, helped update the customs system, helped the ILO with an initial grant to look at labour laws and standards, and even helped with police education. By mid 2013 it was widely recognised that crowd management and issues of trust between the community and police were priorities. The EU ran pilot projects bringing police from Europe who went to see all stakeholders and started to discuss the public role of the police. The police project is particularly important, as with the new laws allowing peaceful protests, and the media being much more critical and vocal, relations between the public and the police force had deteriorated.[100] A multi-ministerial committee to discuss land issues was supported, changing the 'working in silos' tradition where ministries never communicated with each other, even if the issue was related to work across ministries.

With all these developments, the EU has become a prime partner and supporter of the Myanmar reform process. They are however not alone. The other key partner is Japan.

The role of Japan in the economic reform process

Historically speaking, Japan and Myanmar have had a difficult relationship. The Japanese invasion during World War II made Myanmar a war-ravaged colony in Japan's empire. In the post-war years, Japan's relationship with Myanmar improved, with Myanmar government officials being trained by Japanese army officers and civilians. Huge overseas development aid (ODA) cemented the relationship. These payments had started as war reparations in the 1950s, but in the 1960s became loans and grants for economic assistance.[101] In the decade between 1977 and 1988, Japan gave around $3.71 billion in assistance. However, with the advent of the State Law and Order Restoration Council, Japan suspended its ODA. Japan became one of the only Asian countries which heeded the Western sanctions regime, but without suspending aid or the Japan International Cooperation Agency (JICA)'s involvement completely. The relationship remained lukewarm, and Japanese companies stayed away while Chinese and other Southeast and East Asian firms poured in to take advantage of Myanmar's new open-door policy.

In the recent reform process Japan has come back and has been pivotal, becoming the biggest donor offering infrastructure and policy advice. President

Thein Sein's five-day trip to Japan in April 2012[102] resulted in the cancellation of $3.8 billion in debt owed by Myanmar.

> Japan PM Yoshihiko Noda announced that Japan would implement a two-step process to reduce Burma's debt burden: a ¥127.4 billion (US$1.6 billion) debt write-off and the cancellation of ¥176.1 billion (US$2.2 billion) in overdue charges from the past two decades. The cancellation would be contingent on a year of monitoring of the regime's democratic reforms. For its part, Burma will return ¥198.9 billion (US$2.5 billion) in previous borrowings from Japan by taking out new long-term concessionary loans.[103] Noda said that Japan would also provide ¥5 billion (US$62.5 million) in aid to assist Burma's ethnic communities and improve medical care, as well as to support disaster prevention, agriculture, and rural development programs. In addition, Japan and the regime signed an agreement to cooperate on developing the port of Thilawa, a 2,400-hectare Special Economic Zone in Rangoon Division.[104]

All combined, the agreed deals (valued at around $5billion) have made Japan a major player in Myanmar, and are financially much more important than the $76 million US aid package in 2011–12 and the EU's $200 million.[105]

According to interviews in Tokyo, a few well-connected Japanese businessmen made the re-engagement with Myanmar a big priority for the Abe government. Japan was able to build on decades-old ties of the post-war years, when the elites of both countries were close. The Japan–Myanmar Association includes retired government bureaucrats and executives from trading houses Marubeni Corporation and Mitsubishi Corporation. When discussing Japan's current involvement in Myanmar, two names come up regularly: Hideo Watanabe, chairman of the Japan–Myanmar association, and Yohei Sasakawa, who runs the Nippon Foundation and was made Japan's representative to help with the peace process.[106] The Nippon Foundation (NF) was allowed to deliver $64,000 of aid, including rice and medicines, directly to internally displaced persons. It seems that a budget of $3 million has been allocated to support the NF's humanitarian assistance.

The government did not need much prodding by the business community. The first trip since the newly elected Japanese government in 2012 was by Deputy Prime Minister and Finance Minister Taro Aso[107] to Myanmar. Japan's focus on Myanmar has been explained as a revival of the 1977 Fukuda doctrine, where Japan rejected its role as a military power, promoted mutual confidence, mutual trust and a partnership with ASEAN to build a prosperous Southeast Asia. Japan clearly wants a stronger economic presence in Southeast Asia, and Myanmar is an opening market for its industries. This requires a strategic policy with regard to ASEAN countries. Japanese re-engagement must also be seen in light of a deteriorating relationship with China, and many in Myanmar believe that with enough effort Myanmar can realistically compete with what China has done. However, few realise how far China has penetrated over twenty years of engagement, and China's investment amounts to more than $14 billion in 2011, due to investment in energy infrastructure.[108]

Japanese companies have been flooding into Myanmar, complementing the aid package that is driven by government policy. Large high-profile projects that are also seen as helping the Myanmar people include the, 'Development of Participatory Multiplication and Distribution System for Quality Rice Seeds' project in the Ayeyarwady delta, which started in 2011 and will run till 2016; also the 'Rehabilitation of Baluchaung No2 Hydropower Plant' which was constructed in 1960 as part of Japan's war compensation to Myanmar. Then there is the development of the 2,400-hectare Thilawa Special Economic Zone, discussed earlier in this chapter, including a port and an industrial park. Thilawa is being largely financed by a consortium of Japanese companies, including Mitsubishi Corporation, Sumitomo Corporation and Marubeni Corporation, and should be completed in 2015. The good relations continue. In May 2013, Prime Minister Abe visited Myanmar and promised fresh loans of $220 million. Japan clearly sees Myanmar as a strategically important country where, despite some risks, there are huge profits to be made. Given Japan's stagnating economy, the search for new markets is a clear driver in Tokyo's moves.

Overall Myanmar's economic reforms have made a good start, but it will take much energy and determination to stay the course. The country has been growing at 8.5% p.a. and is due to continue with this level of high growth.[109] The path of economic reconstruction will not be smooth or straightforward. The stakes are very high as there has never been anything like this in the country. As with the other reforms, much depends on the 2015 elections and Daw Aung San Suu Kyi's moves. It is unclear what the NLD's economic policies might be. A change of government could negatively impact on the confidence of international investors and multinational firms. Political stability is a prerequisite for the reforms to continue; yet if there is a stand-off on who will become president, stability could quickly be eroded.

There are other possible cases for unrest, not least people's high expectations, and whether these are met quickly enough. The issue of land-grabbing has already impacted negatively on the most vulnerable sections of society and led to loud, albeit peaceful protests. And then there is always the risk of the

'Dutch disease', meaning when dependence on exports of natural resource does not allow for a development of the manufacturing sector with the necessary jobs to counter unemployment. There are issues with labour exploitation as well. Despite the passage of a Minimum Wage Law in 2013, there has been no deal between the employers and workers. The current proposal is $3.24 for a day's work, which activists and labourers are rejecting.[110] The government has to find a coherent vision for balanced development, with a diverse economic base that will allow equitable and inclusive growth. This has to include effective institution building and strategies for industrialisation and sustainable development. Issues that remain include ensuring that the exchange rate remains stable and not over-valued, tackling corruption, protecting against the possibility of rising inflation and dealing with rampant land speculation. At the time of writing this has not yet been achieved.

Myanmar is located between India, China and Southeast Asia. All three key drivers of economic growth, Myanmar could develop as a connective hub between these powerhouses, boosting its own development in the process. However, to do this without harming its own domestic small-scale industries will prove a real challenge in light of the 2015 ASEAN free trade area.

The government has tried to implement its many reforms as quickly as possible, with the 2015 election deadline in mind. However, it has not been able to finalise certain key laws, such as the new investment law, the companies act and the banks and financial institutions law[111] which are all still stuck in parliament.[112] Despite this, Yangon stock exchange is due to open in December 2015.[113] The exchange rate has weakened by around 25% ($1=K1292 at the time of writing), putting further pressure on the economy.[114]

Whilst there has been a slowdown in the last couple of years, this was to be expected as many of the early reforms were 'low-hanging fruit' that could show quick results. Now the more granular level of reforms has to be undertaken, which is more complex with more ministries getting involved. The difficulty is enhanced by the fact that states and regions have been allocated more resources than ever before, and also have to develop a strategy for their area. Such changes take time and need to be coordinated.

Figure 1: Teaching team in Mandalay 2005 (KYH, TMMT, ML, Robert Taylor, Eric Thompson and Rachel Safman)

Figure 2: Social Science summer course for academics University of Yangon 2006

Figure 3: Pre Singapore Conference dinner at Royal Thazin Restaurant in Yangon 2006. Includes Myanmar Egress founders KYH, NWM, SNT and KNK

Figure 4: Ja Nan Lahtaw at the 2006 Singapore Conference

Figure 5: Myanmar Egress 2007 clockwise from top NWM, ML, SNT, KNK, TMT and UHMS

Figure 6: ME delivering aid and doing needs assessments - Pe Aung Zin 2008

Figure 7: NWM meeting Ban Ki Moon 2008

Figure 8: ME graduation ceremony 2009

Figure 9: First ME research methods course 2010

Figure 10: TMT and NWM preparing for the elections 2010

Figure 11: NWM funeral January 2012

Figure 12: DASSK condoles with NWM's mother 2012

Figure 13: ME younger generation Thei Su San, Htike Htike Aung, Nan Thein Gi and MK

Figure 14: Ethnic education leaders meet with CESR staff 2013

Figure 15: ML meets the president. ANO, UHMS, TMT and Zaganar also in the picture

Figure 16: NCA signing ceremony in NPT Oct 2015

6

THE REFORM OF MYANMAR'S EDUCATION SYSTEM

We need more and more human resources of intellectuals and intelligentsia in building a modern, developed democratic nation... Therefore, we will promote the nation's education standard to meet the international level and encourage human resource development... (President Thein Sein, inaugural speech)[1]

These words mark a sea change in official attitude when it comes to Myanmar's education system, where everything foreign was kept at arm's length. Nevertheless, these were the words with which President Thein Sein set out to reform the education system.

During reform processes, it is not unusual for the education sector to become a battleground as the government and various international actors jostle over how best to influence the next generation. Often they are intent on propagating international 'good practice', linked to Western political agendas. Education has always been used as a political tool,[2] and in Myanmar things have been no different. As the government of President Thein Sein developed its reform agenda, education joined the list in fourth place after national reconciliation, ethnic peace and economic reforms, all of which have been discussed in previous chapters. What has happened in the education sector since 2011 is at least as contested as the ethnic peace process and certainly more controversial than the broad economic reforms[3] that seem to have the support of most people at home and abroad. The education reform process not only showcases how different power-hubs within the government (the president, the parliamentary speaker, the NLD and the Ministry of Education) jostle across party lines, but also how INGOs with diverse political agendas fight over what is seen as a crucial area of development in Myanmar.[4] It has been difficult to accommodate the competing domestic and international agendas, and as a result the review and reform processes in education are anything but streamlined, clear or transparent. The debate around education was at the origin of the reform process (as discussed in Chapter 1). Therefore it is clear that education will remain an important factor in the 2015 elections and a crucial problem for the government beyond 2015.

Myanmar has a very diverse education system: the Ministry of Education runs government schools, but there are also monastic schools, other faith-based schools and private schools, as well as a myriad of different ethnic education systems in ethnic majority areas. The section below gives a very brief overview of Myanmar's mainstream education landscape before turning to a survey of 308 teachers who between 2011 and 2012 documented what were Myanmar's prime education problems. The chapter then moves on to look at the competing reform agendas and processes, discussing if and how the actual education problems are being addressed. The chapter ends with a discussion about ethnic education systems and how the education reform process in the ethnic states is disconnected from the peace process, despite the synergies that should bring these processes together.

Education systems in Myanmar

Post-independence Burma's education system was considered advanced compared to the rest of the South/Southeast Asian region, and Rangoon University was known as a beacon of higher education in Asia.[5] However, decades of under-investment and civil strife resulted in the slow and steady decay of the state education system at all levels across the country. During the socialist era (1962–88) school buildings continued to be built both in the cities and in the villages, making schools more easily accessible in rural areas, yet teacher education and pay deteriorated markedly. It was also at this time that Burmese was made the medium for teaching in all schools, abolishing the colonial legacy of English-medium schools for the elite and disallowing the use of ethnic languages in schools in the ethnic majority areas. This in turn had repercussions in universities, as textbooks and other literature were not available in Burmese, leading to a deterioration of standards in higher education. In the 1980s and 1990s only UNICEF and JICA had Memoranda of Understanding with the government and were able to get involved in education at school level. Apart from this, the Myanmar education system was literally cut off from the rest of the world for a few decades.

In 2001–2 the government established a '30-year education development plan' in order to develop a 'learned society' for the knowledge age, involving the expansion of schools as a priority. This was in line with the other meagre reforms spearheaded by SLORC/SPDC in other areas. The government even signed up to the 'Education for All' (EFA) movement in 2003. However, despite the consistently high primary enrolment ratio, there are still not enough schools (today there are a total of 40,992 basic education schools in Myanmar)[6] and there is a very high drop-out rate, estimated at around 34 per cent, as well as a high repetition rate in both rural and urban areas.[7]

In part such a drop-out is based on the high direct costs of sending children to school. Although government schooling is free in principle, parents are expected to contribute to the financing of education, as state expenditure on education as a share of GDP has decreased steadily.[8] Recent research shows that parents and the local community bear 70 per cent of the education costs, as the government only pays teacher salaries, but parents have to pool money for repairs as well as tuition (to supplement teacher salaries) and they bear the cost of books and uniforms.[9] In the rural areas this is compounded by the high opportunity cost for parents who need their children's help at work. Ethnic areas have further problems as Burmese is the only officially recognised language for instruction in schools. The remoteness of many ethnic areas means that it is difficult to secure government-trained teachers for these schools.[10]

Those who cannot afford to go to state schools or are excluded for other reasons go to monastic schools (or other types of community schools) or forego their education altogether. Monastic schools were outlawed during the socialist period as of 1962 and only allowed to return in 1993, when they were allowed to register and gain a certain legal status. At this time some of the biggest monastic networks established themselves, but more schools have continued to emerge and not all are 'counted' by the government. Currently around 1,431 monastic schools have been recognised by the Ministry of Religious Affairs (MoRA) and cater for around 215,000 children by teaching the government curriculum.[11] The monastery provides very basic facilities—often just a large hall or small building, and well-wishers have to pool their funds to pay for teachers' salaries. Needless to say there is often no money for repairs, books, tables or benches. Since Myanmar signed the 'Education for All' declaration, monastic schools are now seen as part of the solution to providing education across all sections of society and across the country where the state does not reach. The ministerial language referring to monastic schools reflects these changes, as what was formerly seen as 'non-formal' education is increasingly referred to as 'formal' education provision.[12] Recently monastic schools have been included in a government-sponsored and UNICEF-run (although limited) in-service child-centred teacher training programme. In 2013 the Ministry of Religious Affairs started to provide a 'donation' to all registered monastic schools to help with teachers' salaries.[13] At the time of writing, it is unclear whether this would translate into a regular donation to support these schools. The immediate effect was that some donors then stopped their support, believing that the state was now going to carry the costs.[14]

A recent alternative to state and monastic schools, albeit only for the rich,[15] is private education. As mentioned earlier, civil society and the emerging middle classes started to develop different types of private schooling in the early 2000s, although the law allowing private schools to register was only passed in 2012.[16] Today private schools exist at pre-elementary, elementary, secondary and higher education level and cater to the popular demands for full schooling as well as specialist training in English, Chinese, computing, accounting and business. Private schools generally do not teach the government curriculum, so children cannot move on to higher education in Myanmar but have to go abroad instead. In the academic year 2010–11 the Ministry of Education granted ten privately-run high schools the right to operate, showing that the government is toying with the idea of increasing education access through the private sector, as long as these schools teach the Myanmar national curriculum.[17]

Education issues today

Despite the different forms of schooling available to different sections of society, the education sector still faces major problems.[18] A survey conducted between 2011 and 2012 in Yangon across state, monastic and private schools revealed that 90 per cent of the teachers who were asked if the education system needed to be reformed felt that this was indeed necessary.[19] Education reforms usually start with an overhaul of the curriculum. It was interesting to note that the teachers surveyed thought that the curriculum (which had been last reformed in 2002) did not need a total overhaul, but rather that separate subjects needed updating and the textbooks needed to be made more student-friendly.

In fact student–teacher ratios were identified as the biggest problem that teachers face. Teachers ideally wanted to see between 30 and 40 students in a class. However in many schools, especially in poorer areas and monastic schools, classrooms will routinely have to accommodate between 60 and 100 students. Government schools in middle-class areas have a more appropriate student–teacher ratio—but even then teachers view it as a problem. The root of this lies in teacher shortages, as the teaching profession is increasingly seen as low status, due to bad pay and difficult conditions. Those who do become teachers tend to move through the ranks from primary schools to secondary schools for their promotion.[20] This results in a glut of urban-based secondary teachers with fewer students, and a dearth of primary school teachers especially in rural areas.

Teachers complained about the time they have to cover the curriculum, especially in middle and high school classes. One teacher gave a typical example: 'We don't have time. Let me say, for biology we need 18 periods for teaching, 4 periods for practicals, so it is altogether 22 periods. But in practice I have only 21 periods for this month. [...] We are in haste every month, we feel like changing it.'

Because of UNICEF and JICA's influence over many years prior to the reforms, the Ministry of Education has theoretically championed the child-centred approach (CCA) across all Myanmar schools. However, these methods were rarely applied in practice as teachers focused on getting the children through the exams and preferred to use rote learning. A concerted effort by INGOs and NGOs in the late 2000s also led to CCA being adopted in many monastic schools.[21] In fact CCA has been pushed across Myanmar schools in an almost crusade-like way, as Western INGOs in particular want to 'improve' teaching in Myanmar classrooms—often without taking note of the realities on the ground. Teachers in turn tend to resist CCA methods, many giving reasons such as: 'But in our opinion we don't think the current syllabus is fit for CCA. Not only children but also teachers prefer CCA, but in the meanwhile a limit of time, lots of lessons to teach, examinations and the number of children, more than we can manage, are things hindering CCA to be successful in current Myanmar schools. [...]' There are also cultural issues.[22] 'CCA is OK for KG, but things like no respect to elders can be prevented only by TCA...' The exam system and monthly end of chapter tests used from Grade 1 to Grade 8 are also seen as incompatible with CCA. To answer the questions in the exams, students need only to memorise what has been taught in the classroom and write down the exact answer. So rote learning persists. After the exams, the students' pass rate is used as an indicator for teacher and school evaluations. If students fail the exams, the teachers have to prepare reports to their respective township education offices and they have to teach the students again in the summer so that they can pass the supply exam and move on to the next grade. Most of the schools skip this process and allow all students to pass in the first stage of exams. Teachers are reluctant to prepare reports and to be disqualified, so students pass even when they have not acquired the necessary knowledge. The exam system was the issue about which many teachers were most vocal. They say that the 'all pass' exam custom is not working. The monthly exam system takes too much time and students tend to forget things after the exam. 'Let all pass system is in a way discouraging students [...] They already know they will pass when time comes.'

Transition to high school is another issue raised by teachers and is complicated by the fact that from Grade 9 science subjects are taught in English,[23] whilst all teaching up to that point was in Burmese. 'We have language problems in teaching Mathematics, Physics, Chemistry, Biology as it is all written in English. So we have to explain them the concepts first. It is an abrupt change as students are to learn in Myanmar till Grade 9.' The fact is that most teachers do not speak English well enough themselves to teach these subjects in English, and this disadvantages students when applying for entry to higher education.

Higher education is also in desperate need of reform. After the turbulent times of the SLORC period (1988–97) when the 1988 student protests led to all universities being closed initially for two years and after another series of student strikes in 1996 and 1998 for a further three years,[24] the government relocated universities to different regions and the undergraduate programmes were moved to campuses far away from any urban centre. The world's largest higher education system by correspondence (locally referred to as Distance Education Programme/University) was allegedly set up to allow poorer students to study whilst living at home. Both these measures made sure that students stayed out of the cities and politics.

Of those students who finish their matriculation, many will go on for further studies to state universities or colleges. They do so at a comparatively young age as they finish school at the age of sixteen. As in many countries in Asia, higher education subjects are viewed in a strict hierarchy. Students who get the top marks are 'encouraged' by parents and society to take up medicine at university. Myanmar has ended up with an excess of doctors who then search for careers outside the medical sector.[25] As one teacher put it: 'they study medicine and then they don't practise—it's a totally useless system'. Studies are supposed to be conducted in English, yet in practice this is hardly ever the case. Due to the declining quality of the state education system, upper- and middle-class students and parents look for better qualifications and study opportunities abroad. They use pre-collegiate programmes that help them apply to foreign universities. The market for international qualifications and the preparation for these courses exist principally in Yangon, and there are quite a number of education agents representing a range of universities from Singapore, Malaysia, USA, UK, Australia, New Zealand and Canada.[26] The expansion of these opportunities means that Myanmar higher education is increasingly seen as a second-class option.

Despite the large number of students who still end up with local higher education degrees, young people find it increasingly challenging to get jobs. An in-house study by Myanmar Egress in 2009 showed that it is impossible to get a job simply with a state education background, even if this includes a university degree. As of 2006 a few civil society training centres emerged. These centres were instrumental in initiating, amongst other things, a public debate around the constitution and the elections. A number of these institutions have taught soft skills and increased political awareness. Since 2012 such institutions have mushroomed, both in the non- and the for-profit sector, as everyone looks for some form of private training in all possible subject areas. Whilst the training offered is mainly taken after university, it is not at 'postgraduate' level.

The education reform process

Given the poor condition in which public education finds itself, and with the middle classes looking for options in the private sector and abroad, the Myanmar government initiated a series of reviews in order to kick-start the education reform process. As discussed earlier, the priorities of President Thein Sein's government have been national reconciliation with the NLD, ethnic peace and economic reform. However, closely linked to both economic reforms and ethnic peace is the issue of education. Education has become the fourth priority of the government.

The 2008 Constitution provides a broad set of principles for education:

The Union shall: (a) earnestly strive to improve education and health of the people; (b) enact the necessary law to enable National people to participate in matters of their education and health; (c) implement free, compulsory primary education system; (d) implement a modern education system that will promote all-around correct thinking and a good moral character contributing towards the building of the Nation. (Article 28)

However, education is neither free nor modern and in dire need of reform. In his inaugural speech on 30 March 2011, the president set out new guiding principles for education:[27]

1. To implement free, compulsory primary education system.
2. To increase the enrolment rate in basic education sector.
3. To ensure new generation as intellectuals and intelligentsia in the human resource development.
4. To improve the capacities of teacher both basic education and higher education sectors.
5. To utilize teaching aids more effectively.
6. To upgrade the quality and socio-economic status of educational personnel.
7. To provide scholarships, stipends and awards for both locally and internationally.
8. To promulgate relevant laws for the participation and contribution of private sector in education services.
9. To collaborate with international and local organization, including UN, INGOs, and NGOs.
10. To upgrade educational standard to international level.

One of the first steps taken by the government included increasing the salaries of civil servants and therefore teachers' salaries (especially for those working in remote, conflict-affected areas). For the first time in 2013 the Ministry of Education also gave small grants for repairs directly to schools,[28] so that headteachers did not have to apply for funds to their township education office (which in turn applies to the state education office that has to write to the MoE in NPT).[29] In addition, a limited number of stipends for very disadvantaged children was also piloted.[30] 'Bonus pay' for teachers in remote and conflict-affected areas was offered for the first time. In the 2013–14 state budget, spending on education was increased to around 5 per cent. To combat teacher shortages in government schools, the MoE encouraged monastic schoolteachers to transfer to the state system though a special scheme. Around 50,000 teachers were recruited on a daily wage in 2013. They are now to be hired as permanent teachers after taking part in an intensive training course. This has resulted in the most experienced monastic schoolteachers leaving for the better-paid state sector.[31]

Given that the 2008 constitution advocates a certain level of decentralisation to the state government level, there has been some discussion in government education circles of how to decentralise education. However, it remains unclear whether this will mean a fiscal decentralisation, and at what level (state/region or township) policy decisions will be made.[32] Education is still a Union subject and important decisions are taken by the Ministry in Nay Pyi Taw. The Framework for Economic and Social Reform (FESR),[33] released in December 2012, discussed the priorities of the government, including the aims for education reforms, focusing especially on 'quick wins' like a review of the education sector and changing the funding structure of basic education. This forms the basis for the deconcentration that included the school grants and students' stipends mentioned above. It also touched on the integration of locally designed curricula and the involvement of community-run education programmes. However, the FESR remains well short of being a framework for decentralisation in education. Decentralisation was also supposed to be aided by the creation of a new administrative level called the *khayaing* (district) level that allows for some responsibilities (such as the authority to move teachers around) to be moved down from the state education office and some (such as data aggregation) to be moved up from the township level. However, at the time of writing the role of the district education offices remains opaque and responsibilities do not seem to have yet been transferred. UNESCO also commissioned a comprehensive report on the decentralisation options open to the government, and then piloted a training course for education planning in the context of decentralised public sector management in February 2014. UNICEF also got onto the decentralisation bandwagon and commissioned a large baseline research project (SITAN) in Mon state, to see what capacity-building local and state officials would need when decentralisation was finally pushed through.

There are a number of challenges in implementing decentralisation to the state level, as until now the education system has been top-down and upwardly accountable. The small school grants and stipends for disadvantaged students that were given directly to schools have been the only signs of some decisions being devolved to schools, but the ministries remain all-powerful.[34] There are actually nineteen ministries involved in education, including the Ministry of Science and Technology, the Ministry of Health and the Ministry of Defence at tertiary level, and the Ministries of Religious Affairs and Border Affairs at basic education level. Policy-wise there has been little coordination between the three regional Basic Education Departments and the Department of Education, Planning and Training which is responsible for teacher training and teacher allocation. Often this results in too few teachers being trained to fill gaps and not enough teachers being allocated to remote areas.

In light of the need for reform, the government embarked on a Comprehensive Education Sector Review (CESR) in the summer of 2012.[35]

> The CESR is required in order to ensure that there is a full and comprehensive understanding of the current status of education in Myanmar, regarding access and quality across the sub-sectors; as well as current strengths and gaps in policy, capacity, management systems, financing and partnership. This will support the implementation of priority reforms and the assessment of realistic policy options to form the basis of a costed, strategic education sector plan. These, in turn, have the potential to address the challenges and greatly accelerate progress towards realisation of Myanmar's education and socio-economic goals. (CESR ToR first phase)

The idea was that in reviewing the situation in education and understanding what did not work, the Ministry of Education team would be able to develop and 'own' a reform programme that was feasible and appropriate. The CESR was divided into three phases: rapid assessment for six months, developing a detailed plan for one year, and costing for six months, with a comprehensive education plan being written by the summer of 2014.[36] Help was sought from the international community to implement the review:

> Myanmar has a wide range of Development Partners (DPs), including multilateral and bi-lateral agencies, UN agencies, INGOs, NGOs and CSOs. The DPs fully support the CESR, sharing with the Government of Myanmar a commitment to the achievement of quality education for all and to broader socio-economic development. The development of a comprehensive policy framework and a costed education sector plan, supported by the establishment of partnership mechanisms, will enable more effective and efficient mobilisation and use of resources for education. It is moreover envisaged that the process of undertaking the CESR will support the development of a clearer, and more widely shared, vision for the Education Sector in Myanmar and the establishment of mechanisms for sustained stakeholder participation in the education sector at all levels. (ToR first phase)

The CESR was created by ministry officials working together with UNICEF, closely supported by donors such as AUSAID and the World Bank amongst others. The review process also saw the return of UNESCO starting to provide technical support to four of the CESR's areas, including overarching policy, legislation and management (PLM), quantitative analysis, technical and vocational education and training (TVET) and higher education (HE). The innovation of this system was that there would be interplay between government officials, international experts and international agencies, and whilst expert advice would be available, the actual process would be led and owned by the Ministry of Education. The focus was mostly on reviewing state education and the formal sector around the country.

However, in parallel, Save the Children, Burnett Institute and World Vision joined hands to focus on monastic, community and ethnic education and feed into the discussions of the review process.

The overarching objectives of the CESR reflected the president's priorities:

a. Develop a knowledge-base on the strengths and challenges in the Myanmar education system and identify areas for reform;
b. Support and contribute to the development of evidence-based policies, legislation and education sector improvements; and
c. Develop costed education sector plans (based on the findings of the review).

The CESR's responsibilities encompassed all sectors of teaching and learning, from early childhood education to higher education and involved a wide range of ministries and departments with a stake in education.[37] After the first phase of work, proposals under consideration by the CESR including increasing basic education from age 11 to 12 years, adding kindergarten, and changing teachers' career structures. The former was intended to resolve the time crunch teachers face to cover the curriculum, although the practicalities of such a transfer are complex. The latter is particularly important as teachers who want to get promoted move to secondary schools, resulting in high student–teacher ratios in primary schools, with the least experienced teachers teaching these classes. The CESR also reviewed language policies (including the teaching of English) and recommended the translation of textbooks into ethnic languages.[38]

The Phase Two in-depth analysis expanded the findings and recommendations of the Rapid Assessment (RA) and prepared draft proposals for two sector-wide costed education plans (one plan for 2014–15 and a five-year plan for 2016–20 to fit with the government's five-year planning cycles). Priorities included quality of secondary education, as well as language of instruction and the use of English language; curriculum, textbook and learner assessment; and supervision, inspection and quality assurance, along with teacher education, NFE, TVET and higher education. To this end data was collected to develop a baseline.[39] In developing this baseline the CESR promised to look at, 'Gender; Ethnicity/language background; economic status/poverty; geographic location (e.g. urban, rural, remote), by State/Region/Township; Disability; as well as other vulnerabilities, for example post conflict communities, immigrants, impact of HIV/AIDS etc.' (ToR Phase 2)

Unfortunately the CESR had little political support from the outset: even the minister of education[40] remained sitting on the fence, ostensibly leaving the running of the CESR to more junior staff.[41] Daw Tin Tin Shu, head of the CESR, was left to coordinate with the international aid agencies and to fend off criticism that came from all quarters, including from inside the government and the opposition parties. The opposition NLD was at first categorically opposed to the CESR. Shortly after the start of the CESR, NLD members and associated civil society and activist groups started to undertake a national education review of their own and created the NNER.[42] Their argument was that the MoE did not have the moral authority to lead the education reform process, that everyone knew what was wrong with the education system (and therefore no review was needed) and that a bid to reform needed to be inclusive of all groups, including ethnic education providers.[43] Although the NNER was more inclusive in its approach, allowing for voices from ethnic education systems to be heard, ethnic education groups have also found that the NNER has a very particular agenda. Inclusiveness has not necessarily meant that other viewpoints are taken on board.[44] The NNER proposal focused mainly on free education, decentralisation and freedom of institutional decision-making. Many of their very progressive ideas are simply not implementable given the state of the education infrastructure, the lack of teachers and the cost of fixing basic faults within the system. The other issue with an education review process led by political parties was that education was being politicised, and Daw Aung San Suu Kyi's party was seen as directly challenging the government's reform process.[45] Lastly the NNER was not linked to a costing exercise, which is crucial when thinking about forthcoming reforms.

At first the CESR process and the NNER operated in parallel without much contact, but after a few months there was some limited collaboration as each review team invited the other to events and shared limited amounts of information. This was largely due to the great diplomatic skills of Daw Tin Tin Shu who was open to suggestions and ideas from all quarters. However, in the end the NNER officially declared that it had lost faith in the government and in the Ministry of Education's reform process. In a press briefing the NNER claimed that the government had broken promises with regard to including them in consultations and inviting them to meetings.[46]

Other matters further complicated the working of the CESR. Since the CESR was the main window through which the INGOs (rechristened as 'development partners') were able to exert influence on the thinking around education reform, the process quickly became dominated by the various agencies sending in experts for areas close to their heart. The British Council, for example, paid for a specialist to advise on English language teaching in schools, and others such as AusAid, the EU etc. also sent in their people to help with issues from early childhood development to higher education. Whilst the help and good intentions were appreciated, the CESR was largely over-run by foreign experts who represented donor interests. There was only limited time available for the actual review and for constructing a coherent education plan, so the Ministry of Education people were rather over-whelmed. This also led to criticisms from inside the government that the development partners were seen as too influential in setting the course of education reforms. The situation was not helped by the fact that the two resident experts in the posts coordinated by UNICEF to help run the ESRC (technical adviser and coordinator) kept changing. The initial rapid assessment was coordinated by Maurice Robson, but he was not given a long enough contract by UNICEF, therefore he left after the first six months for another project.[47] His replacement did not last long, and halfway through Phase Two another expert was sent in.[48] None of these experts had any prior experience of Myanmar and whilst they had previously worked on education reviews and reforms in other countries, each new appointment took a certain time to catch up and understand the workings of the CERS and its complicated political context. This was certainly a strain on the CESR team.[49] In addition the minister of education was taken ill and died at the end of 2013. Despite this, the CESR ploughed on and produced its second set of reports largely on time in 2014.[50]

Finding that the CESR process was taking too long to feed into the legislative process, and wanting to secure a set of education laws well in time for the 2015 elections, the President's Office initiated the Education Promotion Implementation Committee (EPIC).[51] To the surprise of all the development partners who were called at short notice to Nay Pyi Taw on 7 October 2013, the Office convened a National Seminar on Pragmatic Reforms for Education to announce that this new body would take the lead on education.[52] EPIC took up residence very close to the CESR in the Diamond Jubilee Hall on the Yangon University campus. EPIC's three components included a task force of deputy ministers from the thirteen ministries directly involved in education, supported by their director generals, an advisory group consisting of retired MoE officials, academics and other national experts, and eighteen working groups covering specific areas of education reform, with two co-leads (one from government and one from the group of experts), totalling over 200 people. EPIC held some consultations but had limited contact with the CESR teams; the involvement of development partners was severely reduced, not least because all meetings were held in Burmese. The EPIC reports were submitted by end of January 2014.

EPIC was clearly supported by the President's Office and appeared as the answer not only to what was seen as an inefficiently led Ministry of Education process that had accepted too much international interference, but also as a riposte to the Parliamentary Education Promotion Committee (PEPC) that had been encouraged by the speaker of the parliament U Shwe Mann and Daw Aung San Suu Kyi. The PEPC comprised ten USDP members, three NLD members and two MPs from the Shan Nationalities Democratic Party, and was tasked to develop an overarching education 'mother law' to provide a framework for education reforms. The powerful speaker of parliament Thura U Shwe Mann teamed up with Daw Aung San Suu Kyi to push the legislative process in parliament (held quite separately from the CESR work). Parliament had started to challenge government ministries, and parliamentary committees quickly learned to use their new authority to summon officials and hold ministries to account. This has increased as legislation is developed and seems to have been the modus operandi when it came to education reforms. U Shwe Mann and Daw Aung San Suu Kyi started by calling the acting minister of education, Dr Myo Myint, and other officials in November 2013 to criticise the pace of the education reforms and demand a greater involvement of parliament in the process. The Parliamentary Guarantees, Pledges and Undertakings Vetting Committee then also criticised the MoE for failing to deliver on 220 of its commitments.[53] As a result, U Shwe Mann and Daw Aung San Suu Kyi decided to take the lead in parliament with regard to the education reform process, pitching themselves against the president and the Ministry of Education.

The President's Office also tried to remain in control of the legislative process by removing hard-liners and putting presidential allies in the right place. Key actors of the executive branch in education include: Vice President Dr Sai Mauk Kham, who allegedly was close to EPIC and attended many of the policy-planning sessions; the ministers of the President's Office (also known as the 'super cabinet'), mainly U Tin Naing Thein, responsible for social affairs. Other advisers include Dr Aung Tun Thet (a former lecturer at the Yangon Institute of Economics and former Director General in the Ministry of Health); and Dr Yin Yin Nwe (a former Country Representative for UNICEF and former geology lecturer at the University of Yangon).

The Myanmar legislative process of education has encompassed three phases: first in the 1970s the Basic Education Law 1973 (revised 1989), the

University Education Law 1973, the Education Research Law 1973, the Technical, Agricultural and Vocational Education Law 1974, and later the Private Tuition Class Law and the Child Law of 1993. In 2001 the government drafted a 30-year plan for education (2001–31) and signed up Education for All (EFA). In 2003, the Ministry of Education developed an EFA National Action Plan (outlining steps needed to reach EFA by the year 2015). More recently, as part of the reforms, education laws that are either being developed in parliament or have been submitted to parliament by the executive include the Early Childhood Care and Development Law, the Examination Board Law, the Basic Education Law, the University Education Law, the Education Research Law and in September 2014 the Education 'Mother Law'. The disconnection between the legislative processes and the review processes has been staggering. Only the EPIC reports seem to bridge the gap between the review and the legislative debates somewhat, but within a context dogged by power play between key politicians and their departments. The increasing rivalry between the executive and parliamentary branches of government resulted in both working to develop an education 'Mother Law'.

The education law and student protests

In March 2014, the Education Promotion and Implementation Committee (EPIC) drafted the National Education Bill. The bill was submitted to Parliament in July 2014. It then needed presidential approval, but President Thein Sein sent the bill back to parliament with 25 suggested changes. On 30 September 2014 the law was enacted, accepting 19 of the proposed changes.

During the whole process momentum for protest had been increasing as civil society organisations and student and teacher unions accused the government of not taking into account the advice from the relevant stakeholders. The NNER had repeatedly held meetings that decried the law as cementing the centralisation of Myanmar's education system. The meetings had resulted in a set of detailed suggestions that had been submitted to parliament.[54] The main issues that sparked dissent included the teaching of ethnic languages and cultures at universities, the independence of universities including private universities, and the legality of students taking part in political activities.[55]

The Action Committee for Democratic Education (ACDE), comprising members of the All Burma Federation of Students' Unions (ABFSU), the Confederation of University Student Unions and University Student Union

(Myay Latt), started to campaign for the amendment or redrafting of the National Education Law. Demanding a quadripartite meeting between ACDE, NNER, the government and parliament, they held a four-day demonstration over 14–17 November 2014 at various locations in Yangon and other parts of the country. They threatened nationwide demonstrations if the government did not respond within 60 days. Once the 60 days expired, more than 100 people started to match from Mandalay to Yangon on 20 January 2016. Other protesters started to join the march from across the country, including Pakokku, the delta, Dawei and Mawlamyine. The 11-point demand issued by the ACDE on 24 January demanded a meeting with the government and for the law to be amended.[56] The government agreed to meet with the students in February to discuss their demands. Three quadripartite meetings took place during which time the student protests continued. As Dr Thein Lwin had been thrown out of the NLD, the NLD was not seen to be on the side of the NNER and the students. Students maintained that their protests would only stop after the new or amended law had been passed by parliament. At the last meeting an agreement was struck, with the government promising to take into account the 11 demands. The government repeatedly asked the students to suspend their protests, and even a head monk endorsed this position, requesting the students 'to go back to their studies'. However, the tensions grew and as police tried to stop the protesters from marching onto Yangon from Latpadan, things started to become violent. Solidarity protests by students and civil society organisations near Sule Pyia in Yangon were violently broken up by the police in March 2014. The government not only used police to control the protesters and manhandle them, but also civilian thugs who were recruited from poor areas, or who had recently been released from jail. The riots resulted in the arrest of 127 students. Part of the controversy was the fact that the EU had just supported a police training programme, aiming to instruct the Myanmar police force in modern non-violent crowd control techniques, and teaching them about human rights. As the protests broke out and the administration felt that they were losing control on the streets, the police force sent in to control the students turned to violence. Students and civil society activists then returned to the street protesting against the EU, who they said had done a terrible job in training the police. In the meantime in May 2014 more than 70 student activists who had taken part in the protests went on trial on charges of unlawful assembly and rioting.

On 26 March 2014, the Upper House voted to accept amendments to the National Education Law, but with a number of changes to the 11 points that the students had demanded.[57] These included the debate on how much of the national budget the government should spend on education. Whilst the students had insisted that 20 per cent of national spending should go to education, the law vows to increase spending year on year, but without the 20 per cent explicitly guaranteed. Part of the problem in agreeing the amendments of the law was the various competing drafts that had been sent to parliament. The students accused the government of dishonesty, as a draft that had allegedly been discarded at one of the quadripartite meetings was presented to the legislature. In June 2015 the revised bill was voted into law, leaving many disillusioned and disappointed as they felt that the government had broken its promise.[58]

Higher education, Daw Aung San Suu Kyi and Yangon University

Part of the power play in the education reform process was fuelled by the fact that Daw Aung San Suu Kyi has taken an active interest and used her connections to foreign governments and their development agencies to foster her interests. First in line has been the debate around the new higher education bill, as the NLD is campaigning for greater autonomy for universities and the future of Yangon University, which Daw Aung San Suu Kyi wants to have restored to its past glory.[59] Her personal interventions to the British and Australian governments have led to direct support by both embassies as well as AUSAID (now DFAT) and DFID in the higher education sector. Professor Kenneth King from the University of Edinburgh was sent to advise the Parliamentary Higher Education Law (HEL) Committee on the challenges of higher education reform from 4 to 16 February 2013. The British Council subsequently facilitated a visit of the then acting Minister of Education Dr Myo Myint[60] to the UK for a study tour in May 2013.

Progress in higher education has now been made, as undergraduates were re-introduced to Yangon and Mandalay Universities in the 2013 academic year after a fifteen-year ban. The first batch comprised 1,500 students in both universities across twenty disciplines. Yangon University and other institutions in Yangon and Mandalay have also been approached by a myriad of foreign institutions for partnerships and joint programmes. The UK sent a study tour to Myanmar in February 2015, and the institutions visited revealed that they were being approached by international universities on a weekly basis. The expectation from the Myanmar institutions was that the foreign partner will bring the funding for whatever programme they propose. Japan, the US and some European universities have already started linking up with local Myanmar universities, helping reintegrate Myanmar universities into the wider higher education world.

There is a great debate regarding the setting up of private universities, however. Informal enquiries were made by Bard University from the US,[61] asking for a piece of land to allow for a campus to be built. They had proposed a mix of fee-paying and scholarship students, targeting the middle-class market unable to send their children abroad. It is said that this proposal was blocked by Daw Aung San Suu Kyi, who wanted the focus to remain on Yangon University. When another piece of land was discussed in May Myo (PLW), this proposal was again countered by Daw Aung San Suu Kyi.[62] It looks therefore as if proposals related to higher education are firmly in the domain of the NLD and that the government is happy to defer to Daw Aung San Suu Kyi in these matters. However, it is unclear how the whole higher education sector can be reformed if the main focus remains on Yangon University. Universities further afield in the regional capitals or ethnic states, apart from Mandalay University, are not getting much support either.

The role of development partners and diverse political agendas

Until 2012 the only organisations that had any influence on education in Myanmar were UNICEF and JICA, although what they were able to do was very constrained. Both benefited from MoUs with the government. They were active in government schools and advised on teacher training. The British Council has also been an active player in some parts of education, since 1948, with a hiatus during the socialist years in the 1960s; but their focus was more on English language teacher training and since the mid 2000s supporting civil society organisations involved in education.

The Education Thematic Working Group (ETWG) was established in July 2009, following Cyclone Nargis the year before. Once the emergency response was completed, Thematic Working Groups were established, including for education. In addition to the Nargis-affected area, the ETWG then expanded to support coordination across the sector, and more broadly across the country to work together to achieve education for all children. The objectives of the group were to provide a regular opportunity for open dialogue between key education stakeholders, line departments and donor agencies in support of the priority areas in achieving Education for All (EFA) in Myanmar; to help coordinate efforts in education; and to enable capacity-building and sharing of technical expertise and good practice. Technical sub-working groups were established in Early Childhood Care and Development, Non-Formal Education and Disaster Preparedness and Response in Education (DPRE), as well as a Group for Education Discussion. ETWG provided a neutral space for stakeholder dialogue on technical areas of sector reform. At first the engagement with CSOs and non-state actors was the only way that the ETWG could progress, but once the CESR had started, the EWTG also was able to engage with the MoE, increasing communication and building trust. As the Nay Pyi Taw accord of 2013 redefined the relationship between ministries and the development partners, there has been closer cooperation between the ETWG and Myanmar officials.[63]

Until recently development agencies[64] have found direct access to government institutions (primary, secondary and higher) difficult to negotiate. So most have funded UNICEF work through the MDEF programmes.[65] UNICEF continues to lead on the latest MDEF programme, and still receives a large amount of money (mainly from AUSAID/DFAT, DFID and the EU). However, most of these agencies have now carved out priorities in Myanmar's reform process, and so education reform is led by AUSAID/DFAT with support from the other development partners. This has led to some tensions between UNICEF and the funders, who see their prime position threatened. AUSAID/DFAT was able to fund government education programmes directly, and as such became a major contributor to the CESR process, not only through its UNICEF funding. Whilst it is clear that the government does need international financial support in reforming its education system, this type of aid also brings in the political and educational priorities of the funders.

It was also AUSAID/DFAT who led in the initiative to create the Myanmar Education Consortium (MEC) that was to pool the money of the various development partners (in the first instance AUSAID/DFAT collaborated with DFID) when it came to supporting the informal education sector—such as monastic and state education, as well as the local NGOs who support these networks.[66] MEC became operational in the summer of 2013. Local organisations and NGOs who traditionally had direct links to DFID or other development agencies now had to apply to the central pot. This has created a lot of upset amongst Myanmar NGOs, CBOs and CSOs which failed to receive funding for their programmes. Previously their personal relationships with the funders ensured that the programmes could run. The funders had no other outlets and developed good relations with these local organisations. Now it seems that the administrative process relies on organisations being able to prove how they will spend the money, and the old ways based on trust and networks are no longer sufficient.[67]

However, not all agencies are happy being led by AUSAID/DFAT and its close partners DFID and the EU. JICA has stayed away from all pooling of funds and runs its programmes separate from Western aid agencies. Often accused of not being transparent, its role has been further complicated by the work done by the Sasakawa Peace Foundation on the peace process, which also remains opaque. At present JICA has become the lead agency in helping the government with the curriculum and textbook reform process for basic education. The project is due to run from mid 2015 to 2019 and plans to develop a new curriculum framework, new textbooks with matching teachers' guides, and disseminate the whole package, coordinated with pre-service and in-service teacher training.

The World Bank (with AUSAID/DFAT as a partner) has increasingly been involved in education. True to form, its mandate has been to support the decentralisation of education, focusing in particular on the schools grants programme mentioned above as well as the student stipend programme. It is indeed a good thing that headteachers and schools are given more autonomy, as the centralised system as practised till now has not served the schools well. However, headteachers are at the moment under-equipped in dealing with the management of schools, and leadership programmes as piloted by UNICEF would need to be rolled out in parallel for any decentralisation programme to be successful.[68]

Ethnic groups, mother tongue education, decentralisation and reform challenges

As discussed in a previous chapter, ethnic insurgents controlled large parts of the country for a number of decades. During this period Ethnic Armed Groups (EAGs) developed extensive (if under-resourced) administrative regimes, including in some cases parallel government structures, with depart- ments of education, health, finance etc. substituting for government services in the areas under their control and recognised by the local citizens as more legitimate than the institutions championed by the Myanmar government.[69] The divide between the areas administered by the ethnic armies and those ruled by the government was also underlined by different languages, as in EAG-controlled areas the ethnic language was more likely to be used rather than Burmese.

For decades, the Myanmar state education system has insisted on *Bama saga* (Burmese) being used through a national school system, to create a

Myanmar national identity based on *Bamar* culture, with Burmese as a 'unifying' language. Given the diversity of ethno-linguistic groups in Myanmar, there is a strong argument for the country having a *lingua franca* or Union language.[70] However, the promotion of Burmese as a national language under the previous military government did not lead to an inclusive national identity, as ethnic groups were still discriminated against, and the 'national identity' that was promoted was strongly identified with the *Bamar* majority ethnic group.[71] The military government's educational practice included the manipulation of history and textbooks, presenting the Burmese as superior to other ethnic groups.[72] The teaching of and in minority languages was forbidden in state schools, creating an issue for children entering the Myanmar school system in areas where they spoke their mother tongue, one that was usually different from that of their teacher.[73] In essence, the policy remained one of 'Burmanisation': meaning the marginalisation of ethnic identities, segregating ethnic groups and treating them unequally, by which the government made education part of the conflict.[74]

This resulted in different reactions in ethnic areas, depending on whether the government or an EAG was in charge. In government-controlled areas, ethnic civil society actors (particularly faith-based networks e.g. Karen and Kachin Christian churches; Mon and Shan Buddhist monasteries) sometimes managed to provide ethnic language teaching outside school hours, often in informal settings under threat of state suppression.[75] Various ethnic literature and culture committees (some of which were established in the 1950s, although most of these were semi-dormant in subsequent decades) supported the expansion of ethnic language literacy programmes in the 1990s, mainly in summer school settings. Although these (Shan, Mon, Karen, PaO etc.) groups have done much to help keep ethnic languages (and culture) alive, they could not substitute for formal schooling.

In areas more directly affected by armed conflict, and particularly in EAG-controlled areas (which shrank dramatically in the 1980s and '90s),[76] the quasi-governmental 'para-state' structures included education departments that ran schools and produced textbooks in ethnic languages. Some education regimes were fairly closely modelled on the state school curriculum, whereas others developed along separate (indeed, particularly from the 1960s through the 1970s, separatist) lines, using mother-tongue education to promote and reinforce ethnic nationality, ethnic identities and opposition to the militarised state. EAG education regimes represented explicit alternatives to the state, and although they were poorly funded and under-resourced they nevertheless demonstrated the value which ethnic communities place on education.

The various ethnic education groups and departments fall roughly into four categories. There are those like the Mon[77] and the Kachin who have used the government curriculum in translation and whose schools allow for children to learn Burmese as they grow older, so that they can join the government education system either at middle or high school and then go on to state tertiary education institutes if they so wish[78] (and can afford to). Whilst primary school education is conducted in the mother tongue, and older students continue to study their mother tongue and ethnic history alongside the Myanmar national curriculum, these groups generally perceived the value of an education system that does not separate and isolate their young people from the rest of the country. Today the Mon National Education Committee (MNEC) wants to remain independent of the state system, but nevertheless sees the value of expanding mixed schools with Mon language teachers and a more structured and agreed transfer system between MNEC and government schools. Unfortunately—but hardly surprisingly—in the context of renewed armed conflict in Kachin areas over the past three years, the KIO education system seems to be disengaging from that of the state, and adopting a more separatist direction, similar to that of the KNU.

At the other end of the spectrum is the KNU-supported Karen education system which has evolved as a fully separate system, producing graduates who are not only unable to reintegrate into the Myanmar government education system at any age, but also emphasise a clearly articulated Karen (separatist) identity with regard to the *Bamar*-dominated society typified in expressions and reproductions of government-controlled Myanmar.[79]

A third and different example is that of Shan State, where many diverse ethnic groups have set up different, mostly less well organised education systems, allowing children to study in their mother tongue. There is also a Shan education system catering for children whose mother tongue is Shan. However, for the other ethnic minorities in Shan State, Shan and not Burmese is seen as the 'unifying' (or dominating) language, and Burmese is further removed from these communities who learn first in PaO, Kayah or Talang.

Finally a fourth group exists in areas where there are only government schools and where the EAGs have not set up parallel structures. There, NGOs, civil society groups or summer schools organised by the monastic sector try to maintain mother-tongue language. This is the case in Chin and Rakhine States, and the Naga autonomous region in Sagaing Region.

Given the peace process described earlier, the Myanmar state education system is now spreading into areas previously controlled by the EAGs. The education review is proposing education policies that will now affect areas previously under EAG control, and consequently issues of medium of instruction, mother-tongue teaching and the teaching of ethnic languages in schools in ethnic states have become salient points of debate. Thus far, however, ethnic language provision—and particularly the relationship between EAG and government education regimes—has been largely absent in the formal nationwide ceasefire negotiations and the broader peace process. These have focused in the first place on securing and monitoring ceasefires, and on preparations for launching a nationwide political dialogue, including multiple stakeholders (government, parliament, Myanmar army, EAGs, ethnic civil society etc.), that is planned for after the nationwide ceasefire has been signed. Exceptions include efforts by some state governments to introduce ethnic language education into government schools, after discussion with EAG political leaders (the KNU in Tanintharyi Region) or political parties (the above-ground Karen People's Party in Bago Region, and All Mon Regions Democracy Party (AMRD) in Mon State).[80]

Disconnected from the peace process, the state-led education review and reform process include some elements of language reform. The CESR[81] was advised by UNICEF-funded Australian specialist Professor Joseph Lo Bianco on issues pertaining to mother-tongue education, and pressure was put on by the team working on the Early Childhood Education bill to include mother-tongue education for all children at primary level.[82] The role of English in education has been equally hotly debated. Nevertheless, ethnic educators have so far had very little input into the education reform processes. In an attempt to bring the issues of ethnic mother-tongue education and the reform process together, two development partners organised a series of (separate) workshops during the course of 2013 that included the various ethnic education departments and on one occasion made a meeting between them and the CESR team possible. These discussions were highly productive, even though the various ethnic education groups are independent entities that do not have a joint strategy and have not developed a common framework to propose to the government.[83] In line with this, hard-line elements within the ethnic education organisations asked for some of the meetings to be held in Thailand as opposed to Yangon, making further dialogue with the CESR team and other officials impossible.[84] After that the CESR process continued and completed without any ethnic input.

The issues now faced by the ethnic education departments caught between education reform and the peace process are possibly best illustrated by one particular case. The MNEC[85] is one of the largest and best organised ethnic education departments. Because of a long-standing initial ceasefire in Mon State, both Mon National Schools (MNS) and mixed schools were able to expand, offering education in Mon language to Mon families across the state. The MNEC has been largely funded with money from across the border in Thailand, and both local NGOs and INGOs committed to ethnic education have supported the system for many years. In turn Mon families help pay teachers' salaries in cash and kind, and Mon teachers accept a much reduced pay when compared to their Myanmar counterparts. Despite being so well developed, this system has started to unravel in light of the reforms. First, funding from across the border has reduced significantly as money flows directly into Myanmar; development partners have million-dollar budgets to support the Myanmar government in the reform process, but not enough funds to help organisations such as the MNEC.[86] As a result the MNEC is facing a funding crunch. The increased salaries of government teachers have made the Mon teaching profession look even less attractive; and as inflation makes life more expensive, teacher turn-around has increased and teacher recruitment has become more difficult.[87] MNEC has tried to get funding for teachers' salaries from one of the most important development partners in Yangon, but has failed in securing any support.[88] This is despite the fact that MPSI which supports the peace process has lobbied very hard on their behalf, insisting that the MNEC-led education system is not only a model for other ethnic education systems, but could also become a confidence-building measure within the wider peace process in Mon State as the government negotiates with the New Mon State Party. Beyond the peace process the service provided by the MNEC, especially in the more remote areas where government provision does not reach, is essential if the government is to fulfil the new education law that guarantees education to all children at primary level,[89] and in addition promises to provide education for the very young in each child's mother tongue. The Mon State government has recently been made aware that if MNEC schools closed it would cause a great headache, as the government would have to step in and fill the gap. Recently the Mon State parliament declared that the Mon language will be taught in all Mon schools; but since this proposal comes from the All Mon Regions Democratic Party (AMRDP) and not the NMSP which is allied with the MNEC, MNEC teachers are unlikely to be called upon to fulfil these roles.[90] The MNEC does not want to integrate with the government system, but both MNEC and the government have to find a way forward to keep this parallel system of education going in order to fulfil the needs of the local population.[91] Whilst greater decentralisation of the education budget might help, it is unclear if this will happen soon enough to allow for the MNEC to receive limited support from either the Mon State parliament or the Mon State education office. Such support could be justified given that the MNEC schools all teach the national curriculum, but it might also bring pressures to integrate into the government system.

The instance of education in Mon State shows how complex the education reform process has become and how the disconnection between the peace and the education discussions has actually led to a disenfranchisement of those who have for decades assured the education of the ethnic groups. Similar and even more complex problems exist in the other ethnic states, and it is unclear if and how these will be resolved. Given that these organisations mostly serve the poorer sections of society, a move into the self-funding 'private sector' would be impossible.[92] It is however interesting to note that a similar situation pertaining to health reform in Karen State has led to much more cooperative outcomes.[93]

The debate around language as a medium of instruction in Myanmar is not over. Given the importance of language, the ETWG established an education and language sub-working group after the ETWG supported a meeting on 'Language and Social Cohesion' in September 2014, piggy-backing on a regional 'Language Education and Social Cohesion' workshop supported by UNICEF. One of the objectives was to explore the linkages between language and social cohesion, and consider the next steps for multi-lingual education in Myanmar. The meeting allowed for 156 participants from Government, State and Union parliaments, development partners, INGOs, CSOs, universities, private schools, international/national education experts to meet each other and discuss the issue of language and education in Myanmar. The CESR Phase 2 report had recommended the development of an overarching language policy to provide opportunities to learn the mother tongue, Burmese and foreign languages. In parallel, a language policy is being developed by the MoE.[94] It is now one of the key challenges to reach consensus on language education policies that meet the diverse needs and hopes of all groups, to help promote social cohesion and ensure that all children have an equal opportunity to learn effectively across the country.

Education in emergencies

Aside from the legislative wrangling in parliament and the jostling for influence by the INGOs, there have also been two crises where an INGO-led education response became necessary: first after the resumption of hostilities in Kachin State in 2011, and then after the violence in Rakhine State. Both emergencies resulted in large numbers of IDPs, many relocated in camps without access to schools. UNICEF came in with two response plans to help remedy the situation. In Kachin State the problem was remedied in part when the Kachin State government instructed all government schools to accommodate IDP students. UNICEF was able to support 1,300 primary school children in IDP camps in Myitkyina and Waingmaw townships with textbooks and Essential Learning Packages (ELP). One temporary learning space was constructed in Waingmaw township and some psycho-social support was offered to affected families. However, the continuous rise of IDPs has meant overcrowded classrooms and increased pressure on host schools which need more classrooms and teachers. At the time of writing UNICEF estimates there to be around 9,000 children in hard to reach areas unable to access education.[95] Research in the spring and summer of 2015 in Kachin State also showed that the education system in the camps under KIO control was under strain. The conflict has resulted in the KIO schools wanting to dissociate themselves increasingly from the government education system, and with the help of various NGOs the Kachin civil society groups and the KIA are looking into developing a separate curriculum for the schools under their administration. This means that children who will in future study at these schools will no longer be able to switch to Myanmar government schools or higher education institutions.[96]

In Rakhine State's three northern townships most schools closed after the anti-Muslim violence (covered in Chapter 7). There is a problem accessing schools for the displaced communities in Maungdaw. In Sittwe the total estimated displaced population is approximately 6,000 for the 3–5 age group and 10,000 for the 5–10 age group.[97] The children have not been able to leave the camps, and UNICEF has had to construct temporary education facilities, despite this making the displacement more permanent.

The government reform programme has encompassed many sectors, not just education. But as a showcase for political wrangling at both national and international level, there seems no better case study. It will take the best part of a generation to reform the education system properly and reap the results for the young people who are in primary school today. As a result education will remain a central battleground between various governmental and non-governmental organisations well beyond 2015.

THE RISE OF BUDDHIST NATIONALISM

Introduction

The issue of national identity in Myanmar is complex because the country is a multi-ethnic state. Many ethnic Bamar do not see a difference between the word 'Myanmar' and the word 'Bamar' (or 'Burmese'). By contrast, a great many Myanmar nationals of ethnic minority extraction have come to view their identity as their ethnicity.[1] Whilst the mainly ethnic conflict-driven peace process was covered in Chapter 4, this chapter looks at the re-emerging fault-lines between religious groups. For non-Buddhist minority groups, religion has further complicated their relations with the Buddhist majority.

According to Liang Sakhong, part of the problem lies in the misconception between 'nation' and 'state' building, where the Bamar leaders after independence used a process of forced assimilation for ethnic and religious minorities.

> The "nation-building" process with the notion of "one ethnicity, one language, one religion"[2] indeed reflected the core values of Burman/Myanmar "nationalism", which originated in the anti-colonialists motto of "*Amyo, Batha, Thatana*", that is to say, the *Myanmar-lumyo* or Myanmar ethnicity, *Myanmar-batha-ska* or Myanmar language, and *Myanmar-thatana* of *Buddha-bata* or Buddhism, and it has become after independence the unwritten policies of "Myanmarization" and "Buddhistization", and a perceived legitimate practices of ethnic and religious "forced-assimilation" into "*Buddha-bata Mynamar-lumyo*" (that is, to say 'to be a Myanmar is to be a Buddhist'), in multi-ethnic, multi-religious plural society of the Union of Burma.[3]

The issue of nationalism and national identity, and the role and rights of minorities regarding the distribution of power, are compounded by the fact that most ethnic and religious minorities live close to the borders. Steinberg's work discusses how many of Myanmar's neighbours have supported ethnic rebellions against the central government, resulting in Bamar feelings of isolation and xenophobia.[4] To this day there is a real fear of multiculturalism and federalism, as these could weaken the central control of the state and the union government. The minorities in the meantime have battled over land, control over natural resources, cultural, religious and language rights. Steinberg reiterates Liang Sakhong's point that the Myanmar governments over the ages have tried to inculcate an overarching and uniting ideology, to create a nation-state, more often than not using Buddhism as a political tool. It is only after the military coup of 1962 that a more secular approach was preferred, under the banner of the Burma Socialist Programme Party (BSPP). SLORC (later SPDC), which followed after the 1988 protests, also tried to create a secular national identity based on the historic role of the military, conveniently reinterpreted to suit their political needs. Burmese history was rewritten to emphasise the dominance of the military, symbolised by three great Bamar kings, Anawrahta, Bayinaung and Alaungpaya,[5] who allegedly unified the country. This was also reflected in the national school curriculum. Depending on the school, there are daily or weekly prayers. Work done by Rose Metro on the national school curriculum shows that texts are written for Buddhist students and reinforce Buddhist traditions and beliefs, without any reference to non-Buddhist communities. The re-opening of monastic schools (many had been closed under the Burmese Socialist Programme) and the registering of new monastic schools under SLORC/SPDC made primary education much more accessible to the most disadvantaged sections of society, but also reinforced the roles of monasteries in providing Buddhist-centric education. Many monastic schools do accept children of other religious communities, but the ethos in these schools is definitely informed by the majority religion. The army also maintains close relations to the Sangha, with generals often depicted in the press as making merit or paying respects to monks.[6] After the monks' protests in 2007, violently put down by the army, the military tried vehemently to repair its relationship with the Sangha through gifts and a targeted PR campaign. Today the military is completely controlled by Bamar Buddhists; Muslims as well as Christians find it impossible to get promoted above the rank of colonel.[7] However, in the end the Bamar elite-driven nation-state projects have all failed. Ethnic and religious strife testify to the fact that no overarching national identity has been constructed and accepted, and Buddhist nationalism does not transcend localised ethno-linguistic and religious loyalties.[8]

In 2012 the fault-line of religious difference and discrimination started to dominate the domestic and international press headlines: in particular, Buddhist Rakhine violence against the Muslims in Rakhine State who call themselves Rohingya. The difficulty of the issue at hand is compounded by the fact that the two communities have contradictory interpretations over the origins of the Rohingya. Whilst the Rohingya see themselves as descendants of Muslim settlers who arrived many centuries ago, the Rakhine (and official government) view is that the Rohingya were never part of the indigenous national races but migrants from Bengal—who are illegal immigrants.[9]

The displacement and killing of many Rohingya between 2012 and 2014 created a humanitarian and refugee crisis. Western media reports described human rights violations, racism, harassment, extortion, 'stateless people' and the failure of the government to protect a vulnerable minority. This was not the first time—there has been communal violence/persecution against this group in 1942, 1947–54, 1977–8 and 1991–2.[10] This time, however, the presence of NGOs and UNHCR in Rakhine State allowed for close observation and media involvement—something that had not been possible earlier. It also led to an internationalisation of the problem with calls for the government of Myanmar to shoulder its responsibility, whilst representatives of Muslim countries and organisations paid visits and collected donations.

Inter-communal violence in 2012

On 28 May 2012, a Buddhist woman was raped and murdered by a group of Muslim men in Sittwe, Rakhine State. The three were arrested; one died in prison while two were tried and found guilty.[11] This was followed by the murder in Toungup on 3 June of ten Muslim pilgrims who were neither Rohingya nor in any way connected to the May murder. These two incidents triggered a series of violent clashes between the two religious communities across Rakhine State. According to the government, 50 people were killed, 54 wounded, 2,230 homes and 14 places of worship were destroyed.[12] As a result, 75,000 mostly Muslims had to move to camps where UN agencies and NGOs started providing help.[13]

Tensions and clashes started to spread around the country, with protests outside a mosque close to Sule Pagoda, at the heart of Yangon. President Thein Sein appealed to the country for calm on 10 June and the authorities dispatched troops to enforce a state of emergency that had been declared in Rakhine State on the same day.[14] Myanmar also received a visit from United

Nations Special Envoy Vijay Nambiar to the conflict areas. The tensions eased somewhat and the openness of the government resulted in praise from the EU and the US.[15] In addition, the government appointed a 27-person commission to investigate the cause of the clashes and to make recommendations.[16]

The state of emergency automatically ended after three months. But violence erupted again on 21 October 2012 in the townships of Kyaukpyu, Kyauktaw, Minbya, Mrauk-U, Myebon, Pauktaw, Ramree and Rathedaung, all across Rakhine State.[17] In June the attacks had been from both sides of the communal divide, but the October clashes were, according to the ICG, well-coordinated attacks against the Muslim community in general—not only against the Rohingya, but also against other, officially recognised communities such as the Kaman. Government figures said that between 21 and 30 October 89 people were killed, 136 wounded and 5,351 homes burned down, making another 32,231 people homeless.[18] Eid celebrations on 26 October 2012 were cancelled as fear spread across the Muslim communities in Myanmar. The next day hand grenades were thrown at two mosques in Karen State's Kawkareik township. The government attempted to suppress the conflict, imposing a state of emergency in six townships in Rakhine State.[19] Reviews of the violence show that the security forces, especially the police and the Nasaka,[20] were biased, and in some cases that security forces aided and abetted the violence against the Muslim community. The army seemed to have fared better in preventing attacks against Muslim communities in certain areas, some even getting attacked by Rakhine Buddhist mobs.[21] The Nasaka, who clearly sided with the Rakhine Buddhists, were finally disbanded on 12 July 2013 by a presidential order.

Communal clashes are nothing new in Myanmar—Taylor estimates that since the 1930s they happen every decade or so.[22] However, usually they have been quickly brought back under control, whilst communal tensions and grievances are not addressed. The latest violence threatened to destabilise the reform process and consequently there were rumours and suspicions that conservative elements in the government, opposed to the reforms, might be fuelling the communal clashes. A more likely explanation is that that the reforms have lifted the lid on the simmering tensions, and decades of grievances between the communities have poured out. The new freedom of the media, including social media, have allowed for nationalist sentiment to be used to inflame the tensions. The media in effect became a tool to rally nationalists and troublemakers. Militant monks were able to organise protests and use social media to spread nationalist messages of hate.[23] In Rakhine State, monks were present during the riots and actively supported blockades and anti-Muslim boycotts. The president did call for the monks to obey the law and some senior monks spoke out against the violence—but these voices were in the minority.

International involvement also helped fan the flames. In September 2012 Rakhine nationalists met in Sittwe to create an ultra-nationalist manifesto that included proposing the removal of Rohingya villages, and opposing both those relegated to camps being allowed back home and the distribution of national identity cards to Rohingya. In the meantime the Organisation of Islamic Cooperation (OIC) suggested establishing a liaison office in Yangon. This sparked protest demonstrations first in Sittwe and later in Yangon and Mandalay. The government then went back on a signed agreement, not allowing the OIC to establish a mission in Myanmar.[24]

Not only was the OIC unwelcome, even neutral organisations such as Médecins Sans Frontières (MSF) who were providing most of the medical services to the camps had to suspend its operations in Rakhine State in February 2014 due to large-scale local protests. The tensions between the international aid agencies and locals had been rising—in part because of the imminent start of the UN-backed census[25] as well as longer-term grievances about INGOs always being seen to help the Rohingya community, especially those coming back from Bangladesh, with no equivalent help for the Buddhist Rakhine community. Tensions were inflamed by a member of staff from the German NGO 'Malteser' removing a Buddhist flag from a building which the organisation was renting, and rumours that she had done this in a disrespectful manner. This resulted in direct attacks on UN and INGO offices between 26 and 27 March 2014 affecting 33 premises in all, causing $1 million in damage and the evacuation of 300 INGO staff. Humanitarian assistance stopped as the government restricted the movements of all foreigners, affecting the 140,000 displaced people. The humanitarian aid workers who stayed in Sittwe were confined to the single hotel that would have them.[26] It took months for the situation to normalise.

The minorities of both communities have fled their homes and businesses out of fear, preferring to live in camps with those who share their religion, leading to a separation of Muslims and Buddhists in Rakhine State. This has affected both Rohingya[27] as well as Rakhine, although many more Rohingya are in camps. Security forces trying to prevent further clashes have also maintained segregation. The Rohingya, mainly from Sittwe, cannot leave these camps for fear of reprisals, whilst the Rakhine camps are open. According to

ICG, after the residents had left, most of the Rohingya neighbourhoods of Sittwe were 'bulldozed'.[28] This included structures that had not been damaged in the violence.[29] So whilst there is no official policy of long-term segregation, it looks increasingly unlikely that the Rohingya communities will be able to return, not least given the calls from some extreme Rakhine Buddhists for the permanent expulsion of the Rohingya from Rakhine State.

The anti-Muslim violence has not only affected the Rohingya. Another Muslim community in Rakhine State has also suffered: the Kaman, who are recognised as an indigenous group and are therefore entitled to citizenship by birth. They have increasingly been affected by the rise of Buddhist nationalism. In part they are targeted because of a commonly held suspicion that Rohingya who bribed officials to obtain illegal citizenship cards asked to be registered as Kaman. Now the Kaman, even with citizenship cards, require permission to travel due to the risk of violence.[30]

Official responses

As mentioned above, the President established an 'Investigation Commission' on 17 August to look into the March–June 2012 clashes.[31] The commission extended its work in light of the October violence. The commission was asked to look at the causes of the violence and the government response, as well as looking at possible solutions to resolve the situation and suggest a way forward towards reconciliation. Whilst there were no Rohingya on the commission, the members included Muslim, Christian, Hindu and Buddhist representatives, as well as civil society leaders like the comedian (and former dissident and political prisoner) Zarganar and politicians such as former dissident Ko Ko Gyi.[32] The commission report did not use the term 'Rohingya', using instead the term 'Bengali'. 'The commission's position is that had the report chosen to use the term 'Rohingya', it would likely have been interpreted by a majority of domestic readers as an indication of the commission taking sides.[33]

The report came up with a detailed list of very sensible recommendations that addressed issues of IDs, resettlement, livelihoods and schooling. The report for example stated:

> It is becoming extremely urgent to provide the Bengali IDPs with access to safe and secure temporary shelters prior to the monsoon season; There is a pressing need to address overcrowding in camps, provide access to clean water and sanitation; Schools should be reopened and access to education provided for students living in Bengali IDP camps; The Government should immediately review the curricula of

all religious schools and remove any inflammatory texts and teachings to better promote a sense of national pride and mutual understanding between communities; The Government shoulders the responsibility to meet the basic needs of the IDP populations until their livelihoods are restored.

Probably the most controversial part of the report referred to controlling Rohingya population growth:

One factor that has fuelled tensions between the Rakhine public and Bengali populations relates to the sense of insecurity among many Rakhine stemming from the rapid population growth of the Bengali population, which they view as a serious threat. If, as proposed, family-planning education is provided to the Bengali population, the Government should refrain from implementing non-voluntary measures which may be seen as discriminatory or that would be inconsistent with human rights standards.

Whilst the proposal was clear on the voluntary part of the measure proposed, this did result in a reinforcement of the semi-official policy of restricting Rohingya families to two children, which pre-dated the Commission's proposals and had been issued locally.[34]

In the report, 55 per cent of 'Bengali' respondents felt that the main reason for the crisis was because the government had not given rights to those who were citizens and controlled them unfairly. The Commission and Rakhine groups suggested implementing the 1982 Citizenship Act effectively in order to solve the problems: 'The Government should immediately address the citizenship claims of the Bengalis. They will be able to live and coexist with the other citizens only when they themselves become citizens.' U Tin Htoo Aung, Chairman of the Rakhine National Network, said: 'with the existing 1982 law, it is necessary to clarify those who have the right to citizenship and those who are not citizens'.[35] Immigration Minister U Khin Yee said that those who met the criteria of the 1982 Citizenship Act would be issued with a permanent ID card.[36]

The debate brought to light the widespread issue of 'white cards' or temporary IDs. According to an article in *Voice* in 2012, there were over one million Bengali Muslims and about 500,000 of them had been issued with a temporary ID (white cards) in Rakhine State.[37] Prominent lawyer U Bo Min Phyu was widely quoted in the press as saying that white ID cards were illegal: 'The Constitution rules every law. I tried to find White Cards in the constitution. I haven't seen it. These White Cards are not contained in the 1982 citizenship law either. Therefore, claiming for a White Card is a lawless claim.'[38] However, as will be described below, white cards had been used as temporary IDs, leaving the bearers of these cards in legal limbo.[39]

The complex issue of the citizenship laws

Citizenship in the 2008 constitution is described in Chapter VIII entitled 'Citizen, Fundamental Rights and Duties of the Citizens', Articles 345–390. The Union offers citizenship to all those who are born of parents who both hold Myanmar citizenship, or those who on the day the constitution came into effect already held Myanmar citizenship. It then goes on to list rights such as equal treatment before the law, equal opportunities in public employment, occupation, trade etc. and the non-discrimination against women including mothers. The constitution also promises non-discrimination on the basis of race, religion or sex in appointing or assigning civil service personnel (however with the caveat that in those cases where the job is suitable for a man only, only a man should be appointed). With regard to defining who is a Myanmar national, the constitution is actually of very little help and one has to go back to the citizenship laws, the first of which was passed in 1948 when Myanmar gained independence from British colonial rule. The content of this law was based on the country's long history of conflict and diverse ethnic backgrounds. The two Citizenship Acts (The Union Citizenship (Election) Act 1948 and the Union Citizenship Act) were based on sections 10, 11 and 12 of the 1947 Constitution of the Union of Burma.[40] According to the constitution of 1947, the right of citizenship in Burma was defined in the following way:

1. Any person whose parents belong or belonged to any of the indigenous races of Burma,[41] or
2. Any person born in any of the territories included within the Union, at least one of whose grandparents belong or belonged to any of the indigenous races of Burma, or
3. Any person born in any of the territories included within the Union of parents both of whom are, or if they had been alive at the commencement of this Constitution would have been, citizens of Burma, or
4. Any person born in any of the territories which at the time of birth was included within the British colonial dominions, and who has resided in any of the territories included within Burma for a period of not less than eight years in the ten years preceding the date of commencement of this constitution or immediately preceding 1 January 1942, and who intends to reside permanently therein and who signifies his election of citizenship of the Union in the manner and within the time prescribed by law, shall be a citizen of Burma.

(adapted and reproduced from Tun Tun Aung, 2007, pp. 270–71)

Anyone in doubt of their rights to citizenship could apply through the different administrative layers to the Minister of Home Affairs for a decision, as long as this was done by 30 April 1950. According to Tin Maung Maung Than and Moe Thuzar, if the Union Citizenship Act had been effectively implemented in the years following independence, it might have resulted in a clearer legal status for everyone in the country. However, this did not happen.[42]

The 1974 constitution did not change much with regard to citizenship, still decreeing that 'any person, male or female, born of parents both of whom are nationals, has the right by birth to Union citizenship. The constitution also recognises as citizens, any person, male or female, born of parents who became Union citizens by due process of Law after Independence.'[43] In the course of the 1970s the 1948 Citizenship Act was reviewed for six and a half years, and in 1982 the new citizenship law was enacted. According to General Ne Win who introduced the law at the president's house on 8 October 1982, the law was written so as to protect Myanmar (then still called Burma) from foreign subjugation. Ne Win emphasised the fact that Burma had been annexed as of 1824. 'During this period between 1824 and the time when we regained independence in January 1948, foreigners, or aliens, entered our country un-hindered under various pretexts. [...] We, the natives or Burmese nationals, were unable to shape our own destiny.' (Ne Win, 1982) He distinguished between true nationals, guests and those born of mixed unions, and explained the difference between citizens, guests who have registered for citizenship (*eh-naing-ngan-tha*, i.e. associate citizens) and guests who have not registered for citizenship within the legal time frame (*naing-ngan-tha-pyu-khwint-ya-thu*, i.e. naturalised citizens). In his speech Ne Win emphasised that since the grandchildren of these associate and naturalised citizens would become full citizens in the future, there would only be full citizens within two generations.

> There are three types of citizens at present as said earlier. There will be only one type in our country at some time in the future; that is there will be only citizens. [...] When the grandchild is given citizenship, he will, just like any other citizen, become a full citizen. (Ne Win, 1982)

Unfortunately, Ne Win's vision has yet to be realised. The law and its current application is explained below.

The 1982 Citizenship Law

The 1982 Citizenship Law, which is still in effect today, contains special provisions for ethnic groups who came into the country after the beginning of the first Anglo-Burmese War. It also states that the Council of State can determine whether an ethnic group is national or not. Under the 1982

Citizenship Law there are two types of citizenship: (1) Native Citizenship[44] and (2) Legal Citizenship:[45]

(1) Native Citizens: Nationals such as Kachin, Kayah, Kayin, Chin, Bamar, Mon, Rakhine, Shan and other ethnic groups who have been settled in the territory of Myanmar since 1823 and their descendants. No one can revoke their citizenship without a strong reason. A 'Certificate of citizenship' is issued to them.

(2) Legal Citizen: Citizens who are not nationals but qualify to become a Myanmar citizen according to the legal framework. The 3rd generation of residents who arrived before 1948 will be issued 'Certificate of Citizenship' automatically even though they are not 'nationals'.

Within the legal citizenship category there are two sub-types:

(2.1) Associate Citizens:[46] People who became Myanmar citizens according to the 1948 Citizenship Law. A 'Certificate of Associate Citizenship' is issued for this category.

(2.2) Naturalized Citizens:[47] People who had been residing in Myanmar before independence (4 January 1948) and their descendants who have strong supporting evidence and documents that they were eligible for citizenship under the 1948 Citizenship Law. A 'Certificate of Naturalized Citizenship' is issued for this category.

(According to the 1982 Citizenship Act, only a person whose parents have had their naturalisation of citizenship or a certificate of citizenship or a certificate of guest citizenship can be a citizen. So, apart from these criteria, no one can be a citizen. The third generation of residents who do not have these qualifications cannot be a citizen either.)

Citizens of Myanmar hold National Registration Cards as identity cards. There are three types of National Registration Cards (NRC) issued by the Ministry of Immigration and Population. The native citizens and the third generations of legal citizens are issued with pink cards. The associate citizens hold green cards, while the naturalised citizens hold blue cards. Each card records name, sex, religion, race, father's name and the NRC number of the citizen. According to the 2008 constitution, only the native citizens can become President of the Union of Myanmar. In a press release from the Ministry of Immigration, Union Minister U Khin Yi said:

Apart from the recognised ethnic groups of Myanmar (i.e. the 135 ethnic groups of Myanmar), there are Indians, Nepalese, Pakistanis, Bengalis and Chinese residing in Myanmar. They have been issued with Citizenship Cards, Associate Citizenship Cards, Naturalized Citizenship Cards and Temporary Citizenship White Cards according to the existing law.

However, despite the minister's statement, there do not seem to be any definite definitions or criteria for people who have been issued 'Temporary

Citizenship White Cards'.[48] These white temporary citizenship cards raised the issue of how Bengalis (or Rohingya) could become Myanmar citizens. The Ministry of Immigration has argued that they have the same right to apply for legal citizenship as other eligible foreigners and that their documents would be checked according to the 1982 Citizenship Law by a central body.[49]

The main issue that emerged with regard to the debate about the rights of the Rohingya to be recognised as Myanmar nationals and even as Myanmar indigenous race was that of the citizenship laws and illegal migration. President Thein Sein insisted that the four major religions including Islam were protected by the constitution, and any discrimination by religion and ethnicity would not be accepted in Myanmar.[50] However, his words did not seem to have much traction as the issue of who is a Myanmar citizen was debated widely across the press. Thura U Aung Ko, chairman of the Judiciary and Regulatory Committee, said, 'Rakhine are ethnics, Bengali are guest citizens. Therefore, it is necessary that hosts should be lenient to guests and guests should not insult hosts.'[51] In a meeting with American delegates led by Deputy Foreign Minister Mr Joseph Yun, Shwe Saydi Sayadaw explained the Sangha's position:

> it needs to considered in two parts: Bengalis—those who are citizens and those who are not. Those who are citizens should be placed where there is land and house, and those who are not citizens should be placed in refugee camps and the government, international UN agencies and UNHCR should collaborate together. Therefore, it should be separated into two parts to resolve the problem.[52]

U Aung Kyi Nyunt from the NLD said, '... precautions should be taken more seriously than before to prevent the illegal entry of Bengalis and instead of solving the problem after it has happened, one needs to be alert to prevent unnecessary problems.'[53] Dr Aye Maung, a representative of the Hluttaw, said, '... not all Bengalis are terrorists. There are many of them who are innocent. Some people manipulate this [....] As local people, we want it to be calmed.'[54] In the press conference after their trip to Rakhine State, the '88 Generation representative Ko Ko Gyi said,

> ... in our country, there are Chinese nationals who are Myanmar citizens. Kaman nationals with Myanmar citizenship. Therefore, Bengalis want to express themselves as Bengali nationals. There is a right to become a Myanmar citizen if their father, grandfather lived here. If they decide to live here throughout their generations, Bengalis should try for Myanmar citizenship. If they live in accord with Myanmar society, Bengalis have the right to become Myanmar citizens.[55]

U San Kyaw Hla from the Rakhine party RNDP said, 'they want to be regarded as Rohingya ethnics and it will never be possible to be regarded as such in Rakhine State.'[56]

The quotes from the press above clearly showcase the high levels of emotion across society and across the country when it came to recognising the Rohingya.

Who are the 'Rohingya'?

According to extensive research by Jacques Leider (2014), one part of the Muslims in the north of Rakhine State have claimed since the 1950s to be a culturally distinct and separate ethnic group, identifying itself by the name 'Rohingya' and insisting that they have existed in Rakhine State for many generations. This claim has not been accepted either by the Buddhist Rakhine, or by the Myanmar state.[57] The Rohingyas, he says, 'are best defined as a political and militant movement as its foremost aim was the creation of an autonomous Muslim zone'.[58] In fact, separate historical research by Jacques Leider and Derek Tonkin shows that there is no reference to the term 'Rohingya' in the British colonial archives and that the single historical mention of the word is in one late-eighteenth-century text.[59] Whilst there was a Muslim community living in the area of Arakan in the eighteenth century, it is also widely known that under the British administration between 1826 and 1937 there was considerable Bengali migration both as temporary workers and as permanent settlers. It looks as if the original Muslim population was absorbed by the new migrants at the time, as they were more numerous. The population census of 1869 cited by Leider indicates the total of the population of Rakhine as 447,957, of which 24,637 were classified as 'Mahomedans' (5 per cent of the total). Most of the Muslims lived in the Akyab District[60] where they formed 10 per cent of the total population.[61] There was a significant increase in migration from Bengal between the end of the nineteenth century and the start of the First World War, bringing the number of Bengali-speaking Muslims to over 30 per cent of the population by 1912.[62] The large Muslim influx resulted in increased communal tensions between the Muslim and Buddhist communities, especially at the start of the Second World War. When the Japanese arrived in Rakhine in 1942, this became the front line of the war. Communal issues were emphasised by the fact that the Buddhist Rakhine fought on the side of the Japanese and the Muslims on the side of the British, resulting in attacks on each other. During the course of the war the Buddhists fled south to the areas controlled by the Japanese, and the Muslims fled north to where the Allies had their armed forces.[63]

After the war, the Muslim elites in Maungdaw and Buthidaung wanted to affirm their political ambitions. According to Jacques Leider the term

'Rohingya' started to be used after Burma's independence in 1948 by Muslims from these areas identifying themselves with the heritage of the pre-colonial Muslim community in Arakan.[64] The term was also used to set the community apart from the other predominantly Indian Muslims in Myanmar.[65] The same elites created the Mujahid rebels who fought the Burmese government in 1948 for self-determination and for the creation of an exclusive Muslim zone or state in the north of Rakhine.[66] The Mujahid movement was defeated in 1961, but some armed rebel groups remained and continued the struggle.[67] Ne Win's military coup of 1962 resulted in a much harder line taken towards all minorities in Myanmar, and conditions for the Muslim community in Rakhine worsened. There were two periods of substantial exodus of Muslim communities to Bangladesh: the first was in 1977 when the government clamped down on illegal immigration (operation *nagamin*, or 'dragon king'). The communal violence at the time led around 200,000 Rohingya to flee to Bangladesh, returning the following year. Over 60 per cent reportedly held pre-1982 style NRCs, though a small percentage might have been forged or improperly acquired; some 3,000 held Foreign Registration Cards; while the rest were able to provide proof of former residence.[68] In 1992 more than 250,000 Rohingya fled to Bangladesh, of which around 200,000 were subsequently repatriated.[69] The process of repatriation in both cases was negotiated between the Bangladeshi and the Myanmar governments and was supported by UNHCR. Myanmar only accepted refugees back if the displaced could prove some form of residency status. It is understood that in 1992 Myanmar agreed to accept returnees if they could state which village they resided in and who their neighbours were.[70]

The main issue with regard to legal status has been the National Identity Cards. During the 1989 citizenship inspection process, many Rakhine Muslims surrendered their NRCs but did not receive the promised new CSCs (Citizenship Scrutiny Cards) in return, rendering them stateless. From 1995 Temporary Registration Cards (TRCs) or temporary white cards[71] were issued to Muslims who had no documentation. More TRCs were issued in light of the 2010 elections, so as to garner votes for the USDP, angering the Rakhine Buddhists. A report in 2009 alleged that green-coloured cards were being distributed.[72] The regime's Union Solidarity and Development Party (USDP) also promised to grant Rohingya people citizenship as part of an effort to secure the Muslim vote and thereby limit the electoral success of the Rakhine party.[73]

The TRC 'temporary' measure had only recently been addressed when the government initiated a third verification process to issue permanent citizenship cards to those who qualify under the 1982 law.[74] The pilot scheme started in July 2014 in Myebon township in Rakhine State.[75]

Today the Muslims of Rakhine State deny their Bengali roots, saying that they are the descendants of the original Muslim population in the area and that the Rohingya are an unrecognised indigenous race of Myanmar.[76] The historical reality described above shows that the Muslims in the area lived in a single political constituency that was controlled by the British, and that the migration will have inevitably led to the mixing and uniting of Muslim communities in what was a diverse colonial society. This connection is therefore denied by the Rohingya for political purposes and has to be understood in the political context of post-colonial Burma where the Muslims in northern Rakhine neither had the option to unite with East Pakistan at independence nor to create their own independent Muslim state. In effect this community was forced to remain in Burma, and therefore needed to be recognised as a separate ethnic group to ensure its rights of autonomy from the government in Rangoon. Leider explains that 'the two processes, the redefinition of communal identity as a historically local identity and the militant struggle for autonomy, went hand in hand and they cannot be separated'.[77]

The Rakhine perspective

As mentioned above, many Buddhists in Myanmar and especially in Rakhine State fear that with the growth of the Muslim community they will soon become a minority in their own state.[78] The fear is fuelled by high birth rates amongst Muslims,[79] illegal immigration from Bangladesh, and also by the fact that Buddhists from Rakhine often leave their state for work in other areas of Myanmar or even go abroad. Given that the Rohingya community, unlike the Kaman community, does not integrate with the rest of Rakhine society, they are automatically identified as foreigners that could dilute the socio-cultural essence of Rakhine society. Increasingly small businesses are also controlled or owned by the Muslim community, which has created a perceived economic threat. Lastly the recent violence, often sparked by sexual crimes, has created a state of fear where women in particular are seen as being at risk.[80] The grievances and fears of this community might be exaggerated but feel real to them and therefore continue to fuel the anti-Muslim sentiments. In addition there is the issue of using the term 'Rohingya'. The Buddhist community will never agree to the term 'Rohingya' as it believes that using it will imply accepting the historical narrative that goes with the term.[81] They also resent international insistence that the Rohingya be allowed to self-identify as such, and believe that all INGOs are on the side of the Muslims, refusing to understand their problems. This in turn entrenches the anti-Muslim and anti-foreigner feelings, rather than helping resolve what has now become an intractable situation.

Daw Aung San Suu Kyi's lack of reaction

To the dismay of the international community, Daw Aung San Suu Kyi did not unequivocally condemn the discrimination and the violence perpetrated against the Rohingya and other Muslim communities. Responding to questions from the media, Daw Aung San Suu Kyi highlighted the importance of handling the situation with 'delicacy and sensitivity' while also underscoring the need for the rule of law as 'essential [...] to put an end to all conflicts in the country'.[82] She called for more security forces to be deployed. She was unable or unwilling to take a clear stand on how fair the citizenship law was when asked by the international press. Her hesitancy in condemning communal conflict, especially in Rakhine State, led to severe criticisms.[83] Her stand has to be understood in light of her political career, possibly even in light of her desire to become president in the future and therefore not wanting to upset the majority Buddhist population, whose support she needs. But the international community has remained stunned that the icon of non-violence was not willing to take a clearer and tougher position, supporting minorities who were being discriminated against and in some cases murdered due to their different religion.[84] According to ICG, she told the media, 'people want me to take one side or the other, so both sides are displeased because I will not take a stand with them.'[85]

Ordinary views on religion and citizenship

There should be no surprise at Daw Aung San Suu Kyi's views—the right to live in Myanmar and equating Buddhism with citizenship have become mainstream. As part of an EU research project to garner ordinary views on the state and citizenship, data was collected across the whole country between February 2012 and June 2013.[86] Whilst the project had set out to look at issues of rights and responsibilities and particularly at views on political participation, the results, especially when it came to defining citizenship, were startling. The questionnaires deliberately did not ask about religion, so as not to prompt respondents. However, a very large number of respondents within the Buddhist ethnic groups—i.e. not only Bamar respondents but also amongst Mon, Rakhine, Shan and even Karen Buddhists—equated citizenship with religion, or seemed to think that in order to be from Myanmar one must also be Buddhist. Quotes such as 'Myanmars are national united races'; 'Myanmar must be Buddhist';[87] 'Myanmar citizens are Buddhist';[88] 'I think Myanmar is better than every country because there is Buddhism and peace';[89] 'Myanmar peoples respect the Buddha and the dharma'[90] showcase widely held views. The Buddhist respondents in all ethnic groups seemed to think that religion was a key identifier for being from Myanmar. Despite this rather exclusive view, very few responses reflected the position that different ethnic groups or religious groups could not live together. Those who did came from Rakhine State, reflecting the political and social issues of 2012–13. One respondent explained:

> It is impossible to coexist Rakhine and Rohingya, so we must have specific laws. Otherwise the problem will go on. Union must give security for people of Maungtaw because they feel anxious. And support education, with enough teachers for schools. [...] I want to live separately from *kalar*;[91] I don't want chance to live together. All things, we do are only because of their actions. I cannot murder like them.[92]

The anger at those who might allow Muslims to be considered from Myanmar was palpable in the Rakhine sample: 'Myanmar and Rakhine are not the same. Rakhine always keep their promise but Myanmar are not faithful. Some Myanmar married Muslims but Rakhine don't.'[93] However, other respondents referred to the same issue in more oblique ways, expressing weariness of all foreigners: 'Some foreigners moved and resided in some regions of Myanmar. Then, they condensed their population and tried to hold national registration card. If that matter disturbs the food, clothing and shelter of our citizens, we must take action against them.'[94] There were also a small number of responses that equated Myanmar citizenship with being Bamar, in effect excluding the other national races, even if they were Buddhist.[95]

The only real discussion about 'rights' with regard to citizenship was that of the right to live in the country. This response was more frequent in the Rakhine sample, but was also present with non-Rakhine respondents. Given the decades where Myanmar citizens had no 'rights' in the Western sense of the word, it was interesting to see how important the right to reside in the country was to many. Clearly the issue had become more prominent in people's minds as the national press debated the rights of the Rohingya. One respondent said: 'A man resides in Myanmar but we can't say that man is a Myanmar.'[96] But other respondents were vaguer: citizens' rights were equated with being allowed to belong to Myanmar, to live in Myanmar and the duty was to obey the law. 'The *right to belong to my country* and the duty is to have patriotism and responsible for the duty given by the country';[97] 'Right should be given only if they are dutiful citizens for the country';[98] 'A citizen has the right to reside in Myanmar and to do own job. A citizen must obey the law of Myanmar.'[99] Some were more aggressive in their response: 'Right: want to live peacefully and freedom to reside. Duty: must attack aggressors.'[100] In fact, the role of patriotism and nationalism was often linked to culture, religion and sometimes to language, and respondents spoke of braveness, strength and protecting traditions: 'All of the Myanmar citizens need to be patriotic spirit. Myanmar citizens must love our culture, country, nation';[101] 'Myanmar is so brave and has a desire to develop more';[102] 'Myan means "easy to be successful in difficult situations". Mar means "to get patriotism from everything". Myanmar people are patriotic and polite with courage and patriotic, brave, honest, empathy, innocent and patriotic.'[103]

Of course the Muslim views were quite different—indicative of bewilderment and disappointment, not only felt by the Muslims surveyed in Rakhine State, but also in other parts of the country. 'Although I reside in a long line in Myanmar, I'm not a citizen of Myanmar. We should repair the law of 1982. My country is weaker compared with other country because of the constitution';[104] 'There is a project where Government issues national registration cards in state schools. They only provide that service to Buddhist students, so we were left out';[105] 'The military regime after 1988, citizens from religions other than Buddhism cannot join the police service after finishing the matriculation exam. Though I was an outstanding sportsman, I was not selected for the sports team. Also in schools, I was discriminated for my religion. Because of my religion and belief, they define my race or ethnicity as Pakistan–Indian which I have never been to.'[106]

The views above indicate how deeply engrained the role of religion is in defining national identity and the depth of the divide between Buddhist and Muslim communities. It is therefore not surprising that the violence in Rakhine State in 2012 did not remain an isolated incident.[107]

The inter-communal violence of 2013 and 2014

Since 2010 the communal violence has often spread beyond Rakhine State. But in 2013 a new wave of anti-Muslim violence took off, unconnected to the Rakhine incidents. On 20 March 2013, this violence was triggered by a row in a gold shop in Meiktila, when a Buddhist couple tried to sell a gold comb and ended up getting beaten when they allegedly did not accept the price offered by the Muslim shopkeeper.[108] A Buddhist mob assembled and destroyed the shops that were owned by the Muslim community, despite the presence of security forces. The clashes expanded across town as a group of Muslim men, possibly in retaliation for the violence against their community, pulled a Buddhist monk off a motorbike and killed him. The authorities that had not been able to contain the violence against the Muslim shopkeepers were then unable or unwilling to stop the brutal retaliation against the Muslim community across the whole town and neighbouring areas.[109] Muslim neighbourhoods of the town were destroyed, and at least twenty students and several teachers at an Islamic school were murdered. The official death toll was 43 (but could have been higher) and 12,000 Muslims were displaced as their neighbourhoods were destroyed.[110] The shopkeeper was convicted and jailed, whilst the six Muslims who murdered the monk have been charged and may face the death sentence.[111] However, no Buddhists were charged, despite the violence perpetrated against the Muslim community.[112] On 22 March the president declared a state of emergency in Meiktila.

The next bout of violence occurred at the end of April in Okkan, north of Yangon. Dozens of Muslim shops were looted and destroyed and one person killed, with others injured after a Muslim woman allegedly bumped into a novice monk and he dropped his alms bowl as a result. In early May, Muslim shops and houses were attacked in Hpakant, Kachin State. In both these incidents the security forces arrived quickly and the situation was brought under control.

At the end of May 2013 violence erupted in Lashio, Shan State.[113] A Muslim man was accused of setting fire to a young Buddhist woman. He was arrested and charged, whilst the woman was treated for her injuries. However, the incident resulted in Lashio's main mosque and Muslim orphanage/school being torched, as well as a cinema being set on fire. Several hundred Muslims took refuge in a Shan Buddhist monastery in the town.[114] Hundreds of Buddhist men protested on motorcycles, waving iron rods and bamboo poles, as the government appealed for calm. Ye Htut, the presidential spokesman, posted this message on his Facebook page: 'Damaging religious buildings and creating religious riots is inappropriate for the democratic society we are trying to create.'[115] However, the communal violence did not stop. On 24 August 2013, a mob burned Muslim houses and shops again after a sexual assault on a Buddhist woman by a Muslim man. The mob stopped the firefighters from tackling the blaze and those who tried to stop the mob were injured, including the regional security minister. The situation was finally controlled by police reinforcements.[116]

In October 2013 the violence returned to Rakhine State where five Muslims including a 94-year-old woman were killed and dozens of homes were torched in Thandwe when 700 rioters went on the rampage, leading to Muslim families fleeing to the forest. The violence started with an alleged rape of a Buddhist woman by a Muslim man. This happened at the same time as President Thein Sein was visiting Rakhine State to meet leaders from both communities.

Whilst the start of 2014 was rather quiet and did not bring too many communal tensions to the fore, violence erupted in July 2014 in Mandalay when rumours spread that a Muslim teashop owner had raped a Buddhist woman. The allegations in this case proved to be untrue, but a large mob converged on the shop asking for the owner to be handed over. Two died and dozens were injured.[117] This time the police was quick to react. They arrived and arrested 362 rioters. Facebook was blocked so as to stop hate messages from spreading and rioters to get organised.[118] The Mandalay violence came to many as a shock as the anti-Muslim violence was seen as something that only happened in more remote areas, far away from the urban centres with their educated populations. The fact that ordinary residents in Mandalay were able to turn on their Muslim neighbours showed that a fundamentally new attitude had taken hold across the whole country and no area was immune from rising Buddhist nationalism. As mentioned above, anti-Muslim attitudes are not new, but the rapid propagation of such views has been facilitated by the greater freedom of speech, press and movement. In addition the Sangha has also played a key role in this change.

The radicalisation of the Sangha and the 969 movement

Buddhist monks in Myanmar are supposed to live a life apart from politics, and not being allowed to vote is the clearest indication that there should be separation between politics and the clergy. However, as history has shown, monks tend to become politically active at times when political issues pertain to religion, especially to Buddhism. It has already been mentioned above that monks in Myanmar do not necessarily stick with the creed of non-violent protest. Whilst they fortified their image in the West by marching through the streets of Yangon with upturned alms bowls in 2007, protesting against the policies of the military regime, and being beaten and persecuted by the soldiers, there have been other instances when monks have not only actively taken part in violence, but also instigated violence against others. The latest case of this was the riots against the Muslims in Rakhine State and later the Muslims in other Myanmar cities such as Metkila and Lashio, where monks were seen together with the mobs, waving sticks and hounding Muslims, so much so that the president had to interfere and ask the monks to respect the law, reminding them that their behaviour made the country look bad.

The Buddhist–Muslim issue across the country resulted in a rapid and visible radicalisation of the Sangha, coined as the 969 movement. The recently liberalised press with a new 'freedom of speech' ethos allowed for almost anything to be published—even hate speech and pure nonsense. But the anti-Muslim rhetoric did not end with articles in the press, but rather developed into the 969 movement that has engulfed the whole country, showcasing a dark side to civil society movements in Myanmar. The number 969, a holy number for Buddhists,[119] is now used to denote shops and businesses owned and run by Buddhists, so that customers can actively avoid Muslim shops, goods and merchants. The number comes from the Buddhist tradition, but the movement copied the habit that Muslim shops had of denoting places that sold or served halal food products with 786. Different civil society groups are now pitted against each other in their support for the 969 movement, versus those who want to work for a more inclusive civil society. Much of this is played out on social media.

According to an article in *Foreign Policy* the 969 movement was born in Mahamyaing monastery in Moulmein, the capital of Mon State. The head monk ordered the 969 stickers and distributed them under the guise of a Buddhism solidarity movement, not one that discriminates against Muslims. U Wirathu, a prominent monk and abbot of Masoyein monastery in Mandalay, who was jailed in 2003 for inciting anti-Muslim violence, has become its leader. His extreme rhetoric focuses on how the Muslims want to take over Myanmar, in part by marrying Buddhist women. He allegedly said that all rapes in Myanmar were committed by Muslims and none by Buddhists, and that in mixed marriages the Buddhist wives were forced to give up their religion or face torture.[120] Now Wirathu's sermons are published in books, newspapers and distributed through DVDs, easily available to all. He has proudly declared that he is a Buddhist Bin Laden and made the cover of *Time* magazine on 20 June 2013,[121] bringing him worldwide fame. There has always been an irrational fear amongst many Buddhist Bamar that the country could be overrun by foreigners from neighbouring countries and that Buddhism is threated by Islam. One often hears that countries such as Indonesia, Bangladesh, Pakistan and Malaysia used to be home to many

Buddhists, but now have become Muslim countries, something that many feel puts Myanmar at risk. Marriage is often depicted as a key tool through which Islam furthers its conquests, as Muslim women are not allowed to marry non-Muslims and non-Muslim women marrying Muslim men are expected to convert. The anger over this has now resulted in a proposed bill that restricts interfaith marriage, with some monks threatening to campaign for a boycott of parliamentarians who oppose the bill.[122] In November 2014 four controversial 'protection of religion' bills were forwarded to parliament. The laws were passed in August 2015 and restrict religious conversion and interfaith marriage, and enforce monogamy and population control measures.[123] One proposed law even requires anyone wanting to change their faith to get permission from a specially created local authority. The bills are based on drafts written by the 'Committee for the Protection of Nationality and Religion', a monk-led organisation better known as Ma Ba Tha which was founded in June 2013.[124]

Of course there have been protests against the new laws, but there is widespread reluctance to criticise the 969 movement for fear of being seen as critical of Buddhism and the Sangha. The movement is by no means a cohesive front, with many who just see 969 as a Buddhist identifier and not as a symbol of hate. Even monks who do not agree with 969 and see it as intolerant and inconsistent with Buddhism will not criticise it publically for fear of a backlash.[125] The respect for this movement also means that monks are able to reassert their moral authority across society as the country opens up and reforms.

When discussing the rise of Buddhist nationalism and the increasing anti-Islamic sentiment in today's Myanmar, it is important to remember that none of this is new. As Taylor reminds us, Aung San was a firm believer in the separation of politics and religion. Ne Win, he says, 'recognized that one of the biggest problems in maintaining peace in Myanmar's towns and cities was to keep what he referred to as "the bald headed fellows"—Buddhist monks—separate from "the bearded fellows"—Muslims'.[126] This is something that the current government still needs to take to heart.

The census

Religion and the issue of ethnic classification were underlined by one more big policy decision: in mid 2014 Myanmar embarked on a highly controversial Population and Housing Census. Only limited countrywide population data had been collected since 1983 and most 'official' numbers were estimates, based on rough calculations of what population growth was believed to be in certain areas.[127] The controversy that surrounded the census was based on the fact that it was early days for the new government and the collection of highly sensitive data pertaining to people's ethnicity and religion would be a big risk. In addition, international agencies estimated that there were a total of 650,000 internally displaced persons (IDPs) and 120,000 refugees, mainly ethnic minorities, and that there would be challenges to count them accurately.[128] The census was also controversial as it could not be held in certain conflict-affected areas. However, the process was also seen as an opportunity to find out more about the people of Myanmar whose needs had not been heeded by the previous regime. This is why the process was supported and funded by the United Kingdom, Australia, Switzerland, Norway, Germany, Italy and Finland and supervised by the United Nations Population Fund (UNFPA) with a budget of $74 million.[129]

The administration of the census was undertaken by 100,000 junior government schoolteachers between 30 March and 10 April 2014. These (mostly) women did not have any previous canvassing experience, but had been trained by a cascading 'training of trainers' system. Township Immigration and National Registration Department officials held the overall responsibility for ensuring that the enumeration was completed accurately.[130] The official census form was in Burmese and was filled out by the enumerators (including the ticking of the ethnic codes), not the respondents themselves (which again was seen as a cause of potential problems). Most answers to the 41 questions were answered by filling in a bubble, but some questions required answers to be written in Burmese script.

In preparation for the census, it emerged that the biggest issue was the fact that people had to choose one ethnicity (known in Burmese as *lu-myo*, which literally means 'kinds of people')[131] and the ethnicities on offer were based on the 135 national races (plus Indian, Chinese etc.).[132] The alternative was to tick 'other' and write the chosen ethnicity. If a respondent did not give his or her ethnicity, then the father's ethnicity would be recorded. The ethnic classifications therefore did not take into account more recent developments, ignored the issue of mixed race identities (i.e. one could only be Karen or Bamar, but not both, even if one had one parent from each ethnicity). This meant that respondents had to choose one parent's ethnicity and in some cases one ethnicity from a grandparent. Ethnic classifications are often dependent on the environment people live in, and mixed-race individuals might over their lifetime identify differently at different times.[133] A lot of the debate about the census was that a singular identity and the concept of 'racial purity' would not work for many, because of marriage and relocation. Also, mixed race could only be recorded as Myanmar + Foreigner (code 900).[134]

Another worry was how a number of ethnic groups such as the Chin, Kachin, Karen and Shan had been conflated and confused by incorrect labels. Some of the major ethnic groups have five or six sub-groups. However, the census required them to choose to be identified either by that sub-group or the main group. Choosing the sub-group would mean that the main ethnic identity would appear diffused.[135] The converse was also true, as smaller groups such as Kayan and Palaung (Ta-ang) did not want to be subsumed under Kayah and Shan respectively. The classifications and these difficult choices on offer also confused large parts of the population who were not sure what political consequences[136] there would be if they self-identified as the sub-group or main ethnic group on offer. Ethnic organisations, including Chin, Kachin, Karen and Shan, called on their peoples to self-identify only by their collective name (e.g. Kachin, code 101) rather than their sub-group, dialect or clan identities that the census code also lists.

In addition the classification of Rohingya created a lot of problems, as the Rakhine Buddhists protested until the government retracted the possibility that Muslims in Rakhine would be allowed to self-identify as Rohingya, and required them instead to tick the Bengali box. As mentioned above, the Buddhist Rakhine believed that having the term Rohingya on the census would lead to it gaining some political legitimacy. Despite protests by the two Rohingya parties, enumerators were instructed to record 'Rohingya' as 'Bangladesh' (910) or 'Other' (914). This resulted in over 1 million people not being recorded in Rakhine State.[137]

The results of the census were published in August 2014. The big headline was that Myanmar had 'lost' 10 million people, and that unexpectedly the population figure was much smaller than expected.[138] Details on race/ethnicity and religion were withheld. This is largely because of the government's worry that too large a divergence from the 1983 figures could re-enflame communal violence.[139] More results were finally made public in May 2015.[140] Published highlights included:

- Population growth, 0.89 per cent per year, is less than half the 1970s rate and slowing.
- There are only 93 males for every 100 females, reflecting significantly lower male life expectancy and higher migration by men.
- Half the population is under age 27, but the proportion of children has started to fall.

- The average number of children per woman has declined to 2.3 from 4.7 in 1983.
- Life expectancy at birth, 66.8 years, has improved but is still one of the lowest in Southeast Asia. Life expectancy is six years longer for females than males.
- Infant and under-5 mortality rates are high nationwide (62 and 72 per 1,000 live births, respectively), and nearly twice as high in some states as in others.
- Almost 90 per cent of adults are literate, but in Shan State only 63 per cent are.
- 85 per cent of adult males and 50 per cent of females are in the workforce; unemployment is 4 per cent, and nearly twice as high for those aged 15–29.
- Only a third of households have electric lights and a third have mobile phones, but half have televisions.
- Over 70 per cent of homes have improved water and sanitation, but far fewer do in some states.[141]

The gender and literacy data point to the demographics of a more developed country, quite different from Myanmar's immediate neighbours, India and China. However, the urban–rural divide remains stark with over 70 per cent of people still living in rural areas with lower access to electricity, higher infant mortality and less access to sanitary facilities.[142]

CONCLUSION

THE CHALLENGES OF DEMOCRATISATION
IN LIGHT OF THE 2015 ELECTIONS

Leading up to the 2015 elections

The 2015 elections have dominated the administration of this government ever since the SPDC handed over power to President Thein Sein. As of mid 2011 it seemed imperative that this transition time of five years lead to the first free and fair elections in decades, and therefore the president and others in the government have repeatedly promised to deliver. From the time that Daw Aung San Suu Kyi joined the political fray in 2012, her one and only aim has to been to prepare the ground for 2015. Three themes dominated the political headlines: constitutional change, the voting system and the role of political parties, especially the smaller ethnic parties. In concluding the narrative of the reform process, this chapter will discuss these in light of the power struggles between the presidency, the parliament, Daw Aung San Suu Kyi and the chief of staff that played out on the political scene in Myanmar, especially between 2013 and 2015. The chapter ends by reviewing two major challenges that President Thein Sein's government is handing to its successor: the issues pertaining to rule of law and Myanmar's renewed participation in the drug production and trade circuit, neither of which this government has adequately addressed.

Constitutional change

Changing the constitution has been one of the most important debates that emerged after the 2010 elections and was brought to the fore when the NLD joined parliament after the by-elections in 2012. As described in Chapter 3, at the time the NLD MPs under the leadership of Daw Aung San Suu Kyi refused to take the oath that required them to protect the 2008 constitution. The NLD eventually compromised and the MPs took their seats, but the NLD has continually argued that the constitution needs to be revised. The heart of the debate lies around Article 59f that bars Daw Aung San Suu Kyi from the presidency, as her two sons hold foreign nationality. Daw Aung San Suu Kyi has the support of many Western governments when asking for this article to be changed, as they would like to see her president after the 2015 elections. Article 59f is indeed discriminatory and it needs revising because many young Myanmar nationals now have ties to foreign countries, and a number of younger generation former exile returnees have married foreigners and have foreign national children. It is in light of their future participation in politics and potential leadership of the country that the article does need to be looked at again. Having focused the debate solely on Daw Aung San Suu Kyi's potential presidency has however personalised the dispute and pitted the NLD against the 'old guard' in the government.

The amendment of the constitution exemplified the core of the power struggle between the presidency, the parliament, Daw Aung San Suu Kyi and the chief of staff that developed between 2013 and 2015. At the start of 2015 there were three main contenders for the presidency, aside from President Thein Sein himself, who although he is not standing in the elections for a parliamentary seat could have been proposed as a president again. As discussed above, Daw Aung San Suu Kyi has spent most of her time since her election to parliament in 2012 in getting the obstacles that ban her from the top job removed. She did not succeed, as constitutional reforms were blocked by the military MPs in a parliamentary vote in June 2015. She had elucidated the support of Parliamentary Speaker U Shwe Mann. U Shwe Mann, however, was also a contender and has over the past four years used parliament for his own devices, trying to weaken the president. In an intra-party coup in August 2015, U Shwe Mann was removed as USDP chairman, clearly showing the military's support for President Thein Sein. As the election campaign begins, neither Daw Aung San Suu Kyi nor U Shwe Mann are credible presidential candidates any longer. The third potential candidate who remains is the current chief of staff who has let it be known that once retired he would be interested in leading the country. However for him to become president, there would need to be a strong USDP majority in Parliament.

All three have played political games with the president and his office, mainly using the peace process as a political pawn. Chapter 4 explained how

Daw Aung San Suu Kyi and U Shwe Mann weakened the president's envoy U Aung Min's position, saying that the peace process and all negotiations with the EAGs needed the involvement of the parliament. This slowed the process and created new issues of trust between both sides. General Min Aung Hlaing and the military have been less than helpful during most of the ongoing nationwide ceasefire negotiations, going back on agreements that had been reached under U Aung Min's leadership, again weakening the office of the president and his envoy. Given their political ambitions, it seemed to be in the interest of the three 'contenders' to flex their political muscles, and to make sure that the most important part of a new Myanmar—i.e. peace with the ethnic armed groups—would be achieved after 2015, possibly under their own leadership rather than under President Thein Sein. The detrimental legacy of this politicking, however, is an unfinished peace process and a NCA only signed by eight EAGs.

The struggles over the constitution and over who will get the top job next time around have not been the only struggles related to the elections. First there was a small drama around the by-election planned for December 2014 that should have filled the 35 vacant seats in parliament, which was cancelled by the Union Election Commission in September 2014. It was thought that there was too little time to prepare and that the proximity to the 2015 elections made the exercise senseless. Daw Aung San Suu Kyi had agreed, saying that holding these by-elections would be wasting public money,[1] but others disagreed, inferring that the government might resort to cancelling the 2015 elections as well, if they so easily went back on these by-elections. The second, much larger drama was the debate on which voting system Myanmar should use.

FPTP or PR?[2]

Over the past few years it has become clear that Myanmar's electoral system of 'first past the post' (FPTP) allowed for a party that might not receive the majority of votes to control parliament. The system, meant to serve the USDP, suddenly looked as if it might help the NLD control parliament after the 2015 elections, unsettling the USDP. Smaller parties also started to worry that with NLD participation in 2015 the FPTP system could result in their annihilation. In May 2013, the NDF MPs started to discuss the possibility of suggesting changing Myanmar's election system from FPTP to proportional representation (PR).[3] The Union Election Commission (UEC) asked for the resolution to be voted on at the 7th parliamentary meeting, despite the fact that U Tin Aye, UEC chairman, decreed that PR was not suitable for 'young democracies'.[4] In June 2014 the upper house voted on PR as a voting system with 117 votes in favour to 85 votes against.[5] On 24 July U Aung Zin, an NDF MP, proposed the PR system at the 10th Hluttaw Meeting in the Lower House.[6] Although the military MPs from the upper house were against the PR system, the military MPs from the lower house did not vote against it.[7] The USDP, the National Unity Party, the NDF and the Unity and Democracy Party (Kachin State) supported the PR system.[8] The NLD and 38 MPs from the ethnic parties (SNDP, Arakan National Party, Phalom-Sawaw Democratic Party and All Mon Regions Democracy Party) protested by not attending the parliamentary meeting.[9] The National Brotherhood Federation announced that if the PR system would damage ethnic parties, they would protest in the ethnic areas.[10] The whole debate created major confusion amongst the public, and even the press did not seem to be sure what was being proposed by whom and why.[11] At the end of July 2014 the lower house appointed a 24-member commission to help decide which election system would be appropriate for Myanmar. The Electoral Review Commission included five MPs from the USDP, two MPs from the NLD, two MPs from the NDF, one SNDP MP, eight MPs from other ethnic parties, one military MP and five others.[12] In October 2014 the lower house debated the eight voting systems proposed by the Electoral Review Commission.[13] These included hybrid systems that were rejected by the NLD, who insisted that FPTP was the only system that ensured transparency for the public.[14] In the end, by mid November 2014, the parliament decided to stick with the FPTP system after the Constitutional Tribunal concluded that the other electoral systems were inconsistent with the constitution.[15] Whilst it all now looks like a major waste of time, it is significant to see how much debate was invested in the issue, and despite the USDP wanting to change the voting system, that the constitutional tribunal upheld the constitution, siding with the NLD.

The role of political parties in the 2015 elections

The main contenders for 2015 are the NLD and the USDP. At the time of writing, predictions about who will win would be as scientific as looking into a crystal ball. On the one hand an NLD majority is almost expected by observers inside and outside the country; on the other hand the disillusionment with the NLD in urban, ethnic and other minority areas should not be dismissed out of hand.[16] The vote is likely to be a vote of frustration against the government that will be seen not to have delivered reforms quickly enough, rather than a clear endorsement of the NLD whose policies (apart from changing the constitution) are not known. The interesting part of the elections is the question of what will happen to Myanmar's first opposition that emerged in 2010—the ethnic parties.

The ethnic parties

The ethnic political parties were the first legitimate opposition to the USDP-dominated parliaments after the 2010 election. They were able to establish a significant power base in their areas because the NLD had refused to contest the elections. Over the last four years their role and significance have changed. They are an essential part of the forthcoming political dialogue and the continuation of the peace process with the ethnic armed groups. Their influence in the regional parliaments has started to influence policy-making with regard to education and ethnic language use, as well as triggering debates on resource-sharing. Despite the limited decentralisation, the ethnic parties have developed a clear political voice, banding together as the Nationalities Brotherhood Foundation[17] (NBF) that has grown to include fifteen parties. However, in light of the NLD's re-entry into electoral politics and the NLD plan to field candidates in the ethnic states in 2015, the ethnic parties face new challenges.

In preparing for the 2015 elections a small research team went to meet leaders of all ethnic parties across the country to establish their views on political participation in 2015.[18] The research revealed that three issues dominated the ethnic political scene: the participation of the NLD in ethnic states, financing their political campaign and candidates, and the role of armed groups after the nationwide ceasefire.

The role of the NLD

All party representatives who were interviewed spoke positively about the 2015 elections. These elections will need to be free and fair, but most did not seem to think that this would be their biggest challenge. Unsurprisingly, after longer chats, the issue of the NLD was what perturbed the parties most. Whilst acknowledging the fact that the NLD was entitled to campaign around the country and that this was indeed a sign of democratic change, many could not hide their worry about what that would mean for their party. Given Daw Aung San Suu Kyi's popularity, and her decade-long stand against the former regime, the ethnic parties know that they would lose votes to the NLD wherever an NLD candidate is proposed. One Mon leader explained how this would lead to divisions and problems that could demoralise ethnic party representatives, even if these were not visible on the surface. His voice was reminiscent of the fact that it is difficult to criticise Daw Aung San Suu Kyi and her party, whatever they do.

> The NLD used to shout 'ethnic solidarity' everywhere they have done their campaigns and advocacy. If they sincerely respect the ethnic solidarity, they should not come and compete in ethnic areas. It is their rights to compete in ethnic areas, but it is heavily challenging for other ethnic parties to work with. Even though there might not have visible conflicts, ethnic parties will mentally suffer for their unfair act. (Mon party representative, Mon state)

Beyond the fear of losing seats is also the worry that once in power, the NLD will forget about ethnic rights and not be able to represent the ethnic voices adequately. In Shan State one Wa ethnic leader put it succinctly:

> Daw Aung San Suu Kyi usually said that 'ethnic rights should not be neglected whether majority or minority in population/popularity. Minority ethnic rights should be promoted'. She usually raised the voice for ethnic rights almost in every meeting. Therefore, I have a request to NLD. We, minority ethnic political parties would highly appreciate if NLD does not compete in minority ethnic regions. Locals will get confused with multi electoral advocacies. It would be the best if NLD does not compete in ethnic regions. (Political representative of a Wa party, Shan State)

Some parties were less worried than others, saying that there were no NLD offices in the most remote regions, and others saying that their constituents not only had seen what ethnic parties could achieve for them, but also that ethnic solidarity was strong enough not to split the vote. Some even thought that it would be best to see local alliances between the NLD and the local ethnic party, so as not to confuse the electorate. Clearly no one was too worried about the USDP's pulling power; they were only seen as a threat if the elections themselves were not fair and the 'advance votes' trick was pulled again.

The issue of finance and capacity-building

In preparing for the elections across the board, financing the candidates and the campaign is seen as the most challenging issue. In 2010 the ethnic parties received clandestine support, as they were seen as the only viable opposition to the USDP. Given the fact that the NLD will be putting up candidates across the country, the ethnic parties have to worry about how much help and support they can expect this time around. Many candidates are expected to finance themselves, but for those who were elected, the past five years have often meant that they were unable to continue in their line of business. This in turn meant that wives and family members had to become the main bread-winners, making a second term less attractive. Whilst some parties worry less about the financial implications than others, there is a general feeling that finance and capacity-building for candidates are major priorities before the elections. In 2010 the ethnic parties benefited from the training offered by Myanmar Egress and Shalom. Despite this, new MPs found it hard and there was a steep learning curve on the job. A PaO party representative explained why support was needed:

> When we observe MPs elected in 2010 who are now working in the parliament, they are lacking parliamentary concepts, general and political concepts, unfortunately. Therefore we want to provide our MP candidates with political, democratic, parliamentary concepts as well as policy decision-making training. (PaO political party representative, Shan State)

All are aware of the problems they were going to face, but few seemed to have a plan for how these issues could or would be resolved.

The role of the armed groups

Linking back to Chapter 5 and the discussion of the nationwide ceasefire agreement, ethnic parties felt that they have had too little a role to play. The ethnic parties, just like the armed groups, work for the rights and representation of the ethnic people. As such their aims are similar, and even though the EAGs are still technically illegal organisations, often the parties and the armed groups have some sort of relationship with each other. Often this relationship is complicated by the Myanmar laws that do not allow the political parties to communicate with illegal organisations. As a Karen political leader explained:

> [...] the ethnic armed groups remained illegal and it is a struggle for us to negotiate between them and the government. Since we get nearer with them, we know their desire most. The government should provide an opportunity to political parties a legal negotiation power when working with armed groups. Then, the trust building can be more effective too. (Karen political representative)

The NBF brought all the ethnic parties together to devise a draft frame-work for the political dialogue that is supposed to follow the still elusive Nationwide Ceasefire Agreement. However, ethnic parties are unclear as to what will happen to the armed groups after this ceasefire is signed and the political dialogue is engendered. Khin Nyunt's original thinking in the 1990s was that the EAGs would eventually form political parties and join the political process. However, the 2010 elections allowed for the creation of ethnic political parties before the EAGs had mapped out their future. So many ethnic parties wonder what will happen on the ethnic political scene when the armed groups decide to lay down their arms and join in the political process. Many acknowledge that this is not something they need to worry about now, as the peace process will take time. Nevertheless the environment for the EAGs is changing and some ethnic parties worry rightly that the armed groups might form rival parties, splitting the ethnic vote in their areas. Whilst ethnic parties in some regions simply expect the armed group elites to join them, others realistically understand that there could be a power struggle in the making. This is another reason why ethnic parties feel that they ought to be more closely associated with the peace process and the ceasefire arrangements that are taking place at the moment.

In the end the 2015 elections will be the acid test, not only for the Myanmar government, but also for the NLD and the ethnic parties. A lot will depend on how the relationship between parties and the various groups develop in the weeks before the polls. Whilst there are many dangers for the ethnic parties, there are also new opportunities for potential king-makers in the new government. As a Chin political leader explained:

> The Nationalities Brotherhood Federation could grab 300 seats for the ethnic parties [...]. The winning party whether USDP or NLD has to have 51% of votes to have them in the government body. We are in the B3 group with no enemies. We can act as the team maker with the two Bamar rival parties. They can be king of the government only when they can effectively cooperate with us. No king party can stay away from the NBF in politics. (Chin political representative)

Looking forward, Myanmar's remaining challenges

Many challenges will be handed to the next government in 2016. Two that have not been covered in previous chapters stand out: the promotion of the rule of law across society and Myanmar's increased involvement in the drug production and trade cycle.

The rule of law

'The rule of law' has become a battle cry for the NLD, and Daw Aung San Suu Kyi has decreed many times that for Myanmar's reforms to be successful the rule of law is essential. The reality on the ground is that many citizens are not clear on the meaning of the law, and often the law is applied differently depending on the case at hand. There is little trust in the justice system. People believe that justice is meted out selectively, depending on connections and public standing. Despite this, grassroots organisations have used the new political and social space to protest for rights that are guaranteed in the constitution, but that are not being implemented in practice. There has been an upsurge of activism and popular demand for rights. With little or no outside support, a growing number of lawyers, civil society and community groups have been campaigning against land-grabs and other injustices under the banner of human rights. They are routinely denied permits for peaceful assembly and are at risk of arbitrary arrest. Protests are now a regular feature in Myanmar's public space. What is missing is a system that fairly addresses the issues being protested about. More often than not protesters find themselves arrested, as the laws governing public protests are unclear or not followed in the same way in different places.

Establishing 'the rule of law' requires multi-sectoral reforms and a better understanding at government level, so that the government itself becomes embedded in a legal framework and that governmental institutions are competent and fair. Laws need to become public knowledge, be clear and apply to everyone indiscriminately. The rule of law also implies law and order on the ground, something remarkably absent in the religious protests of 2013 and 2014. For this, reforms are not only needed across the public institutions but new mechanisms at grassroots level need to be established so that citizens understand and trust the legal system to impart justice. Currently not only the NLD, but many civil society organisations have called for the rebuilding of Myanmar's crippled justice system so as to ensure citizens' rights. This will be one of the key challenges faced by the new government post-2015.

Drug production and drug trade

Another issue that is likely to have a long-term impact on Myanmar's future is its renewed participation in the international drug trade. In 2008 it was widely believed that the Myanmar government's 15-year programme to eradicate the growing of poppies was successful. At the time, some even spoke of having won the war against the drug trade in the golden triangle. Only seven years later Myanmar is the world's second largest supplier of opium after Afghanistan, and people are asking what has gone wrong.

There has been increased poppy cultivation since President Thein Sein's government took over in 2011. The problem is severe. According to the Myanmar Peace Monitor, Myanmar produces 25% of the world's opium. Poppy cultivation has increased steadily for the last seven years and jumped 17% from 2011 to 2012. The UN says that figures are up again by a staggering 26% in 2013. UNODC estimates that 300,000 Myanmar households engage in poppy cultivation, and research undertaken by Shan Drug Watch shows that 49 out of 55 townships in Shan State are now growing poppies. However, growing poppies is not limited to Shan State, but also occurs in Kachin, Kayah, Rakhine and Chin States as well as Magwe and Sagaing Regions.

The growth of poppies and the production of opium is closely related to the conflict between the Tatmadaw and the ethnic armed groups. In the post-independence era, the Burmese Communist Party (BCP) that was fighting against the Burmese government had an anti-drugs policy and a crop substitution programme. However, when the various ethnic groups that were fighting together under the ambit of the BCP split up, a number of EAGs started to become involved in the broad machinations of the drug trade to finance the conflict. The first set of ceasefires in the early 1990s helped reduce poppy cultivation, and the SPDC developed a 15-year master plan to eliminate drugs between 1999 and 2014. This coincided with an ASEAN-wide policy that aimed to combat the drug trade across all member states. For over a decade poppy cultivation declined and Myanmar's role in the drug trade across the golden triangle was dramatically reduced. Today, however, there has been a sharp rise, posing a severe new problem for President Thein Sein's reformist government.

As the nationwide ceasefire negotiations and the peace process between the Myanmar government and the EAGs have taken shape, it seems that some EAGs have used the new space to increase the opium trade. EAG involvement usually means taxing the farmers who cultivate the poppies, but also getting involved in the production of drugs and sale of the produce across the border. The issue is particularly pertinent with the United Wa State Army, who have recently re-opened Popakyen in Ming Hsat township, a trading hub, despite a government ban. The trading station had been closed after a large drug haul was confiscated in October 2014. The Wa feel that they can defy Nay Pyi Taw as they have 20–30,000 men under arms and their arsenal of heavy weaponry, mostly purchased from China, even includes rocket launchers. Other EAGs are also alleged to be involved in the drug trade, which helps them finance the conflict; but other armed groups have vigorously fought with those who are involved in the drug trade, attacking factories and burning poppy fields. The army is not without blame either. Research has shown that Myanmar military commanders allow People's Militia Forces (PMFs) to establish their own drug production plants and trafficking networks so as to stop the EAGs from making money from drug production and trafficking.

The 15-year drug eradication programme has evidently failed. Ethnic conflict is at the heart of the issue, but there are other problems which the original programme did not resolve and which have helped increase drug production again. The farmers who today choose to cultivate poppy are poor and feel they have no choice. A recent TV documentary on the opium process in Shan State shows that, to date, substitute crops have not worked. This is despite the fact that cultivating poppies is a lot more labour-intensive than other crops. The money that can be made from selling the poppy sap is simply more lucrative than anything else the farmers feel they can grow. A new programme is trying to substitute poppy cultivation with coffee, but the farmers in that area are not convinced and it will be a few years before the crop bears enough fruit for them to be able to decide whether to change their crop permanently. A statement by the Opium Farmer Forum held in September 2015 representing farmers from Kayah, Shan, Kachin and Chin States declares a joint position with regard to drug policies:

> We grow opium in order to ensure food security for our family and to provide our basic needs, and to have access to health and education. We grow opium because of poverty and because we live in isolated and mountainous and high elevated areas, where it is difficult to grow other crops, infrastructure is weak and we face difficulties to transport crops, and where we have difficulty to access markets. We also have little access to land to grow other crops. The large majority of opium farmers are not rich and grow it for their survival. Therefore, they should not be treated as criminals.[19]

Another issue lies at the other end of the market, where the demand comes from. Not only are the drug trade networks across the golden triangle well developed, but increased demand for heroin and amphetamine tablets, especially from China but also other Southeast Asian countries, means that eradication programmes fail in the countries of production. Where there is demand, there will ultimately be supply.

For Myanmar today the issue is not only the drug trade and how this fuels ethnic conflict, but also the increase in local drug use and the HIV epidemic, especially in the border areas. Research by TNI shows that the repressive drug policies have only led to the criminalisation of the users and small-scale dealers, which in turn has led to over-filled prisons and a lack of access to adequate medical care by those requiring rehabilitation and/or HIV treatment. However, those at the heart of the drug trade seem to be able to continue unabated.

The government is aware of the problem. President Thein Sein has on a number of occasions called for better measures to tackle the rampant drug problem, acknowledging that this is one of the issues his government has not managed to control yet, and one that is being left for the new leadership post-2015.

A few words to conclude

The success of the ASEAN chairmanship[20] that concluded at the start of 2015 and the new engagement with Western countries over the past five years has shown that Myanmar has retaken its position on the global political stage. As explained across the book, the military will remain an important stakeholder in the political and social processes. However, Myanmar has turned a page of sorts, allowing for a more inclusive political process to take shape. In allowing the military to retain its position in politics, Myanmar did not transform itself into a Western-style democracy. This was never part of the plan. It was clear to the civil society organisations that prepared for this transitional phase between 2005 and 2010 that the aim was a shift in power relations, not a revolutionary change. It was about creating a new political and social space that can grow, in time, to become a real democracy. The government led by President Thein Sein has started a process that will need to be taken up by whoever wins the 2015 elections. The problems that are being handed over are at least as great as the successes this government has been able to achieve. It remains to be seen how the elections will be held, and what problems will emerge following the results. Whatever the outcome, this book seeks to explain how Myanmar reached a tipping point for change and to document in real time what happened in the five-year transition between 2010 and 2015.

EPILOGUE

THE 8 NOVEMBER ELECTIONS

On Sunday 8th November 2015 Myanmar went to the polls. This is the first full election in which the NLD has been able to take part since 1990. More than 90 parties contested seats for the two houses of parliament as well as the 14 state and regional assemblies.

In the run up to the polls the Union Election Commission and the government faced a number of challenges starting with the question of a legitimate and internationally recognised outcome. A lot hinged on how the elections are perceived both domestically as well as internationally. In March 2014 the government announced that members of the US based Carter Foundation and observers from the EU were invited to monitor the elections. In 2010 foreign observers were not allowed and in the 2012 by-elections only observers from Southeast Asian countries were invited. In 2010 it was widely felt that not all Union Solidarity and Development Party (USDP) seats were won fairly. However the USDP's strategy of using important local personalities as their candidates, such as the local lawyer or doctor, did pay off in many constituencies as well as the fact that many seats were only contested between the USDP and the NUP. For 2015 there was a lot more choice.

International observers deployed across the country confirmed the day after the elections that the voting had been free, although the fact that 25% of the seats are reserved for the military means that it could not be labelled fair. There don't seem to have been any major infringements despite repeated issues with voter lists before the elections. The NLD added to this the issue that candidates had suffered intimidation in the run up to the elections, having filed over 100 complaints over violations of election rules.

Pre election issues

First of all there was an ongoing controversy with regard to voter lists. Citizens were asked to check and correct their details on the published voter list and some found their names missing or other details incorrect. In some cases it was more difficult than it should have been to get these amended.

Second was the issue of religion that crept in by the back door. The ultra nationalist Buddhist movement Ma Ba Tha that had gained traction in the last three years fuelled anti-Muslim feelings across the country, described in chapter 7. Ma Ba Tha's influence did not only result in the four race and religion protection laws being passed last year, it also resulted in Muslim electoral candidates not being able to contest their seats. The ruling USDP did not allow for its three sitting Muslim MPs to stand again in their constituencies allegedly due to citizenship issues. The NLD removed all Muslim candidates from its lists, so as to not offend the conservative Buddhist electorate. Not one of the 1051 NLD candidates was a Muslim. Other Muslim candidates, including from Muslim parties in Muslim majority areas were removed by the Union Election Commission based on citizenship issues, leaving only a handful of Muslim candidates in smaller parties. The result might be a parliament without a single Muslim MP, despite a sizeable number of Muslim citizens.

And then there is the issue of the Muslims who are not citizens, mostly self-identifying as Rohingya. Some would qualify for citizenship if the 1982 citizenship law had been properly applied, others, who are more recent migrants might not. The controversy is that in 2010 many were White Care holders (temporary citizenship cards) and they were allowed to vote. In fact the USDP courted these votes in 2010, trying to defeat the local ethnic Rakhine party. When white cards were declared unconstitutional by Myanmar's constitutional tribunal, all white card holders were disenfranchised overnight.

Elections were not held in nearly 600 village tracts across Kachin, Shan and Karen states. The polls were mostly cancelled due to ongoing conflict between EAGs and the Tatmadaw. However a few areas, which were barred from voting, are in confirmed ceasefire areas, which seemed rather unfair to the affected ethnic populations. Voting was not allowed either in Wa Special Region 2 and Mongla special region 4, affecting five townships, where the EAGs did not allow the Election Commission to compile voters' lists.[1]

The major parties had pre-election issues as well. As mentioned earlier, U Shwe Mann was removed as USDP chair in retaliation for not letting the presidential ministers U Aung Min and U Soe Thane run as USDP candidates in the constituencies of their choice in Kayah State. This highly visible power struggle between USDP factions showed that not all was well within the regime party. The support of many USDP MPs to amend the constitution in the September vote also indicated a major rift between the military and the regime party.

The NLD had issues as well. Candidates were selected by decree, and in some cases local NLD workers who had worked hard for the party and had the backing of the constituents were not allowed to run for their seat as Daw Aung San Suu Kyi took the final decision on the list of candidates. This was reminiscent of 2012 where such undemocratic practices had created some upset. In addition NLD candidates were forbidden from speaking to the press in the pre-election period – a rather odd way of controlling information flows by the NLD 'high command'.

Results

At the time of writing the official declaration is still outstanding, however the Union Election Commission has to date awarded the NLD 390 seats in the bicameral parliament, giving the party an outright majority.[2] In order to control the government the NLD needed 67% of the seats (or 329 seats), so as to balance the 25% of the seats that are held by appointed military MPs. Crossing this threshold means that Myanmar can now become a very different country. The losing USDP has been bitterly disappointed with the result. Nevertheless the outgoing MPs have congratulated the NLD and the regime party has shown dignity in the face of the NLD's landslide victory.

A defeated USDP

The USDP had campaigned hard on the development agenda. It was after all due to their efforts and the leadership of President U Thein Sein that the country had been transformed. As the results started to trickle in, the disappointment across the USDP ranks was intense. Acting USDP chair U Htay Oo lost his seat, as did his predecessor, popular speaker of the house U Shwe Mann. Many of those who felt they had served the country and made change possible have had to concede defeat. This includes the President's peace envoy U Aung Min who almost singlehandedly delivered an unprecedented peace process with the ethnic armed groups (EAGs) and laid the foundations for the NCA that was signed by 8 EAGs on the 15th of October this year. U Soe Thane, who ran as an independent candidate was one of the few who was re-elected.[3]

The night before the elections President Thein Sein gave a speech promising to honour the results of the vote and wishing everyone good health. As the defeat of the USDP became clear he congratulated Daw Aung San Suu Kyi on the NLD win.

The demise of ethnic politics

In some ethnic states many parties and candidates were also licking their wounds. At the time of writing when not all seats had been officially declared, it looks like ethnic parties have taken high losses other than in Rakhine State and some Shan and Chin State areas. A Mon friend said that she hoped that the NLD would rule in an inclusive way, that they would collaborate with the local ethnic parties and hear ethnic voices. She concluded by saying: 'I am hoping that the situation will proceed to the better situation.' The fact that the ethnic electorate chose the NLD over ethnic parties will have been very hard to accept. In essence it now means that ethnic politics is relegated to a Bamar majority party, and that the ethnic voices that had been quite a prominent part of the transition will no longer be heard.

A victorious NLD

The celebrations at the NLD headquarters have been intense as the results started to point to an NLD landslide. Daw Aung San Suu Kyi was re-elected in Kawhmu. Many who had joined her ranks, including Karen activist and leader of the Kare Women's action group Susanna Hla Hla Soe defeated their USDP rivals. In light of the NLD's overwhelming majority Daw Aung San Suu Kyi wrote to President U Thein Sein, the chief of staff Min Aung Hlaing and Speaker of the House U Shwe Mann to ask for a meeting.

Whilst Daw Aung San Suu Kyi can't be president herself, even with a big NLD win, she has nevertheless promised to be 'above the president' and lead the country. No one has any doubt about that—the question that needs to be asked is—will she be able to unite the country?

The challenges ahead

Myanmar's ethnic and religious diversity will not make this an easy task. Muslims have felt discriminated against, even persecuted in certain areas and almost disenfranchised as they had hardly any candidates from their community to vote for. The NLD has not spoken up for the disenfranchised Rohingya either, in fear of being branded foreigner friendly. The NLD's announcement that they will 'protect' Muslims sounds rather feeble. The NLD will need to stand up to Ma Ba Tha to create a more inclusive society.

A second issue includes the representation of ethnic people. Despite local ethnic leaders' misgivings the NLD fielded candidates in all ethnic majority areas. Consequently many locals feared the vote would be split leading to an end of vibrant ethnic politics that had been an unforeseen result of the 2010 elections. The NLD has always maintained that democracy is their first priority and ethnic grievances can be addressed later. Given the protracted and ongoing peace process with the ethnic armed groups, it will be critical for the NLD to hear non-NLD ethnic opinions and to respect these so as to take the political dialogue forward. The NLD now has the great responsibility of representing those ethnic voices that put their trust in Daw Aung San Suu Kyi, deserting their own ethnic parties in the process.

A third issue will be relations with the military. Myanmar has mainland Southeast Asia's largest standing army. The constitution guarantees their place in parliament and control over key ministries. They will remain significant stakeholders in the political system. A divided parliament on military-civilian lines will not be good either for national reconciliation or the peace process. The NLD will have to find a way to cooperate with the chief of staff as well as the military MPs. The NLD's commitment to alter the constitution and in particular change article 436 is likely to bring the party into conflict with the military leadership.

Today euphoria across Myanmar's electorate is high. The results that they had been denied in 1990 have come through 25 years later. Beyond the excitement the NLD will have to satisfy the expectations of a country that has been in waiting for a quarter of a century.

There is some time until the actual transfer of power in the New Year. It has to be hoped that this will go smoothly as planned. These next few weeks will be challenging as those who have held power for so long will have to adjust to a new political reality. It is also a time when the NLD needs to think as to how it will be able to govern not just for its supporters, but for all people of Myanmar.

This book ends with a citation by Ashley South, who in a personal communication after the election said—'I suspect we will see post election triumphalist historic revisionism. We need to recognise the achievements of the current regime and the transitional moment.' I hope this book serves this purpose.

ANNEXES

Annex 1 (Chapter 2)

Daw Aung San Suu Kyi's Open Letter (Unofficial Translation) 28 July 2011

The (post-independence) Union of Burma was co-founded by different nationalities. Like siblings from a single family, all these nationalities had cohabited this land since time immemorial. Therefore, forging peaceful ties and unity among the nationalities is of paramount importance.

Of late, there have been news stories about military conflicts between the country's armed forces and the armed nationalities groups in various regions such as the Kachin, the Shan, the Karen, the Mon and so on. These conflicts are resulting in tragic outcomes such as loss of life, destruction of costly physical infrastructures and economic projects and a condition of general deterioration. Besides causing enormous suffering among local communities, these conflicts come with a potential risk of spilling over and spreading across Burma's immediate neighbourhoods.

The use of force to resolve the conflicts is only going to be mutually harmful to all parties concerned. National reconciliation and unity cannot be built on might. It can only be pursued through political negotiations. Only through political negotiations can genuine national unity be established. Only such unity among nationalities can guarantee the country's (peaceful) future. In the absence of genuine peace and reconciliation, the potential spread of civil war always lurks beneath.

Conflicts between nationalities can surely be resolved on the basis of mutual respect and mutual understanding, leading ultimately to the Union's peace and stability. Only when the Union is genuinely peaceful and stable can nation-building programmes be implemented successfully. Therefore, with the sole purpose of promoting the well-being of all nationalities in the land, I call for immediate ceasefires and the peaceful resolution of conflicts.

On my part I am prepared, and pledge, to do everything in my power towards the cessation of armed conflicts and building peace in the Union.

Signed
Aung San Suu Kyi
54/56 University Avenue, Rangoon
http://www.burmanet.org/news/2011/07/28/
daw-aung-san-suu-kyi's-open-letter-unofficial-translation/

Annex 2 (Chapter 2)

List of meetings with Daw Aung San Suu Kyi after the monks' protests in September 2007 and before her release:

- 2007 September 30, UN Special Envoy Gambari met Aung San Su Kyi in Rangoon. (Burma Campaign UK, 2010)
- 2007 October 25, Aung San Su Kyi met Minister Aung Kyi who had been appointed as liaison officer. No announcement on the discussion was published. (Burma Campaign UK, 2010)
- 2007 November 6, Aung San Su Kyi met UN Special Envoy Mr Gambari. During the visit, the UN envoy proposed a three-way negotiation but the government rejected the UN's proposal. And the government (Minister Kyaw San) said, 'We will welcome positive coordination and cooperation for Myanmar affairs, but will never accept any interference that may harm our sovereignty.' (BBC, BBC News, 2007) (BBC, BBC News, 2008)
- 2008 January 31, Aung San Su Kyi met NLD leaders. After the meeting, the message 'We should hope for the best and prepare for the worst' was sent to the public. (Burma Campaign UK, 2010)
- 2008 March 8, Aung San Su Kyi met UN Special Envoy Mr Gambari. (Burma Campaign UK, 2010)
- 2008 August 21, Global Policy Forum pointed out that UN envoy efforts were heading towards complete failure. An opposition source close to Aung San Su Kyi said that she would not meet the UN envoy if he met top members of the regime. (Jagan, 2008)
- 2009 February 20, Aung San Su Kyi, the UN Envoy Mr Gambari and the NLD leadership met. (Burma Campaign UK, 2010)

- 2009 June 26, Aung San Su Kyi met UN Special Envoy Mr Gambari. (Burma Campaign UK, 2010)
- 2009 July 3, UN Secretary General visited Myanmar and was not allowed to meet Aung San Su Kyi. (Burma Campaign UK, 2010)
- 2009 August 14, Senator Jim Webb visited Myanmar and met with Senior General Than Shwe and Aung San Su Kyi. (Webb J., 2012) After his visit to Myanmar, he called the US government to increase confidence-building gestures in order to pursue a better relationship between the two governments. He also urged Senior General Than Shwe to release Aung San Su Kyi and allow her to participate in the 2010 election. (Webb S. J., 2012)
- 2009 October 3, Aung San Su Kyi met Minister Aung Kyi. (Burma Campaign UK, 2010)
- 2009 October 9, Aung San Su Kyi met the UK ambassador, the deputy heads of the Australian and US missions. (Burma Campaign UK, 2010)
- 2009 November 4, Aung San Su Kyi met the US delegation led by Assistant Secretary of State Kurt Campbell. (Burma Campaign UK, 2010)
- 2009 December 9, Aung San Su Kyi met Minister Aung Kyi. (Burma Campaign UK, 2010)
- 2009 December 16, Aung San Su Kyi met NLD party leaders Aung Shwe, U Lwin and Lun Tin. (Burma Campaign UK, 2010)
- 2010 January 15, Aung San Su Kyi met Minister Aung Kyi. (Burma Campaign UK, 2010)
- 2010 May 10, Aung San Su Kyi met a US delegation led by Assistant Secretary of State Kurt Campbell. (Burma Campaign UK, 2010)
- 2010 November 13, Aung San Su Kyi is released from detention.

Annex 3 (Chapter 2): Election Results 2010

Party	Lower House	Upper House	State & Region Assemblies	Total
Union Solidarity and Development Party*	259	129	496	884
National Unity Party*	12	5	46	63
Shan Nationalities Democratic Party	18	3	36	57
Rakhine Nationalities Development Party	9	7	19	35

All Mon Regions Democracy Party	3	4	9	16
National Democratic Force	8	4	4	16
Chin Progressive Party	2	4	6	12
Pa-O National Organisation*	3	1	6	10
Phalon-Sawaw Democratic Party	2	3	4	9
Chin National Party	2	2	5	9
Palaung National Party*	1	1	4	6
Kayin People's Party	1	1	4	6
Wa Democratic Party*	2	1	3	6
Unity and Democracy Party of Kachin State*	2	1	2	5
Inn Nationalities Development Party	1	–	3	4
Democratic Party (Myanmar)	–	–	3	3
National Democratic Party for Development*	–	–	2	2
Kayin State Democracy and Progressive Party	–	1	1	2
Kayan National Party	–	–	2	2
88 Generation Student of Youths (Myanmar) Party*	–	–	1	1
Ethnic Nationals Development Party	–	–	1	1
Lahu National Development Party*	–	–	1	1
Independent	1	1	4	6
Total	326	168	662	1156

*Assembled from different media outlets.

Annex 4 (Chapter 4): Negotiations and the peace process, 2011–13

Meetings between Government and Armed Groups, 2011
(http://www.mmpeacemonitor.org/)

- 2011 July 31: Government of Myanmar met KIO for ceasefire. The meeting failed to reach agreement, but both parties agreed to continue face-to-face discussion.
- 2011 September 30: Government met UWSA, and government side rejected the key demands of UWSA.

- 2011 October 5: Government and NMSP met for the first time since 1990s and ceasefire breakdown.
- 2011 October 25: Government met DKBA for draft peace proposal.
- 2011 October 29: Government met SSA-N in Naypyidaw.
- 2011 October 31: Government met KNPP for meeting.
- 2011 November 1: Government met KIO for meeting in China.
- 2011 November 12: Government met NMSP for preliminary peace talks.
- 2011 November 18: Government met KNPP, KIO, SSA-S, CNF, and KNU met separately in Mae Sai, Thailand.
- 2011 November 28: Government met KIO's full-scale delegation-level talk, but no agreement reached.
- 2011 November 30: Government met KNPP for preliminary agreement.
- 2011 December 1: Government met SSA-S and signed 8 point-agreement.
- 2011 December 10: Government signed ongoing peace agreement with DKBA.
- 2011 December 18–19: Government met KNU for meeting at Mae Sot, Thailand.
- 2011 December 19: Government met ABSDF, and ABSDF presented four-point ceasefire talk.
- 2011 December 21: Government met NMSP in Thailand.
- 2011 December 22: Government met PNLO in Bangkok for informal peace talks, where UNFC also participated.
- 2011 December 26: Government met NDAA to discuss issues and reached economic agreements.
- 2011 December 25: Government met UWSA and received agreement on trading of timber and construction supplies for infrastructure development.

Meetings between Government and Armed Groups, 2012
(http://www.mmpeacemonitor.org/)

- 2012 January 4–5: CNF signs five-point ceasefire agreement after two days of talks.
- 2012 January 11: KNU signs ceasefire agreement.
- 2012 January 15: SSA-A signs ceasefire agreement. A preliminary ceasefire was signed.
- 2012 January 27: SSA-N signs ceasefire agreement.
- 2012 January 31: NMSP signs ceasefire agreement. The government agreed to a request to allow the Mon language to be used in schools.

- 2012 February 24: NMSP met with government and agreed four-point agreement, based on a five-point agreement initiated at state level on Feb 1.
- 2012 March 6: KNPP signs ceasefire agreement. Karenni liaison offices to be opened in suitable locations and to hold union-level peace talks at a later date.
- 2012 April 5: RSLP signs ceasefire agreement. Formation of peace-making groups for talks at central level on agreed date and venue and allowing negotiated transgression and arms-carrying apart from mutually agreed areas.
- 2012 April 8: NSCN-K signs ceasefire agreement. The National Socialist Council of Nagaland–Khaplang (NSCN-K) signed a 5-point preliminary peace agreement that included coordination for travelling with arms and continued talks between the two sides at Union level.
- 2012 April 9: NMSP met government for stage 2 talks. U Aung Min told the NMSP leaders at the meeting to apply for company licenses for party businesses.
- 2012 May 6: CNF met government to sign peace charter. Signed a 15-point peace charter which included an immediate ceasefire between the CNF and government.
- 2012 May 20: KIO met government for informal meeting in Chaing Rai, Thailand.
- 2012 June 8: KNPP met government and reached Union-level ceasefire.
- 2012 June 19: KIO met government at Majiayang, Kachin: U Aung Min and a KIO delegation led by Maj-Gen Samlut Gun Maw.
- 2012 June 21: SSA-N sign Union-level ceasefire; SSA-North hand over control of different base to Burmese army.
- 2012 June 25: KNU met government for stage 2 talks in Mae Sot, Thailand, to keep the peace-making talks on track.
- 2012 August 5: KNU met government for stage 2 talks at Myawaddy, Thailand. The government and KNU representatives planned to hold a three-day meeting on August 27 in Hpa-an to discuss a ceasefire code of conduct.
- 2012 September 2: Government and KNU met for third round of peace talks in Pa-an, Karen State. Both parties agreed in principle to code of conduct.
- 2012 September 27: Government met SSA-S for second-stage peace talks in Khao Lam.
- 2012 October 5: Government met UWSA and NDAA leaders in Keng Tung for anti-drug meeting.
- 2012 October 10: Government met SSA-N for second-stage meeting in Lashio; both parties agreed to relocation of SSPP/SSA families and IDPs.

- 2012 October 29: Government, SSA-S and UNODC met for anti-drug agreement.
- 2012 October 30: Government met KIO in Ruili, China. Minister U Aung Min agreed to begin political dialogue in November inside Myanmar.
- 2012 November 9: Government met ABSDF in Chiang Mai. During this trip, delegations from Government of Myanmar informally met with UNFC members.
- 2012 November 10: Government informally met with KNPP leaders and discussed observer groups and monitoring the development in Kayah State.
- 2012 November 16: Government met NDAA at border area, and commander of army also met UWSA leaders.
- 2012 December 1: Government met UWSA leaders in Panghsang, capital of Wa Region.
- 2012 December 7: Government met CNF leaders for second Union-level meeting in Yangon; both parties agreed to perform regional development.
- 2012 December 24: Government met ABSDF in Naypyidaw for preliminary meeting.

Meetings between Government and Armed Groups, 2013
(http://www.mmpeacemonitor.org/)

- 2013 January 5–6: Government met KNU leaders for Union-level meeting in Yangon. KNU leaders met President Thein Sein, Vice President Dr Sai Mauk Kham and Commander in Chief, Vice Senior General Min Aung Hlaing.
- 2013 March 11–12: Union Peace Working Committee and Kachin Independent Organisation met in Ruli, China. Four-point press release published.
- 2013 March 23: Union Peace Working Committee met with PNLO for Union-level discussion.
- 2013 April 2: Government delegations met with Kachin Independent Organisation in Ruli, China.
- 2013 May 11: Government met SSPP/SSA at Tant Yan Township, Shan State.
- 2013 May 28: Government met KIO in Myint Kyi Nar, capital of Kachin State.
- 2013 June 19: Government met KNPP in Loi Kaw Township, Kayah State.
- 2013 July 12: Government met UWSA for Union-level meeting.
- 2013 July 22: KIO opened technical advisory office in Myint Kyi Nar, Kachin State.

- 2013 July 31: Government met TNLA for first meeting at Muse Township, Shan State.
- 2013 August 5: Government met ABSDF at Myanmar Peace Center for Union-level meeting.
- 2013 August 31: Government met KNU, RCSS and CNF together in Nay Pyi Taw.
- 2013 September 8: Government and UNFC met for second time for pre-discussion of political dialogue.
- 2013 October 6: Government and RCSS/SSA met in Nay Pyi Taw.
- 2013 October 10: Government met KIO in Myint Kyi Nar, capital of Kachin State.
- 2013 October 22: Government met KNPP for third time in Loi Kaw, capital of Kayah State.
- 2013 November 4: Government and ethnic armed groups met for first meeting of discussion about nationwide ceasefire accord in Myitkyina, Kachin State.
- 2013 December 15: Government met ethnic armed groups to discuss ceasefire around the country.
- 2014 January 5: President met Geneal Mu Tu Sae Poe for fourth time in Nay Pyi Taw.
- 2014 April 5: Government met ethnic armed groups to discuss draft nationwide ceasefire accord to get single text.

Annex 5 (Epilogue)

Party	Pyl Thu Hluttaw	Amyo Thar Hluttaw	State/Region Hluttaw	Ethnic Representative
NLD	254	135	476	17
USDP	30	12	74	2
ANP (Rakhine)	12	10	22	1
SNLD (Shan)	13	3	25	–
Other Parties	13	7	34	5
Individual/Others	1	1	–	–
Total	323	168	631	25

Data Source: Union Election Commission.

7 township could not be allowed for election because of security reasons. The numbers in the table are the number of seats achieved by political parties.

NOTES

INTRODUCTION: REFORMS, CIVIL SOCIETY AND THE CHALLENGE OF DEMOCRATISATION IN THE WAKE OF MILITARY RULE

1. There are various police training programmes underway: one run by the ILO and another funded by the EU and organised by IMG.
2. The censorship board no longer exists, but this does not preclude a certain level of 'self-censorship', especially with regard to sensitive topics such as religion and race, or when driven by the fear of the arbitrary application of laws about criticising the state. I am grateful to one of the anonymous reviewers of the book for pointing this out.
3. His power was cut down to size in August 2015 when he was removed from the USDP leadership. However, the disputes and disagreements between him and the president were a hallmark of the post 2011 government.
4. Violence and intimidation were used during the protests against the education law, as covered in Chapter 6. However, this does not compare to the way the 2007 protests were wiped off the streets, as covered in Chapter 1.
5. The foreign investment law is a case in point.
6. I agree with Egreteau and Jagan that what we are looking at is very much still a praetorian state, where the military is a major stakeholder and has important political and economic interests as well as social influence—possibly in the Indonesian, Thai or even Pakistani tradition.
7. It is important to note, as Mary Callahan has argued, that the reforms were not triggered by intra-military factionalism, popular mobilisations or a defeat in war, and that therefore the current leadership has engendered the reforms from a position of strength without having its hands forced post SPDC 'politics' in Myanmar. Mary Callahan (2012), 'No Longer Necessarily "National Security"', (Myanmar in Reform 2012, HK University symposium, symposium proceedings, selected summaries), pp. 25–7.
8. Pedersen, M. (2005), in Kyaw Yin Hlaing, R. Taylor and Tin Maung Maung Than, *Myanmar: Beyond Politics to Societal Imperatives*, Singapore: ISEAS, p. 161.

9. Although controversially one could argue that, given the way the party operates, the NLD would not offer Western-style democracy either, even if they were in power.
10. Pedersen (2005), in Kyaw Yin Hlaing, Taylor and Tin Maung Maung Than, p. 161.
11. Callahan (2012), p. 25.
12. See Callahan (2012) for a detailed analysis of this, pp. 25–6.
13. See possibly (not out yet, so can only judge from her previous articles) the forthcoming book by Delphine Schrank who maps the post 2008 period from the viewpoints of young NLD activists.
14. T. Kramer (2011), *Civil Society Gaining Ground—Opportunities for Change and Development in Burma*, Amsterdam: TNI/BCN, p. 5.
15. D. I. Steinberg (2001), *Burma—the State of Myanmar*, Washington, DC: Georgetown University Press, p. 103.
16. Ibid.
17. Kyaw Yin Hlaing (2007), 'Associational Life in Myanmar', in N. Ganesan and Kyaw Yin Hlaing (eds), *Myanmar—State, Society and Ethnicity*, Hiroshima: HPI and Singapore: ISEAS, p. 160.
18. Clearly excluding both the Sangha and the SPDC's USDA that is often discussed in the literature on civil society in Myanmar. SLORC created the USDA in September 1993 to underpin its grip on society: 'It may also have considered the need for some mass organization that could propagate the views of the military when the time came as eventually it would, for the promulgation of the new constitution. The decision was therefore not to register this new group as a political party, but rather as a social organization under the ministry of Home Affairs.' Its expansion was rapid: by 1996 it had over 5 million members, and by 1999 over 11 million. Steinberg expected that around 30% of adults became members (pp. 110–11).
19. 'The ground on which such organisations tread is indeed a grey area, for though the government is aware of their existence, they are not hassled as long as they do not challenge the government.' Kyaw Yin Hlaing (2007), p. 165.
20. Such as the free funeral service.
21. Kyaw Yin Hlaing (2007), p. 162.
22. The definition used seven criteria: non-profit; voluntary initiative; relative independence from political parties and organisations, and from government; self-governing; self-perception as accountable in some way to society; disinterest, in the sense of working on behalf of others and not their own staff, as members of committees; socially progressive, that is, having at least one human development or social welfare aim. Cited in Kramer, (2011), p. 11.
23. Paung Ku aims are, 1. To build capacity of civil society organisations, 2. To improve practice within the international development community, 3. To facilitate networking within civil society for learning, sharing and influencing wider change and 4. To enhance advocacy between civil society and policy actors.

24. M. Duffield (2008), 'On the Edge of "No Man's Land": Chronic Emergency in Myanmar', working paper, Centre of Governance and International affairs, University of Bristol, p. 8.

25. M. Callahan (2010), 'The Endurance of Military Rule in Burma: Not Why But Why Not?' in S. Levenstein (ed.), *Finding Dollars, Sense and Legitimacy in Burma*, Washington, DC: Woodrow Wilson International Centre for Scholars, pp. 71–2.

26. 'According to US based writer, Min Zin, for example, inside activists are "third force" wannabes who threaten to "confuse the moral clarity of people's struggle against dictatorship." [...] Other critics go as far as to suggest these "inside" activists are puppets or agents of the regime. When criticised, "inside" reformists find themselves in a bind. They have no credible platform from which to respond, given state control of the media. Additionally, entering into this debate puts the population at risk of greater surveillance by the military.' Callahan (2010), p. 73.

27. Mark SiuSue (2012), 'How Civil Society Can Engage with Policy Making in Myanmar's Transitional Context', *Journal of International Affairs*, Columbia SIPA, http://jia.sipa.columbia.edu/tag/civil-society/ p. 1.

28. ME's training programme (especially the course on social entrepreneurship) and overall ethos was set up to engender the creation of many more CBOs, so as to develop a strong network of organisations that would be able to complement as well as challenge the state. More on this in Chapters 1 and 2.

29. The Farmland Bill that will legalise the purchase and sale of farmland, and the Vacant, Fallow and Virgin Land Management Bill that will regulate the acquisition of land by private enterprise.

30. SiuSue (2012), p. 2.

31. See for example D. Tonkin (2009), 'Burmese Perspectives: Sanctions against Myanmar, Profit and Loss Account, http://www.networkmyanmar.org/images/sanctions.pdf

32. The 1990 elections were not parliamentary elections. See D. Tonkin (2007), 'The 1990 Elections in Myanmar: Broken Promises or a Failure of Communication?' *Journal of Southeast Asia*, vol. 29, no. 1, pp. 33–54.

33. My work in Myanmar in the last decade has been funded by the British Council; the EU; IMG; The American University/UNICEF; DAI/USAID; Shalom Foundation/DFID; Pyo Pin; AUSAID, the Konrad Adenauer Foundation; the Friedrich Ebert Foundation; the Heinrich Böll Foundation and the Friedrich Naumann Foundation.

34. I was fortunate to be able to train a very good small research team in qualitative research methods as of 2010. We have worked together on various funded projects since 2011. Much of the time I took part in the data collection; however for large surveys requiring months in the field, they were the ones who did all the hard fieldwork.

1. HOW MYANMAR GOT FROM 2005 TO 2010: THE ROLE OF CIVIL SOCIETY

1. Myanmar's junta was headed by Senior General Than Shwe; second in command was Senior Vice General Maung Aye; and third (Secretary 1) was General Khin Nyunt. General Khin Nyunt was replaced by General Shwe Mann. Than Shwe and Maung Aye retired in April 2011 at the handover to the civilianised government. General Khin Nyunt was still under house arrest at that time. Shwe Mann was appointed as speaker of the Lower House of Parliament, although he had hoped to become president.

2. It was first announced that Khin Nyunt was retiring on health grounds, but then General Shwe Mann made a speech to top military officials charging Khin Nyunt with corruption, insubordination and an attempt to break up the Tatmadaw. Kyaw Yin Hlaing, R. Taylor and Tin Maung Maung Than (2005), *Myanmar: Beyond Politics to Societal Imperatives*, Singapore: ISEAS, p. 237.

3. Ibid.

4. Kyaw Yin Hlaing (2010), 'Problems with the Process of Reconciliation', in Riffle, L. (ed.), *Myanmar/Burma Inside challenges, outside interests*, Washington, DC: KAF/Brookings Institution Press, p. 41.

5. Kyaw Yin Hlaing, Taylor and Tin Maung Maung Than (2005).

6. The seven-step roadmap to discipline flourishing democracy was announced by General Khin Nyunt on 30 August 2003 in the state media and included: '1. Reconvening the National Convention (NC) that has been adjourned since 1996; 2. After the successful; holding of the NC, step by step implementation of the process necessary for the emergence of a genuine and disciplined democratic system; 3. Drafting a new constitution in accordance with the principles laid down by the NC; 4. Adoption of the constitution through a national referendum; 5. Holding free and fair elections for the pyithu hluttaws according to the new constitution; 6. Convening the hluttaws (assemblies) and 7. Building a modern, developed and democratic nation by the state leaders elected by the hluttaw and the government and other central organs formed by the hluttaw.' (*New Light of Myanmar*, 31 August 2003)

7. This is significant as David Delapraz was unable to secure access to the jails in India. Personal conversations 2005–7.

8. Professor Robert Taylor is probably the only Western Myanmar expert who understood Myanmar's development at that time. Being one of the few Western academics allowed into the country during the late 1970s and 80s, he had a rare overview of the country and contacts at the highest levels of government, giving him a unique insight into how Myanmar was developing.

9. Taylor (2005), in Kyaw Yin Hlaing, Taylor and Tin Maung Maung Than, p. 25.

10. Ibid., p. 25.

11. The formal reform process started in 1988, but with Khin Nyunt's arrest a new political and social space opened.

12. Alan Saw U (2007), in N. Ganesan and Kyaw Yin Hlaing (eds), *Myanmar—State, Society and Ethnicity*, Hiroshima: HPI and Singapore: ISEAS, p. 221.

13. The main ceasefire groups that were represented at the National Convention were: Communist Party of Burma (Arakan); New Democratic Army (Kachin); Kachin Independence Organisation; Kayan National Guard; Karenni Nationalities Peoples Liberation Front; Kayan New Land Party; New Mon State Party; Myanmar National Democratic Alliance Army (Kokang), United Wa State Party; Shan State Army; National Democratic Alliance Army (Eastern Shan State); Kachin Defence Army; PaO national Organisation; Palaung State Liberation Party; Shan State National Army; Shan State Nationalities Liberation Organisation. Seven of these were former allies or breakaway groups of the BCP. Listed by Martin Smith in Kyaw Yin Hlaing, Taylor and Tin Maung Maung Than (2005), p. 78.

14. M. Smith (2007), *State of Strife: The Dynamics of Ethnic Conflict in Burma*, Policy Studies 36, Washington, DC: East–West Center, p. 1. Details of the ceasefire protests and who was negotiating can be found in R. Taylor (2009), *The State in Myanmar*, London: Hurst & Co., pp. 433–45.

15. K. MacLean (2010), 'The Rise of Private Indirect Government in Burma', in Levenstein, S. (ed.), *Finding Dollars, Sense and Legitimacy in Burma*, Washington, DC: Woodrow Wilson International Centre for Scholars, p. 43.

16. Ibid.

17. Smith (2007).

18. D. I. Steinberg (2001), *Burma—the State of Myanmar*, Washington, DC: Georgetown University Press, p. 187.

19. A. South (2007c), Burma, COHRE Country Report, Geneva, p. 133.

20. M. Smith (2005), in Kyaw Yin Hlaing et al. (eds), *Myanmar: Beyond Politics to Societal Imperatives*, Singapore: ISEAS, p. 70.

21. A. South (2008, 2nd edn 2010), *Ethnic Politics in Burma: States of Conflict* (London: Routledge), p. 13.

22. Seng Raw (2001), 'Views from Myanmar: An Ethnic Minority Perspective', in Taylor, R. (ed.), *Burma: Political Economy under Military Rule*, London: Hurst & Co., p. 161.

23. A. South (2007b), 'Burma: the Changing Nature of Displacement Crises', RSC Working Paper no. 39, Refugee Studies Centre, University of Oxford, p. 24.

24. Ibid., pp. 18–19.

25. South (2007c), p. 42.

26. Kyaw Yin Hlaing (2005), 'Myanmar in 2004: Another Year of Uncertainty', *Asian Survey*, 45 (1), pp. 174–9.

27. First convened in 1993 as a first attempt to draft a new constitution.

28. For more on this, see Kyaw Yin Hlaing (2005), pp. 174–9.

29. V. Bowman (2007), 'The political situation in Myanmar', in Skidmore M. and Wilson, T., *Myanmar, the state, community and the environment*, Canberra: ANU Press.

30. Who later became Myanmar's current president.

31. Bowman (2007).

32. It is said that the USDA had over 24 million members in 2007 with associations in most townships. At the time of the elections in 2010 the USDA was converted into a political party—the USDP.

33. *Naypyitaw or Nay Pyi Taw* is often translated as 'the place where the king resides' (see for example Pedersen (2007), p. 219). However, Robert Taylor points out that *Naypyitaw* means capital and that a direct translation means something like 'official sun country'. I am grateful to Bob for pointing out the examples of the use of the word *Naypyitaw*—for example there is a Naypyitaw bus line in Yangon— the 'capital' bus line.

34. Personal conversations in Yangon, 2005–6.

35. Travel between Yangon and NPT today is very easy due to improved roads and flight connections. As NPT has developed its schools and other infrastructure, many families have followed their spouses, and so the trains no longer depart at ridiculous times.

36. A visit to NPT in the summer of 2007 also revealed that some of the construction was so cheap that in some ministries there was damage to the stairs, even before the building had been completed.

37. Association of monk and nuns/monkhood.

38. At first this was only the case in Yangon, but later some private supplementary schools and private schools emerged in Mandalay. Despite the tight regulation on curriculum content, fees and teacher salaries, some larger consortiums managed to set up private schools and education centres around the country. The International Language and Business Centre (ILBC) is such a venture and caters to a wide age group of learners of English and other subjects.

39. Personal conversations with owners of schools and teachers 2005–7 in Yangon.

40. See http://www.myanmar.gov.mm/Perspective/persp1998/9–98/edu.htm

41. Personal conversations with owners of schools and teachers 2005–7 in Yangon.

42. At the time many foreigners living in Myanmar held visas that had nothing to do with their jobs. For example the only child psychologist employed at Pun Hlaing International Hospital was sponsored by a restaurant and held a visa for an assistant cook. Different arrangements were in place for foreigners who came to teach, but usually they received support and sponsorship from a related business of the school owner, as the Ministry of Education would not issue teaching visas.

43. Interview with Ko Tar, July 2014.

44. It is important to note that the NLD's claim to power after winning the 1990 election was rejected by SLORC because of the failure of the party to fulfil the con-

ditions for a transfer of power to a civilian government that included drawing up a constitution that then needed to be ratified by a popular referendum. See Taylor (2009), pp. 412–15; and Derek Tonkin (2007), 'The 1990 Elections in Myanmar: broken promises or a failure of communication?' *Contemporary Southeast Asia*, vol. 29, no. 1, pp. 33–54.

45. U Than Aung was the Education Minister with whom Professor Robert Taylor and Dr Kyaw Yin Hlaing negotiated the first few teaching programmes at Yangon and Mandalay universities. He was replaced by Dr Chan Nyein who cancelled the programme for the Ministry of Education, so it was arranged to move the teaching to the Myanmar Fisheries Federation and the students came from USDA. I am grateful to Bob Taylor for clarifying this point.

46. In Myanmar the brightest students are pushed to study medicine, resulting in a country with a surfeit of medical graduates who are unwilling to practise, and a shortage of doctors actually in the hospitals and surgeries.

47. Mentioned earlier in her role of developing Kachin and other ethnic civil societies after the 1990s ceasefires.

48. At that point, other relatively smaller German foundations started to emulate KAS and FES and were interested in supporting civil society programmes in Myanmar.

49. The Bangkok process itself really took off much later, but the connections had been made.

50. Nay Win Maung dabbled in astrology, so he would have calculated the exact date and time at which to start this endeavour.

51. Both Tin Maung Thann and Nay Win Maung maintained that at the time Kyaw Yin Hlaing's first aim was research and development for the Myanmar academy, rather than using training and education as a means of creating change. This is probably not quite true, but the different approaches between the various ME founders did lead to a lot of tensions and difficulties over the years.

52. Robert Taylor has pointed out that some of the initial funding for Myanmar Egress came from anonymous Western sources. This was not mentioned by any of the ME directors, but is very likely as Nay Win Maung asked a number of friends for financial support at the time.

53. That was me…

54. Interview, summer 2014.

55. Nay Win Maung's mother, Daw Yin Yin, says that she had let it be known to some former students that she hoped Nay Win Maung would not be arrested whilst she was alive. Private conversations, 2013–14.

56. ANO has returned from exile and now works at the Myanmar Peace Centre in Yangon.

57. This was neither a revolution nor was it 'saffron'. Saffron is the colour worn by Thai monks. In Myanmar monks wear maroon. (Some now say that what was meant was 'raw saffron', which is rubbish.)

58. Robert Taylor maintains that the monks' demonstrations in 2007 were linked to the UNGA meeting in New York and not the price of petrol. However, interviews conducted with Nay Win Maung and Tin Maung Thann at the time of the monks' demonstrations in Yangon in September 2007 clearly pointed to the economic issue as a cause of the protests.

59. R. Horsey (2008), 'The dramatic events of 2007 in Myanmar: domestic and international implications', in Skidmore M. and Wilson, T., *Dictatorship, Disorder and Decline in Myanmar*, Canberra: ANU Press, p. 15.

60. Ibid.

61. Largely thugs.

62. I was trying to get a taxi on University Avenue, as I lived nearby, when my husband called my Myanmar mobile telling me that there were reports of protests on the BBC in front of Daw Aung San Suu Kyi's house and I should be careful. However, there was no one on University Avenue at the time—I could see the whole avenue clearly from where I was standing, and the guards blocking the road to Daw Aung San Suu Kyi's house were on duty. Later that day protesters started to arrive at her house. It is a bit of a chicken and egg story, but many Burmese listen to the BBC and the BBC Burmese service must have heard the report and decided to come out and join the crowds in front of her house.

63. Horsey (2008), p. 18.

64. Ibid., p. 19.

65. I am grateful to Bob Taylor for pointing this out.

66. Compare this for example to the 2010 Bangkok protests where 60+ people were killed by the army.

67. Win Min (2008), 'Internal Dynamics of the Burmese Military: Before, During and After the 2007 Demonstrations', in Skidmore M. and Wilson, T., *Dictatorship, Disorder and Decline in Myanmar*, Canberra: ANU Press, p. 37.

68. No facebook at that time in Myanmar.

69. Win Min (2008), p. 42.

70. Appointed as Minister for Labour (2007–12) and later Minister of Information (2012–14).

71. Kyaw Yin Hlaing, (2010), p. 38.

72. 'Contrary to allegations made in Washington, DC by the wife of the then President of the United States, (see "Laura Bush criticizes Burma's cyclone warning", ABC News, 6 May 2008), among others, announcements of the storm and its possible course were announced before it struck land. However, the size of the storm was not then known and it changed from its predicted course, which would have had it passing over the new capital city of Naypyitaw, and proceeded in a more southerly direction which included Yangon and Bago divisions, and Kayin state, as well as Ayeyawaddy division and Mon state.' R. Taylor, 'Responding to Nargis: Political Storm or Humanitarian Rage?' unpublished paper.

73. Tin Maung Maung Tan (2009), 'Myanmar in 2008—Weathering the storm', in Singh, D., *Southeast Asian Affairs 2009*, Singapore: ISEAS, p. 197.
74. I am grateful to Bob Taylor for pointing out that the official version of the government's response can be found in Union of Myanmar, National Disaster Preparedness Central Committee, *Record of Activities during the Emergency, Assistance and Rehabilitation Period in Cyclone Nargis-Affected Areas* (NP: NP, ND [March 2009?]).
75. *Myanmar Alin* and *Kyei Mon*, 4 May 2008. The English-language *New Light of Myanmar* did not appear on 4 May because its presses had no electricity supply. Production resumed the following day. Cited in Taylor (n.d.).
76. Union of Myanmar, op.cit., p. 43, cited in Taylor (n.d.).
77. Tin Maung Maung Than (2009), p. 198.
78. *New Light of Myanmar*, 18 May 2008.
79. See Taylor (n.d.).
80. National Disaster Preparedness Central Committee News Release no. 7, 22 May 2008, *New Light of Myanmar*, 23 May 2008. Cited in Taylor (n.d.).
81. I am grateful to Bob Taylor for pointing this out.
82. This actually resulted in quite a number of INGOs supporting local organisations that had been set up by pro regime cronies or organisations linked to the military. It is unclear how aware of this they were.
83. Taylor also points out that 'the use of natural disasters to change government policies, and impose new economic patterns are not unknown and the incompetence of much well-meaning advice is well documented'.
84. Tin Maung Maung Than (2009), p. 199.
85. This programme had been put in place in response to the 2004 tsunami.
86. There were many more, for example another organisation called the Swanyee Development Foundation (SDF) also became involved by building shelters. T. Kramer (2011), *Civil Society Gaining Ground—Opportunities for Change and Development in Burma*, Amsterdam: TNI/BCN.
87. After the brunt of Nargis was over, the World Bank wanted to do a social impact assessment. NAG, still a part of ME at the time, hired two ME faculty members (known as the twins) who had studied in the US. ME won all follow-up assessments apart from one. Now NAG has developed into a full-fledged independent research institute. NAG subsequently became the Network Action Group.
88. PM Thein Sein was in charge of the relief efforts on the government side.
89. Personal fieldwork at the time in the delta in June 2008.
90. Tripartite Group, 'Monthly Recovery Update', May 2010.
91. Kramer (2011), p. 13.
92. *New Light of Myanmar*, 10 February 2008.
93. Tin Maung Maung Than (2009), p. 203.
94. Interviews with CSOs in Yangon and private conversations with friends across the 'third force' at the time.

95. Tin Maung Maung Than (2009); and interview with Steve Marshall.

96. Unpublished briefing paper by Mael Renault.

97. Conversations with the Ministry of Development in Germany: most international funding went to Egress, Shalom and Metta.

98. Allegedly he had already done this once in 2008, but not met Daw Aung San Suu Kyi.

99. US intervention meant that he was freed and sent back to the US.

100. Kyaw Yin Hlaing (2010), p. 39.

101. Private conversations with Nay Win Maung, 2009 and 2010.

102. Fieldwork in Mon state during the course of 2010 revealed that the NMSP was rearming and expecting a severe army crackdown. Fighting in Karen State had never stopped, and things looked unstable in Shan and Kachin States.

103. 'The sell-off can be seen as a way to transfer state assets and economic rents to the military (through holding companies it controls), regime proxy companies and the private business interests of existing leaders or their cronies.' International Crisis Group report, 'The Myanmar Elections', *Asia Briefing*, no. 105, p. 8. See also Wai Moe and Ba Kaung, 'Junta puts more state-owned properties up for sale', *The Irrawaddy*, 22 January 2010; 'Burmese tycoon takes over fuel imports and sales', *The Irrawaddy*, 27 January 2010; 'Myanmar moves to privatise key state enterprises', *Wall Street Journal*, 19 February 2010; 'Burma to privatise ports', *The Irrawaddy*, 26 February 2010; Ba Kaung, 'Selling off the state silver', *The Irrawaddy*, vol. 18, no. 3, March 2010; 'Myanmar's ruling junta is selling state's assets', *New York Times*, 7 March 2010; and Aung Thet Wine, 'Junta transferring state enterprises to holding company', 10 March 2010.

2. THE ELECTIONS AND THE NEW OPPOSITION: VALIDITY AND PUBLIC DISENCHANTMENT

1. Kyaw Yin Hlaing (2007), *The Politics of State–Society Relations in Myanmar*, South East Asia Research, London: IP Publishing.

2. Ibid.

3. Although this phrase was often associated with civil servants in the Ne Win era, it was used by a number of respondents interviewed to show their pre-election attitude to political participation. Nay Win Maung used it a lot to explain public and societal attitudes at the time.

4. This has been the case since the first constitution was written and not something added to the 2008 constitution.

5. M. Lall and H. Win (2013), 'Myanmar: The 2010 Elections and Political Participation', *Journal of Burma Studies*, vol. 17, no. 1, pp. 181–220.

6. Representatives of the regime have argued previously that a slow transition to democracy is essential, as the people need to be 'educated' under the tutelage of the military.

7. Editor in Chief, *The People's Age*, Yangon, speaking at the Burma Update conference in Canberra, May 2011.

8. Edited by Dr Nay Win Maung.

9. According to interviews there were also veiled references in the state media that allegedly said that if the elections were not a success, then no further change could be expected in the foreseeable future. The elections were presented as a once in a generation opportunity for some form of change.

10. PM Thein Sein as quoted in *New Light of Myanmar*, 29 September 2010.

11. 25% were 18–24 yrs of age and 41% 25–39 yrs of age; the rest were older. 41% were from Yangon, 38% from rural areas, 11% from other cities and 10% from ethnic states.

12. CPCS (2010), 'Listening to Voices from Inside—People's perspectives on Myanmar's 2010 elections', http://www.centrepeaceconflictstudies.org/wp-content/uploads/Ethnic_People_Speak.pdf

13. Lall and Win (2013).

14. Quietly—but not really in secret or under cover.

15. For a full discussion of the research results, see Lall and Win (2013).

16. H. H. Win and Y. M. Aung, (2010), 'Educational Space in Myanmar in Light of 2010 Election', Marseilles: International Burma Studies Conference Press.

17. This included Myanmar Egress, the Asian Network for Free and Fair Elections (ANFREL), the Vahu Development Institute, Shalom Foundation, as well as political parties. (Burma News International, 'Election report 2010, pre-election observations', Myanmar Burma)

18. For a detailed analysis of the election laws, see R. Horsey (2010a), 'Preliminary Analysis of Myanmar's 2010 Electoral Laws', prepared for the Conflict Prevention and Peace Forum, SSRC.

19. This included meetings with Dr Thu Ja, who was trying to get a Kachin party registered, but in the end was not allowed to do so. In Kayah State as well, an independent ethnic party could not be formed because of the authorities.

20. It is understood that the NDF also received support when they decided to split from the NLD.

21. ICG (2010), 'The Myanmar Elections, Asia Briefing', International Crisis Group report no. 105, Jakarta/Brussels, http://www.crisisgroup.org/~/media/Files/asia/south-east-asia/burma-myanmar/B105%20The%20Myanmar%20Elections.ashx, p. 10.

22. Conditions to register as a political party: 'a minimum of 15 persons must apply to the Electoral Commission for permission to carry out the organizational work necessary to establish a new party. These persons must indicate the name of the party they intend to form, and must declare that they meet the personal qualifications stipulated in §4 relating to age, citizenship, and legal status—they must be aged at least 25; be citizens, associate citizens, naturalized citizens or temporary

certificate holders; not be someone who has taken foreign citizenship; not be civil service (or military) personnel; not be members of a religious order; not be serving a prison term; not be a member of an insurgent organization or in direct or indirect contact with same; and not be engaged in illegal drug activities.' R. Horsey (2010b), 'Overview of Registered Political Parties in Myanmar', Conflict Prevention and Peace Forum, 15 June 2010, SSRC, p. 1.

23. Junta authorities are reportedly providing national ID cards to Chinese citizens (classifying them as part of the Lisu ethnic group) in order to reach the 0.1% population quota as required by the junta-drawn constitution for the upcoming general elections, according to sources from the Sino-Burma border. Lisu residents in Shan State North's Namkham and Muse townships reportedly want to have a representative in the Shan State legislature in order to be eligible to become a minister of the state/regional government. However, since the group's population is still less than 59,000, in order to fulfil the required quota Panhsay Kyaw Myint, a well-known militia chief from Namkham, together with officials from Namkham immigration, have been cooperating and providing ID cards to ethnic Chinese in Namkham and Muse and named them as Lisus. If Lisu fill the quota, Sai Kyaw Myint's relative, Sai Htun Maung, would be chosen as a representative of the Lisu nationality and could also become a Lisu minister. During the 2008 referendum, thousands of Chinese citizens were offered temporary cards by the military junta to support its 2008 constitution, which was officially declared to have been approved by more than 90% of eligible voters. Euro-Burma Office Election Monitor, 7–13 August 2010.

24. ICG (2010), p. 5.

25. TNI (2010b), 'Un-level Playing Field: Burma's Election Landscape', Burma Policy Briefing, no. 3, October 2010, p. 2.

26. Later 5 were dissolved, leaving 37 to contest. BNI (2010), 'Hobson's Choice: Burma's 2010 Elections', OSI, p. 30–31.

27. 'A different registration process applied to the 10 parties that were still legally registered under the 1988 party registration law. Under §25, these parties were required to notify the Commission by 6 May that they wished to continue as political parties. Five of the 10 parties gave such notification; the other five—including the National League for Democracy (NLD) and the Shan Nationalities League for Democracy (SNLD)—were automatically deregistered effective 7 May. [...] One of the reasons for the §3 pre-approval process is that, under draconian restrictions on freedom of association and assembly in Myanmar, it would be illegal for people to hold meetings to discuss the formation of a party. Strict censorship provisions are also a serious impediment to party-political activities. The 1962 Printers and Publishers Registration Law requires that permission be obtained in advance from the press scrutiny board for all publications. The authorities have issued a directive that party materials are exempted from censorship, provided that parties

apply for such exemption within 90 days of Election Commission registration, and pay a fee and a deposit.' Horsey (2010b), pp. 2–3.

28. *The Irrawaddy*, 6 September 2010, 'Candidate List Paints Picture of Election Results'.

29. Ibid.

30. A. South (2010), 'Making the Best of a Bad Election', *The Irrawaddy*, July 2010, vol. 18, no. 7, p. 2.

31. *The Irrawaddy*, 15 January 2010, 'Suu Kyi Meets Junta Liaison Officer', http://www.irrawaddy.org/article.php?art_id=17591

32. Daw Aung San Suu Kyi had sent two letters to Than Shwe (25 September 2009 and 11 November 2009) requesting to meet with her party/central committee of her party and proposing to cooperate with the SPDC on lifting sanctions.

33. 'They include Dr May Win Myint of Mayangon Township and Dr Than Nyein, one of the founding members of NLD and brother-in-law of former Military Intelligence Chief and purged Prime Minister, Khin Nyunt. Other newly appointed CEC members include Win Myint, member of NLD's Legal Committee, Dr Win Naing, Thanlyin Township (Rangoon Division), Tun Tun Hein, Naung-Cho Township (Shan State), Nyan Win, Ahpaung Township (Mon State), Han Thar Myint, Butalin Township (Sagaing Division), Thein Nyunt, Thingangyun Township (Rangoon Division), and Ohn Kyaing, member of Central Information Committee. May Win Myint, is a prominent member of the party and led the NLD's Women's Wing before her arrest in 1997. Her appointment will make her the second woman to serve in the NLD hierarchy after detained leader Aung San Suu Kyi.' *Mizzima*, 14 January 2010.

34. An NLD Central Committee meeting had been held on 29 March 2010 to review the electoral laws.

35. See http://www.networkmyanmar.org/index.php/component/content/article?id=73: scroll down to early 2010 for an explanation of the NLD decision.

36. http://www.burmanet.org/news/2009/04/29/national-league-for-democracy-shwegondaing-declaration/

37. The creation of the NDF was a case in point, as the disagreement over whether to take part in the elections or not split the NLD. After the elections such splits have continued with the NDF expelling a sitting MP over internal disagreements. See also Kyaw Yin Hlaing (2007).

38. Note by Network Myanmar: Reports from other sources say that the previous day (22 March) the senior echelons of the party, the Central Committee and Central Executive Committee, decided not to hold a secret ballot on Monday 29 March about whether to register the party for the elections or not, but to leave the decision to Suu Kyi and Chairman Aung Shwe. Those in the NLD who might wish to participate in the elections despite all its flaws would no doubt find other ways of so doing if the NLD itself did not register. The possibility of a split in the party

would now seem to be high. See also 'Suu Kyi opposes party registering for polls', AFP, 23 March 2010.

39. Zöllner, H. B. (2012), 'The Beast and the Beauty: History of the conflict between the Military and Aung San Suu Kyi in Myanmar, 1988–2011, set in a Global Context', Berlin: Regiospectra

40. 'Suu Kyi opposed to NLD registering for the elections', Associated Press, 23 March 2010. 'Personally, I would not even think of registering (the party) under these unjust laws,' Ms Suu Kyi said, according to her lawyer Nyan Win who met with her on Tuesday at her lakeside villa in Yangon. She added: 'I am not instructing the party or the people. They are free to make their decisions democratically,' Nyan Win said.

41. Private email conversation.

42. ICG, no. 105.

43. Myint Maung, 'NLD to plunge itself headlong into social work', *Mizzima News*, 2 April 2010.

44. Myanmar's political landscape beyond 2010.

45. Private email conversation, 2010.

46. BP170310, p. 5. For more on the 1990s elections, see D. Tonkin (2007), 'The 1990 Elections in Myanmar: broken promises or a failure of communication?' *Contemporary Southeast Asia*, vol. 29, no. 1, pp. 33–54.

47. www.myanmarelections2010.com

48. Preliminary Findings report, November 2010.

49. The Western press immediately decried these as largely a farce—unlikely to be free or fair and even less likely to bring change to the long-suffering country. Western concerns centred largely on who was allowed to vote and stand, and the issue around political prisoners. Aung San Suu Kyi was still under house arrest, but not barred from voting.

50. The government did allow a pro-regime Kachin party to be formed.

51. Personal interviews after the elections.

52. As described above, unofficial election observers had been trained and fielded quietly across the country and were reporting back via phone to an HQ at Myanmar Egress where the behaviour was being monitored by Egress staff and foreign supporters. This is also reflected in the report by Special Rapporteur Quintana shortly after the elections, in early 2011.

53. T. O. Quintana (2011), 'Progress report of the Special Rapporteur on the situation of human rights in Myanmar', Human Rights Council,16th session,Agenda item 4,Human rights situations that require the Council's attention, 7 March 2011 General Assembly A/HRC/16/59, p. 4.

54. I am grateful to Derek Tonkin for pointing this out.

55. Quintana (2011), p. 4.

56. Ibid., p. 4.

57. Post-election interviews and conversations in Yangon.
58. In the end very few overturned wins went to court. 'The procedure for filing a complaint about the electoral process as elaborated in the Complaints Procedure for Election Fraud is highly problematic and in fact unprecedented. A non-refundable fee of one million kyat (about $1,200) is required to formally file a complaint. Given that the average annual salary in Myanmar is $459, this fee is prohibitively expensive and appears intended to prevent complaints. In addition to the financial burden of filing a complaint, the Government appears to have issued an implicit threat of further fines and imprisonment for complainants who pursue justice. *The New Light of Myanmar* reported on a letter sent by the Union Election Commission to political parties which stated that some parties had made allegations through foreign radio stations and print media "on the grounds that their candidates were not elected in the elections", and that such allegations went against article 64 of the respective Election Law. Yet article 64 does not refer to general criticism in the media, rather: anyone "found guilty of dishonestly and fraudulently lodging any criminal proceedings against any person regarding offences relating to election shall, on conviction, be punishable with imprisonment for a term not exceeding three years or with fine not exceeding three hundred thousand kyats or with both". In this kind of pronouncement, the intention of the Government appears to be intimidation of candidates from filing complaints. Quintana (2011), pp. 5–6.
59. Won 57 out of the 157 seats it contested.
60. Won 35 out of 44 seats it contested.
61. *Irrawaddy*, 20 November 2010.
62. Thant Myint U (2012), 'White Elephants and Black Swans: Thoughts on Myanmar's Recent History and Possible Futures', in Cheesman, N., Skidmore, M. and Wilson, T. (eds), *Myamar's Transition—Openings, Obstacles and Opportunities*, Myanmar Update Series, Singapore: ISEAS, p. 25.
63. M. Callahan (2010), 'The Endurance of Military Rule in Burma: not why but why not?' in Levenstein, S. L. (ed.), *Finding Dollars, Sense and Legitimacy in Burma*, Washington, DC: Woodrow Wilson International Centre for Scholars.
64. Let us not forget that it is not that different from what has happened in other Southeast Asian countries like Thailand and Indonesia in the 1960s; and like Pakistan and other Asian countries, the military will retain a presence in the wider political life. Also see note below by Richard Horsey. Steinberg maintains that the elections 'may have determined the composition of the new government, but they did not change, and specifically were not intended to change, the distribution of effective power, which still rests with the Tatmadaw (armed forces), and is likely to do so into the indefinite future. Critical in this configuration is the role of the minorities, their ability to articulate their views legally, practice their languages and cultures, and develop locally through access to state-controlled resources.' D. I. Steinberg (2011), 'Myanmar in 2010—the election year and beyond', *Southeast Asian Affairs*, Singapore: ISEAS, pp. 173–4.

65. TNI (2010a), BPB, no. 2, June 2010, p. 8.

66. Thant Myint U (2012), p. 25. This was also often said by Nay Win Maung when he tried to explain the advantages of these elections to foreign diplomats in the course of 2011.

67. Thant Myint U (2012), p. 41.

68. 'Numerology played a role again in the choice of the date and the time of the first session of parliaments. The numerals in the date (31+1+2011=9) sum up to nine as do the numerals of the time 08+55=18; 1+8=9).' ICG (2011), 'Myanmar's Post-Election Landscape', International Crisis Group report no. 118, Jakarta/Brussels, http://www.crisisgroup.org/~/media/Files/asia/south-east-asia/burma-myanmar/B118%20Myanmars%20Post-Election%20Landscape.pdf, pp. 5–6.

69. R. Horsey (2012), 'Myanmar's Political Landscape Following the 2010 Elections: Starting with a Class Nine-Tenth empty?' in Cheesman, N., Skidmore, M. and Wilson, T. (eds), *Myamar's Transition—Openings, Obstacles and Opportunities*, Myanmar Update Series, Singapore: ISEAS, p. 42.

70. 'Dr. Sai Mauk Kham, born 1950, is the owner of a medical clinic in Lashio, Northern Shan State. Besides, he is the chairman of the Shan Literature and Culture Association in Lashio. He was not involved in politics before the elections but had good social contacts to the top military leaders in Shan State.' ICG (2011), pp. 5–6.

71. 'Tin Aung Myint Oo, born 1950, had been quartermaster-general of the army and chairman of two bodies supervising the economy, the Trade Policy Council which was established during the Asian economic crisis in 1997 to strengthening controls on the private sector's economic activities and the Myanmar Economic Corporation, a holding under military control which runs a number of factories. He is regarded as a hardliner.' ICG (2011), pp. 5–6.

72. ICG (2011), pp. 5–6. See also SSRC, prepared for the Conflict Prevention and Peace Forum by Richard Horsey, 14 April 2011, p. 2: 'The new cabinet, appointed by the President, consists of many familiar faces (see appendix 1). Of the thirty ministers: three are serving military officers appointed by the commander-in-chief to the key security portfolios (defence, home affairs, border affairs), as the 2008 Constitution provides; ten were ministers in the previous cabinet who have been reappointed (mostly with the same portfolios, some to different ones); five were deputy ministers in the previous cabinet who have been promoted (again, mostly with the same portfolios, but some to different ones); four are recently-retired senior military officers (Maj-Gen or Lt-Gen) appointed to technical ministries; eight are technocrats who are new to cabinet. Of these, three have military backgrounds but also extensive experience in the technical aspects of their portfolio; the other five are civilian technocrats. The Attorney-General (a civilian) is also well known, having previously held the deputy position. Much has been made in the media of the fact that the vast majority of ministers have a military background. But this should not be surprising in a country where the military has been the pre-

eminent institution for more than half a century, where the best education and career prospects were to be found in military academies, and where civilian education and the civil service have been chronically underfunded and marginalized.'

73. Horsey (2012), pp. 43–4.
74. Ibid., p. 44.
75. Ibid., p. 45.
76. Ibid., p. 46.
77. Ibid., p. 48.
78. *New Light of Myanmar*, 12 March 2011. Parts of the speech were reproduced on page 1 of the state media from March 4 on.
79. Cited in EBO Analysis Paper no. 2, 2011, pp. 2–3n.
80. Cited in EBO Analysis Paper no. 2, 2011, pp. 4–5.
81. Whose small numbers across the parliaments did not reflect the popular support they commanded.
82. Private email conversation.
83. Given the elections and the fact that this was the first week that the new parliament was sitting, the discussions on political awareness and political participation were the most interesting. None of the participants had ever been able to vote before. None had any recollection of 1990. However, all had lived in a highly repressive environment where even talking about politics was taboo. Across the groups it was interesting to note greater political awareness, but substantial reluctance to discuss this openly remained. Fear was still prevalent.
84. 30 people across three groups, one made up entirely of ethnic Karen, one of ethnic Bamar and one of mixed ethnicities, including Bamar.
85. Clearly one cannot generalise on the basis of such small groups. But observers during the campaign noted a different atmosphere across Yangon and other urban areas, where political talk and debate were heard in every teashop. The youth certainly showed interest and this was compounded by the rallies that led up to the by-election in April 2012.
86. On national TV, like *American Idol*.
87. 38 participants attended (26 males + 12 females) and 34 graduated. Most of the participants were representative of the ethnic political parties and some were assistants of members of parliament across all legislatures, representing their ethnic areas. Others were active members of parties nominated by the parties' executive. The programme was conducted as one-time training in Yangon at the Myanmar Egress office at Thamada Hotel. The programme cost US\$ 31,000 in total and FNS funded US\$ 5300 while Egress contributed the rest. The objectives of the programme were as follows:
    1. Provide basic and critical knowledge of governance, policy and development to the participants
    2. Provide forums, role plays and classroom discussions where the participants will get a better understanding of the country's policy issues

3. Provide a unique environment where civic dialogue among various ethnic groups can take place

4. Help those ethnic participants in their daily work in all levels of the legislature or other forums they may be involved in, so they would be able to discuss and make decisions regarding their political platforms, participate and evolve through the political transition

5. Train dynamic citizens of Myanmar so they are able to participate in Myanmar political evolution, advocating good policies for country's development. The training curriculum covered 5 parts:

   1) Governance (10 sub-topics)
   2) Public Policy and Public Administration (5 sub-topics)
   3) Leadership and Public Relations (8 sub-topics)
   4) Development and Economics (9 sub-topics)
   5) Skills for Change Agents (8 sub-topics)

   Moreover, there were three special seminar topics by U Hla Maung Shwe and another two resource persons.

88. Her house arrest had been extended by 18 months after John Yettaw swam across Inya Lake to her house.

89. Quintana (2011), p. 6.

90. Ibid., pp. 8 and 11.

91. ICG (2011), pp. 5–6.

3. NATIONAL RECONCILIATION WITH THE NLD

1. The Depayin Massacre occurred on 30 May 2003 in Tabayin, Sagaing Division, when a government-sponsored mob attacked Daw Aung San Suu Kyi and her NLD entourage. It is believed that around 70 people were killed. Daw Aung San Suu Kyi was put back under house arrest, allegedly for her own safety.

2. For an unofficial translation of the speech, see http://democracyforburma.word-press.com/2010/11/15/unofficial-translated-transcript-daw-aung-san-suu-kyi%E2%80%99s-public-address-nld-headquarters-14-november/ [6.3.2011] Link from Zöllner.

3. From the unofficial transcript of her speech, http://ko-kr.connect.facebook.com/notes/altsean-burma/transcript-daw-aung-san-suu-kyis-public-address-nld-head-quarters-14-november-201/176517152358996 [24.2.3011] Link from Zöllner.

4. The Panglong conference, held on 12 February 1947 at Panglong, Shan State, between Shan, Kachin and Chin leaders, with General Aung San representing the Burmese government. The Karen attended as observers. The Panglong agreement is seen at the basis of the Union of Burma.

5. *Mizzima News*, 9 December 2010.

6. Conversations with Nay Win Maung and ethnic leaders asking about Daw Aung San Suu Kyi's attitude towards ethnic autonomy at the time of her release.

7. Reuters, 28 January 2011.
8. 'Suu Kyi rules out party overhaul'. Agence France-Presse, 17 December 2010, http://www.networkmyanmar.org/index.php/politics/aung-san-suu-kyi/2010–2011
9. H.-B. Zöllner (2011), 'After an Election and a Symbolic Re-election in Myanmar—What Next?' *Internationales Asienforum* 42, 1–2; pp. 47–72.
10. Suu Kyi (1991), pp. 170–73, cited in Zöllner (2011), 'After an Election'.
11. The residents were subsequently threatened with eviction (AP, 20 November 2010). Some days later the authorities revoked the eviction order and continued to extend the registration every week. It is unclear if Daw Aung San Suu Kyi's visit helped the centre or if her visit made their work harder, at least in the short term. (Democratic Voice of Burma, 26 November 2010).
12. The short paper entitled 'Analysis of the Economy' was published on Myanmar's Independence Day, 4 January 2011, http://www.burmapartnership.org/2011/01/economic-analysis-and-vision-of-the-nld/ [7.3.2011]
13. http://www.networkmyanmar.org/images/stories/PDF6/nldsana.pdf [7.3.2011]. For a substantive critique on the statement, see comments made by Derek Tonkin, http://www.networkmyanmar.org/images/stories/PDF6/comment-on-nld-statement.pdf
14. Conversations with Nay Win Maung and a number of ethnic CSO leaders who met her in 2010–11.
15. http://www.stabroeknews.com/2010/archives/11/20/suu-kyi-sees-army-role-in-democratic-myanmar/
16. http://www.rfa.org/english/women/conversation-aungSanSuuKyi/conversation-01112011184908.html, Radio Free Asia, 13 January 2011. It is worth noting that any attempt to refer the military government to the ICC would have resulted in a bitter confrontation, with China and Russia prepared to veto any attempt to do this through the UN Security Council, while referral outside the UN would have been technically difficult if not impossible. (I am grateful to Derek Tonkin for pointing this out, as well as the details that follow.) This is particularly important as before the 1990 elections Col. Kyi Maung threatened Nuremberg-style trials for the junta in an interview with Asia Week on 13 July 1990. Daw Aung San Suu Kyi later made dismissive comments about U Kyi Maung, which led him to resign from the NLD. http://networkmyanmar.org/images/kyi%20maung.pdf For more on this, see Robert Taylor and Derek Tonkin's work on the 1990 elections.
17. The controversy around the 1990 elections centred on the purpose of the elections, with Daw Aung San Suu Kyi conceding during an interview with Dominic Faulder in July 1989 that the military government were insisting on constitution first before any handing over of power: see p. 9 of http://www.networkmyanmar.org/images/stories/PDF5/ele.pdf. A political myth was created later that the elections were parliamentary elections and that the junta did not allow the NLD to assume power.

18. http://www.rfa.org/english/women/conversation-aungSanSuuKyi/conversation-01112011184908.html, Radio Free Asia, 13 January 2011.
19. http://www.networkmyanmar.org/images/stories/PDF8/296newsn.pdf
20. 'To quarrel or to be reconciled', *New Light of Myanmar*, 30 June 2011. Text of reply (in Burmese) from Suu Kyi to the Home Affairs Minister dated 29 June 2011, http://www.networkmyanmar.org/images/stories/PDF8/306newsn.pdf
21. ICG, *Asia Briefing*, no. 127, p. 2.
22. The two had previously met on nine occasions following Aung Kyi's appointment as Minister for Relations with Aung San Suu Kyi in 2007. ICG, *Asia Briefing*, no. 127, p. 2.
23. The text of the statement and a summary of the questions and answers in the press briefing were carried in *New Light of Myanmar* the following day, 26 July 2011, pp. 9, 16.
24. See full text in the Annex.
25. *New Light of Myanmar*, 13 August 2011, pp. 13, 16.
26. ICG, *Asia Briefing*, no. 127.
27. Derek Tonkin has pointed out that General Ne Win had for some years down-played the role of Aung San even before Daw Aung San Suu Kyi arrived on the scene in 1988, possibly as a result of personal jealousy. Daw Aung San Suu Kyi's arrival only added to his resentment.
28. S. Turnell (2012), 'Myanmar in 2011: Confounding Expectations', *Asian Survey*, vol. 52, no. 1, p. 161.
29. ICG, *Asia Briefing*, no. 127, pp. 2–4.
30. Ibid.
31. Conversation with one of the go-betweens who delivered the president's invitation to Daw Aung San Suu Kyi and had to negotiate her travel arrangements.
32. http://www.networkmyanmar.org/index.php/politics/aung-san-suu-kyi/2010–2011, Agence France Presse, 24 August 2011.
33. http://www.dvb.no/news/suu-kyi-'welcome-in-parliament'-says-chief/17766
34. ICG, *Asia Briefing*, no. 127, pp. 2–4.
35. http://www.networkmyanmar.org/images/stories/PDF10/nlm2011–10–01a.pdf
36. 'Myanmar's Suu Kyi could seek parliament seat', Reuters, 29 October 2011, http://www.networkmyanmar.org/index.php/politics/aung-san-suu-kyi/2010–2011
37. Derek Tonkin has pointed out that the reregistration of the NLD required a face-saving device, and the amendment of the Party Law provided a convenient excuse and inducement. For more, see: http://www.networkmyanmar.org/images/stories/PDF10/mbf-no. 9.pdf
38. 'Suu Kyi plans to run in Burma elections', *Bangkok Post*, 1 December 2011, http://www.networkmyanmar.org/index.php/politics/aung-san-suu-kyi/2010–2011
39. http://www.aljazeera.com/news/asia-pacific/2012/01/201211861111501975.html In 1990 Daw Aung San Suu Kyi's application to register as a candidate for Bahan township in Rangoon was at first accepted, then challenged in the Lower

Court and finally rejected by decision of the Higher Court on a challenge brought by a rival candidate from the pro-military National Unity Party, based primarily on her alleged allegiance to a foreign power (UK).

40. http://blogs.wsj.com/davos/2012/01/26/myanmars-aung-san-suu-kyi-addresses-wef-in-video-message/?mod=google_news_blog

41. MHPG, 15 March 2011, 10:00 a.m., Chatrium Hotel.

42. 'Much time has been taken up with matters that are hardly of national importance: the poor state of a township's lampposts, or a request for express trains to stop at a particular suburban station. This shows the in-experience of legislators and that there are no other ways to raise such issues.' ICG, *Asia Briefing*, no. 127, p. 11.

43. This resulted in CSOs who had not been able to register for many years suddenly being invited to resubmit their papers and enter the 'legal fold'.

44. Gwen Robinson, 'Suu Kyi misses opening of parliament', *Financial Times*, http://www.ft.com/cms/s/0/959ae8e4-c57c-11e1-940d-00144feabdc0.html#ixzz3I5H5Vkvn

45. ICG, *Asia Briefing*, no. 127, p. 11.

46. 'Variously introduced between 1988 and 2007, these stated the regime's "four political, economic and social objectives", several versions of the "people's desire" (including an exhortation to "crush all internal and external destructive elements as the common enemy") and criticism of foreign and exile radio stations including the BBC and Voice of America ("do not allow ourselves to be swayed by killer broadcasts designed to cause troubles").' ICG, *Asia Briefing*, no. 127, pp. 2–4.

47. Speech reported in full in *New Light of Myanmar*, 18 August 2011, p. 1 ff. Legislation is being prepared to implement such an offer, which would provide amnesty for offences other than criminal acts against another person. A number of prominent exiles have returned or are in the process of negotiating this. ICG, *Asia Briefing*, no. 127, pp. 2–4. This did result in a number of exiles returning to Myanmar in the course of 2012 and 2013, some of whom started to work with the government on the peace process—such as Aung Naing Oo who had lived in Chiang Mai.

48. http://journal.probeinternational.org/2011/10/10/joy-amid-caution-as-burmese-halt-chinese-mega-dam/

49. State-owned China Power Investment Corp, in a deal with Asia World Company and the Burmese government.

50. Conversations with students and other young people in schools and at CBOs end 2011.

51. 'Burma frees dozens of political prisoners', 12 October 2011, http://www.bbc.co.uk/news/world-asia-pacific-15269259?print=true

52. There were a few more amnesties in 2012 and 2013. M. F. Martin (2013), 'Burma's Political Prisoners and US Sanctions', Congressional Research service, Washington, 2 December 2013.

53. http://www.amnesty.org/en/news/myanmar-political-prisoner-release-2012–01–13.
54. Myanmar has the death sentence, but the last sentence was carried out in 1988 after a North Korean spy had tried to blow up a South Korean delegation in Yangon. There have been no executions of prisoners on death row since.
55. More on this in the chapter on economic reforms.
56. Particularly important as Myanmar had foregone the chair in 2005.
57. 'Burma to chair ASEAN in 2014', http://www.france24.com/en/20111117-burma-chair-asean-myanmar-2014-military-junta-obama-human-rights-political-prisoner/
58. ICG, no. 127, pp. 12–13.
59. In a video address to the US Congress on 22 June 2011, but this pre-dated her recent positive talks with the government.
60. For the full text of the speech in English translation, see *New Light of Myanmar*, 2 March 2012, p. 1.
61. Results of the 7 November 2010 elections in Kawhmu:
    Soe Tint, Union Solidarity and Development Party: 42,716 votes
    Ohn Thaung, National Unity Party: 13,944 votes
    Myint Thaung, National Democratic Force: 4,757 votes
    Win Maung, Modern People's Party: 1,638 votes
62. The USDP, as in the 2010 elections, often chose candidates who were well established and positively regarded in their local community. The choice of the local doctor to run against Daw Aung San Suu Kyi is such an example among many.
63. http://www.independent.co.uk/news/world/asia/suu-kyi-hits-the-campaign-trail-7579429.html
64. The NLD selected 45 candidates for the 2012 by-elections: one was declared ineligible, leaving the NLD to provide another 43 in addition to Daw Aung San Suu Kyi. I am grateful to Derek Tonkin for pointing this out.
65. Interview with local NLD supporter in Mandalay and friend of the rebuffed candidate.
66. M. Martin, 'Burma's April Parliamentary By-Elections', Congressional Research Service Report for Congress, 7–5700, 28 March 2012, p. 5.
67. http://www.smh.com.au/world/suu-kyi-cancels-campaign-tour-20120325–1vs6f.html
68. http://www.bbc.com/news/world-asia-17363329
69. http://www.smh.com.au/world/suu-kyi-cancels-campaign-tour-20120325–1vs6f.html
70. EBO political monitor no. 8 (17–23.32012).
71. AFP (3 April 2012), 'Suu Kyi's party wins 43 seats in parliament'; RFA (3 April 2012), 'NLD, Shan Party Lead Opposition Assault'; Xinhua (3 April 2012), 'Aung San Suu Kyi's party sweeps Myanmar by-election'.

72. Xinhua (2 April 2012), 'Myanmar election commission announces NLD wins overwhelmingly in by-elections'; *Myanmar Times* (9 April 2012), 'NLD sweeps Nay Pyi Taw in surprise win'.

73. One of the NPT seats was won by a popular hip-hop star Zeyar Thaw, who was personally asked by Daw Aung San Suu Kyi to stand. Gwen Robinson, 'The Myanmar rapper and the regime', *Financial Times*, 22 April 2012.

74. Xinhua (2 April 2012), 'Myanmar election commission announces NLD wins overwhelmingly in by-elections'.

75. Tin Maung Maung Thann, SEA Affairs (ISEAS), 2013. Whilst the total number of valid votes cast was 4,091,840, only 146,265 votes (or 3.6 per cent) were advance votes. The voter turnout was 68.19 per cent.

76. *Straits Times* (6 April 2012), 'Now may be the time to end Myanmar sanctions'.

77. RFA (4 April 2012), 'Suu Kyi Won Because of Father'. Derek Tonkin points out that although the results of the 2012 by-elections were a shock to the USDP, there is evidence that the USDP did not pull out all the stops in their campaigning, allowing the NLD to win by a greater margin than they had expected. They are unlikely to make the same mistake at the 2015 elections, where they are likely to offer populist policies and to conduct a much tougher and rougher campaign.

78. A translation of the address has appeared in *New Light of Myanmar*, 15 March 2012, http://www.networkmyanmar.org/images/stories/PDF11/153newsnnld.pdf

79. Reuters (25 April 2012), 'Myanmar's military moves amid Suu Kyi no-show'.

80. NLM (23 April 2012), Republic of the Union of Myanmar Union Election Commission Nay Pyi Taw Notification no. 22/2012 2nd Waxing of Kason, 1374 ME (22 April 2012) 39 Defence Services Personnel Pyithu Hluttaw Representatives substituted; NLM (23 April 2012) Republic of the Union of Myanmar Union Election Commission Nay Pyi Taw Notification no. 23/2012 2nd Waxing of Kason, 1374 ME (22 April 2012) 20 Defence Services Personnel Amyotha Hluttaw Representatives substituted.

81. Tin Maung Maung Than, SEA Affairs, 2013.

82. This is not impossible as the military representatives in parliament have rarely voted 'en bloc'. This information is based on an interview with a UN representative who knows General Min Aung Hlaing personally.

83. *Burma Bulletin*, A month-in-review of events in Burma. Alternative ASEAN Network on Burma campaigns, advocacy and capacity-building for human rights and democracy. Issue 64, April 2012, 'NLD compromises over parliamentary oath of office', pp. 2–3.

84. Reuters (23 April 2012), 'As Myanmar awaits easing of sanctions, row brews over MP no-show'; Xinhua (23 April 2012), 'Myanmar's parliament sessions resume after adjournment'; VOA (23 April 2012), 'Burmese Democracy Party Skips Parliament Opening'.

85. AP (26 April 2012), 'Myanmar's Suu Kyi's hopeful on oath dispute'; Reuters (26 April 2012), 'Myanmar parliament stand-off a "technical matter:" Suu Kyi'; RFA (26 April 2012), 'Oath Dispute Based on "Technicality"'.

86. See Tin Maung Maung Than, SEA affairs, 2013.

87. Xinhua (30 April 2012), 'Myanmar's NLD insists on "respecting" constitution despite decision on parliament debut'; BBC (30 April 2012), 'Suu Kyi backs down over Burmese parliamentary oath'.

88. Specific economic and education reforms will be elaborated on in their respective chapters, 5 and 6.

89. Moe Thuzar, SEA affairs, 2012.

90. Burma abolishes media censorship, http://www.bbc.com/news/world-asia-19315806?print=true It is rumoured that Tint Swe was giving public talks on press freedom after the change—something that is highly bizarre.

91. The riots that broke out across Myanmar will be discussed in a subsequent chapter dealing with the emergence of Buddhist nationalism.

92. ILO child labour and child soldiers, autumn 2012. Decent work in Myanmar—ILO Programme Framework: November 2012—April 2014, November 2012 ILO.

93. Private conversations with Steve Marshall; see also ILO child labour and child soldiers, autumn 2012. Decent work in Myanmar—ILO Programme Framework: November 2012—April 2014, November 2012 ILO.

94. ILO child labour and child soldiers, autumn 2012. Decent work in Myanmar—ILO Programme Framework: November 2012—April 2014, November 2012 ILO.

95. The decision however stands unaltered. See Robert Taylor, *Southeast Asian Affairs*, 2013.

96. 'Myanmar parliament moves against judges', Gwen Robinson, *Financial Times*, http://www.ft.com/cms/s/0/80576cc8-f82b-11e1-bec8-00144feabdc0.html#ixzz3ILWr8eI3

97. http://www.theguardian.com/world/2012/sep/07/burmas-tribunal-judges-resign-impeachment

98. Article 58f of the 2008 constitution.

99. Robert H. Taylor (2013b), 'Myanmar's "Pivot" toward the Shibboleth of "Democracy", *Asian Affairs*, 44:3, pp. 392–400, DOI: 10.1080/03068374.2013.826014 pp. 397–8.

100. 'Democracy Leader Cautions Investors Against "Reckless Optimism" in Myanmar', Thomas Fuller, 1 June 2012, http://www.nytimes.com/2012/06/02/world/asia/myanmar-dissident-cautions-perspective-investors.html?_r=3&

101. 'Suu Kyi misses opening of parliament', Gwen Robinson, *Financial Times*, http://www.ft.com/cms/s/0/959ae8e4-c57c-11e1-940d-00144feabdc0.html#ixzz3I5H5Vkvn

102. 'Burma or Myanmar: The name game', Foreign Policy Blog, 5 July 2012, http://www.networkmyanmar.org/index.php/politics/aung-san-suu-kyi/2012–2013 The previous junta changed the name without consulting public opinion: Daw Aung San Suu Kyi said 'They didn't bother to consider what the public opinion about the new name was. They didn't show any respect to the people.'

103. http://www.networkmyanmar.org/index.php/politics/aung-san-suu-kyi/2012–2013

104. 'Why Suu Kyi still loves Burma's army', Jonathan Owen, 27 January 2013, http://www.independent.co.uk/news/world/asia/why-suu-kyi-still-loves-burmas-army-8468363.html

105. 'Suu Kyi: Burma's Constitution must change', http://www.dvb.no/news/suu-kyi-burma's-constitution-must-change/25678 *Democratic Voice of Burma*, 10 January 2013.

106. http://www.theguardian.com/world/2013/mar/12/burma-confirms-phosphorus-crackdown-mine 'Aung San Suu Kyi support for copper mine outrages Burmese activists', 12 March 2013.

107. 'Farmers turn on Suu Kyi over copper mine', *Sydney Morning Herald*, 16 March 2013, Thomas Fuller, http://www.networkmyanmar.org/index.php/politics/aung-san-suu-kyi/2012–2013

108. 'Suu Kyi's perilous pivot from icon to party boss', Reuters Special Report, 4 October 2012, http://www.reuters.com/article/2012/10/04/us-myanmar-suukyi-idUSBRE8931LA20121004

109. See also E. Prasse-Freeman, *Kyoto Review of SE Asia*, 1 February 2014, http://kyotoreview.org/issue-14/daw-aung-san-suu-kyi-and-her-discontents/and 'The halo slips', *Economist*, 15 June 2013, http://www.economist.com/news/asia/21579512-running-president-comes-risks-halo-slips 'The Lady's star beginning to fade', Joshua Carroll, Anadolu Agency, 21 April 2014, http://www.aa.com.tr/en/rss/316277—myanmar-ladys-star-beginning-to-fade

110. Who will be those she expects to support the NLD during the 2015 elections.

111. 'For example, following the recent ethnic violence between Rakhine Buddhists and Muslim Rohingyas in Burma's northwest, Ms. Suu Kyi said this week the country's citizenship laws should be clarified. But when asked directly whether the stateless Rohingyas ought to be considered Burmese, she said "I do not know". A firmer response to these kinds of challenges will be needed.' 'Aung San Suu Kyi must transition too', *Wall Street Journal*, 20 June 2012, http://online.wsj.com/news/articles/SB10001424052702304898704577477991620165070?mg=reno64-wsj&url=http%3A%2F%2Fonline.wsj.com%2Farticle%2FSB10001424052702304898704577477991620165070.html

112. R. Taylor (2013a), 'Myanmar in 2012—mhyaw ta lin lin or Great Expectations', *Southeast Asian Affairs*, 2013.

113. See comments earlier in the chapter by H.-B. Zöllner on the unanimous election of a leader.

114. Derek Tonkin notes that Daw Aung San Suu Kyi's two sons are formally married and whilst the two sons were registered with the Burmese consulate in London as Burmese citizens and once held Burmese passports, the issue might be made more complicated by the citizenship of their spouses. (I am grateful to Derek Tonkin for pointing this out.) The law also barred General Myint Swe from becoming VP1 as his son had married an Australian national, and he had a foreign daughter-in-law. Article 59f is indeed discriminatory and it needs revising not because of Suu Kyi specifically, but because many other young Myanmar people now have ties to foreign countries. Focusing the debate specifically on Suu Kyi's potential presidency has personalised the dispute and been less than helpful.

115. Over 50 breakfast meetings, according to Tin Maung Thann.

116. 'NLD, 88 Generation to Hold Rallies, Nationwide Campaign for Constitutional Reform', Yen Snaig, *Irrawaddy*, 5 May 2014, http://www.irrawaddy.org/burma/nld-88-generation-hold-rallies-nationwide-campaign-constitutional-reform.html

117. Suu Kyi Urges Public to 'Test Parliament' With Charter Change Campaign 2014–05–27, http://www.rfa.org/english/news/myanmar/constitutional-reform-05272014184433.html

118. 'The fight for Myanmar's constitution', Simon Roughneen, 29 May 2014, http://asia.nikkei.com/print/article/33208

119. 'Myanmar's Constitutional Uncertainty', Sebastian Strangio, 21 July 2014, http://thediplomat.com/2014/07/myanmars-constitutional-uncertainty/

120. 'The Central Executive Committee (CEC) today was also reshuffled, excising loyalists to U Shwe Mann and inserting a new cast of former military elites. During a 15-minute press conference, the outgoing party members were referred to as being "allowed to resign". Several former military officials who had recently resigned to join the party were promoted to the CEC, including U Hla Htay Win, Thura U Thet Swe, U Myint Soe, U Wai Lwin. Some ministers those have also been reassigned to take part in the new CEC, including U Thet Naing Win, U Pike Htway, U Maung Maung Htay, U Than Tun, U Kyaw Kyaw Htay and Daw Win Maw Tun. Former CEC members closely allied with U Shwe Mann were also axed. Thura U Aung Ko, U Maung Maung Thein, U Aung Thein Linn and others were granted permission by the president to leave their posts.' http://www.mmtimes.com/index.php/national-news/15998-president-axes-shwe-mann.html

121. 'The whole of Kayah State has a population of less than 287,000—divided into seven townships and hence 14 state-level constituencies, 7 lower house constituencies, and (like all states and regions) 12 upper house constituencies.' This results in townships with less than 30,000 population, making it easier to win a vote. See Richard Horsey's IMG note on elections and ethnic areas. There have been reports that U Soe Thane has been campaigning hard in the Kayah constit-

uency where he will stand as an independent candidate. See http://www.
irrawaddy.org/election/news/soe-thane-backs-spending-splash-in-karenni-state
122. http://www.bbc.co.uk/news/world-asia-33974550
123. 'Section 396 states that a representative can be "recalled" for one of a number of
reasons: high treason; breach of any provision of the constitution; misbehaviour;
disqualification prescribed in this constitution; and inefficient discharge of duties.
According to the constitution, a minimum of 1 per cent of the original voters in
the representative's constituency must then submit a complaint to the Union
Election Commission against the representative. The UEC will conduct an investigation in accord with the law. The representative will have the right to defend
themselves in person or through a representative. If the UEC considers that the
allegation is true and that the MP should not continue to serve as a representative, the commission shall proceed in accord with the law.' http://www.mmtimes.
com/index.php/opinion/16253-why-mps-fear-the-right-of-recall-bill.html

4. THE PEACE PROCESS

1. The CIA Factbook estimates Burman 68%, Shan 9%, Karen 7%, Rakhine 4%,
Chinese 3%, Indian 2%, Mon 2%, other 5%. A census took place April 2014. While
this may give better data, there is also a risk of reinforcing the unhelpful and essen-
tialisation of ethnicity in Myanmar.
2. Sai Kham Mong (2007), in Ganesan, N. and Kyaw Yin Hlaing (eds), *Myanmar—
State, Society and Ethnicity*, Singapore: ISEAS, and Hiroshima: Hiroshima Peace
Institute, p. 261.
3. M. Gravers (1999), *Nationalism as Political Paranoia in Burma: An Essay on the
Historical Practice of Power*, Richmond, Surrey: Curzon, p. 109.
4. Thant Myint-U (2001), *Making of Modern Burma*, Cambridge: Cambridge
University Press.
5. R. H. Taylor (2005), 'Do States Make Nations? The Politics of Identity in Myanmar
Revisited', *Southeast Asia Research*, vol. 13, no. 3, p. 274.
6. Taylor (2007), in Ganesan and Kyaw, pp. 75–6.
7. Sai Kham Mong (2007), in Ganesan and Kyaw, p. 259. This is not unusual: the
British had similar policies in India at the time that today affect both India and
Pakistan.
8. D. I. Steinberg (2001), *Burma—the State of Myanmar*, Washington, DC:
Georgetown University Press, p. 184; also see M. Walton (2008) 'Ethnicity,
Conflict and History in Burma: the Myths of Panglong', *Asian Survey* 48:6,
pp. 889–910.
9. Taylor (2005), p. 280; Sai Kham Mong (2007) in Ganesan and Kyaw, p. 265.
10. The official state promotion of Buddhism started in the early 1960s. The issue of
Buddhism and Myanmar/Burmese national identity is further discussed in the
chapter on the re-emergence of Buddhist nationalism.

11. Alan Saw U (2007), in Ganesan and Kyaw, p. 220.

12. For more on this important historic period that cannot be covered here, see M. Smith (1999), *Burma: Insurgency and the Politics of Ethnicity*, London: Zed Books; and A. South (2008), *Ethnic Politics in Burma: States of Conflict*, London: Routledge.

13. Steinberg (2001) p. 185.

14. Taylor (2007), in Gansen and Kyaw, p. 85.

15. Sai Kham Mong (2007), in Ganesan and Kyaw, p. 256.

16. G. Houtman (1999), *Mental Culture in Burmese Crisis Politics: Aung San Suu Kyi and the National League for Democracy*, Tokyo: Tokyo University of Foreign Studies.

17. Smith (1999).

18. Smith (2005), in Kyaw, p. 67.

19. Not carrying rations or supplies.

20. A. South (2011), 'Burma's Longest War: Anatomy of the Karen Conflict', Netherlands: Transnational Institute/Burma Centre, pp. 31–2: 'The first semi-permanent refugee settlements in Thailand were established in Tak Province in 1984, as Karen civilians fled from fighting and human rights abuses in Burma. The Royal Thai Government (RTG) allowed these people temporary refuge, so long as the task of providing basic assistance was taken up by a small number of international NGOs. In the late 1980s the main NGO consortium assisting the refugees was reorganised, as the Burmese Border Consortium (BBC); in 2004 it was re-named the Thailand Burma Border Consortium (TBBC). In January 2011, the refugee caseload verified by TBBC was 141,549 people, living in nine camps strung out along the middle section of the border. The previous three years had been marked by the resettlement of some 30,000 Karen and other Burmese refugees to third countries abroad.'

21. South (2008, 2011).

22. South (2004), p. 238.

23. Adapted in part from M. Lall (2009), 'Ethnic conflict in light of the 2010 elections in Burma/Myanmar', Chatham House briefing paper.

24. Smith (1999).

25. Min Zaw Oo (2014), 'Understanding Myanmar Peace Process', Swisspeace, http://www.swisspeace.ch/fileadmin/user_upload/Media/Publications/Catalyzing_Reflections_2_2014_online.pdf, p. 8.

26. Myint Thu (2014), *An Unexpected Long Journey*, pp. 625–60: Chronological Events of Ceasefire Efforts in 1990s:

1989 November 3, Ministry of Home Affairs and Ministry of Religious announced order 3/89. In this order, KIO, KNU, KNPP and MNSP were declared black listed organisations.

1989 December 15, Military Government and the KIA No. (4) Battalion signed a ceasefire agreement.

1990 December 18, NCGUB was established in the KIA control area, Ma Nal Pa Law. Later, NCGUB moved to the USA.

1991 February 1, Pao National Organization (PNO) and Military Government signed ceasefire agreement.

1991 September 24, Government and Shan State Army (SSA) signed ceasefire agreement.

1991 October 4, Army and KNU guerrilla skirmished in the Delta Region of the Ayeyarwaddy Division.

1992 February 24, Military Government and Kachin Independent Organization (KIO) signed ceasefire agreement.

1992 July 31, National Council of Union of Burma had been established.

1994 December 24, Buddhist Karen separated from Karen National Union (KNU) and formed Democratic Karen Buddhist Association (DKBA).

1996 January and February, Mong Tai Army surrendered to the Tatmadaw.

2001 March 21, Karen National Liberalization Party (KNLP), KNPLF, NMSP, PSLO, SNPLO, SSA and SSNA signed ceasefire agreement with Government.

27. South (2007b), p. 16.
28. Min Zaw Oo (2014), p. 11.
29. Only 1996 KNPP ceasefire broke down, after 3 months. I am grateful to Ashley South for pointing this out to me.
30. Jan Nan Lahtaw (2007) in Ganesan and Kyaw, pp. 236–7.
31. According to Ashley South, Shalom was part of the KIO strategy as well as a 'reward' to Saboi Jum for his role in the ceasefire.
32. South (2004), p. 248.
33. Personal conversation, Yangon, July 2007.
34. South (2004).
35. Smith (2007), p. 53.
36. Ibid., p. 53.
37. The main non-ceasefire groups are: Arakan Liberation Party; Arakan Rohingya National Organisation; Chin National Front; Hongsawatoi Restoration Party; Karen National Union; Karenni National Progressive Party; Lahu Democratic Front; Mergui-Tavoy United Front; Nationalist Socialist Council of Nagaland; National United Party of Arakan; Rohingya Solidarity Organisation; Shan State Army (South); Wa National Organisation. See Martin Smith (2005), in Kyaw, p. 80.
38. For more on this see South (2011).
39. Smith (2005), in Kyaw, p. 58.
40. South (2011), p. 10.
41. Ibid., p. 13.
42. At the beginning there were 40 separate ethnic armed groups. Later some ethnic armed groups merged into a single group, so there were only 25 ethnic armed groups before the 2010 election.

43. Min Zaw Oo (2014), p. 13. See also Transnational Institute (2012), 'Burma at the Crossroads: Maintaining the Momentum for Reform', Burma Policy Briefing no. 9, Amsterdam: Burma Centrum Nederland.
44. I am grateful to Ashley South for pointing this out.
45. ICG Asia Briefing N°127 Jakarta/Brussels, 22 September 2011 Myanmar: Major Reform Underway p. 6.
46. It is unclear who started to shoot: each side accuses the other side of starting the conflict. I am grateful to Ashley South for pointing out that at the time there were a number of other killings of civilians at the edge of KIO-controlled areas, and that the Tatmadaw was trying to provoke the KIO/KIA.
47. Since he had been taken from the liaison office and not from the battlefield, the torture allegations seem to be the more likely cause of his injuries. BCPR–BP 2 (2012).
48. ICG (2011), p. 7.
49. Ibid., p. 7.
50. A. South (2015), 'Governance and Political Legitimacy in the Peace Process' in *Myanmar: the Dynamics of an Evolving Polity*, Lynne Reinner, ed. David Steinberg).
51. N. Farelly (2012), 'Ceasing Ceasefire? Kachin Politics beyond the Stalemates', in Cheesman, N., Skidmore, M. and Wilson, T. (eds), *Myanmar's Transition—Openings, Obstacles and Opportunities*, Myanmar Update Series, Singapore: ISEAS.
52. Human Rights Watch (2012), 'Untold Miseries: Wartime Abuses and Forced Displacement in Burma's Kachin State', New York.
53. President's speech on meeting with individuals from social and economic sectors, 17 August 2011.
54. By then a large number of EAGs had signed preliminary agreements and ceasefires with the new government, but the continuing war in Kachin State made it impossible to make the peace process a nationwide process.
55. President's speech at Pyi Htaung Su Hluttaw, 1 March 2012.
56. 'The Klo Htoo Baw Battalion (formerly DKBA Brigade 5) signed a ceasefire with the government on 3 November 2011, the Restoration Council Shan State/Shan State Army—South signed an initial ceasefire agreement with a union level peace group on the 3 December 2011 this was followed by the Chin National Front (CNF) on 6 January 2012, the Shan State Progress Party signed two peace agreements on 28 January 2012, the Karen National Union on 12 January 2012 and the New Mon State Party on 1 February 2012.' See Burma Centre Analysis Paper no. 1, January 2012.
57. ICG (2011).
58. ICG (2011).
59. There were credibility issues with Thein Zaw in Kachin State. Allegedly he had offered large sums of money to community leaders if they would establish a political party to challenge the main Kachin party (which was ultimately denied registration); no one accepted this offer.

60. South (2011).

61. 'In addition, the KNU's strategy in attempting to formulate an agreement with the regime has often been shaped by KNU founder Saw Ba U Gyi's four principles which state: 1. For us surrender is out of question; 2. The recognition of Karen state must be complete; 3. WE shall retain our arms; 4. We shall decide our ow political destiny.' (Paul Keenan—Burma's ethnic ceasefire agreements, BCRP Briefing paper 1 Jan 2012, p1)

62. While a reluctance to compromise the above principals shaped early negotiations, the later talks in March 2005, allowed the KNU to retain its arms and provide some limited authority over Karen controlled areas. In addition, the offer also included resettling internally displaced Karens to areas under the KNU's control and thus providing a more secure environment for vulnerable Karen populations. This final offer in 2005, prior to the breakdown of the talks due to the regime blaming the KNU for its participation in a number of bombings of in Rangoon, consisted of the KNU being given a trial period of two years and an offer of renegotiation afterwards. This was seriously considered by the leadership. However, the KNU leadership found itself deeply divided by those who are were more acceptable to the Junta's overtures and a number of hardliners whose trust in the regime had been eroded by previous failed peace attempts.' P. Keenan, 'Burma's ethnic ceasefire agreements', BCPR Briefing paper, 1 Jan 2012, p. 6.

63. I am grateful to Ashley South for pointing out that in part the ceasefire did not happen because exile opposition leaders did not want a KNU ceasefire.

64. BCPR, Keenan (2012), p. 6.

65. BCES-AP 4 (2012), p. 1.

66. This is the way that MPC was conceived. MPC however became first and foremost the government's secretariat in the peace process. Its research/think tank roles have become secondary.

67. U Aung Min and U Soe Thane actually used their own money to travel to the various meetings with the EAGs. The directors of ME, in particular Tin Maung Thann and U Hla Maung Shwe, also helped financially and sometimes accompanied the ministers.

68. Australian Agency for International Development (AusAID), Centre for Peace and Conflict Studies (CPCS), Columbia University, Department for International Development (DFID), European Union (EU), Institute for Security and Development Policy (ISDP), Inter-mediate, Internews, International Crisis Group (ICG), International IDEA, International Management Group (IMG), International Media Support (IMS), Japan International Cooperation Agency (JICA), Japan Platform (JPF), Ministry of Foreign Affairs of Japan, Norwegian Ministry of Foreign Affairs (NMFA), Norwegian People's Aid (NPA), Norwegian Refugee Council (NRC), Peace Donor Support Group (PDSG), Peace Nexus (PN), Swiss Federal Department of Foreign Affairs, The Centre for Humanitarian Dialogue

(HD Centre), The Nippon Foundation (TNF), United Nations (UN), World Bank Group (WB).

69. Private discussion with U Hla Maung Shwe at the side of one of these meetings on a Saturday morning in May 2015.

70. This quote is hung in the main meeting room at the Myanmar Peace Centre.

71. One-on-one interviews were conducted with the Minister of Immigration, Minister of Forestry, Minister of Electrics, the Deputy Attorney General, the Vice President of Union Peace Making Working Committee (USDP), U Soe Thane in Nay Pyi Taw in December 2013 and U Aung Min in Yangon in August 2014. A summary of their views and thoughts is reproduced here. The data were gathered as part of an EU-funded project on peace and legitimacy between 2012 and 2014.

72. One can argue that this is from the perspective of those holding the guns; however, as the ministers interviewed made clear, anyone who has been at war has a much better incentive in wanting to make peace.

73. Most of the interviews were confidential, in that the interviewees were promised anonymity. Those who agreed to be on the record are named.

74. Minister 1.

75. Clearly not everyone agrees that this process has been inclusive.

76. Minister 3.

77. It was interesting to note that the USDP representatives blamed the conflict on misunderstanding and the British colonial legacy. Whilst these are not uncommon views, he was the only one of this group to frame the issue in these terms, showing that President Thein Sein's selection of advisers is indeed more progressive than the old guard.

78. Minister 2.

79. Minister 1.

80. It is clear that this realisation is only shared by a few of the ministers, and in the case of AM and others grew over time. Nevertheless, this is a very important demonstration that change is possible, even for elite actors.

81. Minister 3.

82. http://www.atimes.com/atimes/Southeast_Asia/SEA-01-240314.html. The Tatmadaw maintains that the Myanmar army is already 'federal' in that it allows for all ethnic nationalities to join the army. The EAGs see a federal army as an institution that would not be dominated and controlled by one ethnic group, allowing an ethnic person to rise to the rank of commander in chief. It is unclear how the Tatmadaw and the government are interpreting the practicalities of the demand for a federal army.

83. Minister 1.

84. Ashley South has argued that the window for a meaningful political dialogue before the elections has now closed. Since the nationwide ceasefire negotiations process has slowed, the government has started to discuss the peace process at par-

liamentary levels, without the participation of the armed groups. South argues that whilst the armed groups are important stakeholders, they are not the only stakeholders and they could be marginalised after the 2015 elections. It would therefore be important for them to agree a comprehensive ceasefire with the Tatmadaw, including a code of conduct before the 2015 elections. See South (2014), http://www.irrawaddy.org/contributor/next-burmas-peace-process.html

85. This process was supported by the Norwegian Refugee Council http://www.the-mimu.info/sites/themimu.info/files/documents/Report_Lessons_Learned_Sup-porting_the_Peace_Process_MPSI_Mar2012-Mar2014.pdf, p. 29.

86. Myanmar Peace Support Initiative (MPSI) (2014), 'Lessons learned from MPSI's work supporting the peace process in Myanmar', Yangon, p. 81.

87. Ibid., p. 81.

88. Ibid., p. 81.

89. Ibid., p. 5.

90. MPSI-associated projects have been undertaken across five ethnic states (Chin, Shan, Mon, Karen and Kayah) and two regions (Bago and Tanintharyi). Projects have been delivered in partnership with seven Ethnic Armed Groups, thirteen local partners (four of which are consortia) and nine international partners. MPSI (2014), p. 5.

91. Ibid., p. 5

92. Ibid., pp. 27–9. The Norwegian Refugee Council (NRC) has supported the Ministry of Immigration and Population in issuing Citizen Scrutiny Cards (full Myanmar ID cards) to communities in remote and conflict-affected areas, estab-lishing a 'one-stop shop' model that covers, free of charge, all the steps involved in issuing the Citizen Scrutiny Cards on the same day. MPSI has provided support in mobilising funding for this work, and helped NRC to gain access to conflict-affected (including pilot project) areas. From June 2012 to September 2013, 79,399 national identity cards were issued to citizens in conflict-affected areas of Karen State; from November 2012 to September 2013, 14,402 ID cards were issued in Kayah State; and from April to September 2013, 11,038 ID cards were issued for Southern Shan State. ID card activities commenced in Mon (Thaton office) in October 2013 and in Tanintharyi (Dawei office) in December 2013. MPSI (2014), p. 29.

93. Within the pilot projects, the main roles MPSI has taken on include: (i) consult-ing with, and facilitating discussions among, relevant stakeholders (Ethnic Armed Groups, civil society organisations, local communities and, to a varying degree, with local government and military authorities); (ii) supporting the establishment of CBO consortia and platforms for the planning and implementation of pilot projects; (iii) supporting communities and CBOs to articulate their needs and concerns; (iv) brokering access to conflict-affected areas; (v) linking donors and implementing partners (mostly international NGOs) to locally-initiated projects;

(vi) supporting local partners proposing pilot projects to formulate actions and budgets in terms required by funders; (vii) providing advice and information to stakeholders about 'best practice' across the different kinds of projects proposed; (viii) responding quickly to needs articulated by key stakeholders; (ix) learning from interventions, and where appropriate feeding back into the peace process. MPSI (2014), p. 16.

94. MPSI (2014), p. 15. Most armed groups have their HQs in neighbouring countries and are considered illegal and illegitimate organisations by the Myanmar government.

95. Ibid., p. 19.

96. A critical example is funding for MNEC. MPSI encouraged MNEC to apply for funds to one of the major donors, just for hopes to be raised and then turned down, twice. This also shows that the international donor community often had little knowledge how confidence in the peace process could be eroded by uninformed behaviour.

97. Ibid., p. 18.

98. The Ethnic Peace Resources Project (EPRP) emerged towards the end of 2012 out of the work of the MPSI. The EPRP seeks to empower ethnic people to participate in the emerging political dialogue of Myanmar's peace process. Ibid., p. 34.

99. 'Problems of land-grabbing are compounded by the negative impacts of the 2012 Farmland Act, and 2012 Vacant, Fallow and Wasteland Act.' Ibid., p. 27.

100. 'Most new business activities in conflict-affected areas are extractive (logging, mining etc.) and often connected to local or national power-holders. Business activities in newly accessible conflict-affected areas are often associated with land-grabbing (e.g. for plantation agriculture). As well as the negative social and environmental impacts, such activities can undermine communities and other stakeholders' trust and confidence in the peace process. [...] Ethnic communities are concerned about major infrastructure projects. Myanmar undoubtedly needs economic and infrastructure development, especially in remote and conflict-affected areas. However, ethnic communities are deeply concerned that the peace process will see the construction of major infrastructure projects (e.g. hydroelectric dams) depriving them of ancestral lands, and undermining human security and livelihoods. Large-scale projects should only be implemented after free, prior and informed consultation with all stakeholders and following proper impact assessments.' Ibid., p. 27.

101. 'For example, before the KNU ceasefire, villagers often had to flee from fighting, and to avoid forced conscription and portering. Post-ceasefire, people report greatly decreased levels of fear. Many of those who spoke with MPSI said that for the first time in decades they did not have to worry about fleeing into the jungle, to avoid being subjected to serious human rights abuses. In some cases, dis-

placed people are beginning to return to previous settlements and attempting to rebuild their lives. Many villagers mentioned that before the ceasefire they were unable to travel or visit their farms—or could only do so by paying bribes. Even then, villagers were severely restricted in terms of the amount of food or other supplies they could carry while travelling, as they risked being accused of supporting the KNU. Villagers told terrible stories of abuse at the hands of the Myanmar Army, including beatings and killings—even the beheading of suspected insurgents. After the ceasefire however, villagers have been able to travel much more freely and to tend their rice fields. Levels of taxation, paid to either the Myanmar Army or Ethnic Armed Groups, have decreased significantly over the past two years in both Karen and Mon areas. In many communities, livelihoods have improved as a result of villagers' better access to their farms, and a reduction in predatory taxation.' Ibid. See also http://www.peacedonorsupport-group.com/reflections—one-year-on.html Ashley South has pointed out that MPSI was always intended to be a short-term initiative, light and flexible, coming in behind the agreement of ceasefires. The intention was to widen down MPSI, once a better established peace infrastructure was in place. Therefore MPSI will close at the beginning of 2015. PDSG is supposed to take over from MPSI. There is also advanced talk about establishing a Multi-Donor Peace Support Fund for Myanmar, as well as bilateral donor channels. Nevertheless, the peace-support infrastructure in Myanmar is still very 'supply-led', based primarily on the assumptions and agendas of international donors, rather than responding to local needs. Furthermore, the PDSG has yet to achieve effective coordination, let alone real strategic leadership.

102. There is more money from JICA. See http://www.mmpeacemonitor.org/stake-holders/nippon-foundation.
The aid package was officially launched on 22 December 2012 in Mon State.
22 December 2012: NMSP—$70,000 worth of emergency supplies, including 50 tonnes of rice, medical supplies for hospitals and 500 boxes of traditional medicine.
12 January 2013: PNLO—Donated 1,200 bags of rice.
12 February 2013: KNU—US$ 30,000 of emergency supplies to displaced people in Karen State, incl. 70 tonnes of rice.
103. Interviews in Tokyo consistently refused in 2013 and 2014.
104. https://www.dvb.no/analysis/japans-lack-of-transparency-threatens-burmas-development-myanmar/34024
105. Harn Yawnghwe is a Shan politician who lived for many decades in exile; he was youngest son of Myanmar's first president.
106. BCPR—BP 2 (2012).
107. UNFC members (previously of CEFU): Kachin Independence Organisation (KIO), New Mon State Party (NMSP), Shan State Army—North (SSPP/SSA), Karen National Union (MNU), Karenni National Progressive Party (KNPP),

Chin National Front (CNF). There are five new members: Lahu Democratic Union (LDU), Arakan National Council (ANC), Pa-Oh National Liberation Organisation (PNLO), Ta-ang National Liberation Army (TNLA) and Wa National Organisation (WNO)

108. It is the smaller UNFC member groups that emerge in 2015 as issues in the UNFC demand for an all-inclusive ceasefire.

109. Confidential interview with one of the main ethnic leaders who was involved in the NCA negotiations in Yangon, August 2014. He became part of this by being called in through the 'intellectuals'.

110. BCES—BP 16 (2013).

111. '...including provision for a framework for political negotiations, ceasefire monitoring arrangements, agreement of a Code of Conduct governing the behaviour of armed elements, and other issues, including how best to assist and provide 'peace dividends' to conflict-affected communities, and the vexed issues of land rights. Participants in such talks would initially include key EAGs, senior government officials (including parliamentary representation through the Central Committee for Union Peace-making and Working Committee for Union Peace-making) and the Myanmar Army. Subsequently, it would be necessary to include ethnic political parties and civil society actors in comprehensive discussions.' A. South (2015), 'Governance and political legitimacy in the peace process', in Steinberg, D., *Myanmar, the Dynamics of Evolving Polity*, Boulder, CO: Lynne Rienner Publishers, p. 364.

112. I am grateful to Ashley South for pointing out that there was a fierce debate at the conference regarding whether this was a UNFC event or not.

113. Although, according to Ashley South, questions remain regarding the degree to which key groups, such as the RCSS, and particularly the UWSA, endorsed this approach.

114. BCES BP 19 (2013).

115. I am grateful to Ashley South for pointing this out. For more on the KNU, see South (2011).

116. There have been discussions since the meeting in Myitkyina that the government was playing 'good cop—bad cop' and that this had been a premeditated strategy; however, it appeared to those who attended this meeting that U Aung Min was taken aback by the army's document and position. (Interview with a member of the NCCT a few days after the meeting)

117. BCES BP 19 (2013).

118. http://www.burmalibrary.org/docs17/BCES-BP-20-Law_Khee_Lah-orig-red.pdf

119. Three from the executive/cabinet, led by U Aung Min; three from parliament, led by ex-general U Thein Zaw; and three from the Myanmar Army. South (2015), pp. 367–8.

120. Confidential interview with ethnic leader after his return from Laiza.

121. Former exiled activist, now working at MPC.
122. Aung Naing Oo (2014a), 'The nationwide ceasefire agreement at a glance, 30 July 2014', http://www.mmtimes.com/index.php/national-news/11219-the-nation-wide-ceasefire-agreement-at-a-glance.html This refers to the third draft and things have moved on since.
123. 'The first chapter is about basic principles. Here, all sides are to agree on union, rather than secession, and respect of sovereignty. Other key basic principles include a commitment to peaceful dialogue rather than war, inclusiveness and recognition of diversity, and establishment of pledges toward federalism rooted in multi-party democracy.

     The second chapter focuses on the aims and objectives of the agreement, including the long-awaited political dialogue process and a ceasefire monitoring mechanism. It also emphasises that the agreement should be signed by all groups that are part of the peace process.

     The third chapter deals directly with ceasefire issues. It talks about joint ceasefire monitoring mechanisms, troop relocations, freedom of movement without weapons for troops, freedom of movement for civilians, protection of civilians and humanitarian assistance. One word that is often repeated here is collaboration. Civilian protection alone has 20 sub-headings ranging from refraining from establishing military bases at social, religious, health or education buildings to the protection of women and children in armed conflict.

     The fourth chapter is an agreement to draw up codes of conduct once the agreement is signed, which is a crucial step for strengthening ceasefires. Without these and the joint ceasefire monitoring, it would be impossible to maintain an effective ceasefire.

     The next chapter focuses on political guarantees and the holding of a political dialogue. It sets out the key steps toward peace, starting with the nationwide ceasefire agreement, followed by the development of the framework for political dialogue, which is the basis on which political dialogue will be implemented. One of the provisions of this chapter is on the ratification of political and peace agreements by the nation's parliament. [...]

     The sixth chapter is about transitional arrangements and future plans. One of the most important agreements will be the suspension of the Unlawful Associations Act for all signatories to the agreement, which has been a thorn in the side of the peacemaking efforts.

     Chapter 7—the final chapter—deals with the official language, validity and signing of the agreement.' Aung Naing Oo (2014a).
124. The six points have been translated as: 1. To have a keen desire to reach eternal peace; 2. To keep promises agreed in peace deals; 3. To avoid capitalising on the peace agreement; 4. To avoid placing a heavy burden on local people; 5. To abide

strictly by the existing laws; 6. To march towards a democratic country in accord with the 2008 constitution. http://www.nationmultimedia.com/aec/Tatmadaw-outlines-6-point-policy-for-peace-talk-30243970.html

125. At the time of writing, a number of permutations for a potential political dialogue have emerged. The ethnic political parries under the leadership of the NBF called a meeting of all parties (NLD and USDP did not attend or were not invited) and came up with one possible option. The six-party talks between the president, the commander in chief, the NLD and the political parties have also been discussing a possible structure of the political dialogue. The EAGs see their involvement in the dialogue as key, but others, including the political parties, do not necessarily subscribe to this view. At the time of writing it is too early to know how the political dialogue will be structured or if indeed it will start at all before the 2015 elections.

126. A key UNFC demand.

127. This is based on the founder of the KNU, Ba U Gyi's four principles that are still held as the guiding Principles of the Revolution of the Karen National Union:

1. Surrender is out of the question.
2. The recognition of the Karen State must be completed.
3. We shall retain our arms.
4. We shall decide our own political destiny.

128. '... the UNFC cannot truly speak on behalf of all the ethnic armed organizations as it claims. The United Wa State Army with 30,000 troops, Restoration Council for Shan State with 7,000 troops National Democratic Alliance Army with 2,000 troops, and the National Socialist Council of Nagaland (Kaplan) with at least 1,000 troops in Myanmar, are not members of the UNFC nor the NCCT which is negotiating a Nationwide Ceasefire Agreement (NCA) with the Government. Those not represented by the UNFC total 45,000 troops (if the KNU leaves the UNFC). In contrast, the biggest group within the UNFC is the KIO with 10,000 troops. Add to this the twelve other smaller groups and the grand total is about 18,000 troops. Given this discrepancy, the government needs to ensure that the negotiations being conducted by the NCCT is in line with the opinion of the other groups. Otherwise, they may not agree to sign the NCA.' *Political Monitor, 20*, 30 August—5 September 2014, http://www.euro-burma.eu/activities/research-policy/ebo-political-monitors/

129. None were KIA cadets but from Arakan Army, ABSDF, CNF and TNLA, all KIA allies.

130. It is important to remember that the NCA was an idea that emanated from the president that was kind of 'sold' to the Ethnic Armed Groups. This also explains why the government has been trying so hard to get the accord signed as soon as possible. It is their desire, but both sides have a lot to lose if the NCA is not signed before the 2015 elections.

131. EBO brief number 01 2015 Deed of Commitment https://euroburmaoffice.
s3.amazonaws.com/filer_public/fc/1f/fc1f9cec-4462–4e18-a8ac-5e8ef531a3ea/
ebo_brief_no012015_deed_of_commitment.pdf

132. 'The UWSA, NDAA and SSPP asked for time to consult with their headquarters. The ABSDF, ALP, CNF, PNLO, and NMSP felt that the Deed should be
discussed in-depth before signing. The NSCN-K did not speak but it is understood that they want a Greater Nagaland straddling India and Myanmar.' EBO
brief number 01 2015, Deed of Commitment.

133. 'Initially, the President and the VPs and Speakers were only to act as witnesses,
not sign the Deed, so it was not necessary for the Commander-in-Chief to be
present. President Thein Sein surprised everyone by signing the Deed himself
and others had to follow. But while Min Aung Hlaing did not come to the signing ceremony, he had personally negotiated the wording for the Deed after he
arrived back. So as was arranged initially, he assigned three top Lieut-Generals
involved in NCA negotiations to represent the Tatmadaw. They were given direct
orders by him to sign.' EBO brief number 01 2015, Deed of Commitment.

134. It also led to some anti-Chinese sentiments being aired, especially on Facebook,
where Myanmar citizens of Chinese origin were being written about in the same
vein as other Chinese, or in fact the ethnic Chinese in the Kokang conflict.

135. http://www.channelnewsasia.com/news/asiapacific/myanmar-rebels-
agree/1757654.html

136. https://euroburmaoffice.s3.amazonaws.com/filer_public/49/a3/49a3ea40-fef6–
46a7–94a7–5deff91856e5/ebo_background_paper_-_the_arakan_army_involve-
ment_in_rakhine_state.pdf

137. http://www.burmalink.org/ethnic-armed-organizations-summit-statement-law-
khee-lar-karen-state-2-9-june-2015/

138. 'Myanmar's Peace Process: A Nationwide Ceasefire Remains Elusive', Crisis Group
Asia Briefing no. 146, Yangon/Brussels, 16 September 2015.

139. 'The MNDAA, reportedly under Chinese pressure, announced a unilateral cease-
fire on 11 June. The government responded by demanding it surrender; the
MNDAA's two allied groups indicated they would continue to fight.' Crisis
Group Asia Briefing no. 146, 16 September 2015.

140. As has been pointed out by EBO briefing paper 3/15 (August 2015), 'the issue
here is not the all-inclusiveness of all ethnic groups as the UNFC 16+1 do not
include NDAA, RCSS, UWSA and NSCN-K. The issue here is about the unity
of the UNFC members. The government's grouping of 14+1 includes the NDAA,
RCSS, UWSA and NSCN-K, that are not part of the UNFC but excludes six
groups (ANC, LDU, WNO, AA, TNLA and MNDAA), that are part of the
UNFC.'

141. Although the issue is really about three groups, there are actually six groups that
are excluded; the three others are the Lahu Democratic Union (LDU), Arakan

National Council (ANC), Wa National Organization (WNO), but they have no significant armed wing and are therefore also excluded from signing a 'ceasefire'.

142. Crisis Group Asia Briefing no. 146, 16 September 2015.

143. http://uk.reuters.com/article/2015/09/09/uk-myanmar-rebels-idUKKCN0R 90EC20150909

144. KNU, DKBA, KNU peace council. RCSS, PNLO, ALP, CNF and ABSDF. These organisations were removed from the list of illegal and terrorist organisations before the signing ceremony. 'Many say that this cannot be called a 'nationwide ceasefire agreement' as not all have signed.

145. This is reminiscent of the conflict between the Karen and the Tatmadaw. Ashley South (2011), in his analysis of the Karen conflict, describes how on several occasions the KNU was egged on by the hard-line Karen diaspora to continue the fight and not sign a ceasefire, as the Karen expected the international community to support them in what they felt was a 'just war'. In the end the KNU was severely weakened by the breakaway of the DKBA and the loss of a large part of its 'liberated zone' in the 1990s, something which might have been avoided had the KNU come to an agreement with the government, as so many other EAGs did at the time. The Kachin position was also confirmed by further fieldwork in Kachin State, where it emerged that KIO schools and educators were moving away from using the government curriculum in translation, a clear sign of disengagement from the Union. For more on this, see South and Lall (forthcoming), *Language, Education and the Peace Process*.

146. They are still not united, as Wa and Mongla are separate, and not all groups have joined the NCCT, but this is the first time that there is some form of unity.

147. Interviews were held as part of an EU-funded project on peace and legitimacy. The groups that agreed to be interviewed included the KNU, NMSP, KNPP, DKBA, CNF, PNLO, ANP. All interviews were held in Yangon just after the July 2014 Liza meeting. An interview with the KIA was held in July 2015 in Chiang Mai.

148. South (2015), p. 363.

149. In the first three months after joining the parliament, Daw Aung San Suu Kyi had 57 meetings with the speaker U Shwe Mann. There were subsequent, less frequent meetings, but the exact number could not be verified. It was rumoured that the frequency of these meetings caused problems in U Shwe Mann's household. (Confidential interview)

150. 'Many political parties have expressed resentment at being excluded from the ceasefire process. They feel uneasy at the manner in which the government—and by extension, international supporters of the peace process—have welcomed Ethnic Armed Groups as political players via the peace arena. Political parties feel they have significant legitimacy derived from the electoral support of com-

munities, which is not reflected in their marginal roles in the peace process. 34 ethnic political party MPs were elected to the Upper House, 54 to the Lower House, and 110 to State/Regional assemblies. In four of the seven ethnic State legislatures (Chin, Karen, Rakhine and Shan), ethnic parties gained more than 25% of the seats.' MPSI (2014), p. 34.

151. Petrie, C. and South, A. (2013), 'Mapping of Myanmar Peacebuilding', Brussels: Civil Society Dialogue Network (CSDN), pp. 6–8.

152. 'For the peace process in Myanmar to be sustained and deepened, it is essential that members of the ethnic Burman community gain better understandings of the grievances, aspirations and realities of their minority brethren.' Petrie and South (2013), p. 12.

153. 'For some border and exile-based activist groups, the changes in Myanmar are perceived as threatening. Over the past two decades exile-based activist groups and networks have become used to controlling the political agenda, framing ethnic conflict in Myanmar for international consumption, and in the process channeling donor funds to their own client conflict-affected populations. Local opposition groups face a dilemma: whether and how to reinvent themselves and work for change around the new peace scenario, or to become increasingly marginalised in the borderlands and overseas, frustrated and angry as the political narrative shifts "inside" Myanmar.' Petrie and South (2013), p. 17.

154. Two focus groups about the peace process were held in NPT, one with MPs from the lower house and one with MPs from the upper house. A number of them represented ethnic parties, although the NLD was represented as well.

155. MPs from Lower House FGD

156. The peace process, as explained in this chapter, is rather complicated as neither the government side nor the EAG side was united. Only over the period of two years did the government on the one hand develop a united position, and the armed groups decided on a structure that allowed them also to speak with a more united front to the government. It is in light of this that political parties and parliament, and even the army, were not involved at first.

157. MPs from Lower House FGD

158. MPs from Upper House FGD

159. Of the 1,329, 45% were female and 55% were male; 37% were Bamar, 6% Kachin, 5% Kayah, 9% Karen, 9% Chin, 4% Mon, 8 % Rakhine and 8% Shan; 7% self-identified as mixed and 12% as other. On age, 37% were 18–25 years of age, 30% were 26–40, and 27 were 40–60; the rest were over 60. On education, 47% were graduates and 30% had completed secondary education; there were very few postgraduates, and 6% said they had only completed primary education. On class, only 13 % were working class (casual and agricultural work), another 17% were students, with the rest working in government jobs, NGOs, the private sector or their own business. The data were collected as part of an EU-funded project on peace and legitimacy.

160. In fact 84% said they wanted to participate in the peace process in some form.

161. Most of the poll was conducted before the military became involved, and the rest at a time when it was unclear how much the military would be involved.

162. Aung Naing Oo (2014b), 'In praise of peace dividends, 13 October 2014', http://www.mmtimes.com/index.php/opinion/11935-in-praise-of-peace-dividends.html

163. 'In 2012 there were an estimated 500,000 Internally Displaced People (IDPs) in the south-east alone, plus some 150,000 predominantly Karen refugees living in a series of camps along the Thailand-Burma border, and several million private 'economic migrants' in neighbouring countries. In the nearly two years since the start of ceasefire negotiations in late 2011, the number of displaced people in southeast Myanmar has reduced, while numbers have increased dramatically in Kachin and Rakhine States as a result of war and communal violence.' South (2015), p. 356.

164. According to the Ministry of Border Affairs, a total of K1.242 billion (US$ 1.25 million) has been spent, http://www.mmtimes.com/index.php/opinion/11935-in-praise-of-peace-dividends.html

165. South (2015), p. 371.

166. http://mizzima.com/mizzima-news/politics/item/13840-ethnic-parties-merge-plans-for-political-peace-talks

167. http://mizzima.com/mizzima-news/politics/item/14463-framework-for-peace-dialogue-developed-by-56-of-myanmar-s-smaller-political-parties

168. http://english.dvb.no/news/56-parties-approve-framework-for-political-dialogue-burma-myanmar/46181

169. Some armed group leaders have significant economic agendas, and questionable records in terms of human rights and governance in their areas of authority. See Ashley South's argument about the future of the peace process in *The Irrawaddy*, 8 December 2014, http://www.irrawaddy.org/contributor/next-burmas-peace-process.html

5. ECONOMIC REFORMS AND RE-ENGAGEMENT WITH THE INTERNATIONAL COMMUNITY

1. Cited in L. Rieffel (2012), 'The Myanmar Economy: Tough Choices, Global Economy and Development', WP 51, Washington, DC: Brookings Institute, p. 1.

2. As opposed to most difficult—which is the peace process. However, in terms of size and effect on the population, this is more multifaceted and cannot be resolved through negotiations.

3. According to the IMF, annual per capita income was around US$ 900 in fiscal year 2011/12 (1 April 2011 to 31 March 2012), and approximately 25% of its population live below the national poverty line. Data available at IMF (2013), Myanmar—

2013, Article IV, 'Consultation and First Review under the Staff-Monitored Programme', IMF Country Report No. 13/250, http://www.imf.org/external/pubs/ft/scr/2013/cr13250.pdf [25/11/2013].

4. The census revealed a total of 51,419,420 population at midnight on 29 March 2014: http://countryoffice.unfpa.org/myanmar/2014/08/30/10473/unfpa_press_release_myanmar_releases_population_count_from_census/

5. Myanmar is ranked 149 out of 187 countries in the 2011 UN Human Development Index. World Bank (2013), Public Expenditure and Financial Accountability, 'Republic of the Union of Myanmar, Public Financial Management Performance Report, March 2012', Report No. 75897-MM (PEFA, March 2013) p. 3.

6. World Bank (2013), p. 3.

7. Trade Policy Review Body (2014), Myanmar Report by the Secretariat, WTO WT/TPR/S/293, 21 January 2014, p. 7.

8. See http://www.imf.org/external/pubs/ft/scr/2014/cr1491.pdf

9. I am grateful to Derek Tonkin for pointing this out. http://www.ash.harvard.edu/extension/ash/docs/creating.pdf

10. Trade Policy Review Body (2014), p. 7.

11. Sanctions are discussed later in the chapter: Western sanctions were 'suspended' in 2012 for a year, but are now effectively cancelled and could not be reinstituted without the unanimous agreement of all 28 EU Member States. The difficulty with sanctions, as both the EU and the US discovered, is that the only really effective ones would have been financial sanctions to interdict natural gas and jade revenues. But that would have involved action against China, Thailand, Singapore and possibly other countries where revenues were held, and that never was a practical option. See also: http://www.un.org/en/ga/search/view_doc.asp?symbol=S/PV.7323

12. A study on the Triumph undergarment factory which closed because of sanctions showed that a number of the women working there then went into prostitution as they were unable to get any other jobs.

13. Details on the ineffectiveness of sanctions in Derek Tonkin's 'Burmese Perspectives, Letter from Guilford', available on www.networkmyanmar.org. See for example the Burmese perspective on 5 July 2009 and 5 March 2010.

14. 'The Bay of Bengal Initiative for Multi-Sectoral Technical and Economic Co-operation (BIMSTEC), which Myanmar joined on 22 December 1997, is not yet functioning. BIMSTEC is a forum to facilitate and promote trade, investment, and technical cooperation among participating countries: Bangladesh, Bhutan, India, Nepal, Sri Lanka, Myanmar, and Thailand. It identifies 13 broad sectors for cooperation, including: trade and investment, technology, tourism, transport and communication, energy, agriculture, fisheries, poverty alleviation, and counter-terrorism and transnational crimes. In 2004, BIMSTEC parties agreed to establish a BIMSTEC Free Trade Area Framework Agreement in goods, services, and

investment. Article 3 of the Agreement provides that goods, except those included in the Negative List, will be subject to tariff reduction or elimination according to different time frames. Myanmar had tariff reductions and eliminations for its fast track products before June 2011, and the tariffs on its normal track products are to be reduced or eliminated before June 2017. Rules of origin have not yet been agreed among BIMSTEC countries.' Trade Policy Review Body (2014), p. 24.

15. Trade Policy Review Body (2014), p. 22.

16. The GMS programme covers nine priority sectors: transport, energy, telecommunications, environment, human resource development, tourism, trade, private-sector investment and agriculture. The GMS countries have ratified an agreement to facilitate the cross-border movement of goods and people, which is being implemented on a pilot basis at key border crossings, and is being prepared for full implementation in the GMS corridors. There are no preferential tariff arrangements under the GMS. Trade Policy Review Body (2014), p. 25.

17. S. Turnell (2011), 'Fundamentals of Myanmar's Macroeconomy: A Political Economy Perspective', *Asian Economic Policy Review* 6 (1), pp. 136–53.

18. World Bank (2014), 'Myanmar—Ending poverty and boosting shared prosperity at a time of transition, a systematic country diagnosis', November 2014, p. 3.

19. ADB (2012), 'Opportunities and Challenges', Philippines: Mandaluyong City, August 2012, p. 22.

20. World Economic Forum (2013), 'New Energy Architecture: Myanmar', prepared in collaboration with Accenture and the Asian Development Bank, p. 16.

21. Most urban Myanmar people I have spoken to say that the banking system is totally dysfunctional, but since now people can access money through ATMs, things are starting to improve, albeit slowly.

22. Although clearly the revenues of the gas sales should have helped develop infrastructure.

23. ADB (2012), p. 20.

24. L. Jones (2013), 'The Political Economy of Myanmar's Transition', PREPT (no page numbers)

25. Term coined by Stuart Larkin, see http://www.burmalibrary.org/docs12/Stuart_Larkin-Myanmar_at_the_Crossroads.pdf

26. BTI (2012), Myanmar Country Report © 2012 Gütersloh: Bertelsmann Stiftung, http://www.bti-project.org, p. 18.

27. Tin Maung Maung Than (2005), 'State Dominance in Myanmar: The Political Economy of Industrialization', Singapore: ISEAS. p. 380.

28. N. Freeman (2014), 'Navigating the Economic Reform Process', *Southeast Asian Affairs*, pp. 224–39.

29. http://www2.irrawaddy.org/article.php?art_id=21193

30. U Myint is also a good friend of Daw Aung San Suu Kyi. The appointment of the

presidential advisers surprised many. See https://www.dvb.no/news/presidential-'advisors'-raise-eyebrows/15438

31. ICG (2011), 'Myanmar: Major Reform Underway', P8–10, Asia Briefing no. 127, Jakarta/Brussels, 22 September.

32. Ibid.

33. See Chapter 3 for details on national reconciliation.

34. ICG (2011).

35. World Bank (2013), pp.v-vi.

36. Ibid., pp.v-vi.

37. Ibid., pp.v-vi.

38. See also U Myint (2011), 'Myanmar Kyat Exchange Rate Issue', Yangon, 25 June 2011 (presented to the National Workshop on Reforms for Economic Development of Myanmar, Naypyitaw, 19–21 August 2011). Cited in ICG briefing no. 12.

39. The real rate oscillated between 900 and 1200 kyats for a dollar between 2004 and 2011.

40. IMF (2012), 'Exchange rate unification', IMF Country Report no. 12/104, Myanmar—2011, Article IV, p. 4.

41. ICG (2011), p. 11.

42. IMF (2012), p. 4.

43. Around 850 kyat to a dollar at the time.

44. Trade Policy Review Body (2014).

45. World Bank (2013), p. 4. However, Derek Tonkin points out that the slow decline in the value of the kyat is both managed and long overdue. There is no evidence of any free market rate emerging.

46. Rieffel (2012).

47. http://www.irrawaddy.org/business/burmas-central-bank-awards-9-foreign-lenders-operating-licenses.html

48. Trade Policy Review Body (2014), p. 12.

49. GoM (2012), 'Framework for economic and social reforms, Policy Priorities for 2012–15 towards the Long-Term Goals of the National Comprehensive Development Plan', NPT.

50. Nixon, H., Joelene, C., Kyi Pyar Chit Saw, Thet Aung Lynn and Arnold, M. (2013), *State and Region Governments in Myanmar*, NPT: MDRI and Asia Foundation NPT, p. 21.

51. Trade Policy Review Body (2014), p. 18.

52. 'Prior to June 2012, all imports into Myanmar required a non-automatic import license. This has changed since June 2012, when the Government eased import licensing requirements for 166 commodities (these correspond to more than 1,900 tariff lines) by allowing their importation with an automatic license. Subsequently, in April 2013, all licensing requirements for these commodities were abolished. Nonetheless, under the provisions of the Control of Imports and Exports

(Temporary) Act 1947, most goods imported into Myanmar still require an import license. Import licenses are issued by the Department of Commerce and Consumer Affairs of the Ministry of Commerce.' Trade Policy Review Body (2014), p. 37.

53. '... extraction and sale of teak; cultivation and conservation of forest plantation (except village-owned fire-wood plantation cultivated by villagers for their personal use); exploration, extraction, and sale/export of petroleum and natural gas; exploration, extraction, and export of pearl, jade, and precious stones; breeding and production of fish and prawns in fisheries, which have been reserved for research by the Government; postal and telecommunications services; air transport services, railway transport services; banking services and insurance services; broadcasting services and television services; exploration, extraction, and export of metals; electricity generating services (other than those permitted by law to private and cooperative electricity generating services); manufacture of products relating to security and defence, which the Government has, from time to time, prescribed by notifications.' Trade Policy Review Body (2014), p. 48.

54. However, Romain Caillaud comments that this might no longer be true. He notes that urbanites benefit more, but recent trips to rural areas have convinced him that the reforms are having an impact even at the village level—access to mobile phones, mechanisation of agriculture also, thanks to cheaper, liberalised import procedures, etc. I am grateful to him for pointing this out.

55. When mobile phones first came to Myanmar, the government chose a system that was incompatible with Western phones, so that Western mobiles could not pick up the local signal. SIM cards were rationed and very expensive—around $2,000 in 2004. Mobile phones became a real status symbol, and only the rich and those with connections could afford to own one. The price started to come down in the course of 2006–8, and more and more urban people were able to afford SIM cards. Around 2007 the government also started to sell pre-paid SIM cards with limited credit on them. These had to be thrown away after they ran out of credit. Since 2010/11 SIM cards have been relatively cheap and widely available.

56. Ericson and Deloitte (2013), 'The Potential Economic Impact of Mobile Communications in Myanmar 2012–2013'.

57. Freeman (2014), p. 235.

58. Buddhist nationalist movement; see Chapter 7.

59. Informal conversations with young people in Yangon, summer 2014.

60. World Economic Forum (2013), p. 6.

61. 'The majority of Myanmar's production is accounted for by two offshore fields: Yadana (5.7 TCF) and Yetagun (3.16 TCF), which were the source of 95% of Myanmar's total gas production in 2011. Both fields have been supplying natural gas to Thailand since 2000, with 755 mmcfd coming from Yadana and 424 mmcfd from Yetagun. In 2004, Daewoo announced the discovery of the Shwe gas field, off the coast of Rakhine state. Purchasing rights were awarded to the PRC in June

2008, under an agreement to export 6.5 TCF over 30 years. These supplies will be moved overland to Southwest PRC via an 870 km gas pipeline running from Kyaukpyu to Muse in Myanmar before entering the PRC at the border city of Ruili in Yunnan Province. The pipeline is scheduled for completion in late 2013 at an estimated cost of US$ 2.01 billion. South-East Asia Pipeline (SEAP) Company Limited, a Hong Kong-registered entity created by China National Petroleum Company (CNPC), and the Shwe Consortium members are in charge of constructing and operating this onshore pipeline. PRC's CNPC will construct a crude oil pipeline parallel to the gas pipeline at a cost of US$ 2.25 billion, which should be complete by the end of 2013. The crude oil pipeline will be 771 km andwill stretch into Yunnan and eventually into Chongqing in PRC.The pipeline will transport oil from the Middle East and Africa to south-western PRC. The project also involves the construction of a new deep-water crude unloading port and oil storage facitilieson Myanmar's Maday Island. CNPC controls a 50.9% stake in the pipeline through its wholly-owned subsidiary, SEAP. MOGE controls the remaining 49.1%. SEAP will be responsible for the construction and operation of the pipeline, while Myanmar's government will provide security.' p. 19, 'The Myanmar-PRC pipeline is expected to generate a significant amount of revenue for Myanmar. In accordance with international practice, a 16% value added tax will be levied on the crude oil transported through the pipeline, raising US$ 900 million (excluding the transport tariff) in foreign exchange earnings each year. A further US$ 900 million annually is expected to arise from the sale of natural gas to the PRC over the next 30 years, bringing the total revenue generated by the project to US$ 1.8 billion each year.' World Economic Forum (2013), pp. 14–15.

62. World Economic Forum (2013), p. 12
63. See also Transnational Institute (2013), 'Access Denied Land Rights and Ethnic Conflict in Burma', BCN Burma Policy Briefing no. 11, May 2013.
64. 'Proximity to trade corridors, where logistics are cheap, cluster-effects are possible and supply-chains can develop, characterise many of East Asia's most successful SEZs.' http://asiapacific.anu.edu.au/newmandala/2014/10/23/myanmar-special-economic-zones-part-i/
65. http://www.bangkokpost.com/business/news/448934/officials-to-meet-on-dawei-initial-phase
66. I am grateful to Romain Caillaud for pointing this out.
67. 'State and region governments consist of a partially elected unicameral *hluttaw*, an executive led by a Chief Minister and cabinet of state/region ministers, and state/region judicial institutions. The *hluttaw* is composed of two elected members per township, representatives for "national races", and appointed military representatives equal to one quarter of the total. The Chief Minister is selected by the President from among elected or unelected *hluttaw* members, and confirmed by the *hluttaw*. The Chief Minister selects the civilian ministers from among *hluttaw*

representatives or other candidates, and these are assigned portfolios by the President. The state/region Minister for Border and Security Affairs is a military officer nominated by the Commander-in-Chief. In general, judicial appointment procedures and structures are centralized and limit judicial independence. The President, in consultation with the Chief Justice of the Union, nominates the state/region Chief Justice. There is a state or region Advocate General, nominated by the Chief Minister. A Constitutional Tribunal of the Union considers constitutional disputes between regions, states and the union. Schedule Two of the Constitution lists areas over which the state or region government has legislative powers; it also assigns the states and regions executive or administrative authority over the same areas, and new responsibilities may be added under union law. These areas are divided among eight sectors, each with specific responsibilities, and several of which are deferred for further definition. In most of the sectors the specified responsibilities are quite narrow, and they also exclude certain major areas such as health and education.' Nixon et al. (2013), NPT pp.v-vi.

68. World Bank (2013), p. 5.
69. Nixon et al. (2013), p.vi.
70. Ibid., p.xii
71. 4 April: 'US Secretary of State Hillary Clinton announced that the US would ease financial and investment sanctions on Burma. The partial lifting of sanctions included the following measures: 1.Seeking agreement with the regime for a fully accredited ambassador;2.Establishing an in-country USAID mission and supporting a country program for the UNDP; 3.Allowing US private non-profit organizations to pursue a broad range of activities from democracy building to health and education;4.Facilitating travel to the US for Burmese MPs and select regime officials; and5.The targeted easing of the ban on the export of US financial services and investment. 17 April: The US Treasury's Office of Foreign Assets Control issued a general license authorizing financial transactions for a range of not-for-profit projects and programs in Burma including democracy-building and good-governance projects and educational activities. 25 April: The US ruled out an immediate end to its main sanctions on Burma. In his testimony before the House Foreign Affairs Committee, US Assistant Secretary of State for East Asian and Pacific Affairs Kurt Campbell said that the US would only lift sanctions on Burma in certain prescribed areas. Campbell stressed that the reform process must extend to the country as a whole and that the US remained concerned over reliable reports of ongoing human rights violations and the regime's ties to North Korea.' *Burma Bulletin* (2012), 'Alternative ASEAN Network on Burma: campaigns, advocacy and capacity-building for human rights and democracy', Issue 64, pp. 8–9.
72. *Burma Bulletin* (2012), pp. 8–9.
73. I was personally present at the meeting. It was always known that within the EU there were countries that favoured engagement and the dropping of sanctions,

such as Germany, and those who were considered 'hard-liners' and wanted to maintain sanctions, such as Britain.

74. See for example Daw Aung San Suu Kyi's discussion with John Bercow on the NNC Today programme in December 2014: http://www.bbc.co.uk/programmes/p02fvkp6. According to Derek Tonkin, Daw Aung San Suu Kyi said in response to John Bercow's unsupported assertion that 'frankly many voices in the UK are suggesting that perhaps they [sanctions] should be reintroduced', Suu Kyi made it clear that: 'I don't like going backwards, I like going forwards, so I think that rather than reintroducing old methods, I think what would help greatly would be if everybody seriously put their minds to doing whatever they can to encourage negotiations to take place.' http://www.networkmyanmar.org/index.php/sanctions

75. 'The actions and policies of the Government of Burma continue to pose an unusual and extraordinary threat to the national security and foreign policy of the United States. For this reason, the national emergency declared on May 20, 1997, and the measures adopted to deal with that emergency in Executive Orders 13047 of May 20, 1997; 13310 of July 28, 2003; 13448 of October 18, 2007; 13464 of April 30, 2008; 13619 of July 11, 2012; and 13651 of August 6, 2013, must continue in effect beyond May 20, 2015. Therefore, in accordance with section 202(d) of the National Emergencies Act (50 U.S.C. 1622(d)), I am continuing for 1 year the national emergency with respect to Burma declared in Executive Order 13047.' http://www.networkmyanmar.org/index.php/sanctions

76. Conflict Risk Network (2012), 'Not open for business: Despite elections, investor risk remains high in Burma', April 2012, p. 4.

77. Came out at the same time as the exchange rate unification.

78. Conflict Risk Network (2012), p. 4.

79. Freeman (2014), p. 231.

80. GoM (2012) NPT, p. 5.

81. Cited in ICG (2011).

82. See the next chapter for details on education reform and how in some ethnic states ethnic languages are now taught in state schools.

83. Transnational Institute (2013), pp. 1–3.

84. Ibid., pp. 1–3.

85. Ibid., pp. 3–5.

86. Allegedly this time in a consultative manner (thanks to Romain Caillaud for pointing this out).

87. McKinsey Global Institute (2013), 'Myanmar's moment: Unique opportunities, major challenges', Copyright © McKinsey & Company 2013, p. 75. This is a poor record compared with other developing Asian peers. For example, about 30% of workers in Vietnam and Thailand have a secondary education; in Indonesia the share is almost 50%, and in China and Malaysia it is about 60%.

88. See the next chapter on education reforms.

89. McKinsey Global Institute (2013), p. 78.

90. Ibid., p. 78.

91. GoM (2012), NPT, p. 24.

92. Rieffel (2012), pp. 12–13.

93. Ibid., p. 9.

94. Ibid., p. 9.

95. Ibid., pp. 9–10.

96. McKinsey Global Institute (2013), p. 29.

97. Interview with the WB in August 2014.

98. IMG interview.

99. One of these was the Ministry of Education, which only really opened to change after the minister of education died in 2013. See chapter on economic reforms.

100. See http://mizzima.com/opinion/features/item/13656-eu-training-helps-police-force-build-a-better-image

101. Loan aid started in 1968 and grant aid in 1975.

102. It was the first visit to Japan by a Myanmar head of state in 28 years. *Burma Bulletin* (2012), p. 7.

103. *Japan Times* (22 April 2012), 'Japan to cancel 60% of Myanmar's debt'.

104. Cited in *Burma Bulletin* (2012), p. 7. One of the anonymous reviewers says that Thilawa was initially funded in the 1990s by money out of Hong Kong (Chinese company), but it was not possible to verify this. Interviews in Japan point to the fact that Thilawa was first discussed between Sasakawa san and the president or another high official. Again, this could not be verified.

105. http://in.reuters.com/article/2012/10/02/japan-myanmar-idINDEE89109420121002

106. See chapter on the peace process.

107. Also known for his hard-line views on China.

108. http://in.reuters.com/article/2012/10/02/japan-myanmar-idINDEE89109420121002

109. 'Myanmar risks overheating: IMF', http://www.mmtimes.com/index.php/business/16567-myanmar-risks-overheating-imf.html

110. Shibani Mahtani, 'Myanmar's Business and Finance Laws Stuck in Pre-Election Limbo, http://blogs.wsj.com/frontiers/2015/09/02/myanmars-business-and-finance-laws-stuck-in-pre-election-limbo/

111. Ibid.

112. Parliament has suspended debates in light of the start of the election campaign. So this is left for the next government to pick up.

113. Htin Lynn Aung, Sandar Lwin, 'Stock exchange to open in December', Monday, 31 August 2015, http://www.mmtimes.com/index.php/business/16222-stock-exchange-to-open-in-december.html

114. 'Myanmar risks overheating: IMF', http://www.mmtimes.com/index.php/business/16567-myanmar-risks-overheating-imf.html

6. THE REFORM OF MYANMAR'S EDUCATION SYSTEM

1. Cited in EBO (2011), 'President Thein Sein's Inaugural Speech', Euro Burma Office, Analysis Paper no. 2/2011, https://euroburmaoffice.s3.amazonaws.com/filer_public/6d/67/6d67b1e2–19b8–450a-9983–63a8844ba616/ebo_analysis_paper_no_2__2011_-_presidents_speech_on_30_march_2011_english.pdf, p. 4.
2. M. Lall and E. Vickers (2009), *Education as a Political Tool in Asia*, London: Routledge.
3. There are of course big issues within economic reforms as well, such as land, mining etc.
4. The main development partners in Myanmar are UNICEF, UNESCO, AUSAID, DFID, JICA and the EU.
5. Although Cheesman writes about the state having to expand education massively in the 1950s to meet populist post-independence demand, and the system rapidly buckling under the strain of the expansion then—especially if you consider extent to which the state itself almost collapsed (more than once) in the early years of independence. Thanks to Emily SM for pointing this out.
6. Of these, 28,967 are Basic Education Primary Schools, 6,553 are Basic Education Post-Primary Schools, 3,121 are Basic Education Middle Schools, and 2,351 are Basic Education High Schools. A total of 8,200,595 students are officially enrolled in basic education schools (JICA, 2013). Cited in Pyoe Pin (2014), *The Political Economy of Basic Education in Myanmar*, Yangon.
7. Khin Maung Kyi, Ronald Findlay, R. M. Sundrum, Mya Maung, Myo Nyunt, Zaw Oo et al. (2000), *Economic Development of Burma; a vision and a strategy*, Stockholm: Olof Palme International Centre, p. 145. See ADB reports on secondary education for CESR for drop-out statistics.
8. Although now slowly increasing: http://www.irrawaddy.org/burma/govt-proposes-20-budget-rise-boosting-education-defense-health.html
9. On the government expenditure side, salary payments dominate the budget, taking up 80–90 %, leaving very little for goods, services and maintenance expenses. Construction expenditure take ups over 90% of the capital budget, leaving little for equipment. Unpublished UNICEF SITAN report on Mon state, 2014.
10. Especially as the teacher recruitment and placement system is so flawed, and so teachers are not recruited and posted on the basis of their likelihood to remain in rural areas/speak the language. The latter part of the chapter deals with the various ethnic education regimes, mother tongue and peace issues.
11. During 2010–11 academic year there were a total of 1,431 Monastic Schools with 0.215 million students, including novices and nuns. These include 1,071 Primary, 246 Post-Primary, 112 Middle and 2 High Schools. Government of the Republic of the Union of Myanmar (2012), Ministry of Education, 'Education for All: Access to and Quality of Education in Myanmar', Conference on Development Policy Options with Special Reference to Education and Health in Myanmar, 13–16 February, 2012, Nay Pyi Taw, p. 13.

12. M. Lall (2010), *Child centred learning and teaching approaches in Myanmar*, Yangon: British Council.
13. This was calculated on the basis of number of registered students per school, therefore not covering all teacher salaries.
14. Conversation with local supporters of monastic schools.
15. Some families in the middle classes are prepared to spend 25–50% of their household income on fees.
16. http://www.myanmar-business.org/2013/06/myanmar-allows-opening-of-62-private.html
17. The 10 pilot-run private high schools in Yangon region were listed as Maha Myagyuntha, Zinyaw, EC Education Center, Educational Palace, Success, N-3, Maths-Than Sein, Thein Naing (Academic), Arr Mann, Shwe Pin Shwe Thi.
18. Pyoe Pin Programme Report (2014), *The Political Economy of Education in Myanmar*, Pyoe Pin, Yangon. p. 8. 'Primary school enrolment is 74%, however, this figure masks high levels of attrition as they are recorded by township education officers in the first week of term during annual enrolment drives. There are significant regional disparities. Tanintharyi Region's primary enrolment rate is 93 % while Shan State's primary enrolment rate is 58% (UNICEF, Ministry of Health, and Ministry of Planning, 2011). Enrolment in primary education in rural areas is only 3.6% lower than in urban areas (JICA, 2013, p. 29). The government reports that 80% of children are currently less than a 30 minute walk away from a primary school (UNICEF, 2010, p. 18). 54.2% of children who enter primary school complete its five grades (UNICEF, Ministry of Health, and Ministry of Planning, 2011). There are significant regional and income disparities in completion rates. Only 31.2% of the poorest quintile of students complete grade five (MQBEP, 2010, p. 4). Only 31.7% of students in Rakhine complete primary school (UNICEF, Ministry of Health, and Ministry of Planning, 2011). There is a regional dimension to drop-out rates, with the rural–urban enrolment gap at the secondary level being approximately 30% (JICA, 2013, p. 29).'
19. For more information on the survey, see M. Lall et al. (2013), *Teachers' Voice—What Education Reforms Does Myanmar Need?* Yangon and Bangkok: Myanmar Egress and FNS.
20. This is about to change as the education reforms plan to offer different career tracks for primary and secondary school teachers.
21. For difficulties with this, see Lall (2010).
22. Ibid.
23. English is taught from Grade 1 onwards, but not to a standard that students can then follow instruction in English.
24. In Yangon the university was closed for 10 years out of 12.
25. The Myanmar Egress research team is full of doctors, and all testify to the fact that they would not have chosen medical studies had they not been pressured. Others

who are interested in being a doctor often cite reasons of hardship in government postings in remote areas at the start of careers as putting them off. There is a nascent private medical system emerging, which might make it more interesting for young people to remain in the medical field, but this will then make proper medical care unaffordable for the poor.

26. One needs to remember, however, that the situation in Yangon is atypical of Myanmar in general. Whilst there are similar trends to be observed in Mandalay, other state capitals have fewer alternatives to offer to the failing state system.

27. The Government of the Republic of the Union of Myanmar (2012). In March 2011, at the first regular session of Pyidaungsu Hluttaw (parliament) on the 18th day, the Head of State, President U Thein Sein, gave guidance to give special focus on the implementation of the following tasks for the upgrading of national education.

28. They were also issued with a strict list of what they could use the money for, even if that wasn't what they needed money for. The World Bank (2013) notes that in 2012/13 school year, school grants were piloted in 40,000 schools. These are small school budgets managed directly by each principal to purchase consumables such as chalk and cleaning supplies. The amount of these grants is estimated to be $324 on average to primary schools, $1,216 on average to middle schools, and $1,822 on average to high schools. The World Bank is now collaborating with the government to expand the school grants programme for school year 2014/15.

29. In fact a recent study M. Lall (2014), *Head teachers and leadership training needs in Myanmar*. British Council, Yangon (unpublished report) reveals that many headteachers simply refer to the school board and ask parents where possible to fund repairs, as the centralised system takes too long and is not reliable.

30. The stipend project allowed for headteachers to nominate their most disadvantaged children for financial help. Priority was given to orphans. However, this required a large amount of paperwork and only very few children actually received the stipend. The school grants and stipend programme is now being revamped and expanded with help from the World Bank.

31. It is likely to have affected the ethnic schools as well, although at the time of writing I had no direct evidence of ethnic teachers leaving.

32. November 2012 Draft Framework for Social and Economic Reforms (FESR), quoted below, indicates that the GoM plans to work with a *distributed (or deconcentrated) model of education management*. (Emphasis added). 'GOM attaches high priority to developing a participatory process of local budgeting, which should reflect local priorities and needs while corresponding with national policy directions, by delegating decision-making authority over expenditure compositions (between recurrent and capital expenditure) as well as inter-sectoral allocations (between sectors) under the guidance of local parliaments. *However, GOM still retains the budgetary controls over health and education expenditure for transitional*

adjustments, which may be a future subject of decision for fiscal decentralization. In the meantime, GOM plans to ensure that the initial imbalances of decentralization can be corrected through a gradual process of coordination and delegation, which can ultimately reinforce the legitimacy and capacity of the state and regional governments particularly for those that are contributing to parallel process of peacebuilding and regional development.' (FESR, November 2012 Draft, p. 34) '… While GOM strengthens regulatory policies to streamline various private and community-run educational programs, it is also moving ahead with the *decentralization of education management in line with the requirements of the Constitution* by integrating locally-designed teaching curriculum as well as non-formal programs in basic education system. This reform policy and strategy will focus on the need to expand the system of basic education from eleven to twelve years, *on child-centred teaching methodologies, upgrading teacher training and other curriculum reforms necessary to enhance the quality of basic education, on teacher remuneration and broader issues of education financing, on establishing a rigorous system for education quality assessment and performance, and on further reforms in the management of basic education including the importance of active engagement in the process by the parents themselves. In addition, GOM will also pay attention to other supportive measures that can address high drop-out rates and out-of-pocket cost burdens on the families."* (FESR, November 2012 Draft, p. 29)

33. Also discussed in Chapter 5.

34. During 2012/13 the MoE transferred an estimated $324 on average to primary schools, $1216 to middle schools and $1822 to high schools in direct support for them to spend on goods and services. The programme supported 40,000 schools and cost $18 million. It is said that these amounts are to double in the 2013/14 school year. (World Bank Education Mission, June 3–14, 2014)

35. This was agreed in February 2012, but the actual process started a few months later.

36. At the time of writing things had been delayed and the CESR was drafting the National Education Sector Plan and had not reached the costing stage yet. There was a Quick Wins budget in October/November 2014 to tide things over. Thanks to Emily SM for pointing this out.

37. Ministry of Education (MoE), Ministry of Social Welfare, Relief and Resettlement (MoSWRR), Ministry of Religious Affairs (MoRA), Ministry of Science and Technology (MoST), Ministry of Labour (MoL), Ministry of Border Affairs (MoBA), Ministry of Defence (MoD), Ministry of Health (MoH), Ministry of Agriculture and Irrigation (MoAI), Ministry of Cooperatives (MoC), Ministry of Finance and Revenue (MoFR), Union Attorney General's Office (UAGO).

38. Allegedly some policy advice to the CESR regarding language was literally lost in translation, as texts were translated into Burmese, then final versions back into English, losing some of the text in the process. Thanks to ESM for pointing this out.

39. The themes for Phase 2 covered 1. Policy, Legislation, Management (PLM) and Financing; 2. Early Childhood Development and Basic Education (ECDBE) (including Early Childhood Education (ECD), Primary and Secondary Education, Language of Instruction, Curriculum, Textbook and Learner Assessment, and Supervision, Inspection and Quality Assurance); 3. Teacher Education; 4. Non Formal Education (NFE); 5. Technical and Vocational Education and Training (TVET); and 6. Higher Education (HE).

40. U Mya Aye died in at the end of 2013 and was first replaced by Dr Myo Myint, who became acting minister when U Mya Aye became ill. He continued to be acting minister until Dr Khin San Yee was appointed Minister of Education. She is the second female minister in the government.

41. As seen in earlier chapters, not all ministers were equally reform-friendly and a few were worried that if perceived as too reformist, they would be targeted if there was a military backlash later. The 'hard-liners' and loyalists to Than Shwe are still perceived as too powerful.

42. At the time of writing the NLD has disowned the NNER and removed the head of the NNER, Dr Thein Lwin, from its central executive committee.

43. Conversation at an NNER event with Dr Thein Lwin, who heads the NNER 2013.

44. Conversations with various ethnic education stakeholders, 2013–14.

45. This is despite Daw Aung San Suu Kyi's own involvement in the Higher Education Reform process at government level. It also needs to be noted that the NLD later distanced itself from the NNER, as is discussed later in the chapter.

46. The repeated breaking of promises, cancelling previously agreed arrangements and spreading false news, as documented above, have caused us to lose all faith in EPIC and the Ministry of Education's process of education reform. NNER (2014), 'NNER's position regarding its loss of faith in the government and Ministry of Education's education reform process', Yangon, 7 March 2014, http://www.burmalibrary.org/docs21/UTL-07—2014-03-07-NNER_Letter_to_Public-en.pdf

47. He later came back in another capacity.

48. The selection of experts was often problematic. The CVs received by UNICEF and reviewed by the development partners were at times seen as not being impressive enough for such a high calibre job. It is unclear if this was due to the short notice or if the posts offered were simply not long enough. (Conversations with various development partners).

49. The CESR was also affected by the international staff not recognising the politics of reform. UNICEF's terrible contracting arrangements led to delays (which QBEP MTR strongly criticised). None of the DPs/QBEP-funders had an education expert in their missions, and people contracted in as experts were often not listened to.

50. Although translated versions took longer and were only shared at the end of 2014.

51. Another factor (briefly mentioned above) was that the President's Office was also fed up with the increasing influence of various development partners and wanted to return the process to Myanmar leadership.

52. The development partners were assured that this was not to replace the CESR nor to do similar work twice, but that EPIC and the CESR were complementary to each other. In reality, however, this was a move to retake control of the process without having to shut the CESR down or make the development partners' work redundant. (Conversation with relevant people in the President's Office).

53. This committee is charged with monitoring whether or not ministries and departments are delivering on specific reform pledges and delivery targets. The committee found that the MoE was 'the worst performing ministry' and that it had failed to deliver on 220 of its commitments. Pyoe Pin (2014), pp. 19–20.

54. http://www.burmapartnership.org/ updates-national-education-law-student-protest/

55. http://www.mmtimes.com/index.php/national-news/11994-student-unions-vow-to-%20continue-protests-against-education-law.html

56. The 11 points demanded by the ACDE:
    1. Inclusion of representatives of teachers and students in legislation process of education policies and laws, by-laws and other related laws
    2. the right to freely establish and operate student and teacher unions and legal recognition for them
    3. establishment of National Education Commission and University Coordination Committee mentioned in the approved National Education Law
    4. self-determination and self-management on educational affairs of individual state/regions and schools
    5. modifying current examination and university matriculation system
    6. modifying teaching methods to such that ensure freedom for thinking and self-studying of students
    7. inclusion of a provision in National Education Law that ensure freedom for the practice of ethnic languages and mother tongue based multi-lingual education for ethnic populations and tribes
    8. inclusive education for all children including children with disabilities
    9. resumption of enrolment for students previously expelled from schools due to the student uprisings
    10. allocation of 20 percent of national budget for education
    11. regulating of free compulsory education up to middle school level rather than primary level.

57. http://www.irrawaddy.org/burma/upper-house-approves-education-law-amendments.html

58. http://www.rfa.org/english/news/myanmar/reform-06192015175225.html

59. Whilst the NNER is concerned with all education sectors, Daw Aung San Suu

Kyi seems much less interested in primary and secondary education. A number of critics have argued that the money she wants spent on Yangon University would be better placed in getting basic education right.

60. Accompanied by Hon. Prof. Dr Mya Oo, Member of Upper House of Parliament; Dr Mya Oo, Member of Lower House of Parliament, Secretary of Education Development Committee (Pyithu Hluttaw), Secretary of National Education Law Committee, Secretary of Higher Education Law Committee; Prof. Dr Aung Kyaw Myat, Director General, Ministry of Science and Technology, Member of Education Development Committee.

61. One of the trustees at Bard, U Ba Win, is of Myanmar origin.

62. Discussions with Dr Nay Win Maung's mother, whose granddaughter was going to Bard at the time and who tried to help facilitate the deal between Bard and the government. It is unclear why Daw Aung San Suu Kyi would be against the campus in MM unless this was solely to get credit for progress in HE herself.

63. Of course there is also the Joint Education Sector Working Group, which is a high-level mechanism for policy dialogue between the government and development partners. The JESWG is co-chaired by the Ministry of Education, UNICEF and Australia. See http://www.themimu.info/sector/education

64. Apart from JICA, who have always had a closer relationship with the Myanmar government.

65. This programme document presents the Myanmar Quality Basic Education Programme (QBEP). The QBEP represents a joint partnership between UNICEF and the donors of the Myanmar Multi Donor Education Fund (MDEF), currently the European Union (EU), Australia (AusAID), United Kingdom (DFID), Denmark and Norway. The first phase of support to education through the UNICEF/MDEF partnership (MDEF1) ran from 2007 to 2011 and achieved successes in addressing access and quality issues and building capacity and partnerships. The current context of political change, steps towards decentralisation and greater openness to external assistance provides an important opportunity to build on this. There is the potential to combine strengthened and expanded programming to directly address quality, access and equity issues, with system-building and policy/strategy development. Development of a coherent strategic sector framework would in turn make it possible in future for increased levels of financial and technical assistance that would greatly accelerate progress. The QBEP has the Purpose (Outcome) of *increased number and proportion of children accessing and completing quality basic education in targeted townships*. The four key Outputs (Results) are: 1) *expand coverage of quality early childhood development (ECD) services*, 2) *improve quality of teaching and learning*, 3) *enhance planning, management and monitoring and* 4) *enhance coverage, quality and relevance of second chance education*. The direct beneficiaries of QBEP will be an estimated 650,000 children annually.

66. 'The Myanmar Education Consortium (MEC), established in 2012 and funded through the Australian and UK Governments, has the overall goal of increasing the number and proportion of children in Myanmar accessing and completing quality basic education, including monastic education. As part of the MEC, the Burnet Institute Myanmar (BIMM) and the Monastic Education Development Group (MEDG) are working to build the capacity of the Monastic School system to provide quality education and school facilities (including water, sanitation and hygiene) in a targeted number of schools across Myanmar. Burnet Institute and Monastic Education Development Group (2014), *Monastic schools in Myanmar—a baseline study*.

67. MEC is not very transparent in who receives funding and who does not. There have been rumours big organisations received funding, as opposed to the local NGOs but this was impossible to verify. The lack of transparency speaks for itself.

68. The World Bank programme also focuses on a national reading assessment project to assess teaching and learning quality.

69. M. Smith (1999), *Burma: Insurgency and the Politics of Ethnicity*, London: Zed Books; A. South (2008), *Ethnic Politics in Burma: States of Conflict*, London: Routledge.

70. This is not unusual in countries with different ethnic and linguistic groups—see Pakistan and Indonesia, for example.

71. More on this in the chapter on the peace process, as well as in the chapter on religious identity.

72. N. Salem-Gervais, and Metro, R. (2012), 'A Textbook Case of Nation-Building: The Evolution of History Curricula in Myanmar', *Journal of Burma Studies*.

73. Research by Shalom shows that ethnic minority children in remote areas do not understand the teacher, and consequently there are high drop-out rates.

74. G. Houtman (1999), *Mental Culture in Burmese Crisis Politics: Aung San Suu Kyi and the National League for Democracy*, Tokyo: Tokyo University of Foreign Studies.

75. South (2008); M. Lall and South, A. (2013), 'Comparing models of non-state ethnic education in Myanmar: the Mon and Karen national education regimes', *Journal of Contemporary Asia*, vol. 44, issue 2, pp. 298–321.

76. A. South (2003), *The Golden Sheldrake: Mon Nationalism and Civil War in Burma*, London: Routledge Curzon.

77. The Mon National Schools were able to expand into government-controlled territory due to the first ceasefire. The MNEC was also able to develop a structure of locally negotiated 'mixed' schools whereby a Mon language and history teacher works in a government school. M. Lall and South, A. (2013).

78. They have to be able to afford it. Students also have to be allowed to transition by the government school, which is currently discretionary—there is no obligation for relevant officials to recognise a child's learning in a non-state education insti-

tution. However, there are local arrangements in place in a number of areas where MNS operate.

79. Lall and South (2013).

80. Saw Tun Lin, 'Govt Confirms Karen Language will be Taught in Pago Schools', Karen News, 15 December 2013, http://karennews.org/2013/12/govt-confirms-karen-language-will-be-taught-in-pago-schools.html/

81. CESR Rapid Assessment report: Recommendations related to ethnic and mother tongue education:

   • Develop coordination strategies for networking among ethnic-minority organisations operating in education (e.g. Karen, Chin and Mon organisations); the network of monastic education schools; religious, economic and social organisations, as well as organisations focused on gender equality and women's development organisations; and organisations for inclusive education.

   • Strengthen direct connections existing between state/division governments and state/division education sectors.

   • Use education as a tool to strengthen peaceful coexistence among ethnicities and exchange strategies.

   • Encourage more cooperation between the MoE and international/local NGOs in border areas and areas that have no peace. In doing so, the Ministry should first develop trust from the people and then collaborate according to the Nay Pyi Taw Accord. Detailed studies should be conducted in the CESR Phase 2.

82. Pyoe Pin (2014), p. 8. 'There are 273,516 basic education teachers registered with the Ministry of Education (JICA, 2013). 70% of teachers working in ethnic areas are not able to speak the local language/dialect even though 30% of all rural school children will not have heard the Burmese before entering school (UNICEF, 2010). The literacy rate for women in Myanmar is approximately 72%. This is 11% lower than for men (Belak, 2003, p. 131). This difference is more severe for minority groups, with only 50–60% of Karen women and less than 50% of young Mon women being literate (Belak, 2003, p. 131). This gender parity index for both primary and secondary school attendance is, however, at 1.01, indicating no statistically significant disparity in this regard (MQBEP, 2010, p. 4). While women make up 82% of teachers, they are only 39% of school heads (UNICEF, 2010, p. 12).'

83. All agree that mother-tongue education is important, but the organisations have different views on whether Burmese should be taught, and if so at what age and for how long. Some would prefer simply to teach their own language and English. Recently a network of ethnic education organisations has been created—Myanmar Indigenous Network for Education, MINE. However, there are issues of one group appearing to impose its views on other groups, so not all members are happy.

84. The hard-line elements are now spearheaded by the Karen mobile teacher training/mobile schools that are directed by Scott O'Brian.

85. All based on interviews and talks with MNEC officials, as well as taking part in

various education workshops trying to bring the MNEC and the state education system closer together.

86. There has also been a general deprioritisation of support to ethnic groups in the course of the general re-alignment of development partners towards the government.

87. This is also due to the fact that the Mon national cause is less attractive now that the nationwide peace process makes a resumption of ethnic conflict in Mon State highly unlikely. Young people prefer to look for jobs in Thailand or Yangon.

88. Many INGOs/donors do not pay teacher salaries.

89. 'Once free, compulsory education has been successfully implemented at the primary level; it shall be extended step by step (to higher grades).'

90. http://www.irrawaddy.org/burma/mon-state-likely-pass-mother-tongue-teaching-bill.html

91. At the time of writing, some limited funding has been offered by the Norwegian government, but it is unclear if this funding will be extended beyond the one year of the original offer, simply postponing the current financial issues facing MNEC.

92. From a legislative point of view, this certainly would have been the easiest solution for the Myanmar government.

93. Conversations with Kim Jolliffe, who was advising on health reforms in the border area. It is still early days, but the collaboration in Karen State seems to work more smoothly than anything seen in in the ethnic education sectors to date. See also, 'A Federal, Devolved Health System for Burma/Myanmar' authored by the Health Convergence Core Group, not yet in the public domain at the time of writing.

94. The Myanmar Language Commission has been renamed as the Myanmar and Ethnic Languages Commission (announced at the National Education Law consultation with DPS in November 2014).

95. About US$1 million is estimated to be required for education support in Kachin State and Northern Shan State. The Kachin Response Plan is prepared under the leadership of the United Nations Humanitarian Coordinator, with the support of UNOCHA, UN agencies and NGOs, providing assistance in Kachin State, including UNDP, UNHCR, UNICEF, WFP, FAO, HPA, KBC, KMSS, LDO, Metta, Oxfam, Save the Children, Shalom, Solidarites International, SVS, WPN, Trocaire and World Vision, March 2012–Feb 2013.

96. More on this in Lall and South (2013).

97. The Rakhine Response plan is a document agreed by all humanitarian partners with operations in Rakhine State, July to December 2012 (UN document, unpublished).

7. THE RISE OF BUDDHIST NATIONALISM

1. Tun Aung Chain (2000), 'Historians and the Search for Myanmar Nationhood', at 16th Conference of the International Association of Historians of Asia, Kota Kinabalu: International Association of Historians of Asia in Cooperation with Universiti Malaysia Sabah; A. South (2008, reprint edn 2010), *Ethnic Politics in Burma: States of Conflict*, London: Routledge.

2. Derek Tonkin has pointed out that the notion of 'one ethnicity, one language, one religion' contrasts with Aung San's, 'What we want is a strong state administration as exemplified in Germany and Italy. There shall be only one nation, one state, one party, one leader. There shall be no parliamentary opposition, no nonsense of individualism'—words he is said to have written under Col. Suzuki's guidance around 1942.

3. L. Sakhong (2012), 'The Dynamics of Sixty Years of Ethnic Armed Conflict in Burma', Analysis Paper no. 1, January 2012, BCRP, pp. 1–2. 'Nationalism, for both U Nu and Ne Win, was simply based on the notion of "one ethnicity, one language, one religion", that is, the *Myanmar-lumyo* or Myanmar ethnicity, *Myanmar-bathaska* or Myanmar language, and the *Myanmar-thatana* of Buddhism. Although their approaches to ethnic and religious "forced-assimilation" were different, U Nu and Ne Win both had the same goal of creating a homogeneous people in the country. While U Nu opted for cultural and religious assimilation into Buddhism as a means of "forced-assimilation", Ne Win removed the rights of the country's religious and cultural minorities, especially minority's language right, as a means of creating a homogeneous unitary state, under the motto of "one voice, one blood, and one nation", and adopted the "national language policy" as a means of ethnic "forced assimilation". U Nu and Ne Win thus complemented each other, although their approaches in depriving cultural and religious minorities of their rights were different in nature.' pp. 7–8.

4. D. Steinberg (2012), 'The problem of democracy in the republic of the Union of Myanmar, neither nation-state nor state-nation,' *Southeast Asian Affairs*, Singapore: ISEAS, p. 222. 'East Pakistan (later Bangladesh), with Middle Eastern funding, supported the Rohingya (Muslim) rebels along its frontier in Rakhine (Arakan). India assisted various cross-border ethnic groups in its Northeast Region. China helped the Burma Communist Party and at times the Kachin. Thailand materially assisted a variety of rebellions to create "buffer states" between what was regarded as a radical regime in Rangoon and a conservative one in Bangkok. The Thais at various unofficial levels have harboured Burmese dissidents as well. Elements of the United Kingdom had promoted Karen independence, and the United States clandestinely assisted the Kuomintang (Chinese Nationalist) rebels along the China frontier, and other dissidents in Thailand.'

5. 'General Than Shwe may have perceived himself as the fourth of these unifiers'. Steinberg (2012), pp. 224–5.

6. 'Since the days of the State Peace and Development Council and its predecessor, the State Law and Order Restoration Council, wags in Yangon often joked that Myanmar color television only had two colors—maroon for monks' robes and green for soldiers uniforms. Almost daily, some general would be seen paying obeisance to well-known Buddhist monks. Now it is civilian ministers doing the same.' R. H. Taylor (2014), http://asia.nikkei.com/Politics-Economy/Policy-Politics/ Robert-Taylor-What-would-Ne-Win-have-thought-of-today-s-Myanmar

7. Steinberg (2012), p. 230.

8. Ibid., p. 225.

9. Tin Maung Maung Than and Moe Thuzar (2012), 'Myanmar's Rohingya Dilemma', *ISEAS perspectives*, Naypyidaw, 9 July 2012, p. 4. I am grateful to Derek Tonkin for pointing out that the Bengalis migrated to Arakan after 1879 quite legally in British eyes. The British were willing to grant them permanent domicile under the terms of the 1941 Indo-Burma Agreement. The 1948 Citizenship Act would seem to uphold this position. It is unclear how they are retroactively regarded as 'illegals'" by Nay Pyi Taw.

10. J. Leider (2012), EFEO presentation (unpublished). There is also a debate as to whether Bengalis fled into Rakhine State during the independence war from West Pakistan in 1971. Rakhine scholars like Khin Maung Saw claim that up to 2 million Bengalis fled as war refugees into Burma in 1971, but there is no corroborative evidence for this. Email conversations between Derek Tonkin and Wakar Uddin point to only a handful of refugees.

11. R. H. Taylor (2013), 'Myanmar in 2012, Mhyaw ta lin lin or great expectations', *Southeast Asian Affairs*, Singapore: ISEAS, p. 201. It would seem that the man who died in prison, by the name of Htet Htet, was a Buddhist orphan adopted by a Muslim family. It would not seem that the three called themselves 'Rohingya'. Htet Htet (also known as Rawshe), Mahmud Rawphi (aka Hla Win) and Khochi (aka Myint Swe) were found guilty of raping, murdering and robbing Thida Htwe from Thabyaychaung village in Ramee township on her way home from a sewing lesson on 28 May 2012. There has been debate amongst some about whether the doctor who did the post mortem examination certified that she had been raped. I am grateful to Derek Tonkin for pointing this out.

12. Taylor (2013), p. 201. See also http://www.bbc.co.uk/news/world-asia-1832 4614

13. ICG (2012), 'Myanmar: Storm Clouds on the Horizon', Asia Report no. 238, 12 November 2012.

14. Tin Maung Maung Than and Moe Thuzar (2012), p. 3. The death toll (including the rape victim and the 10 Muslim men) now stands at 62 in the period 28 May to 21 June, according to a local government official. (Xinhua, 21 June 2012, 'Death toll rises to 62 in Myanmar's riot-hit Rakhine state: official') Over 2,000 residential homes and at least one mosque were also destroyed during the riots.

15. Tin Maung Maung Than and Moe Thuzar (2012), p. 1.
16. Taylor (2013), p. 201. The commission is discussed later in this chapter.
17. ICG (2012), pp. 1–3.
18. Ibid.
19. Taylor (2013).
20. 'The Nasaka, or "Border Immigration Headquarters" as it is sometimes known, is an inter-agency force established in 1992 and comprised of around 1200 immigration, police, intelligence and customs officials. It operates in the Muslim-majority northern part of the state, near the Bangladesh border.' http://blog.crisisgroup.org/asia/2013/07/16/myanmars-nasaka-disbanding-an-abusive-agency/
21. ICG (2012), pp. 4–5 The army, recruited nationally and rotated into the region, has been better at maintaining security, for example preventing attacks against the majority Muslim residents of Buthidaung township, which has a large army presence, and guarding the last Muslim-majority neighbourhood in downtown Sittwe.
22. Taylor (2013), p. 201.
23. Buddhist monks are often viewed in the West as non-violent. This is fundamentally incorrect: in Myanmar monks have been part of the nationalist independence movement. Similar situations of monks involved in violence have also been observed in Sri Lanka.
24. ICG (2012).
25. Rakhine Buddhists started as a boycott campaign against the UN-backed census by Rakhine groups who were opposed to the plan to allow Rohingya to self-identify as such. ICG (2014), 'Myanmar: The Politics of Rakhine State', Asia Report no. 261, Jakarta/Brussels, http://www.crisisgroup.org/~/media/Files/asia/south-east-asia/burma-myanmar/261-myanmar-the-politics-of-rakhine-state.pdf, p. 13.
26. ICG (2014), p. 13.
27. Who is classified as Rohingya can also depend on political pressures of unity in the light of adversity. See http://www.networkmyanmar.org/images/M-Ali.pdf
28. It is understood that uninhabited land where structures are destroyed returns to the state, meaning that those who lived in these structures beforehand have in effect become homeless.
29. ICG (2012), pp. 5–6.
30. ICG (2014), p. 23.
31. This is different from the Myanmar Human Rights Commission, established in September 2011. 'The 15-member body largely consists of civilians—including ethnic Chin, Karen, Kachin and Shan representatives—such as those from academia (three retired professors), foreign affairs (three retired ambassadors) and civil servants.' http://www.irrawaddy.org/news-analysis/empowering-the-myanmar-human-rights-commission.html The MHRC is seen as largely ineffective, having refused to look into abuses in ethnic conflict zones and not having tackled

any case referred to it to a satisfying degree: http://www.burmapartnership.
org/2014/09/
the-myanmar-national-human-rights-commission-continues-failing-to-deliver/

32. ICG (2012), p. 6.
33. ICG (2013), 'The Dark Side of Transition: Violence Against Muslims in Myanmar', Asia Report no. 251, 1 October 2013, p. 9.
34. I am grateful to Derek Tonkin for pointing out that the Population Control bill (no English translation yet available) reportedly requires a compulsory spacing of births by 36 months in designated communities. It is due to be discussed at the next session of parliament.
35. *7 Day News Journal*, vol. 12, no. 14, 12 June 2013, p. 8.
36. *Daily Eleven*, 30 June 2013, p. 17.
37. *The Voice*, vol. 8, no. 30, 16–22 July 2012, p. 3.
38. *Weekly Eleven*, vol. 8, no. 51, 30 Sept 2013, supplement. See also *Myanmar Times*, 4 Oct 2013, http://www.mmtimes.com/index.php/national-news/8350-speaker-pledges-support-for-rakhine-people.html
39. In early 2015 a controversy over the voting rights of white card holders erupted. The president decided to cancel all white cards and they lost their validity on 31 Match 2015, leaving former white card holders with no ID at all. This affected mostly the 600,000–700,000 Rakhine Muslims who self-identity as Rohingya. They will now not be able to vote in the November 2015 elections either. http://www.mmtimes.com/index.php/national-news/13106-president-backtracks-on-white-cards.html
40. Section 11 of the 1947 constitution specified that citizenship was granted to every person, both of whose parents belonged to any of the indigenous races of Burma and were/would have been citizens of the Union; every person born in any of the territories included within the Union if their grandparent(s) belonged to any of the indigenous races of Burma; and every person born in any of the territories which at the time of birth was included within the British dominions and who had resided in any of the territories included in the Union for a period of not less than eight years in the ten years immediately preceding the date of the commencement of the Constitution or 1 January 1942. More importantly, recognition was given to the intent to reside permanently in the Union, thus signifying the choice to be a citizen of the Union. Tin Maung Maung Than and Moe Thuzar (2012), p. 5.
41. Indigenous races of Burma meant the 'Arakanese, Burmese, Chin, Kachin, Karen, Kayah, Mon or Shan race and racial groups as have settled in any of the territories included within the Union as their permanent home from a period anterior to 1823 AD (1185 BE)'. Tin Maung Maung Than and Moe Thuzar (2012), p. 5.
42. Tin Maung Maung Than and Moe Thuzar (2012), p. 5.
43. Chapter V Principles on the Citizens' Fundamental Rights and Responsibilities, 1974 Constitution.

44. This term is not legally used in the act, but this word is translated from the Myanmar context for easy understanding.

45. This term is not legally used in the act, but this word is translated from the Myanmar context for easy understanding.

46. 1982 Citizenship Law, Naturalized Citizen: Persons who have entered and resided in the State anterior to 4th January, 1948, and their off springs born within the State may, if they have not yet applied under the union Citizenship Act, 1948, apply for naturalized citizenship to the Central Body, furnishing conclusive evidence.

47. The language is as stated in the 1982 Citizenship law. Applicants for naturalized citizenship are required to be of 18 years of age, to be fluent in one of the national languages, be of good character and be of sound mind. Tin Maung Maung Than and Moe Thuzar (2012).

48. White cards seem to have been issued in Rakhine State as the 2010 elections approached so that the people could vote. This has created great controversy as those who were issued with white cards expected to be 'upgraded' later, and the authorities have not done much about the legal limbo that the white card holders are in.

49. 1982 Citizenship Law:

    Any person may apply to the Central Body when it is necessary for a decision as to his citizenship, associate citizenship or naturalized citizenship.

    The Central Body shall (a) permit the applicant the submission of application with supporting evidence; (b) decide in accordance with law; (c) inform its decision to the applicant.

    The Council of Ministers shall form the Central Body as follows: (a) Minister Chairman Ministry of Home Affairs (b) Minister Member Ministry of Defence (c) Minister Member Ministry of Foreign Affairs.

    The Central Body has the authority:

    (a) to decide if a person is a citizen, or an associate citizen or a naturalized citizen;

    (b) to decide upon an application for associate citizenship or naturalized citizenship;

    (c) to terminate citizenship or associate citizenship or naturalized citizenship;

    (d) to revoke citizenship or associate citizenship or naturalized citizenship;

    (e) to decide upon an application regarding failure as to registration or affirmation.

    The Central Body shall give the right of defence to a person against whom action is taken:

    (a) A person dissatisfied with the decision of the Central Body may appeal to the Council of Ministers in accordance with the procedure laid down.(b). The decisions of the council of ministers is final.

50. *Mon Tehh Nay*, vol 1. no. 35, 25 August 2013, p. 3.

51. *The Voice*, vol. 8, no. 43, 29 October—4 November 2012, p. 4.

52. *Narinjara*, 10 September 2012.

53. *The Messenger*, vol. 3, no. 23, 27 October 2012, p. 9.

54. Ibid.

55. *The Flower News*, vol. 8, no. 31, 14–20 August 2012, p. 21.

56. *Narinjara*, 10 September 2012.

57. For a detailed analysis of the history of the Rohingya issue, see D. Tonkin (2014), 'The Mujahid Rebellion in Arakan: a 1952 Analysis by the British Foreign Office'; D. Tonkin (2014), 'The R-word, and its ramifications'; D. Tonkin (2014), 'The Rohingya Identity: Arithmetic of the Absurd'; D. Tonkin (2014), 'The "Rohingya" Identity—Further Thoughts'; D. Tonkin (2014), 'The "Rohingya' Identity— British experience in Arakan 1826–1948'; D. Tonkin (2014), 'Whither Myanmar?' All available at www.networkmyanmar.org on the page entitled Rohingya/Muslim issues.

58. J. Leider (2014), 'Rohingya—the name, the movement, the quest for identity', http://www.burmalibrary.org/docs21/Jacques-P-Leider-2014-01-28-Rohingya-The_Name-The_movement-The_quest_for_identity-en.pdf, p. 4.

59. See D. Tonkin (2014), 'The "Rohingya" Identity—Further Thoughts'; and Leider (2014,) p. 10: 'What we learn from Hamilton is, on the one hand, that there was a Muslim community in Rakhine at the moment of the conquest in 1784 and, on the other hand, that both Muslims and Hindus were among those hundreds or thousands of Rakhine who had been deported and resettled in Upper Myanmar. These Muslims spoke an Indian language of their own in which they called themselves "Rooinga," to state the place where they came from. In the absence of any other evidence, an interpretation of the word as being more than a plain reference to the geographic origin of the Muslims is debatable.'

60. Akyab under the British administration used to include the whole of Northern Rakhine Division, including Sittwe. A separate Maungdaw District was created later, including Maungdaw and Buthidaung. Sittwe District today excludes these two townships.

61. J. Leider (2014) p. 12

62. 'Among a total population of 529,943 in Akyab district, 181,509 were said to be Bengali speakers while 178,647 were categorized among various Muslim denominations.' Leider (2014), p. 14.

63. ICG (2014), p. 3; and ICG (2013), p. 4.

64. Derek Tonkin points out that the term 'Rohingya' really only started to be used in the 1960s.

65. Leider (2012).

66. P.19: 'Hopes put on alleged British promises for independence were vain. Overtures made by Northern Rakhine militants to Ali Jinnah in April 1947 were turned

down in July and the secession option was a dead end as Ali Jinnah and Aung San agreed that the international border at the Naf River was not going to be negotiated.'

67. *Guardian*, '290 Mujahid rebels surrender: Rohinja is one of the Minorities of the Union', 6 July, 12 November, 16 November 1961, http://www.networkmyanmar. org/images/stories/Mujahid-Surrenders-1961.pdf

68. I am grateful to Derek Tonkin for pointing this out. See p. 5 of http://www.networkmyanmar.org/images/stories/PDF18/CB-1979.pdf

69. ICG (2013), p. 5.

70. Tin Maung Maung Than and Moe Thuzar (2012).

71. There are severe restrictions on those holding TRCs. Permission to marry must be obtained from the authorities, and at various times in the past there have been orders limiting couples to two children. There are also severe restrictions for TRC holders on freedom of movement outside the village-tract or between townships, limiting work opportunities and access to government services.

72. 'A resident from Maungdaw also confirmed that the delegation met with prominent religious leaders and local Muslims and sharing the regimes plans for the 2010 elections. "We had a meeting with them after Jumma prayers last Friday in Myoma Mosque. They told us to support the authorities in the coming poll, so as to get full citizen rights like other people in the country and that no one or no party except the SPDC government can make our community developed." [...] According to an intelligence source, Burmese authorities issued similar cards just before the 2008 constitutional referendum to some Indian tribes, known locally as Manipuri or Kathay, who have been settled in a jungle village near Ngaranchaung Village in Maungdaw township since 1993.' Euro-Burma Office Election Monitor, 'Muslims to be issued green registration cards before election', 8 23.11–27.11.2009.

73. The Rohingya have five legislative representatives, all of whom are from the USDP. There are four Rohingya political parties, none of which currently holds any seats: National Democratic Party for Development, Democracy and Human Rights Party, National Development and Peace Party, and Union Nationals Development Party. ICG (2014), p. 6.

74. Ibid., pp. 10–11.

75. Ibid., pp. 19–20.

76. Not all members of the Rohingya ethno-linguistic group accept the term itself as it has come to be linked to a particular political/religious agenda and is identified mainly with communities in the northern part of Rakhine State near the Bangladesh border. ICG (2013), p. 3.

77. Leider (2014), pp. 17–18.

78. 'In particular, by the time of the 2012 violence there was a belief that Sittwe itself was close to having a Muslim majority, fuelling concerns of the political elite in the state capital, and raising the prospect—alarming to many—that the city might return a Muslim representative in a future election.' ICG (2014), pp. 14–15.

79. Who are also believed to have multiple wives.

80. ICG (2014), pp. 14–15.

81. For many Rakhine, the term now simply has very negative connotations, of a radical political agenda by a religiously conservative group with links to mujahidin insurgents. ICG (2014), p. 17.

82. Tin Maung Maung Than and Moe Thuzar (2012), p. 196.

83. Taylor, (2013), p. 1.

84. She also refuses to condemn the violence perpetrated in Kachin State since the resumption of the conflict between the KIA and the Tatmadaw in 2011. This is covered in Chapter 5.

85. ICG (2012), pp. 1–2.

86. A mixed methods questionnaire was administered to respondents from seven states (Mon, Karen, Kaya, Shan, Kachin, Chin and Rakhine) and four regions (Yangon, Bago, Mandalay, Sagain) in urban, rural and semi-urban settings. A total of 2,007 (out of around 2,050) respondents of Bamar, Kachin, Kaya, Karen, Chin, Shan, Mon and Rakhine ethnic groups returned the questionnaire. There were also small samples of Pa-O, Phalaung, Lisu, In Thar, Naga, Kaman, Pathi, and Maramagyi ethnic representatives.

87. Rakhine, Buddhist RAK-1649.

88. Mon, Buddhist MON-0651.

89. Bamar, religion not given, YGN 0422.

90. Mon, Buddhist, Mon 0690.

91. 'Kalar' is used as a derogatory term for Indian and Muslims, meaning 'black'. White people are referred to as 'kalar phyu'.

92. Rakhine, Buddhist, RAK 1753.

93. Rakhine, Buddhist, RAK 1637.

94. Bamar, Buddhist, KYN-0800.

95. For example Burma, Buddhist, YGN 0324.

96. Rakhine, Buddhist, RAK 1660.

97. Italics added, Bamar, Buddhist, YGN 0296.

98. Bamar, Buddhist, YGN 0442.

99. Kayin, Buddhist, KYN 0842.

100. Mon Buddhist, MON 0637.

101. Bamar, Buddhist, Mon 0703.

102. Bamar, Buddhist, YGN 0299.

103. PaO, Buddhist, Shan 1486.

104. Other, Muslim RAK-1811.

105. Bamar, Muslim, YGN-1939.

106. Bamar, Muslim, MDY-1874.

107. It is also important to note how there are increasing anti-Chinese feelings being propagated by the media and social media. This form of racism, which is not new,

falls under the religious and ethnic differences and the discrimination between different citizenship status, rather than under the heading of ethnic conflict. Much of the anti-Chinese tension was fuelled by the resumption of conflict between the MNDAA (Kokang) and the Tatmadaw (as covered in Chapter 4).

108. The press reports the shopkeeper breaking the comb to check the gold content and then offering too low a price, as well as refusing to repair the comb.

109. 'The response of the security forces was clearly inadequate. Witnesses described police officers standing by while people were killed in front of them, and video footage shot by police has depicted this. The only time when police reportedly fired their weapons was when a rock thrown by the crowd struck an officer. When the mob surrounded a large group of Muslims who had sought refuge in a compound, the police did escort some of them to safety, but were apparently unable to prevent several being killed by the mob while under escort.' ICG (2013), pp. 12–13.

110. 'Burma riots: Muslim gold shop workers jailed', http://www.bbc.com/news/world-asia-22124346?print=true

111. BBC (2013), 'Six Muslims charged over monk's death in Burma's Meiktila', http://www.bbc.com/news/world-asia-22433871?print=true. However, Myanmar has not executed anyone since 1988.

112. 'Footage filmed by the police and given to the BBC showed young Muslim men chased from their burning homes and hacked with machetes. In almost an hour of material, clearly identifiable men and monks were seen destroying Muslim shops and mosques.' BBC (2013).

113. 29 May 2013, http://news.yahoo.com/2nd-day-anti-muslim-violence-strikes-ne-myanmar-130258237.html

114. ICG (2013), p. 14.

115. http://news.yahoo.com/2nd-day-anti-muslim-violence-strikes-ne-myanmar-130258237.html

116. ICG (2013), p. 15.

117. http://www.irinnews.org/report/100345/grassroots-moves-to-quell-myanmar-s-communal-violence

118. http://thediplomat.com/2014/07/the-meaning-of-the-mandalay-riots-in-myanmar/

119. 969 represents the nine attributes of Buddha, the six attributes of his teachings, and the nine attributes of the Sangha.

120. http://www.foreignpolicy.com/articles/2013/04/22/the_monks_who_hate_muslims#sthash.6lwjeJne.dpbs

121. 'The Face of Buddhist Terror', Time Magazine, 20 June 2013.

122. This is nothing new: a British colonial inquiry into anti-Indian riots in Yangon in 1938 noted that 'one of the major sources of anxiety in the minds of a great number of Burmese was the question of the marriage of their womenfolk with

foreigners in general and with Indians in particular'. ICG (2013), pp. 17–18. I
am grateful to Derek Tonkin for pointing out that Professor Pearn's paper in
1948 reveals that the anti-Muslim riots of 1938 also affected Maung Daw and
Buthidaung; see last sentence of paragraph 7 at: http://www.networkmyanmar.
org/images/stories/PDF18/Pearn-1952-rev.pdf

123. The four bills were sent to the government in 2013, and in February President
U Thein Sein submitted them to parliament. However, they were sent back to
the government to be rewritten. In March, President U Thein Sein set up a
12-member commission headed by Deputy Attorney General U Tun Tun Oo to
draft two of the laws, while two others were sent directly to government ministries. The laws were returned to parliament in November 2014 and signed into
law in August. For more details see http://www.loc.gov/lawweb/servlet/lloc_
news?disp3_l205404604_text. Adapted excerpts below: *Monogamy law*

The monogamy legislation makes it a criminal offence to have more than one
spouse or to live with an unmarried partner who is not a spouse. An estimated
five per cent of Burma's population is Muslim, and some members of this group
reportedly practise polygamy, but the government has denied that the new law
targeted Muslims. Signed into law 31 August 2015.

Religious Conversion Law and Interfaith Marriage Law

The Religious Conversion Law requires that a Myanmar citizen who wishes to
change his/her religion must obtain approval from a newly established
Registration Board for religious conversion, set up in townships. The person must
also undergo an interview and engage in religious study for a period not to exceed
90 days from the date of application, but extendable to 180 days at the applicant's
request. If after that period the applicant still wishes to convert, the Registration
Board will issue a certificate of religious conversion. The law prescribes punish-
ments for forced conversion or for applying to convert with the intention of
harming a religion. Chapter 6 of the Religious Conversion Law includes penal-
ties for violating its various provisions.

The Myanmar Buddhist Women's Special Marriage Law regulates the marriages
of Buddhist women to non-Buddhist men. If the woman is under 20 years of age,
she must have parental consent. The law allows local registrars to publicly post
marriage applications for 14 days, to determine whether there are any objections
to the proposed unions. A couple may get married only if there are no objections;
if there are objections, the issue can be taken to court. Both signed into law
26 August 2015.

Population Control Law

This law imposes on women in certain regions the requirement to space the birth
of their children 36 months apart. The draft Population Control Law as adopted
by the Union Parliament on 27 April 2015 provides that governments of divi-

sions and states have the authority "to request a presidential order limiting reproductive rates if it is determined that population growth, accelerating birth rates, or rising infant or maternal mortality rates are negatively impacting regional development", or that there exists an "imbalance between population and resources, low socio-economic indicators and regional food insufficiency because of internal migration". Under the above-mentioned circumstances, the regional government is to work with "experts" (not defined in the law) to make the determination, and "[i]f the president approves the request, a 'special region' is designated, triggering the law's provisions, including the birth spacing restriction and the formation of a 'delivery services body' to administer health care in coordination with the Ministry of Health." The designation of an area as a special region can be repealed if found to be no longer needed.' Signed into law May 2015.

124. Ma Ba Tha members say that an existing marriage law introduced in 1954 is not strong and the new draft law would protect women from being forced to convert to their husband's religion. http://www.burmanet.org/news/2014/12/01/the-myanmar-times-controversial-religion-bills-submitted-to-parliament-ei-ei-toe-lwin/

125. ICG (2013), pp. 17–18.

126. http://asia.nikkei.com/Politics-Economy/Policy-Politics/Robert-Taylor-What-would-Ne-Win-have-thought-of-today-s-Myanmar

127. The last British census in Burma was undertaken in 1931. In 2005 at an interview with UNICEF I was informed that child immunisations were conducted according to the numbers supplied by the government and that consequently UNICEF often had to immunise more (or less) than 100% of the children as the numbers on the ground differed to the governmental estimates. However, predating the 2014 census, Myanmar had undertaken an agricultural census in 2010: http://www.fao.org/fileadmin/templates/ess/documents/meetings_and_workshops/APCAS23/documents_OCT10/APCAS-10-24_-Myanmar.pdf; a housing census (also covering fertility issues) in 2007: http://countryoffice.unfpa.org/myanmar/?publications=7694; and a living conditions survey in 2006: http://www.undp.org/content/dam/myanmar/docs/Publications/PovRedu/MMR_FA1_IA1_TechnicalReportAppendix_Eng.pdf. These are not covered here, as they pre-date the reform period. I am grateful to one of the anonymous reviewers of this book of having pointed these out to me.

128. Burma/Myanmar (2014), 'TNI Ethnicity without Meaning, Data without Context—The 2014 Census, Identity and Citizenship', Burma Policy Briefing no. 13, February 2014, p. 2.

129. Ibid., p. 14.

130. There were some sanctions, if that was not the case.

131. 'lu-myo' is a concept of differentiation rooted in the belief of objective, verifiable, fixed, and blood-borne lineage and is far closer to the English concept of 'race'

than 'ethnicity'. Ibid., p. 3. 'Departing from earlier citizenship requirements, the 1982 law defines those who "belong" in the country as members of groups of "lu-myo" ("kinds of people" or "race")—that have been designated as "*taingyinthar*" (literally, "sons/offspring of the geographical division"). [...] Denoting what have become regarded as the eight major races in the country, Section 3 of the 1982 law explained: "Nationals such as the Kachin, Kayah, Karen, Chin, Burman, Mon, Rakhine or Shan and ethnic (*taingyinthar*) groups as have settled in any of the territories included within the State as their permanent home from a period anterior to 1185 B.E. (1823 A.D.) are Burma citizens." In contrast, any races determined by the State Council not to have been present within the modern boundaries are considered non-*taingyinthar* (i.e., non-native) and eligible for lesser "associate" or "naturalized" citizenship, but not full citizenship.' Ibid., p. 5.

132. The current list is almost identical to one first deployed during the Socialist era (1962–88) and resurrected during the early years of the previous military government (1988–2011). These, in turn, were derived from a flawed British census in 1931. Ibid., p. 2.

133. See for example http://www.foreignpolicy.com/articles/2013/12/19/burmas_senseless_census#sthash.QatXk0DQ.dpbs

134. Burma/Myanmar (2014), p. 17.

135. 'For example, the Kachin nationalist movement has always considered that there are six or seven ethnic Kachin sub-groups, but the census demarcates eleven (codes 102–112). But given that enumerators will record only one "*lu-myo*" code for each member of a household, this means that ethnic identities will appear diffused; for example, someone of the majority Kachin sub-group will have to choose between Jinghpaw (code 104) and Kachin (code 101).' Ibid., p. 16.

136. This pertains to the elections: 'Since Burma's most recent constitution guarantees special political representation if a *lu-myo* achieves 0.1 percent of the population, ethnicity will be a powerful means for groups to fight for their interests—but only for the ones that qualify. The census, then, will help determine which groups matter in Burma, and which don't.' http://www.foreignpolicy.com/articles/2013/12/19/burmas_senseless_census#sthash.QatXk0DQ.dpbs The census data 'could have adverse impact on political representation'. Burma/Myanmar (2014), p. 2.

137. http://countryoffice.unfpa.org/myanmar/2015/05/29/12209/census_results_highlight_myanmar_rsquo_s_development_needs/ See also http://www.aljazeera.com/news/2015/05/myanmar-criticised-excluding-rohingyas-census-150529045829329.html

138. http://unstats.un.org/unsd/demographic/sources/census/2010_phc/Myanmar/MMR-2014-08-28-provres.pdf

139. Burma/Myanmar (2014), p. 15. The last census in 1983 reported the national population to be 89.4 per cent Buddhist, 4.9 per cent Christian and 4.4 per cent Islamic.

140. Full data available at http://themimu.info/census-data
141. http://countryoffice.unfpa.org/myanmar/2015/05/29/12209/census_results_highlight_myanmar_rsquo_s_development_needs/
142. http://www.lowyinterpreter.org/post/2015/06/12/Myanmar-census-reveals-huge-urban-rural-divide.aspx

CONCLUSION: THE CHALLENGES OF DEMOCRATISATION IN LIGHT OF THE 2015 ELECTIONS

1. *The Voice Weekly*, 4 August 2014.
2. Thanks to the MERI team that checked the discourse in the Myanmar press.
3. 31.5.2013. http://ndfmyanmar.org/?p=1142
4. http://ndfmyanmar.org/?p=1142 and http://burma.irrawaddy.org/news/2014/06/16/60474.html, 16 June 2014
5. http://myitmakhamediagroup.com/post 3 August 8, 2014
6. http://burma.irrawaddy.org/news/2014/07/29/62518.html
7. http://burma.irrawaddy.org/news/2014/07/26/62410.html
8. http://burma.irrawaddy.org/news/2014/07/31/62596.html
9. http://burma.irrawaddy.org/news/2014/07/31/62596.html
10. http://myanmar.mmtimes.com/index.php/national-news/11094–2014–07–10–09–02–30.html
11. http://www.mmtimes.com/index.php/opinion/11302-u-shwe-mann-directs-pr-drama.html
12. http://7daydaily.com/story/17379#.U99J8KDmrvw
13. https://www.dvb.no/elections/nld-rejects-hybrid-voting-system/45450
14. Clearly the NLD prefers this system, because it would allow it to dominate parliament in 2015.
15. https://www.dvb.no/elections/lower-house-rejects-pr-system-burma-myanmar/45888
16. This includes the controversial way that the NLD has selected its candidates, sometimes against the wishes of the actual constituency where they are to stand.
17. The NBF started in 2011 as the Nationalities Brotherhood Forum.
18. The research was undertaken by speaking to all existing ethnic political parties, those who won seats and those who did not. Interviews were conducted with the party leaders or another senior member of the party. Focus group discussions were held with party members and the elected MPs of the local legislative assemblies. In NPT, focus group discussion were held with the elected MPs from the different parties together. Interviews and focus groups were held in all seven ethnic states, Yangon and NPT. M. Lall et al. (2015), *Myanmar's Ethnic Parties and the 2015 Elections*, Yangon: EU and IMG.
19. TNI (2015), 'Statement of the 3rd Myanmar Opium Farmer Forum', 12 September, https://www.tni.org/en/article/statement-of-3rd-myanmar-opium-farmer-forum

20. There has been no space in this book to detail the changes for Myanmar at a foreign policy level. This would need to be covered in a separate volume. A good review is NBR's *Myanmar's Regional Role* (2014). In this report Morten Pedersen writes (p. 60): 'The government has thus moved aggressively to normalize Myanmar's international relations, rebalance bilateral relations with the major powers, and further integrate the country into the region. At the same time, it has taken steps to ensure that new foreign aid, trade, and investment genuinely benefit the country and its people rather than just a narrow economic elite.' The ASEAN chairmanship and hosting the SEA games were a major part of Myanmar normalising its relationship with the region and the outside world. Myanmar's foreign policy priorities have also included revitalising its relationship with Japan. Some of this is covered in the chapter on economic reforms.

EPILOGUE: THE 8 NOVEMBER ELECTIONS

1. http://www.mmtimes.com/index.php/national-news/15885-no-election-in-wa-mong-la-regions.html
2. At the time of writing the NLD had won 255 seats in the Lower House, 135 seats in the Upper House and 492 seats across Region and State Parliaments. The USDP had won 29, 12 and 73 respectively. The largest ethnic parties are the SNLD with 12, 3 and 25 seats and the ANP with 12, 10 and 23 seats respectively. 11 seats in remote areas still need to be confirmed.
3. He has been accused of spending large sums of money to develop the constituency where he was running. http://www.irrawaddy.org/election/news/soe-thane-backs-spending-splash-in-karenni-state

BIBLIOGRAPHY BY CHAPTER

References for Introduction

Callahan, M. (2010), 'The Endurance of Military Rule in Burma: not why but why not?'. in Levenstein, S. (ed.) *Finding Dollars, Sense and Legitimacy in Burma*, Washington, DC: Woodrow Wilson International Centre for Scholars.

—— (2012), 'No Longer Necessarily "National Security"' (Myanmar in Reform 2012, HK University symposium, symposium proceedings, selected summaries), pp. 25–7.

Duffield, M. (2008), 'On the Edge of "No Man's Land": Chronic Emergency in Myanmar', working paper, Centre of Governance and International affairs, University of Bristol.

Kramer, Tom (2011), *Civil Society Gaining Ground—Opportunities for Change and Development in Burma*, Amsterdam: TNI/BCN.

Kyaw Yin Hlaing (2007), 'Associational Life in Myanmar', in Ganesan, N. and Kyaw Yin Hlaing (eds) (2007), *Myanmar—State, Sociey and Ethnicity*, Hiroshima: HPI and Singapore: ISEAS.

Mark SiuSue (2012), 'How Civil Society Can Engage with Policy Making in Myanmar's Transitional Context', *Journal of International Affairs*, Columbia SIPA, http://jia.sipa.columbia.edu/tag/civil-society/.

Pedersen, M. (2005) in Kyaw Yin Hlaing, Taylor, R. Tin Maung Maung Than, *Myanmar: Beyond Politics to Societal Imperatives*, Singapore: ISEAS.

Steinberg, D. I. (2001), *Burma—the State of Myanmar*, Washington, DC: Georgetown University Press.

Tonkin, D. (2007), 'The 1990 Elections in Myanmar: Broken Promises or a Failure of Communication?' *Journal of Southeast Asia*, vol. 29, no. 1, pp. 33–54.

—— (2009) 'Burmese Perspectives: Sanctions against Myanmar, Profit and Loss Account', http://www.networkmyanmar.org/images/sanctions.pdf.

BIBLIOGRAPHY BY CHAPTER

References for Chapter 1

Alan Saw U in Ganesan, N. and Kyaw Yin Hlaing (eds) (2007), *Myanmar—State, Society and Ethnicity*, Singapore: ISEAS and Hiroshima: Hiroshima Peace Institute.

Bowman, V. (2007), 'The Political Situation in Myanmar', in Skidmore M. and Wilson, T., *Myanmar, the State, Community and the Environment*, Canberra: ANU Press.

Hewison, K. and Prager Nyein, S. (2010), 'Civil Society and Political Opposition in Burma', in Li Chenyang and Hofmeister Wolhelm (eds), *Myanmar—Prospects for Change*, KAS and Yunnan University, Select Publishing (Kunming).

Horsey, R. (2008), 'The dramatic events of 2007 in Myanmar: domestic and international implications', in Skidmore M. and Wilson, T., *Dictatorship, Disorder and Decline in Myanmar*, Canberra: ANU Press.

Kyaw Yin Hlaing (2005), 'Myanmar in 2004—Why Military Rule Continues', *South East Asian Affairs in 2005*, Singapore: ISEAS.

——(2005), 'Myanmar in 2004: Another Year of Uncertainty', *Asian Survey*, 45 (1), pp. 174–9.

—— (2010), 'Problems with the Process of Reconciliation', in Riffle, L. (ed.), *Myanmar/Burma Inside challenges, outside interests*, Washington, DC: KAF/Brookings Institution Press.

MacLean, K. (2010), 'The Rise of Private Indirect Government in Burma', in Levenstein, S. (ed.), *Finding Dollars, Sense and Legitimacy in Burma*, Washington, DC: Woodrow Wilson International Centre for Scholars.

Pedersen, M. (2007), 'Myanmar—the future takes form—but little change in sight', in Singh, D. and Salazar, L., *Southeast Asian Affairs 2007*, Singapore: ISEAS.

Seng Raw (2001), 'Views from Myanmar: An Ethnic Minority Perspective', in Taylor, R. (ed.), Burma: Political Economy under Military Rule, London: Hurst & Co.

Smith, M. (2005), in Kyaw Yin Hlaing et al. (eds), *Myanmar: Beyond Politics to Societal Imperatives*, Singapore: ISEAS, p. 62.

—— (2007), *State of Strife: The Dynamics of Ethnic Conflict in Burma*, Policy Studies 36, Washington, DC: East–West Center, p. 2.

South. A. (2007a), 'Karen Nationalist Communities: The "Problem" of Diversity', *Contemporary Southeast Asia*, vol. 29, no. 1, pp. 55–76.

—— (2007b), 'Burma: the Changing Nature of Displacement Crises', RSC Working Paper no. 39, Refugee Studies Centre, University of Oxford.

—— (2007c), Burma, COHRE Country Report, Geneva.

—— (2008, 2nd edn 2010), *Ethnic Politics in Burma: States of Conflict* (London: Routledge), p. 128.

Steinberg, D. I. (2001), *Burma—the State of Myanmar*, Washington, DC: Georgetown University Press.

Taylor, R. (2005), 'Pathways to the Present', in Kyaw Yin Hlaing, Taylor, R. and Tin Maung Maung Than, *Myanmar: Beyond Politics to Societal Imperatives*, Singapore: ISEAS.

———. (2009), *The State in Myanmar*, London: Hurst & Co.

——— (n.d.), Responding to Nargis: Political Storm or Humanitarian Rage? unpublished paper.

Tin Maung Maung Than (2009), 'Myanmar in 2008—Weathering the storm', in Singh, D., *Southeast Asian Affairs 2009*, Singapore: ISEAS.

Tonkin, D. (2007), 'The 1990 Elections in Myanmar: Broken Promises or a Failure of Communication?' *Journal of Southeast Asia*, vol. 29, no. 1, pp. 33–54.

Tripartite group, 'Monthly Recovery Update', May 2010.

Win Min (2008), 'Internal Dynamics of the Burmese Military: Before, During and After the 2007 Demonstrations', in Skidmore M. and Wilson, T., *Dictatorship, Disorder and Decline in Myanmar*, Canberra: ANU Press.

References for Chapter 2

Burma News International (BNI) (2010), Election report 2010, pre-election observations, Myanmar Burma.

BNI (2010), 'Hobson's choice: Burma's 2010 elections', OSI.

Callahan, M. (2010), 'The Endurance of Military Rule in Burma: Not Why but Why Not?' in Levenstein, S. L. (ed.), *Finding Dollars, Sense and Legitimacy in Burma*, Washington, DC: Woodrow Wilson International Centre for Scholars.

CPCS (2010), 'Listening to Voices from Inside—People's perspectives on Myanmar's 2010 elections', http://www.centrepeaceconflictstudies.org/wp-content/uploads/Ethnic_People_Speak.pdf.

Horsey, R. (2010a), 'Preliminary Analysis of Myanmar's 2010 Electoral Laws', prepared for the Conflict Prevention and Peace Forum, 31 March, SSRC.

——— (2010b), 'Overview of Registered Political Parties in Myanmar', Conflict Prevention and Peace Forum, 15 June 2010, SSRC.

——— (2012), 'Myanmar's political landscape following the 2010 elections: starting with a class nine-tenth empty?' in Cheesman, N., Skidmore, M. and Wilson, T. (eds), *Myamar's Transition—Openings, Obstacles and Opportunities*, Myanmar Update Series, Singapore: ISEAS.

ICG (2010), 'The Myanmar Elections, Asia Briefing', International Crisis Group report no. 105, Jakarta/Brussels,. http://www.crisisgroup.org/~/media/Files/asia/south-east-asia/burma-myanmar/B105%20The%20Myanmar%20Elections.ashx.

——— (2011), 'Myanmar's Post-Election Landscape', International Crisis Group report no. 118, Jakarta/Brussels,. http://www.crisisgroup.org/~/media/Files/asia/south-east-asia/burma-myanmar/B118%20Myanmars%20Post-Election%20Landscape.pdf.

Kyaw Yin Hlaing (2007), *The Politics of State–Society Relations in Myanmar*, South East Asia Research, London: IP Publishing.

Lall, M. and Win, H. (2013), 'Myanmar: The 2010 Elections and Political Participation', *Journal of Burma Studies*, vol. 17, no. 1, pp. 181–220.

Myint Maung, 'NLD to plunge itself headlong into social work', *Mizzima News*, 2 April 2010.

Pe Myint (2012), 'The Emergence of Myanmar Weekly News Journals and Their Development in Recent Years', in Cheesman, N., Skidmore, M. and Wilson, T. (eds), *Myanmar's Transition—Openings, Obstacles and Opportunities*, Myanmar Update Series, Singapore: ISEAS.

Quintana, T. O. (2011), 'Progress report of the Special Rapporteur on the situation of human rights in Myanmar', Human Rights Council, 16th session, Agenda item 4, Human rights situations that require the Council's attention, 7 March 2011 General Assembly A/HRC/16/59.

Raynaud, M. (2010), 'Myanmar's political landscape beyond 2010 June 2010', unpublished paper.

South, A. (2010), 'Making the Best of a Bad Election', *The Irrawaddy*, July 2010, vol. 18, no. 7.

Steinberg, D. I. (2011), 'Myanmar in 2010—the election year and beyond', *Southeast Asian Affairs*, Singapore: ISEAS, pp. 173–89.

Thant Myint U (2012), 'White Elephants and Black Swans: Thoughts on Myanmar's Recent History and Possible Futures', in Cheesman, N., Skidmore, M. and Wilson, T. (eds), *Myamar's Transition—Openings, Obstacles and Opportunities*, Myanmar Update Series, Singapore: ISEAS.

TNI (2010a), 'Burma's 2010 Elections: Challenges and Opportunities', Burma Policy Briefing, no. 2, June 2010.

—— (2010b), 'Un-level Playing Field: Burma's Election Landscape', Burma Policy Briefing, no. 3, October 2010.

Tonkin, D., Burmese perspectives, BP170310.

—— (2007), 'The 1990 Elections in Myanmar: broken promises or a failure of communication?' *Contemporary Southeast Asia*, vol. 29, no. 1, pp. 33–54.

Hla Hla Win and Yan Ming Aung Y. M. (2010), 'Educational Space in Myanmar in Light of 2010 Election', Marseilles: International Burma Studies Conference Press.

Zöllner, H. B. (2012), 'The Beast and the Beauty: History of the conflict between the Military and Aung San Suu Kyi in Myanmar, 1988–2011, set in a Global Context', Berlin: Regiospectra.

Other newspaper articles.

The Irrawaddy, 15 January 2010, 'Suu Kyi Meets Junta Liaison Officer', http://www.irrawaddy.org/article.php?art_id=17591.

—— 6 September 2010, 'Candidate List Paints Picture of Election Results'.

—— 20 November 2010, 'Main ethnic parties plan to sit in new parliament', http://www.irrawaddy.org/article.php?art_id=20134.

Mizzima News, 14 January 2010, 'NLD restructures top decision-making body', http://www.mizzima.com/news/inside-burma/3379-nld-restructures-top-decision-making-body.html.

BIBLIOGRAPHY BY CHAPTER

References for Chapter 3

Alternative ASEAN Network on Burma: campaigns, advocacy and capacity-building for human rights and democracy, Issue 64, April 2012.

Burma Bulletin (2012), a month-in-review of events in Burma.

Euro Burma Office (2012), Political Monitor no. 8 (17-23.32012), EBO Brussels.

ICG (2011), 'Myanmar: Major Reform Underway', ICG Asia Briefing no. 127, Jakarta/Brussels, http://www.crisisgroup.org/~/media/Files/asia/south-east-asia/burma-myanmar/B127%20Myanmar%20-%20Major%20Reform%20Underway.pdf.

ILO (2012), 'Decent work in Myanmar', ILO Programme Framework, November 2012—April 2014, Geneva: ILO.

Martin, M. (2012), 'Burma's April Parliamentary By-Elections', Congressional Research Service Report for Congress', 7-5700, 28 March 2012.

Moe Thuzar (2012), 'Myanmar: No turning back', *Southeast Asian Affairs*, Singapore: ISEAS, pp. 203–19.

Prasse-Freeman, E. (2014), 'Daw Aung San Suu Kyi and her discontents', *Kyoto Review of SE Asia*,. http://kyotoreview.org/issue-14/daw-aung-san-suu-kyi-and-her-discontents/.

Taylor, R. H. (2013a), 'Myanmar in 2012: Mhyaw ta lin lin or Great Expectations', *Southeast Asian Affairs*, Singapore: ISEAS, pp. 191–203.

—— (2013b), Myanmar's 'Pivot' toward the Shibboleth of 'Democracy', *Asian Affairs*, 44:3, pp. 392–400.

Tin Maung Maung Than (2013), 'Myanmar's 2012 By-elections, the return of the NLD', *Southeast Asian Affairs*, Singapore: ISEAS, pp. 204–19.

Turnell, S. (2012), 'Myanmar in 2011: Confounding Expectations', *Asian Survey*, vol. 52, no. 1, pp. 157–64.

Zöllner, H. B. (2011), 'After an Election and a Symbolic Re-election in Myanmar—What Next?' *Internationales Asienforum* 42, 1–2; pp. 47–72.

References for the Annex to Chapter 3

BBC (2007, November 7), BBC News. Retrieved 13 October 2014 from BBC News: www.bbc.co.uk/news/world-asia-pacific-7082422.

—— (2008, March 8), BBC News. Retrieved 10 October 2014 from BBC News: www.bbc.co.uk/news/world-asia-pacific-7284850.

—— (2011, July 25), BBC News. Retrieved 17 October 2014 from BBC News: www.bbc.co.uk/news/world-asia-pacific-14271464.

Burma Campaign UK (2010). Myanmar Briefing (updated June 2011, vol. no. 6), London: Burma Campaign UK.

CNS (n.d.), CNS News. Retrieved from CNS News: www.cnsnews.com/news/article/democratic-senator-call-drop-burma.

Jagan, L. (2008, August 21), Global Policy Forum. Retrieved 11 October 2014 from Global Policy Forum: www.globalpolicy.org.

Jha, P. G. (n.d.). JNU. Retrieved 23 October 2014 from JNU: www.jnu.ac.in.

Network Myanmar (n.d.). Retrieved 15 October 2014 from Network Myanmar: www.networkmyanmar.org/index.php/external-relation/.

Webb, J. (2012, May 4), US Senate. Retrieved 14 October 2014 from US Senate: http://webb.senate.gov/newsroom/pressreleases/2012-05-04.cfm.

—— (2012), Six Year Legislative Report. Washinton, DC: United States Senate.

Wikipedia (n.d.). Retrieved 15 October 2014 from Wikipedia: en.wikipedia.org/wiki/Aung_San_Suu_Kyi.

Xinhua (2011, July 25), Xinhua News. Retrieved 24 October 2014 from Xinhua News: news.xinhuanet.com/english2010/world/2011-07/25/c-131007960.html.

References for Chapter 4

Aung Naing Oo (2014a), 'The nationwide ceasefire agreement at a glance, 30 July 2014', http://www.mmtimes.com/index.php/national-news/11219-the-nation-wide-ceasefire-agreement-at-a-glance.html.

—— (2014b), 'In praise of peace dividends,13 October 2014',. http://www.mmtimes.com/index.php/opinion/11935-in-praise-of-peace-dividends.html.

Burma Centre for Ethnic Studies (BCES) and Burma Centre for Peace and Reconciliation (BCPR): note that all papers are available on http://www.burmalibrary.org/show.php?cat=2864.

BCES—AP 1 (2012), 'The Dynamics of Sixty Years of Ethnic Armed Conflict in Burma', Burma Centre for Ethnic Studies, Yangon.

BCES—AP 4 (2012), 'Realising change in Karen Politics', Burma Centre for Ethnic Studies, Yangon.

BCES—BP 16 Keenan, P. (2013), 'The UNFC and the peace process', Burma Centre for Ethnic Studies, Yangon.

BCES—BP 19 Keenan, P. (2013), 'The Laiza agreement', Burma Centre for Ethnic Studies, Yangon.

BCPR—BP 1 Keenan, P. (2012), 'Burma's ethnic ceasefire agreements', Yangon.

BCPR—BP 2 Keenan, P. (2012), 'The conflict in Kachin State', Yangon.

BCPR—BP 6 'Establishing a common framework: The role of the United Nationalities Federal Council in the peace process and the need for an all-inclusive ethnic consultation', Yangon.

CIA Factbook Burma, https://www.cia.gov/library/publications/the-world-factbook/geos/bm.html.

Farelly, N. (2012), 'Ceasing Ceasefire? Kachin Politics beyond the Stalemates', in Cheesman, N., Skidmore, M. and Wilson, T. (eds), *Myanmar's Transition—Openings, Obstacles and Opportunities*, Myanmar Update Series, Singapore: ISEAS.

Ganesan, N. and Kyaw Yin Hlaing (eds) (2007), *Myanmar—State, Society and Ethnicity*, Singapore: ISEAS, and Hiroshima: Hiroshima Peace Institute.

Gravers, M. (1999), *Nationalism as Political Paranoia in Burma: An Essay on the Historical Practice of Power*, Richmond, Surrey: Curzon.

Houtman, G. (1999), *Mental Culture in Burmese Crisis Politics: Aung San Suu Kyi and the National League for Democracy*, Tokyo: Tokyo University of Foreign Studies.

Human Rights Watch (2012), 'Untold Miseries: Wartime Abuses and Forced Displacement in Burma's Kachin State', New York.

International Crisis Group (2011), 'Myanmar: A New Peace Initiative', Asia Report N214.

Kyaw Yin Hlaing et al. (eds.) (2005), 'Myanmar: Beyond Politics to Societal Imperatives', Singapore: ISEAS.

Lall, M. (2009), 'Ethnic conflict in light of the 2010 elections in Burma/Myanmar', Chatham House briefing paper, London: Chatham House.

Min Zaw Oo (2014), 'Understanding Myanmar Peace Process', Swisspeace, http://www.swisspeace.ch/fileadmin/user_upload/Media/Publications/Catalyzing_Reflections_2_2014_online.pdf.

Myanmar Peace Support Initiative (MPSI) (2014), 'Lessons learned from MPSI's work supporting the peace process in Myanmar', Yangon.

Petrie, C. and South, A. (2013), 'Mapping of Myanmar Peacebuilding', Brussels: Civil Society Dialogue Network (CSDN).

Smith, M. (1999), *Burma: Insurgency and the Politics of Ethnicity*, London: Zed Books.

———. (2007), 'State of Strife: The Dynamics of Ethnic Conflict in Burma', Policy Studies 36, Washington, DC: East–West Center.

South, A. (2004), 'Political Transition in Myanmar: A New Model for Democratization', *Contemporary Southeast Asia*, vol. 26, no. 2, pp. 233–55.

——— (2007b) 'Burma: the Changing Nature of Displacement Crises', RSC Working Paper no. 39, Refugee Studies Centre, University of Oxford.

——— (2008), *Ethnic Politics in Burma: States of Conflict*, London: Routledge.

——— (2011), 'Burma's Longest War: anatomy of the Karen conflict', Netherlands: Transnational Institute/Burma Centre.

——— (2015), 'Governance and political legitimacy in the peace process', in Steinberg, D. I., *Myanmar, the dynamics of evolving polity*, Boulder, CO: Lynne Rienner Publishers.

Steinberg, D. I. (2001), *Burma—the State of Myanmar*, Washington, DC: Georgetown University Press.

Taylor, R. H. (2005), 'Do States Make Nations? The Politics of Identity in Myanmar Revisited', *Southeast Asia Research*, vol.13, no. 3, pp. 261–86.

Thant Myint-U (2001), *Making of Modern Burma*, Cambridge: Cambridge University Press.

Transnational Institute (2012), 'Burma at the Crossroads: Maintaining the Momentum for Reform', Burma Policy Briefing no.9, Amsterdam: Burma Centrum Nederland.

Walton, M. (2008), 'Ethnicity, Conflict and History in Burma: the Myths of Panglong', *Asian Survey* 48:6, pp. 889–910.

References for Chapter 5

ADB (2012), 'Opportunities and Challenges', Philippines: Mandaluyong City.

BTI (2012), 'Myanmar Country Report', Gütersloh: Bertelsmann Stiftung, http://www.bti-project.org.

Burma Bulletin (2012), 'Alternative ASEAN Network on Burma: campaigns, advocacy and capacity-building for human rights and democracy', Issue 64.

Conflict Risk Network (2012), 'Not open for business: Despite elections, investor risk remains high in Burma', April 2012.

Ericson and Deloitte (2013), 'The Potential Economic Impact of Mobile Communications in Myanmar 2012–2013'.

Freeman, N. (2014) 'Navigating the Economic Reform Process', *Southeast Asian Affairs*.

GoM (2012), Framework for economic and social reforms, Policy Priorities for 2012–15, towards the Long-Term Goals of the National Comprehensive Development Plan, NPT.

ICG (2011), 'Myanmar: Major Reform Underway', Asia Briefing no. 127, Jakarta/Brussels,. http://www.crisisgroup.org/~/media/Files/asia/south-east-asia/burma-myanmar/B127%20Myanmar%20-%20Major%20Reform%20Underway.pdf.

IMF (2012), 'Exchange rate unification', IMF Country Report no. 12/104, Myanmar—2011, Article IV.

——— (2013), 'Consultation and First Review under the Staff-Monitored Programme', IMF Country Report no. 13/250, Myanmar—2013, Article IV, http://www.imf.org/external/pubs/ft/scr/2013/cr13250.pdf [25/11/2013].

Jones, L. (2013), 'The Political Economy of Myanmar's Transition', PREPT (no page numbers), http://www.academdia.edu/48414475/The_Political_Economy_of_Myanmar_s_Transition.

McKinsey Global Institute (2013), 'Myanmar's moment: Unique opportunities, major challenges', McKinsey & Company.

Nixon, H., Joelene, C., Kyi Pyar Chit Saw, Thet Aung Lynn and Arnold, M. (2013), *State and Region Governments in Myanmar*, NPT: MDRI and Asia Foundation, pp.v-vi.

Rieffel, L. (2012), 'The Myanmar Economy: Tough Choices, Global Economy and Development', WP 51, Washington, DC: Brookings Institute.

Tin Maung Maung Than (2005), 'State Dominance in Myanmar: The Political Economy of Industrialization', Singapore: ISEAS.

Transnational Institute (2013), 'Access Denied Land Rights and Ethnic Conflict in Burma', BCN Burma Policy Briefing no. 11.

Turnell, S. (2011), 'Fundamentals of Myanmar's Macroeconomy: A Political Economy Perspective', *Asian Economic Policy Review* 6 (1), pp. 136–53.

U Myint (2011), 'Myanmar Kyat Exchange Rate Issue', Yangon, 25 June 2011, presented to the National Workshop on Reforms for Economic Development of Myanmar, Naypyitaw, 19–21 August 2011, cited in ICG briefing no. 12.

World Bank (2013), 'Public Expenditure and Financial Accountability, Republic of the Union of Myanmar, Public Financial Management Performance Report, March 2012', Report no. 75897-MM.

—— (2014) 'Myanmar—Ending poverty and boosting shared prosperity at a time of transition, A systematic country diagnosis', p. 3.

World Economic Forum (2013), 'New Energy Architecture: Myanmar', prepared in collaboration with Accenture and the Asian Development Bank.

WTO Trade Policy Review Body (2014), 'Myanmar Report by the Secretariat', WT/TPR/S/293, 21 January 2014, p. 7.

Websites and newspapers

http://www.imf.org/external/pubs/ft/scr/2014/cr1491.pdf.

http://countryoffice.unfpa.org/myanmar/2014/08/30/10473/unfpa_press_release_myanmar_releases_population_count_from_census/.

https://www.dvb.no/news/presidential-'advisors'-raise-eyebrows/15438.

http://asiapacific.anu.edu.au/newmandala/2014/10/23/myanmar-special-economic-zones-part-i/.

http://www.bangkokpost.com/business/news/448934/officials-to-meet-on-dawei-initial-phase.

http://in.reuters.com/article/2012/10/02/japan-myanmar-idINDEE89109420121002.

References for Chapter 6

Burnet Institute and Monastic Education Development Group (2014), 'Monastic schools in Myanmar—a baseline study'.

CESR, ToR first phase (unpublished).

—— ToR second phase (unpublished).

—— Rapid Assessment report.

EBO (2011), 'President Thein Sein's Inaugural Speech', Euro Burma Office, Analysis Paper no. 2/2011,. https://euroburmaoffice.s3.amazonaws.com/filer_public/6d/67/6d67b1e2-19b8-450a-9983-63a8844ba616/ebo_analysis_paper_no_2__2011—presidents_speech_on_30_march_2011_english.pdf.

BIBLIOGRAPHY BY CHAPTER

Government of Myanmar (2008), Constitution of the Republic of the Union of Myanmar, Nay Pyi Taw: Ministry of Information.

Government of the Republic of the Union of Myanmar (2012), Ministry of Education, 'Education for All: Access to and Quality of Education in Myanmar', Conference on Development Policy Options with Special Reference to Education and Health in Myanmar, 13–16 February, 2012, Nay Pyi Taw.

Government of Myanmar (2012), 'Framework for Social and Economic Reforms' (FESR).

Health Convergence Core Group (n.d.), 'A Federal, Devolved Health System for Burma/Myanmar', unpublished paper.

JICA (2013), 'Data Collection Survey on Education Sector in Myanmar', Final Report.

Khin Maung Kyi, Ronald Findlay, R. M. Sundrum, Mya Maung, Myo Nyunt, Zaw Oo et al. (2000), *Economic Development of Burma; a vision and a strategy*, Stockholm: Olof Palme International Centre.

Lall, M. (2009), 'Education in Myanmar—the interplay of state, civil society and business', in Skidmore, M. and Wilson, T., *Dictatorship, Disorder and Decline in Myanmar*, Canberra: ANU E-Press, pp. 127–50.

—— (2010), *Child centred learning and teaching approaches in Myanmar*, Yangon: British Council.

—— (2011), 'Pushing the child centred approach in Myanmar—the role of cross-national policy networks and the effects in the classroom', *Critical Studies in Education*, vol. 52, no. 3, pp. 219–33.

Lall, M. and South, A. (2013), 'Comparing models of non-state ethnic education in Myanmar: the Mon and Karen national education regimes', *Journal of Contemporary Asia*, vol. 44, issue 2, pp. 298–321.

M. Lall and E. Vickers (2009), *Education as a Political Tool in Asia*, London: Routledge.

Lall, M. et al. (2013), *Teachers' voice—what education reforms does Myanmar need?* Yangon and Bangkok: Myanmar Egress and FNS.

NNER (2014), 'NNER's position regarding its loss of faith in the government and Ministry of Education's education reform process', Yangon, 7 March 2014, http://www.burmalibrary.org/docs21/UTL-07—2014-03-07-NNER_Letter_to_Public-en.pdf.

Pyoe Pin (2014), *The Political Economy of Basic Education in Myanmar*, Yangon.

Salem-Gervais, N. and Metro, R. (2012), 'A Textbook Case of Nation-Building: The Evolution of History Curricula in Myanmar, *Journal of Burma Studies*.

Saw Tun Lin (2013), 'Govt Confirms Karen Language will be Taught In Pago Schools', Karen News, 15 December 2013, http://karennews.org/2013/12/govt-confirms-karen-language-will-be-taught-in-pago-schools.html/.

Smith, M. (1999), *Burma: Insurgency and the Politics of Ethnicity*, London: Zed Books.

South, A. (2003), *The Golden Sheldrake: Mon Nationalism and Civil War in Burma*, London: Routledge Curzon.

—— (2008), *Ethnic Politics in Burma: States of Conflict*, London: Routledge.

UNICEF, Programme Document presenting the Myanmar Quality Basic Education Programme (QBEP).

—— The Rakhine Response plan, unpublished documents.

—— The Kachin Response plan, unpublished documents.

World Bank (2013), School grants and student stipends, unpublished documents.

World Bank Education Mission, 3–14 June 2014, unpublished documents.

References for Chapter 7

BBC (2013), 'Six Muslims charged over monk's death in Burma's Meiktila', http://www.bbc.com/news/world-asia-22433871?print=true.

Burma/Myanmar (2014), 'TNI Ethnicity without Meaning, Data without Context—The 2014 Census, Identity and Citizenship', Burma Policy Briefing no. 13, February 2014.

Government of Myanmar (2008), Constitution of the Republic of the Union of Myanmar, Naypyitaw: Ministry of Information.

ICG (2012), 'Myanmar: Storm Clouds on the Horizon', Asia Report no. 238, Jakarta/Brussels, http://www.crisisgroup.org/~/media/Files/asia/south-east-asia/burma-myanmar/238-myanmar-storm-clouds-on-the-horizon.

—— (2013), 'The Dark Side of Transition: Violence Against Muslims in Myanmar', Asia Report no. 251, Jakarta/Brussels,. http://www.crisisgroup.org/~/media/Files/asia/south-east-asia/burma-myanmar/251-the-dark-side-of-transition-violence-against-muslims-in-myanmar.pdf.

ICG (2014), 'Myanmar: The Politics of Rakhine State', Asia Report no. 261, Jakarta/Brussels, http://www.crisisgroup.org/~/media/Files/asia/south-east-asia/burma-myanmar/261-myanmar-the-politics-of-rakhine-state.pdf.

Lall, M. et al. (2014), *Citizenship in Myanmar—contemporary debates and challenges in light of the reform process*, Yangon and Bangkok: Myanmar Egress and FNS.

Leider, J. (2012), EFEO presentation (unpublished).

—— (2014), 'Rohingya—the name, the movement, the quest for identity',. http://www.burmalibrary.org/docs21/Jacques-P-Leider-2014-01-28-Rohingya-The_Name-The_movement-The_quest_for_identity-en.pdf.

Sakhong, L. (2012), 'The Dynamics of Sixty Years of Ethnic Armed Conflict in Burma', Analysis Paper no.1, January 2012, BCRP, pp. 1–2.

South, A. (2008, reprint edn 2010), *Ethnic Politics in Burma: States of Conflict*, London: Routledge.

Steinberg, D. I. (2012), 'The problem of democracy in the republic of the Union of Myanmar, neither nation-state nor state-nation?' *Southeast Asian Affairs*, Singapore: ISEAS.

Taylor, R. H. (2013a), 'Myanmar's "Pivot" toward the Shibboleth of "Democracy"', *Asian Affairs* 44:3, pp. 392–400, DOI: 10.1080/03068374.2013.826014.

—— (2013b), 'Myanmar in 2012, Mhyaw ta lin lin or great expectations', *Southeast Asian Affairs*, Singapore: ISEAS.

—— (2014), http://asia.nikkei.com/Politics-Economy/Policy-Politics/Robert-Taylor-What-would-Ne-Win-have-thought-of-today-s-Myanmar.

Tin Maung Maung Than and Moe Thuzar (2012), 'Myanmar's Rohingya Dilemma', *ISEAS perspectives*, Naypyidaw, 9 July 2012.

Tonkin, D. (2014), 'The Mujahid Rebellion in Arakan: a 1952 Analysis by the British Foreign Office'.

—— (2014), 'The R-word, and its ramifications'.

—— (2014), 'The Rohingya Identity: Arithmetic of the Absurd'.

—— (2014), 'The "Rohingya" Identity—Further Thoughts'.

—— (2014), 'The "Rohingya" Identity—British experience in Arakan 1826–1948'.

—— (2014), 'Whither Myanmar?'.

All Tonkin articles available at

http://www.networkmyanmar.org/images/stories/PDF17/Rohingya-Identity-II.pdf.

Tun Aung Chain (2000), 'Historians and the Search for Myanmar Nationhood', at 16th Conference of the International Association of Historians of Asia, Kota Kinabalu: International Association of Historians of Asia in Cooperation with Universiti Malaysia Sabah.

Tun Tun Aung (2007), 'An introduction to Citizenship Card under Myanmar Citizenship Law', no. 38, pp. 265–90.

References for Conclusion

Lall, M. et al. (2015), *Myanmar's ethnic parties and the 2015 elections*, Yangon: EU and IMG.

TNI (2015), 'Statement of the 3rd Myanmar Opium farmer forum', 12 September,. https://www.tni.org/en/article/statement-of-3rd-myanmar-opium-farmer-forum.

The Voice Weekly, 4 August 2014.

http://ndfmyanmar.org/?p=1142 31.5.2013.

http://burma.irrawaddy.org/news/2014/06/16/60474.html, 16 June 2014.

http://myitmakhamediagroup.com/post 3, 8 August 2014.

http://burma.irrawaddy.org/news/2014/07/29/62518.html.

http://burma.irrawaddy.org/news/2014/07/26/62410.html.

http://burma.irrawaddy.org/news/2014/07/31/62596.html.

http://burma.irrawaddy.org/news/2014/07/31/62596.html.

http://myanmar.mmtimes.com/index.php/national-news/11094-2014-07-10-09-02-30.html.

http://www.mmtimes.com/index.php/opinion/11302-u-shwe-mann-directs-pr-drama.html.

http://7daydaily.com/story/17379#.U99J8KDmrvw.

https://www.dvb.no/elections/nld-rejects-hybrid-voting-system/45450.

https://www.dvb.no/elections/lower-house-rejects-pr-system-burma-myanmar/45888.

INDEX

Abe, Shinzo, 156, 157
ACLEDA Bank, 152
Action Committee for Democratic
    Education (ACDE), 173–4
Afghanistan, 217
AGD Bank, 84
agriculture, 15, 32–3, 41, 56, 73,
    131–2, 134, 137, 138, 139, 147–8
aid agencies, 1, 2, 6, 10, 14, 21, 109,
    111, 152–7, 170–2, 176–8, 181–3
AIDS (acquired immune deficiency
    syndrome), 38, 68, 169, 220
Aik Pao, 89
Air Bagan, 84
Akyab District, 196
Alaungpaya, King of Burma, 186
Aljazeera, 72
All Burma Federation of Students'
    Unions (ABFSU), 173
All Burma Monks' Alliance, 30
All Burma Student Democratic Front
    (ABSDF), 103
All Mon Regions Democratic Party
    (AMRDP), 87, 181, 182, 212
Alliance Française, 61
Amytha Hluttaw, see Upper House
Anawrahta, King of Burma, 186
Anglo-Burmese War

First (1824–6), 193
Third (1885), 93
Anti-Corruption Commission, 146
Ar Yone Oo, 36
Arakan, 196–7
Arakan Army (AA), 117, 118
Arakan League for Democracy (ALD),
    144
Arakan Liberation Party (ALP), 109
Arakan National Council (ANC), 121,
    123
Arakan National Party (ANP), 212
Aris, Michael, 52
army, see Tatmadaw
Asia World Co., 41, 136
Asian Development Bank (ADB), 28,
    135, 152, 153
Asian Institute of Technology (AIT),
    23, 35, 103
Aso, Taro, 156
assimilation, 185
Association of South East Asian Na-
    tions (ASEAN), 19, 34, 41, 76, 78,
    111, 133, 136, 149, 154, 156–7, 158,
    218, 220
ATMs (automatic teller machines), 138
Aung Ko, 195
Aung Ko Win, 135

Aung Kyi, 32, 40, 49, 71, 72

Aung Kyi Nyunt, 195

Aung Min, 11, 82, 91, 102–6, 111, 114, 115, 124, 126, 128, 211

Aung Naing Oo, 28, 103, 115, 131

Aung San, 11, 51, 65, 71–2, 94, 205

Aung San Suu Kyi, 2, 3, 5, 12, 29–30, 32, 60, 151, 157, 170, 175–6, 199, 209, 210, 211, 213–14, 216

   2003 sentenced to house arrest, 64–5, 67

   2007 greets protesting monks at gate of house, 30

   2009 John Yettaw incident; sentenced to further house arrest, 39–40, 67

   2010 meetings with Aung Kyi; announcement of NLD election boycott, 49–52; released from house arrest, 29, 64–5, 67–8

   2011 meeting with Tomás Ojea Quintana, 65; addresses World Economic Forum, 69; reminded by government of illegal status of NLD, 70; attends National Workshop on Reforms for Economic Development, 137 voices support for UN Commission of Inquiry, 76; meeting with Aung Kyi, 71; meeting with Thein Sein, 11, 65, 71–2; announces intent to run for parliament, 73–4, 144

   2012 addresses World Economic Forum, 73; by-election campaign; elected MP for Kawhmu, 77–9, 144; warns against foreign investment at Bangkok conference, 82–3; tour of Europe, 83; appointed chair of Committee for Rule of Law, 82; chairs commission on Letpadaung mine, 84; meets with Barack Obama, 85; criticism over crony donations to NLD and stance on ethnic conflicts, 84–5

   2013 re-elected chairperson of NLD, 86; heckled at Letpadaung mine, 84; criticizes pace of education reform, 172

   2014 campaign for constitutional change, 86–92, 124; attends four-way talks on constitutional change, 89; talks on NCA, 132; supports cancellation of by-elections, 211

   2015 threatens election boycott, 90

Aung Thaung, 101

Aung Tun Thet, 172

AUSAID, 12, 168, 171, 177–8

Australia, 82, 108, 144, 165, 175, 181, 206

Aye Maung, 195

Aye Mya Hlaing, 24, 27

Ayeyarwady River, 23, 27, 32, 72, 157 delta region, 23, 27, 32–6, 38, 45, 63, 72–3, 86, 111, 157, 174

Bagan, Mandalay Region, 72

Bagan Capital, 144

Bago Region, 31, 71, 102, 109, 181

   Kyaukkyi, 102

   Latpadan, 174

   Pyay, 31

Bali, Indonesia, 76

Baluchaung Power Plant, Kayah State, 157

Bamar ethnicity, 5, 14, 62, 85, 93–4, 104, 117, 120, 124–5, 129, 131, 178–9, 185–6, 194, 200, 204, 206, 216

Bamo, Kachin State, 31

Bangkok, Thailand, 26, 28, 45

Bangkok process, 24, 28, 104
Bangladesh, 34, 36, 97, 189, 197, 198, 204, 207
banking, 135, 138, 152, 158
Baptists, 93, 102
Bard University, New York, 176
Basic Education Departments, 167
Basic Education Law, 172, 173
Bay of Bengal Initiative for Multi-Sectoral Technical and Economic Cooperation (BIMSTEC), 134
Bayinaung, King of Burma, 186
Belgium, 23
Bengali Muslims, see Rohingya
biomass, 140
Biz Fifteen, 136
Bo Min Phyu, 191
Border Area Development Programme, 16
border guard forces (BGF), 40, 97, 98, 101
bridges, 16, 99
Britain, see United Kingdom
British Council, 170–1, 175, 176
Brussels, Belgium, 23
Buddhism, 12, 19, 29–32, 44, 65, 68, 84, 94, 142, 179, 185–91, 195–208, 222
    monastic schools, 20, 44, 160, 161–2, 163, 166, 169, 177, 179, 186
    nationalism, 185–91, 195–208
    Sangha, 12, 19, 29–32, 44, 52, 186, 188, 195, 203–5
bureaucracy, 3, 82, 95, 146
Burma Campaign UK, 102, 145
Burma Center Netherlands (BCN), 147, 148
Burma Socialist Programme Party (BSPP), 186
Burma Studies, 24

Burmanisation, 94, 160–1, 179
Burmese Communist Party (BCP), 15, 16, 95, 218
Burmese Perspectives, 52
'Burmese Way to Socialism', 94
Burnett Institute, 169
Buthidaung, Rakhine State, 196
by-elections, 76, 78–9, 144, 209, 211

Callahan, Mary, 5, 8
Cambodia, 45, 47, 135
cameras, 30, 31
Canada, 144, 165
Carnegie Endowment for Peace, 85
Carter Foundation, 221
ceasefires, 11, 15–17, 40–1, 54, 65, 87, 95–132, 182
censorship, 1, 2, 57, 72, 79–80, 153
Centre for Economic and Social Development (CESD), 136–7, 139, 153
Centre for Legal Affairs, 137
Centre for Peace and Conflict Studies (CPCS), 45
Centre for Strategic and International Studies, 137
Chevening Scholarship, 28
Chiang Mai, Thailand, 112, 115, 118
child labour, soldiers, 80
Child Law, 173
child-centred approach (CCA), 163
Chin ethnicity, State, 48, 54, 93–4, 101, 107, 109, 180, 194, 207, 216, 219, 218
    Chin Hills Regulation, 93–4, 120
    Chin National Front (CNF), 101, 121, 123
    Chin National Front (CNP), 54, 109, 112
    Chin Progressive Party, 54, 87
China, 14, 16, 22, 34, 41, 48, 75, 76, 84, 86, 95, 97, 100, 101, 118, 120,

134, 135, 140, 142, 149, 150, 155, 157, 158, 194, 195, 208, 218

Chit Khine, 136

Christian Democratic Union of Germany (CDU), 21

Christianity, 93, 94, 100, 102, 179, 186, 190

Chyang Ying, 99

citizen reporting' 52

citizenship law, 191–201

Citizenship Scrutiny Cards (CSCs), 197

citizenship, 10, 43, 46–7, 61, 62, 64

civic education, 46–7, 61–4

civil service, 4, 48, 56, 57

Civil Society Organisations (CSOs), 1, 5, 6–9, 10–11, 16, 18, 20, 24, 32, 36–7, 39, 41, 45–7, 51, 52, 57, 61–2, 64, 70, 74–5, 97, 104, 109, 119, 120, 124–9, 130, 132, 139, 153, 162, 165, 168, 174, 176, 177, 179, 183, 204, 217

coal, 150

Cold War, 95

Committee for Rule of Law and Peace and Stability, 82

Committee for the Emergence of Federal Union (CEFU), 112

communal violence, 85, 187–91, 197, 199, 201–3, 207, 222

Communist Party of Burma (CPB), 15, 16, 95, 218

Community Based Organisations (CBOs), 7–9, 39, 103, 108, 109, 177

Comprehensive Education Sector Review (CESR), 12, 168–72, 177, 181, 183

Confederation of University Student Unions, 173

Conflict Risk Network, 145

Constitution, 3, 14, 15, 17–18, 22, 37–

9, 44, 50, 58, 79, 81, 85, 86–91, 98, 112, 115, 121, 122, 124, 127, 128, 142, 165, 166, 192, 195, 209–11

Constitutional Tribunal, 81, 212

consumer protection, 20

Control of Import/Export Temporary Law, 139

copper, 84, 86, 150

corruption, 58, 71, 135, 145–6, 158

cronyism, 33, 35, 41, 48, 84, 86, 135–6

currency, 11, 58, 76, 101, 137–41

curriculum, 163, 169, 178, 179, 180, 186

Cyclone Giri (2010), 73

Cyclone Nargis (2008), 7, 10, 32–9, 73, 75, 111, 176

dams, 8, 16, 75, 99

Davos, Switzerland, 69, 73

Dawei SEZ, Tanintharyi Region, 141–2, 174

DDR (disarmament, demobilization and reintegration), 96

decentralisation, 10, 56–7, 105–6, 122, 142–3, 147, 166–7, 177, 213

Deed of Commitment, 116–17

Delapraz, David, 14

Delhi, India, 14

delta region, 23, 27, 32–6, 38, 45, 63, 72–3, 86, 111, 157, 174

Democratic Karen Benvolent Army (DKBA), 98, 101, 109, 116, 120, 122

democratisation, 3–5, 106

Denmark, 108

Department for International Development (DFID), 12, 36, 175, 177–8

Department of Education, Planning and Training, 167

Department of Foreign Affairs and Trade (DFAT), 175, 177–8

Depayin massacre (2003), 67

Desert Island Discs, 83

development partners, 170–2, 176–8, 181–3

devolution, 56

diaspora, exiles, 8, 24, 28, 60, 74, 76, 102, 103, 106, 119, 136, 144, 210

Disaster Preparedness and Response in Education (DPRE), 177

'discipline-flourishing democracy', 3

distance education, 164

drug-trafficking, 16, 216–20

'Dutch disease', 158

duties, 44, 61, 62

Early Childhood Care and Development, 173, 177, 181

East Pakistan, 198

ECODEV, 35

Economic Advisory Board, 136

economic reforms, 3, 4, 11, 22, 58, 83, 133–58

Eden Group, 136

education, 2, 3, 10, 11, 12, 14, 15, 16, 19–28, 38, 44, 46, 61, 74, 106, 109, 122, 130, 138, 139, 147, 148, 151, 159–84, 186, 200, 208, 213

All Burma Federation of Students' Unions (ABFSU), 173

All Burma Student Democratic Front (ABSDF), 103

Basic Education Departments, 167

Basic Education Law, 172, 173

Burmanisation, 160–1, 179

child-centred approach (CCA), 163

Child Law, 173

civic education, 46–7, 61–4

class sizes, 162–3, 169

Comprehensive Education Sector Review (CESR), 12, 168–72, 177, 181, 183

Confederation of University Student Unions, 173

curriculum, 163, 169, 178, 179, 180, 186

development partners, 170–2, 176–8, 181, 182, 183

Disaster Preparedness and Response in Education (DPRE), 177

Essential Learning Packages (ELP), 184

distance education, 164

Early Childhood Care and Development, 173, 177, 181

Education for All (EFA), 161, 173, 176

Education Mother Law, 172, 173

Education Promotion Implementation Committee (EPIC), 12, 171–3

Education Research Law, 173

Education Thematic Working Group (ETWG), 176–7, 183

ethnic education systems, 12, 160, 161, 169, 170, 178–84, 200, 213

Examination Board Law, 173

examinations, 20–2, 163–4, 201

foreign teachers, 20, 21

funding, 161–2, 166, 182

higher education, 20, 21, 25, 148, 160, 162, 164–6, 168–9, 171, 175–6, 184

Higher Education Law, 175

IDP students, 184

Konrad Adenauer Stiftung (KAS), 21, 26

monastic schools, 20, 44, 160, 161–2, 163, 166, 169, 177, 179, 186

National Education Bill, 173–5

National Network for Education Reform (NNER), 12, 170, 174

Non-Formal Education (NFE), 169, 177
languages, 19–20, 26, 87, 151, 160–2, 164, 169, 171, 173, 176, 178–82
overseas study, 20, 165
Parliamentary Education Promotion Committee (PEPC), 172
primary education, 20, 162, 163, 165, 166, 169, 177, 180, 181, 182, 184
private schools, universities, 19–20, 74, 160, 162, 173, 176, 183
Private Tuition Law, 19, 173
rote learning, 163
secondary education, 20, 162, 163, 164, 169, 177, 180
state education, 44, 160, 162, 165, 166, 168, 177, 178, 179, 180
student protests, 21, 29, 31, 164, 173–5
teacher shortages, 163, 166, 182
Technical, Agricultural and Vocational Education Law, 173
technical and vocational education and training (TVET), 168, 169
textbooks, 160, 162, 169, 178, 179, 180
University Education Law, 173
universities, 21–2, 85, 160, 164, 165, 173, 175–6, 183
Eid al-Fitr, 188
88 Generation, 29, 75, 88, 195
8888 Uprising, 21, 22, 29, 30, 31, 43, 95, 186
Eike Htun, 135
Election Commission (EC), 47, 49, 51, 55, 79, 89, 91, 211, 221
Electoral Review Commission, 212
electricity, 18, 36, 107, 135, 136, 140–1, 142, 145, 149, 157

electronic media, 30–1
English language, 19–20, 26, 151, 160, 162, 164, 169, 171, 176, 181
environmental protection, 8, 17, 38, 69, 74, 75, 141, 153
Essential Learning Packages (ELP), 184
ethnic communities, 93–4
    Civil Society Organisations (CSOs), 6, 7, 10, 24, 46, 47, 120, 124–9, 179, 184
    communal violence, 85, 187–91, 197, 199, 201–3, 207, 222
    discrimination against, 57, 85, 187, 192, 195–205
    education, 12, 26, 56, 160, 161, 169, 170, 178–84, 200, 213
    Ethnic Armed Groups (EAGs), 2, 5, 10, 11, 14–17, 20, 40, 49, 65, 71, 84–5, 87, 94–132, 178, 180–1, 184, 211, 215–16, 218–19
    national identity, 185–6
    political parties, participation, 45–50, 52–6, 59–60, 61–4, 68, 70, 213, 214
Ethnic National Council (ENC), 112
Ethnic Nationalities Solidarity and Cooperation Committee, 112
Euro-Burma Office, 112, 113
European Karen Network, 102
European Union (EU), 11, 12, 26, 40, 46, 53, 59, 78, 103, 108, 110, 144, 152–5, 156, 171, 174, 177, 178, 188, 199, 221
Examination Board Law, 173
examinations, 20–2, 163–4, 201
exchange rates, 58, 76, 137–41, 145
exiles, diaspora, 8, 24, 28, 60, 74, 76, 102, 103, 106, 119, 136, 144, 210
Export and Import Law, 139
exports, 134, 136, 137, 138, 158
Extractive Industries Transparency Initiative (EITI), 146

Facebook, 202, 203

Farmland Administration Body (FAB), 148

Farmland Law, 147

Federal Democracy Alliance, 89

federalism, 17, 87, 105, 107, 112, 115, 116, 125, 129, 142, 186

Federated State Act, 121

Financial Commission, 143

financial sector, 58, 135, 137, 138, 139, 152, 158, 178

Finland, 108, 206

first past the post (FPTP), 211–12

Fisheries and Aquatic Technicians Association, 23

fishing, fisheries, 23, 32

focus groups, 60–4

forced assimilation, 185

forced labour, 17, 38, 80–1

foreign aid, 1, 2, 6, 10, 14, 21, 109, 111, 152–7, 170

Foreign and Commonwealth Office, 145

foreign direct investment (FDI), 1, 2, 81, 82–3, 84, 85, 134, 139, 141, 144, 147, 148, 149, 150

Foreign Exchange and Management Law, 139

Foreign Investment Law, 139

Foreign Registration Cards, 197

foreign teachers, 20, 21

forestry, 153

'four cuts' strategy, 95

fourth estate, 76, 80

Framework for Economic and Social Reforms (FESR), 139, 146, 149, 167

France, 34

freedom of speech/association, 1, 2, 4, 7, 23, 44, 57, 72, 80, 81, 106, 153, 173, 204

Friedrich Ebert Stiftung (FES), 21, 25, 26

Friedrich Naumann Stiftung (FNS), 45, 46, 47

fuel prices, 29

Fuji Coffee House, Yangon, 25

Fukuda Doctrine, 156

Gambari, Ibrahim, 28

Gambira, 75

gas, 134, 140, 142, 145

gems, 15, 145, 150

general systems preferences (GSP), 153

Germany, 21, 23, 24, 25, 26, 189, 206

gold, 17, 150

golden triangle, 217

Greater Mekong Sub-region (GMS), 134–5

green cards, 194, 197

Hague, William, 85

halal food, 204

Han Thar Myint, 88

hardliners, 64, 65, 82, 101, 151, 154, 172

Harn Yawnghwe, 112

Hayzer, Noeleen, 28

health services, 14, 15, 16, 38, 138, 139, 147, 178

hierarchy, 50, 62, 68

higher education, 20, 21, 25, 148, 160, 162, 164–6, 168–9, 171, 175–6, 184

Higher Education Law, 175

Hinduism, 190

Hiroshima Peace Institute, 21

HIV (human immunodeficiency virus), 38, 68, 169, 220

Hla Maung Shwe, 23, 27, 35, 47, 48, 103, 104

Horsey, Richard, 57

Hpa Ahn, Karen State, 102, 114

Hpa Kant, Kachin State, 202

Htay Myint, 35, 135

Htay Oo, 27, 79, 89
Htoo Group, 41, 136
human resources, 136, 159, 166
Human Rights Watch, 76
human rights, 20, 69, 73, 76, 85, 95, 174, 187
human trafficking, 80
hydropower, 8, 16, 75, 99, 140, 145, 157

ID cards, 48, 109, 131, 189, 190, 191, 194, 197, 200, 222
illegal association law, 120
illegal immigration, 187, 195, 197, 198
IMG, 152–5
imports, 138, 139, 141
in camera trials, 74
income divide, 1–2
Independent, 77
India, 14, 34, 36, 41, 97, 150, 158, 194, 201, 208
Indonesia, 41, 76, 204
industrialisation, 82, 135, 148–51, 158
inflation, 2, 34, 158, 182
information technology (IT), 19–20, 135
infrastructure, 1, 14, 15, 16, 103, 122, 135, 136, 142, 148–51, 155, 157
Inland Water Transport Board, 34
Insein Prison, Yangon, 74
interfaith marriage, 205
internally displaced persons (IDPs), 107, 111, 184, 187, 190–1, 206
International Committee of the Red Cross (ICRC), 14
International Criminal Court (ICC), 70
International Crisis Group (ICG), 48, 51, 65, 188, 190, 199
International Labour Organisation (ILO), 38, 74, 80–1, 155

International Monetary Fund (IMF), 11, 28, 76, 134, 138
International Organisation of Supreme Audit Institutions (INTOSAI), 137
International Peace Support Group, 108
Internet, 80, 140, 150, 202, 203, 204
investment, 1, 2, 8, 59, 81, 82–3, 84, 85, 133, 134, 139, 141, 144, 147, 148, 149, 150, 158
Investment Commission, 82
Investment Guarantee Agency (IGA), 152
iron, 134, 150
Irrawaddy River, *see* Ayeyarwady River
Irrawaddy, The, 49, 80
Islam, 57, 80, 84–5, 140, 142, 184, 186–91, 195–208, 222
Israel, 118
Italian-Thai Development Company, 141
Italy, 206

Ja Nan Lahtaw, 16, 24, 96, 97
jade, jadeite, 17, 134, 150
Japan, 11, 21, 36, 94, 103, 110–11, 118, 142, 151, 152, 153, 155–7, 175, 196
Japan International Cooperation Agency (JICA), 30, 155, 160, 163, 176, 178
Japan-Myanmar Association, 156
Jimmy (Kyaw Min Yu), 88
Joint Nationwide Ceasefire Drafting Work Group, 114
Jones, Lee, 136
Judiciary and Regulatory Committee, 195
Jung, Kerstin, 35

Kachin ethnicity, State, 11, 12, 15,

16, 31, 53, 55, 75, 84–5, 93, 94, 96,
98–100, 107, 114, 119, 131, 179,
180, 184, 194, 202, 207, 212, 218,
219, 222
Kachin Hill Tribes Regulation, 93,
120–1
Kachin Independence Army (KIA),
71, 98–100, 101, 117, 119, 120
Kachin Independence Organisation
(KIO), 96, 98–100, 101, 112,
118, 119, 180, 184
Kachin State Progressive Party, 99
Kaman people, 188, 190, 195
Karen ethnicity, State, 12, 17, 48, 49,
53, 63, 77, 93–4, 96, 97, 101, 102–3,
107, 109, 110, 116, 131, 179, 181,
183, 194, 200, 206, 207, 215
Democratic Karen Benevolent Army
(DKBA), 98, 101, 109, 116, 120,
122
European Karen Network, 102
Karen Baptist Convention, 102
Karen National Union (KNU), 17,
97, 101, 102–3, 109, 113–17,
119–21, 123, 128, 144, 180, 181
Karen Peace Council (KPC), 102,
116
Karen People's Party (KPP), 181,
127, 128
Karen Women's Empowerment
Group, 126
Karen Women's Organisation, 116
Karenni ethnicity, see Kayah
Karenni National Progressive Party
(KNPP), 97, 101, 109, 112, 120,
128
Kawhmu, Yangon Region, 72–3, 77
Kawthoolei, 102
Kayah ethnicity, State, 15, 91, 94, 96,
101, 107, 109, 110, 131, 180, 194,
207, 218, 219

khayaing (district), 167
Khin Aung Myint, 89
Khin Maung Swe, 50, 89
Khin Nyunt, 10, 13–15, 19, 20, 22, 24,
27, 28, 29, 40, 75, 95, 96, 102, 216
Khin Ye, 103, 191, 194
Khin Zaw Win, 24
Khun Htun Oo, 89
King, Kenneth, 175
Ko Ko Gyi, 88, 190, 195
Ko Ko Hlaing, 136
Ko Tar, 20, 125
Kokang ethnicity, region, 17, 41, 98,
117
Konrad Adenauer Stiftung (KAS), 21,
26
Kramer, Tom, 7
Kuala Lumpur, Malaysia, 21
Kunming, Yunnan, 142
Kyaukpyu SEZ, Rakhine State, 141,
142
Kyaukkyi, Bago Region, 102
Kyaukpyu, Rakhine State, 188
Kyaw Ni Khin, 23, 24
Kyaw Soe Hlaing, 103
Kyaw Swar Min, 77
Kyaw Thu, 24
Kyaw Win, 135
Kyaw Yin Hlaing, 13, 19, 21, 23–5,
27–8, 31, 43, 103
Kyi Toe, 78

labour, 38, 57, 74, 80–1, 141–2, 149,
155, 158
Labour Organisation Law, 81
Laiza, Kachin State, 11, 100, 113, 114,
116
land bills, 8, 147
land reform, rights, 8, 80, 109, 110,
131–2, 147–8, 157–8, 217
land use certificates (LUCs), 8, 147

languages, 19–20, 26, 87, 151, 160–2, 164, 169, 171, 173, 176, 178–82
Laos, 34, 135
Lashio, Shan State, 27, 202, 204
Latpadan, Bago Region, 174
Laukkai, Shan State, 117
Law, Steven, 41, 135
Law Khee Lah, Kayin State, 114, 117
lead, 150
Least Developed Country (LDC), 133, 153
Legal Advisory Board, 136
legislative assemblies, 3, 53, 79, 142
Leider, Jacques, 196, 198
Letpadaung mine, Sagaing Region, 84, 86
Liang Sakhong, 185, 186
Light Infantry Divisions (LIDs), 31, 33, 99
limestone, 150
lingua franca, 178
Link Emergency Aid & Development (LEAD), 36
Living Colour, 22, 25
Lo Bianco, Joseph, 181
logging, 15, 17, 22, 134
London, England, 21, 84, 145
Lower House (Pyithu Hluttaw), 5, 55, 56, 79, 81, 90, 129, 149, 212
lu-myo, 206

Ma Ba Tha, 205
Magwe Region, 53, 218
    Pakokku, 29–30, 174
Mahamyaing monastery, Moulmein, 204
Mai Sai, Thailand, 102
Malaysia, 20, 21, 41, 97, 116, 165, 204
Malteser, 189
Mandalay Region, 20, 23, 53, 63, 77, 88, 130, 131, 174, 189, 203, 204

Bagan, 72
Mandalay University, 21, 175
Meiktila, 201–2, 204
Pyin Oo Lwin, 27, 176
Mannerplaw, Karen State, 114
manufacturing, 134, 135, 140, 148–9
Marshall, Steve, 38, 80
Martyrs' Day, 71, 88
Marubeni Corporation, 156
Masoyein monastery, Mandalay, 204
Mauk Kham, 57, 89, 172
Maung Aye, 13, 22, 28, 31
Maungdaw, Rakhine State, 184, 196, 200
Mawlamyine, Mon State, 174
Max Group, 41, 136
Maymyo, see Pyin Oo Lwin
McKinsey, 148
Médecins Sans Frontières (MSF), 189
media, 1, 2, 8, 22, 30–1, 44, 56, 69, 72, 74, 79–80, 204
medicine, study of, 164
Meiktila, Mandalay Region, 201–2, 204
Mekong River, 134–5
Metro, Rose, 186
Metta Development Foundation, 16, 35, 96
microfinance, 58, 152
middle classes, 1–2, 5, 19–20, 25, 41, 43, 45, 100, 140, 150, 162, 165, 176
Military Intelligence (MI), 11, 13, 14, 19, 27, 28, 96
military, see Tatmadaw
Min Aung Hlaing, 5, 79, 89, 90, 116–17, 211
Min Ko Naing, 88
Min Zaw Oo, 103
Minbya, Rakhine State, 188
minerals, mining, 15, 41, 84, 134, 145, 150

Ming Hsat, Shan State, 218
Mingaladon airport, Yangon, 34
Minimum Wage Law, 158
Ministry of Agriculture and Irrigation, 27, 38, 148
Ministry of Border Affairs, 16, 38, 58, 167
Ministry of Commerce, 153
Ministry of Defence, 137, 167
Ministry of Education, 12, 38, 159, 160, 162, 163, 166, 167, 168, 169, 170, 171, 172, 175, 177, 183
Ministry of Electrics, 107
Ministry of Finance and Revenue, 144, 149, 153
Ministry of Forestry, 153
Ministry of Health, 38, 153, 167
Ministry of Home Affairs, 7, 136, 192
Ministry of Immigration, 107, 191, 194, 195
Ministry of Labour, 38, 74
Ministry of Religious Affairs, 161, 162, 167
Ministry of Science and Technology, 153, 167
Ministry of Social Welfare, Relief and Resettlement, 38
missionaries, 93
Mitsubishi Corp, 156
Mizzima, 49, 80
mobile phones, 1, 2, 140
Moe Thuzar, 193
Mon ethnicity, State, 12, 15, 45, 87, 96, 101, 107, 109, 110, 131, 179, 180–3, 194, 200, 204, 214
  All Mon Regions Democratic Party (AMRDP), 87, 181, 182, 212
  Mon National Education Committee (MNEC), 180, 182–3
  Mon National Schools (MNS), 182
  Mon Women's Organisation, 126

New Mon State Party (NMSP), 98, 101, 109, 112, 121, 122, 123, 126, 182
monarchy, 68, 93, 186
monastic schools, 20, 44, 160, 161–2, 163, 166, 169, 177, 179, 186
Mongla ethnicity, 101
monks, *see* Sangha
Mori Yuji, 118
Morning Dawn, 36
Moshe, 116
Moulmein, Mon State, 204
Mountbatten, Louis, 1st Earl Mountbatten of Burma, 121
Mrauk-U, Rakhine State, 188
Mujahid, 197
multinational companies, 142, 146–7, 150–1
Muse, Shan State, 13
Mutu Sae Poe, 116
Mya Aye, 88
Myanmar
  1947 Panglong Conference, 68, 70, 94, 116, 120, 121; promulgation of Constitution, 192
  1948 independence, 94, 192, 193, 197; Mujahid rebellion in Rakhine, 197
  1949 Karen National Union (KNU) rebellion begins, 102
  1960 construction of Baluchaung Power Plant begins, 157
  1961 Mujahid rebels defeated, 197
  1962 Ne Win comes to power, 94–5, 134, 160, 161, 176, 186, 197
  1974 promulgation of Constitution, 193
  1977 Operation Nagamin; exodus of Rohingya, 197
  1979 Chinese funding for EAGs dries up, 14–15, 95

1982 new Citizenship Law enacted, 193–4, 198, 201

1988 8888 Uprising, 21, 22, 29, 30, 31, 43, 95; SLORC seizes power, 7, 134, 155, 164, 186, 201

1989 ceasefire process with EAGs begins, 15, 20, 40, 95, 216; initiation of Border Area Development Programme, 16; citizenship inspection process, 197

1990 NLD wins general election; junta refuses to recognise result, 21, 30, 38, 50, 52, 68, 70; Western sanctions imposed, 9, 22

1992 Ministry for Progress of Border Areas and National Races established, 16, 93; exodus of Rohingya, 197

1993 foundation of USDA, 18; KIO agrees to ceasefire, 98; monastic schools re-legalised, 161

1995 fall of KNU's Mannerplaw headquarters, 114

1996 student strikes, 164

1997 accession to ASEAN, 134; MNDAA announces opium ban, 16; SLORC reconstituted as SPDC, 7

1998 foundation of Myanmar Fisheries Federation (MFF), 23; foundation of Metta Development Foundation, 96; student strikes, 164

1999 ICRC permitted to inspect prisons, 14

2001 establishment of Ethnic National Council (ENC), 112; establishment of '30 year education plan', 161; signing of Education for All declaration, 161, 173

2002 Nay Win Maung arrested, 27;

MNDAA opium ban comes into effect, 16

2003 banking crisis, 135; Depayin massacre, 67; Aung San Suu Kyi sentenced to house arrest, 64–5, 67; Khin Nyunt demoted to prime minister, 13; announcment of Roadmap to Discipline-flourishing Democracy, 3, 14, 17–18, 22; Education for All plan drawn up, 161, 173; U Wirathu arrested for inciting violence, 204

2004 peace talks with KNU, 102; re-opening of National Convention, 17; KAS run programme at Yangon University, 21; conflict between army and intelligence in Muse, 13; Khin Nyunt arrested, 10, 13–14, 19, 20, 24, 28, 29, 96; Khin Zaw Win released from prison, 24

2005 Tin Maung Thann organises MFF lectures, 23; formation of Myanmar Egress (ME), 22; KAS run programme at Yangon and Mandalay Universities, 21; establishment of new capital at Nay Pyi Taw announced, 18

2006 ME holds first official meeting, 24; KAS run programme at Yangon University, 21; Burma Studies conference in Singapore, 24, 28

2007 beginning of Bangkok process, 24, 104; establishment of Paung Ku, 8; ME sets up office in Thamada Hotel, 24–5; KAS refused permission to teach at Yangon University, 21; police question ME about research project in Lashio, 27; KIO submit proposal to National Convention, 98; Saffron Revolution, 10, 29–32, 43, 75, 186, 203

2008 Cyclone Nargis, 7, 10, 32–9, 73, 75, 111, 176; constitutional referendum, 37–8, 44, 50, 98; ILO negotiates with government on forced labour issue, 38; promulgation of Constitution, 3, 79, 85, 97, 112, 115, 121, 122, 128, 142, 165, 166, 192

2009 Shwegondaing Declaration, 50; John Yettaw incident; Aung San Suu Kyi sentenced to further house arrest, 39–40, 67; conflict in Kokang, 41, 98; Joseph Stiglitz gives lecture in Nay Pyi Taw, 28; construction of Myitsone dam begins, 8; USDP allegedly distributes green cards, 197

2010 election legislation released, 47; Thein Sein resigns from armed forces; USDP registered as political party, 48; NLD announce election boycott; formation of NDF, 49–51, 55, 60, 63, 68; establishment of ETWG, 176; Cyclone Giri, 73; USDP wins general election, 5, 7, 14, 41, 44, 53–5, 85, 98, 121, 197; Aung San Suu Kyi released from house arrest, 64–5, 67–8

2011 Aung San Suu Kyi meets with Tomás Ojea Quintana, 65; NLD refused registration, 68; Aung San Suu Kyi addresses World Economic Forum, 69; foundation of UNFC, 112; Thein Sein sworn in as president, 2, 11, 218; ethnic parties release anti-sanctions statement, 59; Thein Sein's inaugural speech, 58, 101, 133, 159, 166;

Thein Sein appoints advisory boards, 136; political prisoners released, 75, 144, 153; launch of economic workshops, 137; Aung San Suu Kyi reminded of illegal status of NLD, 70; Martyrs' Day; Aung San Suu Kyi meets with Aung Kyi, 71; conflict re-erupts in Kachin State, 11, 71, 84, 99–100, 184; exile groups write to Barack Obama, 76; Thein Sein meets with Aung San Suu Kyi, 65, 71–2; Thein Sein urges exiles to return home, 74; Derek Mitchell appointed US Special Representative, 76; arrival of IMF delegation, 76; ceasefire agreements with UWSA, NDAA and DKBA, 101; suspension of Myitsone dam project; political prisoners released, 75, 144, 153; NLD announces intention to re-register as party, 72; licensing of money-changing counters, 138; Hillary Clinton makes visit; ASEAN summit, 76; peace talks with KNU, 102; Aung San Suu Kyi announces intent to run for parliament, 73–4, 144

2012 KNU agrees to ceasefire, 102; Aung San Suu Kyi addresses World Economic Forum, 73; political prisoners released; death sentences commuted, 75, 144, 153; William Hague makes visit, 85; SEZ Law enacted, 141; EAG conference, 112; Thein Sein addresses Union Assembly, 76, 100; establishment of MDRI, 136; Aung San Suu Kyi tours country; delivers campaign speech, 78; Thein Sein invites international monitors, 78; Labour Organisation Law comes into effect, 81; Farmland and VFV Laws enacted, 8, 147; launch of Myanmar Peace Support Initiative (MPSI), 108; by-elections, 76, 78–9, 144, 209; floating of currency, 138; EU suspends sanctions, 144; Thein Sein visits Japan, 156; communal riots begin, 187–8; Aung San Suu Kyi warns against foreign investment, 82–3; Sasakawa Yohei appointed 'ambassador for ethnic minorities', 111; Italian-Thai Development Company withdraws from Dawei project, 141; launch of CESR, 168; resignation of Tin Aung Myint Oo, 82; Investigation Commission on communal violence launched, 188, 190; censorship board abolished, 80, 153; Aung San Suu Kyi appointed chair of Committee for Rule of Law, 82; World Bank opens office in Yangon, 143; Export and Import Law enacted, 139; Rakhine nationalists meet in Sittwe, 189; 500 NLD members quit in Pathein, 86; communal riots re-erupt, 188; opening of Myanmar Peace Centre (MPC), 103, 153; Barack Obama makes visit, 85; protests at Letpadaung mine, 84; Foreign Investment and Exchange Laws enacted, 139; revelations of crony donations to NLD, 84; release of FESR, 139, 167

2013 Taro Aso makes visit, 156; foundation of NEMC, 140; Nay Pyi Taw Accord for Effective Development Cooperation, 151, 177; Kenneth King advises HEL Committee, 175; Aung San Suu Kyi re-elected chairperson of NLD, 86; Aung San Suu Kyi heckled at Letpadaung mine, 84; ACLEDA sets up microfinance institution, 152; communal violence erupts in Meiktila and Okkan, 85, 201–2, 204; Shinzo Abe makes visit, 157; UNFC withdraws from WGEC, 113; telecoms contracts awarded, 140; Myo Myint makes study tour of UK, 175; communal violence erupts in Lashio, 202, 204; foundation of Ma Ba Tha, 205; Nasaka disbanded, 188; RCSS and KNU agree to National Ceasefire Accord, 113; launch of public administration reform, 143; establishment of Anti-Corruption Commission, 146; EAG conference in Laiza, 11, 113; peace talks with EAGs in Myitkyina, 11, 114; accession to Investment Guarantee Agency (IGA), 152; National Seminar on Pragmatic Reforms for Education, 171; communal violence erupts in Rakhine, 203, 204; MPs criticize pace of education reform, 172

2014 ASEAN chairmanship begins, 76, 220; peace talks EAGs in Law Khee Lah, 114; MSF withdraws from Rakhine State, 189; Carter Foundation and EU invited to monitor elections, 221; Aung San Suu Kyi starts campaign for constitutional change, 88, 124; Union Assembly votes on constitutional change, 89–90;

pilot citizenship verification process in Rakhine, 197; Upper House votes for PR system, 212; Martyrs' Day, 88; EAG conference in Laiza, 114–15; communal violence erupts in Mandalay, 203; Population and Housing Census begins, 205–7; Electoral Review Commission launched, 212; committee on constitutional change finishes review, 87–8; KNU pulls out of UNFC, 115; National Education Bill enacted; student protests, 173–5; ETWG meeting on Language and Social Cohesion, 183; by-elections cancelled, 211; four-way talks on constitutional change, 89; high-level talks on Nationwide Ceasefire Agreement (NCA), 132; formation of PPIC, 132; shelling of KIA cadet college in Laiza, 116; parliament votes for FPTP system, 212

2015 Deed of Commitment on federalism, 116; conflict re-erupts in Kokang, 98, 117; Aung San Suu Kyi threatens election boycott, 90; Thein Sein's New Year message, 2; drafting of NCA, 117, 119; fighting erupts between military and AA, 117; UK delegates make study tour, 175; Population and Housing Census published, 207; EAG meeting on NCA in Law Khee Lah, 117–18; revised National Education Bill enacted, 175; USDP coup removes Shwe Mann, 91, 210; protection of religion bills enacted, 205; Thein Sein meets with EAG leaders, 118; signing of NCA in Nay Pyi Taw, 119, 181, 211, 215; general election, 2, 3, 9, 11, 88–9, 124, 132, 157, 158, 160, 209–20, 221

Myanmar Development Resource Institute (MDRI), 136–7, 153

Myanmar Economic Corporation (MEC), 41, 136, 149

Myanmar Education Consortium (MEC), 177

Myanmar Egress (ME), 6, 8, 10, 22–8, 31–2, 35–6, 39, 40, 45, 46–8, 53, 63, 103, 148, 165, 215

   Bangkok process, 24, 28, 104

   civic education, 46–7, 63

   E001, 25, 26

   E002, 25, 26, 39, 46

   Project Cycle Management, 39

   Shwepyitaw document, 47

Myanmar Electric Power Enterprise (MEPE), 149

Myanmar Fisheries Federation (MFF), 23, 24, 26, 35

Myanmar Information Management Unit (MIMU), 36

Myanmar Investment Commission (MIC), 148

Myanmar Multi Donor Education Fund (MDEF), 177

Myanmar National Democratic Alliance Army (MNDAA), 16, 98, 117, 118

Myanmar Oil and Gas Enterprise (MOGE), 149

Myanmar Peace Centre (MPC), 11, 103–4, 108, 110, 115, 117, 126, 153

Myanmar Peace Monitor, 218

Myanmar Peace Support Initiative (MPSI), 11, 108–10, 131, 182

Myanmar Post and Telecommunications (MPT), 140, 149

Myanmar Times, 115

Myay Latt, 174
Myebon, Rakhine State, 188, 198
Myeik, Tanintharyi Region, 78
Myint, 71, 136, 137
Myint Swe, 31, 36, 82
Myitkyina, Kachin State, 11, 31, 99, 114, 115, 184
Myitsone dam, Kachin State, 8, 75, 99, 153
Myo Myint, 172, 175

Naga autonomous region, Sagaing Region, 180
Nambiar, Vijay, 116, 117, 188
Nant Bwa Bwa Phan, 102
Nargis Action Group (NAG), 35
Nasaka, 188
nation-building, 59, 94, 128, 185, 223
National Ceasefire Coordination Team (NCCT), 113, 114–15, 117–18, 124
National Comprehensive Development Plan (NCDP), 139
National Convention, 14, 17–18, 96, 98
National Democratic Alliance Army (Mongla), 101
National Democratic Force (NDF), 48, 49–51, 53–4, 68, 87, 89, 211–12
National Disaster Preparedness Central Committee (NDPCC), 33
National Education Bill, 173–5
National Energy Management Committee (NEMC), 140
national identity, 12, 44, 105, 185–208
National League for Democracy (NLD), 2, 4, 5, 6, 8, 11, 12, 17, 38, 44, 49–51, 53–5, 58, 59, 65, 67–73, 77–9, 82, 84, 85–92, 159, 165, 170, 172, 174, 175–6, 195, 209–10, 211–14, 216–17, 221–2

National Network for Education Reform (NNER), 12, 170, 174
national reconciliation, 4, 5, 11, 16, 30, 58, 65, 69, 71, 73, 92, 105, 123, 165
national reconsolidation, 16, 100
National Registration Card (NRC), 107, 194, 197, 200, 206; see also ID cards
National Security Council, 31
National Seminar on Pragmatic Reforms for Education, 171
National Unity Party (NUP), 53, 55, 87, 89, 125, 127, 129, 212, 221
National University of Singapore (NUS), 21
National Workshop on Reforms for Economic Development, 71, 137
nationalism, national identity, 12, 44, 105, 185–208
Nationalities Assembly, see Upper House
Nationalities Brotherhood Federation (NBF), 89, 132, 212, 213, 215–16
Nationwide Ceasefire Agreement (NCA), 2, 11, 87, 98, 104, 107, 113–19, 181, 211, 215
Naw Zipporah Sein, 103
Nay Pyi Taw Union Territory (capital of Myanmar), 1, 9, 11, 18, 28, 40, 64, 65, 71, 74, 78, 88, 104, 119, 137, 142, 143, 152, 154, 166, 171, 177
Nay Pyi Taw Accord for Effective Development Cooperation, 151
Nay Win Maung, 22–8, 31, 36, 40, 48, 52, 62–4, 104
Nayaka, 20
Ne Win, 94–5, 134, 193, 197, 205
Nepal, 194
Netherlands, 108
networks, 9
'new economic complexes', 15

New Light of Myanmar, 55
New Mon State Party (NMSP), 98, 101, 109, 112, 121, 122, 123, 126, 182
New Zealand, 165
newspapers, 1, 2, 22, 25, 44, 72, 74, 204
969 movement, 204
Nippon Foundation (NF), 110–11, 118, 156
Noda, Yoshihiko, 156
non-governmental organisations, (NGOs)
   local non-governmental organisations, (LNGOs), 7–9, 10, 16, 26, 34, 35, 36, 38–9, 41, 58, 75, 96, 108, 109, 128, 130–1, 148, 168, 177, 180, 182, 184, 187
   international non-governmental organisations, (INGOs), 8, 34, 36, 38, 39, 58, 95, 108, 152, 160, 163, 166, 168, 170, 182, 183, 189, 199
Non-Formal Education (NFE), 169, 177
non-interference, 34
Norway, 11, 108, 140, 144, 152, 206
Nu, 94
Nu Nu Yin, 23
nuns, *see* Sangha
Nyan Tun, 82, 89
Nyan Win, 50–1, 88

Obama, Barack, 65, 76, 85
Office of the Auditor General (OAG), 137
Ohn Kyaing, 88
oil, 142
Okkan, Sagaing Region, 202
Ooredoo, 140
Operation Nagamin, 197
opium, 16, 217–20
Organisation of Islamic Cooperation (OIC), 189

Organisational Development and Process Development (ODPD), 47
overseas development aid (ODA), 155
overseas study, 20, 165

P'doh David Taw, 102
Pakistan, 194, 198, 201, 204
Pakokku, Magwe Region, 29–30, 174
Palaung (Ta'ang) ethnicity, 15, 180, 207
   Ta'ang National Liberation Army (TNLA), 117, 118
Panglong Conference (1947), 68, 70, 94, 116, 120, 121
Pangsang, Shan State, 117
PaO ethnicity, 15, 101, 179, 180, 215
   PaO National League, 87
   PaO National Liberation Organisation (PNLO), 123
Parajuli, Bishow, 73
Paris Club, 152
Parliamentary Committee on Education, 12
Parliamentary Education Promotion Committee (PEPC), 172
Parliamentary Guarantees, Pledges and Undertakings Vetting Committee, 172
parliament, 1, 2, 3, 11, 12, 37, 38, 48, 49, 50, 52, 53, 55, 56–9, 65, 72, 74, 79, 81, 83, 88–91, 100, 124, 125–6, 129, 132, 141, 149, 159, 172, 174, 183, 195, 212
   Lower House, 5, 55, 56, 79, 81, 89, 90, 129, 149, 183, 212
   Union Assembly, 56, 57, 58, 72, 76, 89–90, 132, 183
   Upper House, 55, 56, 79, 89, 90, 129, 149, 174, 183, 212
'passive politicians', 43
Pathein, Ayeyarwady Region, 33, 86

Pauktaw, Rakhine State, 188
Paung Da Oo monastery, Mandalay, 20
Paung Ku, 8
Pe Myint, 44
Peace and Politics Implementation Committee (PPIC), 132
Peace Donor Support Group (PDSG), 108
pearls, 150
Pedersen, Morten 3–4
Penang, Malaysia, 20
pensions, 137
People's Assembly, *see* Lower House
People's Militia Forces (PMFs), 219
People's Parliament Election Law, 50
Petrie, Charles, 108, 124–5
petroleum, 29, 134
Phalom-Sawaw Democratic Party, 87, 212
Pheung Kya-shin, 98
phosphorus, 84
Phyo Min Thein, 49
Planning and the Finance Committee (PFC), 137
policy, legislation and management (PLM), 168
Political Advisory Board, 136
political participation, 43–7, 55, 60–4, 109
Political Party Registration Law, 50
political prisoners, 2, 14, 24, 38, 65, 75, 144, 153, 190
pollution, 141
Population and Housing Census, 205–8
Post and Telecommunications Department, 140
Post Nargis Recovery and Preparedness Plan (PONREPP), 38
poverty, 1–2, 7, 14, 38, 58, 133, 134, 136, 137, 169

presidency, 11, 12, 65, 91, 92, 171, 172, 209–10
Press Scrutiny and Registration Department (PSRD), 80
primary education, 20, 162, 163, 165, 166, 169, 177, 180, 181, 182, 184
prisons, prisoners, 2, 14, 24, 38, 65, 74, 75, 144, 153, 190
private investments, 8
private schools, universities, 19–20, 74, 160, 162, 173, 176, 183
private sector, 5, 85, 147, 148, 150, 152, 165, 182
Private Tuition Law, 19, 173
privatisation, 41, 136, 137
Project Cycle Management, 39
proportional representation (PR), 211–12
protection of religion bills, 205
protests, 2, 8, 21, 22, 29–32, 164, 173–5
Public Accounts Committee (PAC), 137
public sector, 137
pulses, 134
Pyabon, Sagaing Region, 35
Pyay, Bago Region, 31
Pyidaungsu Hluttaw, *see* Union Assembly
Pyin Oo Lwin, Mandalay Region, 27, 176
Pyinmana, Naypyidaw Union Territory, 18
Pyithu Hluttaw *see* Lower House
Pyithu Khit, 72
Pyone Cho (Mtay Win Aung), 88

Qatar, 140
quantitative analysis, 168
Quintana, Tomás Ojea, 55, 64–5

'racial purity', 206

Radio Free Asia, 70, 72
railways, 18, 135, 150
Rakhine ethnicity, State, 15, 45, 47, 48,
    53–4, 57, 73, 86, 101, 117–18, 131,
    141–2, 180, 184, 187–91, 194–208,
    218, 222
    Arakan Army (AA), 117, 118
    Arakan League for Democracy
        (ALD), 144
    Arakan Liberation Party (ALP), 109
    Arakan National Council (ANC),
        121, 123
    Arakan National Party (ANP), 129,
        212
    Rakhine National Network (RNN),
        191
    Rakhine Nationalities Development
        Party (RNDP), 47, 54, 55, 87,
        195
    Rakhine Nationals Progressive Party
        (RNPP), 144
Ramree, Rakhine State, 188
Rapid Assessment (RA), 169
Rathedaung, Rakhine State, 188
Raynauld, Mael, 52
real estate, 136
Red Cross, 14, 33
reformers, 64, 65, 154
regional assemblies, 53–4
rent-seeking, 133, 136
responsibility to protect' (RTP), 34
Revolutionary Council of Shan State
    (RCSS), 109, 113, 116
rice, 33, 68, 134, 137, 157
Rieffel, Lex, 149, 150
rights, 20, 38, 43, 46, 61, 62, 109
Roadmap to Discipline-flourishing De-
    mocracy, 3, 10, 14, 17–18, 22, 58–9
roads, 16, 99, 135, 142, 150
Robinson, Gwen, 74
Robson, Maurice, 171

Rohingya ethnicity, 12, 80, 85,
    187–91, 194–208, 222
rote learning, 163
Royal Thazin Restaurant, Yangon, 24
rubies, 150
rule of law, 59, 78, 82, 199, 209,
    216–17
rural areas, 1–2, 45, 61, 64, 133, 136,
    137, 160, 163, 208
Russia, 76

Saboi Jum, 16, 96
Saffron Revolution (2007), 10, 29–32,
    43, 75, 186, 203
Sagaing Region, 180, 218
    Letpadaung mine, 84, 86
    Naga autonomous region, 180
    Okkan, 202
    Pyabon, 35
Sakura Tower, Yangon, 31
sanctions, 9, 22, 40, 59–60, 67, 69, 76,
    134, 144–6, 150, 152, 153
Sangha, 12, 19, 29–32, 44, 52, 186,
    188, 195
Sao Yawd Serk, 116
Sasakawa Yohei, 111, 156
Sasakawa Peace Foundation, 111, 178
Save the Children, 34, 169
secondary education, 20, 162, 163,
    164, 169, 177, 180
Seng Raw, 16, 96
service sector, 134, 135
seven-step roadmap, see Roadmap to
    Discipline-flourishing Democracy
Shalom, 16, 24, 96, 215
Shan ethnicity, State, 15, 16, 45, 48, 53,
    54, 55, 84, 94, 96, 97, 99, 101, 107,
    109, 117, 131, 179, 180, 194, 202,
    207, 214, 219, 222
    Shan Drug Watch, 218
    Shan Nationalities Democratic Party

(SNDP), 49, 55, 78, 87, 89, 172, 212

Shan Nationalities League of Democracy (SNLD), 89, 144

Shan State Army-North (SSA-N), 101, 112

Shan State Army-South (SSA-S), 97, 101, 109, 116

Shan State Progressive Party (SSPP), 112

Shwe gas pipeline, 142

Shwe Mann, 2, 5, 12, 23, 27, 28, 31, 35, 81–2, 87, 89, 91, 124, 172, 210, 221

Shwe Saydi Sayadaw, 195

Shwedagong pagoda, Yangon, 30

Shwegondaing Declaration, 50

Shwepyitaw document, 47

SIM cards, 2, 140

Singapore, 21, 24, 28, 41, 165

Sit Aye, 136

Sittwe, Rakhine State, 184, 187, 189–90

SiuSue, Mark, 8

skills gap, 148

Sky Net, 84

Slim, William Joseph, 1st Viscount Slim, 121

Smith, Martin, 15, 95, 97

Social Democratic Party of Germany (SPD), 21

social media, 80, 202, 203, 204

social welfare, 7, 17, 51, 70

socialism, 9, 14, 94–5, 134, 160, 161, 176, 186

Soe Thein, 11, 36, 73, 82, 91, 103, 104, 144

Soe Tint, 77

Soe Win, 89

Sonny Nyunt Thein, 23, 25, 26

South, Ashley, 16, 49, 97, 100, 124–5

Special Branch, 27

special economic zones (SEZs), 2, 83, 141–2, 156, 157

SSR (security sector reform), 96

state education, 44, 160, 162, 165, 166, 168, 177, 178, 179, 180

State Law and Order Restoration Council (SLORC), 7, 16, 135, 147, 150, 155, 161, 186

State Peace and Development Council (SPDC), 7, 15, 16, 17–18, 34, 50, 58, 101, 161, 186, 209

State-owned Economic Enterprises (SEEs), 139, 149

steel, 134

Steinberg, David, 7, 186

Stiglitz, Joseph, 28

stock exchange, 158

student protests, 21, 29, 31, 164, 173–5

Sule Pyia, Yangon, 174, 187

Sun Guoxiang, 118

Swan Arr Shin, 29–30, 37

Switzerland, 108, 206

Ta'ang National Liberation Army (TNLA), 117, 118

Tanintharyi Region, 78, 109, 141–2, 181
  Dawei SEZ, 141–2, 174
  Myeik, 78

tariffs, 33, 58, 153

Tatmadaw, 1, 3, 5–7, 9, 10, 13–18, 19, 22, 27–8, 31–3, 37, 41, 43, 48, 50, 52, 56–7, 58, 62, 65, 70, 76, 78, 79, 80, 83, 89, 90–1, 94–5, 97–8, 99–100, 102, 106–7, 115, 116, 117, 119, 123, 126, 131, 135–6, 145, 186, 218, 221

taxation, 135, 136, 138, 139, 141

Tay Za, 41, 135, 136

Taylor, Debby Aung Din, 28

Taylor, Robert, 14, 33, 82, 85, 93, 94, 188, 205

tea, 56

teacher shortages, 163, 166, 182

teak, 22

technical and vocational education and training (TVET), 168, 169

Technical, Agricultural and Vocational Education Law, 173

telecommunications, 135, 140, 142, 150

Telenor, 140

Temporary Registration Cards (TRCs), 197

textbooks, 160, 162, 169, 178, 179, 180

Thailand, 6, 23, 24, 26, 34, 36, 41, 45, 95, 97, 102, 112, 115, 118, 120, 134–5, 140, 141–3, 149, 181

Thamada Hotel, Yangon, 24–5, 26, 39

Than Htay, 84

Than Shwe, 5, 11, 16, 18, 22, 28, 31, 32, 35, 40, 50, 57, 58, 59, 65, 69, 151

Thant Myint, 55

Thant Myint Oo, 28

Thein Lwin, 174

Thein Phyu (TP), 138

Thein Sein, 4, 5, 9, 18, 73, 91–2, 104, 108, 152, 165, 195, 209, 210, 211, 220

2008 convenes National Disaster Preparedness Central Committee (NDPCC), 33

2010 resigns from armed forces; runs for president, 48

2011 sworn in as president, 2, 11, 57–8, 209, 218; inauguaral speech, 58, 101, 133, 159, 166; appoints advisory boards, 136; meeting with Aung San Suu Kyi, 65, 71–2; offer of peace talks to EAGs, 112; urges exiles to return home, 74; suspension of Myitsone dam project; political prisoners released, 75, 144, 153

2012 Union Assembly address, 76, 100; invites international monitors to observe by-elections, 78; visit to Japan, 156; calls for calm after communal riots, 187, 189; launch of Investigation Commission on communal violence, 188, 190; censorship board abolished, 80, 153; request for clarification of parliamentary committee powers, 81; Aung San Suu Kyi appointed chair of Committee for Rule of Law, 82; snubs Bangkok conference after Aung San Suu Kyi invited to speak, 83

2013 launch of public administration reform, 143; establishment of Anti-Corruption Commission, 146; disbanding of Nasaka, 188

2014 attends four-way talks on constitutional change, 89; convenes high-level talks on NCA, 132

2015 Deed of Commitment on federalism, 116; drafting of NCA, 117; New Year message, 2; meeting with EAG leaders, 118; signing of NCA, 119

Thein Tun, 89, 135

Thein Zaw, 101

Thet Tun, 102–3

Thilawa SEZ, Yangon Region, 141, 156, 157

Thingyian, 65, 74

third force, 8, 37

three pillars, 62

duties, 44, 61, 62

political participation, 43–7, 55, 60–4, 109

rights, 20, 38, 43, 46, 61, 62, 109

Thu Wei, 125

tilapia, 23

timber, 15, 17, 22, 134, 150, 153
Time, 204
Tin Aung Myint Oo, 57, 78, 82, 151
Tin Aye, 89, 212
Tin Htoo Aung, 191
Tin Maung Maung Than, 33, 193
Tin Maung Thann, 22–8, 31, 35, 36, 48, 103
Tin Myo Win, 78
Tin Naing Thein, 172
Tin Tin Shu, 170
Tint Swe, 80
Tokyo Foundation, 111
Tonkin, Derek, 52, 83, 144, 196
Toungup, Rakhine State, 187
tourism, 30, 59, 136
Township Immigration, 206
Traders Hotel, Yangon, 31
Transnational Institute (TNI), 219
transport, 136, 142, 150
Tripartite Core Group (TCG), 34, 38, 39
troika, 1, 13
Tu Ja, 99
Tun Myint Naing, 136
Tun Tun Aung, 192
Tun Tun Hein, 88
Turnell, Sean, 41, 135

unemployment, 135
Union Assembly (Pyidaungsu Hluttaw), 56, 57
Union Citizenship Act, 192–3
Union Day, 116
Union Democratic Party (UDP), 48–9
Union Election Commission (UEC), 47, 49, 51, 55, 79, 89, 91, 211, 221
Union of Myanmar Economic Holdings Limited (UMEHL), 41, 136, 149
Union of Myanmar Federation of
Chambers of Commerce and Industry (UMFCCI), 23
Union Peacemaking Working Committee (UPWC), 11, 103, 104, 118, 124
Union Solidarity and Development Association (USDA), 18, 29, 33, 37, 38
Union Solidarity and Development Party (USDP), 48, 52, 53–5, 57, 77, 78–9, 87, 88, 89, 90, 91, 99, 104, 172, 197, 210, 212–14, 216, 221–2
United Kingdom (UK), 19, 28, 36, 85, 93–4, 108, 120–1, 145, 165, 170–1, 175, 192, 196, 198, 206
United Nationalities Alliance, 89
United Nationalities Federal Council (UNFC), 11, 107, 111–16
United Nations (UN), 12, 28, 34, 58, 64–5, 73–4, 76, 80, 108, 116, 137, 153, 160, 162, 163, 166, 167, 168, 171, 172, 176, 177, 178, 181, 183, 184, 187–8, 189, 195, 197
Children's Fund (UNICEF), 12, 160, 162, 163, 167, 168, 171, 172, 176, 177, 178, 181, 183, 184
Commission of Inquiry, 76
Economic and Social Commission for Asia and the Pacific (UNESCAP), 28
Educational, Scientific and Cultural Organization (UNESCO), 167, 168
High Commissioner for Refugees (UNHCR), 187, 195, 197
Millennium Development Goals (MDGs), 153
Office for Project Services (UNOPS), 35
Office for the Coordination of Humanitarian Affairs (OCHA), 36
Population Fund (UNFPA), 206
Strategic Planning Process, 73

INDEX

United States (US), 11, 18, 28, 34, 36, 40, 65, 76, 78, 85, 89, 144, 145, 156, 160, 165, 176, 188, 195

United Wa State Army (UWSA), 98, 101, 218

United Wa State Party (UWSP), 117

Unity and Democracy Party, 212

universities, 21–2, 85, 160, 164, 165, 173, 175–6, 183

University Education Law, 173

University of Edinburgh, 175

University of London, 21

Upper House (Amyotha Hluttaw), 55, 56, 79, 90, 129, 149, 174, 212

urban areas, 1–2, 5, 8, 43, 44, 45–7, 54, 60, 61, 63, 134, 148, 163, 208

Vacant, Fallow, and Virgin Land Law (VFV Law), 8, 147

Vahu Development Institute, 103

Vietnam, 135

Voice, 22, 25, 44, 191

Wa ethnicity, region, 15, 17, 35, 54, 101, 214, 218, 222
  United Wa State Army (UWSA), 98, 101, 218
  United Wa State Party (UWSP), 117

Wah Thin Kha, Yangon Region, 77

Waingmaw, Kachin State, 184

Wan Bao Mining Company, 84

War Office, 136

War Veterans Organisation, 33

Watanabe, Hideo, 156

welfare, 7, 17, 51, 70

White Cards, 191, 194–5, 222

white phosphorus, 84

White Tiger Party, *see* Shan Nationalities Democratic Party

Wikileaks, 40

Wilton Park, 28

Win Htain, 88

Win Min, 31

Win Myint, 31, 88

Win Tin, 72

Wirathu, 204

Women's Affairs Federation, 33

women's rights, 126, 192

wood products, 134

Working Group for Ethnic Coordination (WGEC), 112–13

World Bank, 1, 11, 28, 133, 135, 137, 138, 139, 143–4, 149, 152, 168, 178

World Economic Forum, 69, 73, 82–3

World Health Organisation (WHO), 34

World Vision, 169

World War II (1939–45), 94, 155, 196

xenophobia, 186, 199

Yangon Region, 1, 2, 6, 18, 20, 24–8, 29–32, 33, 34, 37, 38, 41, 51–3, 55, 60, 61, 63, 71, 82, 88, 94, 104, 111, 117, 125, 130, 131, 133, 139, 140, 143, 148, 152, 174, 181, 187, 189, 198
  Fuji Coffee House, 25
  Insein Prison, 74
  Kawhmu, 72–3, 77
  Mingaladon airport, 34
  Royal Thazin Restaurant, 24
  Sakura Tower, 31
  Shwedagong pagoda, 30
  Sule pagoda, 174, 187
  Thamada Hotel, 24–5, 26, 39
  Thilawa SEZ, 141, 156, 157
  Traders Hotel, 31
  Wah Thin Kha, 77
  Yangon Institute of Economics, 172
  Yangon University, 21, 85, 160, 171, 172, 175–6

INDEX

Ye Htut, 89, 202
Ye Mya Thu, 23
Ye Naing Win, 22
Yeo, George, 34
Yettaw, John 40, 67
Yin Nu, 116
Yin Yin Nwe, 172
Yun, Joseph, 195

Yunnan, China, 135, 142

Zaganar, 75, 190
Zaw Oo, 28
Zaw Zaw, 41, 135, 136
Zaw Zaw Han, 35
zinc, 150
Zöllner, Hans-Bernd, 50–1, 68